CONSCIOUSNESS . MEDITATION . WATCHER ON THE HILLS

ON KAWARA
CONSCIOUSNESS . MEDITATION . WATCHER ON THE HILLS

les presses du réel **IKON**

This book has been published on the occasion of an exhibition by
On Kawara, *Consciousness. Meditation. Watcher on the hills*
organised by Ikon Gallery, Birmingham and Le Consortium, Dijon.

Touring worldwide and clockwise.

Contents

Franck Gautherot / Jonathan Watkins
Foreword

No artist's statement here, as ever, no portrait of the artist and no interview. Furthermore there are no newspaper cuttings to provide a commentary of current affairs for Date Paintings, and no colourful postcards.

Being "still alive" for almost forty years is embodied essentially in this exhibition, forty years that take up four lines in the twenty books of two million years. Counting them down, year by year, day by day, is conducive to meditation …

… is conducive to a consciousness that equates a kindergarten child with an esoteric philosopher, a professor of mathematics with a seemingly self-taught-man, a cave man with a watcher on the hills.

There is too much and therefore nothing for the artist to say.

Kahlil Gibran

Osho

Kajin Yamamoto

Jiddu Krishnamurti, David Bohm

Ikuro Adachi

Stuart Hameroff, Roger Penrose

Kahlil Gibran
On Friendship

And a youth said, Speak to us of Friendship.

And he answered, saying:

Your friend is your needs answered.

He is your field which you sow with love and reap with thanksgiving.

And he is your board and your fireside.

For you come to him with your hunger, and you seek him for peace.

When your friend speaks his mind you fear not the "nay" in your own mind, nor do you withhold the "ay."

And when he is silent your heart ceases not to listen to his heart;

For without words, in friendship, all thoughts, all desires, all expectations are born and shared, with joy that is unacclaimed.

When you part from your friend, you grieve not;

For that which you love most in him may be clearer in his absence, as the mountain to the climber is clearer from the plain.

And let there be no purpose in friendship save the deepening of the spirit.

For love that seeks aught but the disclosure of its own mystery is not love but a net cast forth: and only the unprofitable is caught.

And let your best be for your friend.

If he must know the ebb of your tide, let him know its flood also.

For what is your friend that you should seek him with hours to kill?

Seek him always with hours to live.

For it is his to fill your need, but not your emptiness.

And in the sweetness of friendship let there be laughter, and sharing of pleasures.

For in the dew of little things the heart finds its morning and is refreshed.

And then a scholar said, Speak of Talking.

And he answered, saying:

You talk when you cease to be at peace with your thoughts;

And when you can no longer dwell in the solitude of your heart you live in your lips, and sound is a diversion and a pastime.

And in much of your talking, thinking is half murdered.

For thought is a bird of space, that in a cage of words may indeed unfold its wings but cannot fly.

There are those among you who seek the talkative through fear of being alone.

The silence of aloneness reveals to their eyes their naked selves and they would escape.

And there are those who talk, and without knowledge or forethought reveal a truth which they themselves do not understand.

And there are those who have the truth within them, but they tell it not in words.

In the bosom of such as these the spirit dwells in rhythmic silence.

When you meet your friend on the roadside or in the market place, let the spirit in you move your lips and direct your tongue.

Let the voice within your voice speak to the ear of his ear;

For his soul will keep the truth of your heart as the taste of the wine is remembered When the colour is forgotten and the vessel is no more.

And an astronomer said, Master, what of Time?

And he answered:

You would measure time the measureless and the immeasurable.

You would adjust your conduct and even direct the course of your spirit according to hours and seasons.

Of time you would make a stream upon whose bank you would sit and watch its flowing.

Yet the timeless in you is aware of life's timelessness,

And knows that yesterday is but today's memory and tomorrow is today's dream.

And that that which sings and contemplates in you is still dwelling within the bounds of that first moment which scattered the stars into space.

Who among you does not feel that his power to love is boundless?

And yet who does not feel that very love, though boundless, encompassed within the centre of his being, and moving not from love thought to love thought, nor from love deeds to other love deeds?

And is not time even as love is, undivided and spaceless?

But if in your thought you must measure time into seasons, let each season encircle all the other seasons,

And let today embrace the past with remembrance and the future with longing.

Kahlil Gibran, "On Friendship", from the book *The Prophet*
Published by Alfred A. Knopf, New York, 1998, P58-63

Now the first technique: *Each thing is perceived through knowing. The self shines in space through knowing. Perceive one being as knower and known.*

Whenever you know something, it is known through knowing. The object comes to your mind through the faculty of knowledge. You look at a flower: you know this is a roseflower. The roseflower is there and you are inside. Something from you comes to the roseflower, something from you is projected on the roseflower. Some energy moves from you, comes to the rose, takes its form, colour and smell, and comes back and informs you that this is a roseflower.

All knowledge, whatsoever you know, is revealed through the faculty of knowing. Knowing is your faculty; knowledge is gathered through this faculty. But knowing reveals two things: the known and the knower. Whenever you are knowing a roseflower, your knowledge is half if you forget the knower who is knowing it. So while knowing a roseflower there are three things: the roseflower – the known; and the knower – you; and the relationship between the two – knowledge.

So knowledge can be divided into three points: knower, known and knowing. Knowing is just like a bridge between two points – the subject and the object. Ordinarily your knowledge reveals only the known; the knower remains unrevealed. Ordinarily your knowledge is one-arrowed: it points to the rose but it never points to you. Unless it starts pointing to you, that knowledge will allow you to know about the world, but it will not allow you to know about yourself.

All the techniques of meditation are to reveal the knower. George Gurdjieff used a particular technique just like this. He called it self-remembering. He said that whenever you are knowing something, always remember the knower. Don't forget it in the object. Remember the subject.

Just now you are listening to me. When you are listening to me, you can listen in two ways. One, your mind can be focused towards me – then you forget the listener. Then the speaker is known but the listener is forgotten. Gurdjieff said that while listening, know the speaker and also know the listener. Your knowledge must be double-arrowed, pointing to two points – the knower and the known. It must not only flow in one direction towards the object. It must flow simultaneously towards two directions – the known and the knower. This he called self-remembering.

Looking at a flower, also remember the one who is looking. Difficult, because if you do try it, if you try to be aware of the knower, you will forget the rose. You have become so fixed to one direction that it will take time. If you become aware of the knower, then the known will be forgotten. If you become aware of the known, then the knower will be forgotten.

But a little effort, and by and by you can be aware of both simultaneously. And when you become capable of being aware of both – this Gurdjieff calls self-remembering. This is one of the oldest techniques that Buddha used, and Gurdjieff again introduced it to the Western world.

Buddha called it *samyak smriti* – right mindfulness. He said that your mind is not in a right mindfulness if it knows only one point. It must know both. And then a miracle happens: if you are aware of both the known and the knower, suddenly you become the third – you are neither. Just by endeavouring to be aware of both the known and the knower, you become the third, you become a witness. A third possibility arises immediately, a witnessing self comes into being, because how can you know both? If you are the knower, then you remain fixed to one point. In self-remembering you shift from the fixed point of the knower. Then the knower is your mind and the known is the world, and you become a third point, a consciousness, a witnessing self.

This third point cannot be transcended, and that which cannot be transcended is the ultimate. That which can be transcended is not worthwhile, because then it is not your nature – you can transcend it.

I will try to explain it through an example. In the night you sleep and you dream. In the morning you wake and the dream is lost. While you are awake there is no dream; a different world comes into your view. You move in the streets, you work in a factory or in an office. Then you come back your home, and again you fall asleep at night. Then this world that you knew while you were awake disappears. Then you don't remember who you are. Then you don't know whether you are black or white, poor or rich, wise or foolish. You don't know anything. You don't know if you are young or old. You don't know if you are man or woman. All that was related with the waking consciousness disappears; you enter the world of dreams. You forget the waking world, it is no more. In the morning, again the dreaming world disappears. You come back.

Which is real? – because while you are dreaming, the real world, the world that you knew you when you were awake, is no more. You cannot compare. And while you are awake the dreaming world is no more. You cannot compare. Which is real? Why do you call the dreaming world unreal? What is the criterion?

If you say, "Because it disappears when I am awake," this cannot be the criterion, because your waking world disappears when you are dreaming. And really, if you argue this way, then the dreaming world may be more real, because while you are awake you can remember the dream, but while you are dreaming you cannot remember the waking consciousness and the world around it. So which is more real and more deep? The dreaming world completely washes away the world that you call real. Your real world cannot wash away the dreaming world so totally; it seems more solid, more real. And what is the criterion? How to say? How to compare?

Tantra says that both are unreal. Then what is real? Tantra says that the one who knows the dreaming world and the one who knows the waking world, he is real – because he is never transcended. He is never canceled. Whether you dream or whether you are awake, he is there, uncanceled.

Tantra says that the one who knows the dream, and the one who knows that now the dream has stopped, the one who knows the waking world, and the one who knows that now the waking world has disappeared, is the real – because there is no point when it is not, it is always there. That which cannot be canceled by any experience is the real. That which cannot be transcended, beyond which you cannot go, is your self. If you can go beyond it, then it was not your self.

This method of Gurdjieff's, which he calls self-remembering, or Buddha's method, which he calls right-mindfulness, or this tantra sutra, lead to one thing. They lead within you to a point which is neither the known nor the knower, but a witnessing self which knows both.

This witnessing self is the ultimate, you cannot go beyond it, because now whatsoever you do will be witnessing. Beyond witnessing you cannot move. So witnessing is the ultimate substratum, the basic ground of consciousness. This sutra will reveal it to you.

Each thing is perceived through knowing.
The self shines in space through knowing.
Perceive one being as knower and known.

If you can perceive in yourself one point which is both knower and known, then you have transcended object and subject both. Then you have transcended matter and mind both; then you have transcended the outer and inner both. You have come to a point where the knower and the known are one. There is no division.

With the mind, division will remain. Only with the witnessing self division disappears. With the witnessing self you cannot say who is the known and who is the knower – it is both. But this has to be based on experience; otherwise it becomes a philosophical discussion. So try it, experiment.

You are sitting near a roseflower: look at it. The first thing to do is be totally attentive, give total attention to the rose, so that the whole world disappears and only the rose remains there – your consciousness is totally attentive to the being of the rose. If the attention is total then the world disappears, because the more the attention is concentrated on the rose, the more everything else falls away. The world disappears; only the rose remains. The rose becomes the world.

This is the first step – to concentrate on they rose. If you cannot concentrate on the rose, it will be difficult to move to the knower, because then your mind is always diverted. So concentration becomes the first step towards meditation. Only the rose remains; the whole world has disappeared. Now you can move inwards; now the rose becomes the point from where you can move. Now see the rose, and start becoming aware of yourself – the knower.

In the beginning you will miss. When you shift to the knower, the rose will drop out of consciousness. It will become faint, it will go away, it will become distant. Again you will come to the rose, and you will forget the self. This hide-and-seek play will go on, but if you persist, sooner or later a moment will come when suddenly you will be in-between. The knower, the mind, and the rose will be there, and you will be just in the middle, looking at both. That middle point, that balancing point, is the witness.

Once you know that, you have become both. Then the rose, the known, and the knower, the mind, are just two wings to you. Then the object and the subject are just two wings; you are the centre of both. They are extensions of you. Then the world and the divine are both extensions of you. You have come to the very centre of being. And this centre is just a witness.

Perceive one being as knower and known.

Start by concentrating on something. When the concentration has come to be total, then try to move inwards, become mindful of yourself, and then try to balance. It will take time – months, even years. It depends on how intense is your effort, because it is the most subtle balancing to come between the two. But it happens, and when it happens you have reached the centre of existence. In that centre you are rooted, grounded, silent, blissful, in ecstasy and duality is no more. This is what Hindus have called *samadhi*. This is what Jesus called the kingdom of God.

Just understanding it verbally will not be of much help, but if you try, from the very beginning you will start to feel that something is happening. When you concentrate on the rose, the world will disappear. This is a miracle – when the whole world disappears. Then you come to understand that it is your attention which is basic, and wherever you move your attention, a world is created, and from wherever you remove your attention, the world drops. So you can create worlds through your attention.

Look at it in this way. You are sitting here. If you are in love with someone, then suddenly only one person remains in this hall; everything else disappears, it is not there. What happens? Why does only one person remain when you are in love? The whole world drops really; it is phantomlike, shadows. Only one person is real, because now your mind is concentrated on one person, your mind is totally absorbed in one person. Everything else becomes shadowlike, a shadow existence – it is not real for you.

Whenever you can concentrate, the very concentration changes the whole pattern of your existence, the whole pattern of your mind. Try it – on anything. You can try it on a buddha statue or a flower or a tree or anything, or just on the face of your beloved or your friend – just look at the face.

It will be easy, because if you love some face it is very easy to concentrate. And really, those who tried to concentrate on Buddha, on Jesus, on Krishna, they were lovers. So it was very easy for Sariputta or for Maudgalyan or for the other disciples to concentrate on Buddha's face; they loved Buddha. The moment they looked at Buddha's face they were easily flowing towards it. The love was there; they were infatuated.

So try to find a face – any face you love will do – and just look in the eyes and concentrate on the face. Suddenly, the whole world drops; a new dimension has opened. Your mind is concentrated on one thing; then that person or that thing becomes the whole world.

When I say this, I mean that if your attention is total towards anything, that thing becomes the whole world. You create the world through your attention. Your world you create through your own attention. And when you are totally absorbed, flowing like a river towards the object, then suddenly start becoming aware of the original source from where this attention is flowing. The river is flowing; now become aware of the origin.

In the beginning you will get lost again and again; you will shift. If you move to the origin, you will forget the river and the object, the sea towards which it is flowing. It will change; if you come to the object, you will forget the origin. It is natural, because the mind has become fixed to either the object or to the subject.

That's why so many people go into retreats, they just leave the world. Leaving the world basically means leaving the object so that they can concentrate on themselves. It is easy. If you leave the world and close your eyes and close all your senses, you can be aware of yourself easily, but again that awareness is false because you have chosen one point of duality. This is another extreme of the same disease.

First you were aware of the object – the known, and you were not aware of the subject – the knower. Now you are fixed with the knower and you have forgotten the known, but you remain divided in duality. And this is the old mind again in a new pattern. Nothing has changed.

That's why my emphasis is not to leave the world of the objects. Don't leave the world of the objects. Rather, try to become aware of both the subject and the object simultaneously, the outer and the inner simultaneously. If both are there, only then can you be balanced between them. If one is there you will get obsessed with it.

Those who go to the Himalayas and close themselves, they are just like you only standing in a reverse position. You are fixed with the objects, they are fixed with the subject. You are fixed with the outer, they are fixed with the inner. Neither you are free nor they, because you cannot be free with the one. With the one you become identified. You can be free only when you become aware of the two. Then you can become the third, and the third is the free point. With one you become identified. With two you can move, you can shift, you can balance, and you can come to a midpoint, an absolute midpoint.

Buddha used to say that his path is a middle path – *majjhim nikai*. It has not been really understood why he insisted so much on calling it the middle path. This is the reason: because his whole process was of mindfulness – it is the middle path. Buddha says, "Don't leave the world, and don't cling to the other world. Rather, be in-between. Don't leave one extreme and move to the other; just be in the middle, because in the middle both are not. Just in the middle you are free. Just in the middle there is no duality. You have come to one, and the duality has become just the extension of you – just two wings."

Buddha's middle path is based on this technique. It is beautiful. For so many reasons, it is beautiful. One: it is very scientific, because only between two can you balance. If there is only one point, imbalance is bound to be there. So Buddha says that those who are worldly are imbalanced, and those who have renounced are again imbalanced in the other extreme. A balanced man is one who is neither in this extreme nor that; he lives just in the middle. You cannot call him worldly, you cannot call him otherworldly. He is free to move; he is not attached to any. He has come to the midpoint, the golden mean.

Secondly: it is very easy to move to the other extreme – very easy. If you eat too much you can fast easily, but you cannot diet easily. If you talk too much you can go into silence very easily, but you cannot talk less. If you eat too much, it is very easy not to eat at all – this is another extreme. But to eat moderately, to come to a midpoint, is very difficult. To love a person is easy; to hate a person is easy. To be simply indifferent is very difficult. From one extreme you can move to the other.

To remain in the middle is very difficult. Why? Because in the middle you have to lose your mind. Your mind exists in extremes. Mind means the excess. Mind is always extremist: either you are for or you are against. You cannot be simply neutral. Mind cannot exist in neutrality: it can be here or there – because mind needs the opposite, it needs to be opposed to something. If it is not opposed to anything it disappears. Then there is no functioning for it; it cannot function.

Try this. In any way become neutral, indifferent – suddenly mind has no function. If you are for, you can think; if you are against, you can think. If you are neither for nor against, what is left to think?

Buddha says that indifference is the basis of the middle path. *Upeksha*, indifference – be indifferent to the extremes. Just try one thing, be indifferent to the extremes. A balancing happens.

This balancing will give you a new dimension of feeling where you are both the knower and the known, the world and the other world, this and that, the body and the mind. You are both, and simultaneoulsy neither – above both. A triangle has come into existence.

You may have seen that many occult, secret societies have used the triangles as their symbol. The triangle is one of the oldest occult symbols just because of this – because the triangle has three angles. Ordinarily you have only two angles, the third is missing. It is not there yet, it has not evolved. The third angle is beyond both. Both belong to it, they are part of it, and still it is beyond and higher than both.

If you do this expriment you will help to create a triangle within yourself. The third angle will arise by and by, and when it comes then you cannot be in misery. Once you can witness, you cannot be in misery. Misery means getting identified with something.

But one subtle point has to be remembered — then you will not even get identified with bliss. That's why Buddha says, "I can say only this much – that there will be no misery. In samadhi, in ecstasy, there will be no misery. I cannot say that there will be bliss." Buddha says, "I cannot say that. I can simply say there will be no misery."

And he is right, because bliss means when there is no identification of any type – not even with bliss. This is very subtle. If you feel that you are blissful, sooner or later you will be in misery again. If you feel you are blissful, you are preparing to be miserable again. You are still getting identified with a mood.

You feel happy: now you get identified with happiness. The moment you get identified with happiness, unhappiness has started. Now you will cling to it, now you will become afraid of the opposite, now you will expect it to remain with you constantly. You have created all that is needed for misery to be there and then misery will enter, and when you get identified with happiness, you will get identified with misery. Identification is the disease.

At the third point you are not identified with anything: whatsoever comes and passes, comes and passes; you remain a witness, just a spectator – neutral, indifferent, unidentified.

The morning comes and the sun rises and you witness it. You don't say, "I am the morning." Then when the noon comes, you don't say, "I have become the noon." You witness it. And when the sun sets and darkness comes and the night, you don't say, "I am the darkness and the night." You witness it. You say, "There was morning, then there was noon, then there was evening and now there is night. And again there will be morning and the circle will go on and I am just an onlooker. I go on witnessing."

If the same becomes possible with your moods – moods of the morning and moods of the noon and moods of the evening and the night, and they have their own circle, they go on moving – you become a witness. You say, "Now happiness has come – just like a morning. And now night will come – the misery. The moods will go on changing around me, and I will remain centred in myself. I will not get attached to any mood. I will not cling to any mood. I will not hope for anything and I will not feel frustrated. I will simply witness. Whatsoever happens, I will see it. When it comes, I will see; when it goes, I will see."

Buddha uses this many times. He says again and again that when a thought arises, look at it. A thought of misery, a thought of happiness arises – look at it. It comes to a climax – look at it. Then it starts falling down – look at it. Then it disappears – look at it. Arising, existing, dying, and you remain just a witness; go on looking at it. This third point makes you a witness, *sakshin*, and to be a witness is the highest possibility of consciousness.

Osho, "Know the Knower and the Known", from *The Book of Secrets, The Science of Meditation, A Contemporary Approach to 112 Meditations Described in the Vigyan Bhairav Tantra* Published by St. Martin Press, New York, 1998, Chapter 61, P861-6

An Introduction

"Cosmic philosophy," which many readers may have never heard of before, is literally a study of knowledge that concerns the Universe – both the internal one (consciousness/mind) and the external one (time/space/matter). This branch of philosophy might possibly have history older than our earth.

The Universe itself constitutes an ego (self) of immense magnitude. Seen from our human perspective, its "personification" in all areas of its expanse appears supernatural. I have called this functioning "self-cognition of the Universe." It is indeed a "conscious" – as well as spiritual and intellectual – functioning. That is to say, the Universe is transforming itself, together with its vast Time and Space, into one unparalleled self-conscious entity. This consciousness of the Universe, so infinite that it intuitively knows that its transformation makes every being as part of it, is not only the governing principle but also the root cause of all kinds of creation, perception, and evolution. At the same time, it is the principle of life, ego, and things.

"Personification," or self-actualisation of the Universe, extends to all areas of its expanse through its own "perceptual agency," and all beings exist as a manifestation of this agency. Needless to say, humans are a realisation of the Universe's infinitely developing faculty of perception and eternally recurring force of life. Nothing is thus impossible for humans. In this book, I endeavour to examine the essence of the Universe and the infinite capacity of humans, in order to explain as fully and plainly as possible how to unleash the potential of humans, perceptual or otherwise.

In this book, I have assigned the general term "cosmic faculty of perception" to the extraordinary perceptual and other abilities latent in humans. It means the sense, or consciousness, that a being innately possesses about the Universe. Furthermore, I define the Universe's consciousness, or Cosmic Consciousness, as follows:

Definition 1: Cosmic Consciousness is the root cause of all laws. As such, it is the supreme principle of the Universe.
Definition 2: Cosmic Consciousness is a consciousness common to all beings.
Definition 3: Cosmic Consciousness is the power to enable beings to exist, the knowledge to know it, and the will to desire limitlessly.

These definitions have been deduced from my reflection on consciousness, as will be outlined in Chapter 1: "What Is Consciousness?" in this book. That which is thus defined thoroughly satisfies the following necessary and sufficient conditions for Cosmic Consciousness to be the supreme principle of all:

1) It must contain within itself the object of its own consciousness as a cause of its own consciousness.

2) Accordingly, it must at once engender the cause (or basis) of its own consciousness and prompt the act of becoming an object of its own consciousness. That is to say, this act itself must be the cause of its own consciousness (self-consciousness).

3) What 2) means is same as creating an object within itself in such a way that the object (object of cognition) of its own consciousness is also the cause of self-perception. Thus, consciousness is the act of becoming itself an object, manifesting itself as a phenomenon.

The "consciousness" that fully satisfies these conditions then comes to assume the following characteristics worthy of the supreme principle of all:

1)' It is at once an act of objectifying (actualising) a sense that it is alive (self-consciousness of life) and a consciousness that it is alive.

2)' It is at once an act of objectifying (actualising) a sense that it exists (self-consciousness of being) and a consciousness that it exists.

3)' It is at once an act of objectifying (actualising) a sense that it understands (self-consciousness of knowledge) and a consciousness that it understands.

It is thus understood, through these characteristics, that all beings and phenomena of the Universe are objectified within the Universe itself as objects of self-consciousness of the Universe (consciousness). It is my hope that readers will learn from this book how this consciousness is formed, what will result from this consciousness, and what it will make possible and how.

In this book, the following definitions are established with regard to the Universe:

Definition of the Universe
The Universe is:
1) itself an ego of immense magnitude;
2) itself a conscious entity;
3) a consciousness that is being "personified";
4) life itself; and
5) a site in which all beings function.

A human rule over the Universe (site of life) will become possible only when we fuse ourselves with Cosmic Consciousness, which is the principle of our own, and work with all beings in a unified and inseparable manner. The Universe presents no programme that makes this project difficult.

Chapter 1: Essence of Consciousness
Section 1: What Is Consciousness?

When we try to put in practice that which is theoretically explored in this book – the development and application of the perceptual faculty, and the fusion with Cosmic Consciousness – questions inevitably arise concerning consciousness, perception, senses, and the mind, all of which are the paramount subjects in philosophical inquiries. Therefore, we must here begin by gaining a clear understanding of and a further insight into consciousness.

For example, we use the word "consciousness" (or "to be conscious") in the sense of "awareness" (or "to be aware") of a certain thing or condition:

1) She is conscious of her own strengths and shortcomings. An actor is conscious of the audience's response.

2) He lost consciousness.

Notably, there is a distinct difference between the first and second usage. In addition, there is another rather unusual case: consciousness in the dream state. I would like to examine each of these three instances.

Concerning 1): "to be conscious" typically signifies the psychological experience of the said person directing her/his attention to an object (including an image or idea occurring in her/his mind). Here, consciousness means an attentive or awakened state of mind. However, such an explanation proves quite arbitrary, and even contradictory, if we further consider 2) and the dream-state consciousness. For 2): the reference to consciousness is made in terms of the connection between an object of consciousness and sensory organs – or the sensory function of internal organ – as aptly expressed by the phrase, "to lose consciousness." For some reason, the said person is no longer cognisant of anything, with her/his sensory functions being disrupted.

Let us next consider the "dream" state, wherein the sensory connection with the external world appears to be disrupted but some sign of consciousness can be observed. Generally speaking, this is the state of "unconsciousness" in an objective sense. Whether or not a person asleep is dreaming can be easily determined by observing the movement of her/his eyeballs, intermittently uttered unintelligible words, and lip movements. Scientists have even invented such "dream-monitors" as brain-wave sensors. When a person is asleep, it is possible to talk to her/him gently enough not to wake her/him up and extract her/his responses. So long as the right questions are asked and the state of sleep is appropriate for such questioning, the person asleep, without exception, responds vocally, enabling the interrogator to extract the content of her/his dream. However, s/he will hardly remember the conversation during sleep, when asked about it after waking up. Even if s/he does remember it, s/he thinks that it was an "event in the dream," in which the interrogator made an appearance in some capacity. In other words, the said person has no "objective" recollection of having uttered any words while asleep. There are countless other instances of strange correlation observed between consciousness and sensory organs, which all indicate that "consciousness" and the "mind" are neither identical nor working on the same plane, so to speak. In the case of 1), the said person "knows" that s/he is cognisant of a certain fact or object (i.e., internally recognises the state of self-awareness), whereas in the case of the person dreaming, s/he does not have any such objective "object-sense" (i.e., sense about an object) – which is the same as "having no consciousness" about an object-sense. Granted that when a person dreams in sleep with no external interference (voice or motion), s/he has an object-sense about the images in the dream. Still, this is a subjective experience, completely different from the object-sense one generally has while awake.

If so, how does one know that her/his object-sense is objective as an object of cognition? In other words, where does the self-awareness (consciousness) that "I am sensing it" reside? And why does such self-awareness arise?

Since the manner in which these questions are posed is very important, I would like to rephrase them. Can the whole event of "I am sensing it" constitute an immediate object of another sensory agency? This first question is essential in proving the existence of Cosmic Consciousness that is the comprehensive and principal consciousness serving as the ultimate principle of all cognition and in codifying such Cosmic Consciousness as the primal mode of ego (self). When I sense a certain object, if that sense itself is an object of cognition within a certain consciousness, two questions must be asked: "What" makes my sense that allows me to sense a rose true? and "What" enables me to know it?

These "What" must be discovered and understood, because I do not sense the rose, but blindly and merely know that the said object is "being sensed" as a rose, and I have no idea why I sense it as a rose when directing my eye toward it. Let me repeat: I merely know that the object is being sensed, yet I do not know why, or how, that sense arises. We must know why. By knowing it, we will know that "I who sense" is in itself an immediate object of cognition for consciousness, separate from the consciousness of "I."

Section 2: Cosmic Consciousness

When I am cognisant of a certain object, there always exists a distance, both spatial and temporal, between myself and the object. This distance is also a psychological and mental gap between myself and the object. Such a gap exists not only when we are cognisant of an object, but also when we "act" – when we try to create something or do something to somebody. This indicates that since our cognition is directed toward a certain "objective" thing as an object, it excludes the mental dimension. Then it logically follows that our sense or action always involves an object. When an object of cognition is not an objective entity but a fantasy, memory, or dream – that which exists in one's subjectivity – it becomes an object of her/his "self-reflection" or "self-sense" (i.e., sense of the self).

That is to say, there is a consciousness of "I" invoked by an object-sense. It distinguishes among the "first person" (I), "second person" (you), and "third person" (s/he), based on its relationship with this object, and discerns the "passive" and "active" modes, based on "who does what to whom." We may call the state of consciousness thus differentiated by an object-sense "consciousness as phenomenon" or "consciousness of differentiation." In addition, I would like to call an action on or reaction to the object made through this consciousness the "mind as phenomenon."

Let us now turn to the "root cause of phenomenon (thing)" unencumbered by the above-described object-sense about an objective thing. It is easily imagined that all things visible to the eye are differentiated from invisible "causes," which are also called "laws." However, the law that is the cause of a phenomenon, in turn, results from another cause. Such a higher cause is called a "principle." It can thus be understood as the cause of all causes. When Cosmic Consciousness is called the supreme principle, it means precisely that it is the cause of all laws.

The word Cosmic ("of the Universe") is conceptually equivalent to "universal" ("pertaining to all"): its straightforward meaning is "all that are perceived constitute itself within its consciousness." That is why it is called the "principle." Since this leads to a bold and surprising insight, let me explain in simpler terms.

Since Cosmic Consciousness is the ultimate cause, it has no cause for its own phenomenon, unlike all other phenomena. There is no cause, existence, or phenomenon outside its cause. Our object-sense is caused by an object (i.e., where there is an object, our object-sense arises). How, then, is Cosmic Consciousness's object-sense formed? Since "consciousness" – be it subjective or objective – is a consciousness "about" an object, Cosmic Consciousness, which is defined as the cause of all causes, must also be a consciousness about something. However, it would be a contradiction if Cosmic Consciousness, which is the supreme cause and which exists unto itself, had an object of consciousness outside itself, just as we have our objects of consciousness outside ourselves. Should an object-sense arise within Cosmic Consciousness, or should Cosmic Consciousness itself be nothing but some sort of object-sense about something, it would not exist objectively, as our consciousness does. Therefore, the first thing we can think of is that Cosmic Consciousness's object-sense may be subjective – i.e., Cosmic Consciousness is "convinced" that such an object should exist, even though there is no such object of perception. Suppose that its object-sense is a mere conviction – i.e., an illusion or a one-actor play, so to speak. Still, as far as we know from our experience, there is no play that is absolutely about the solo actor alone. That is to say, consciousness never "on its own" (though this is a funny expression) creates an object-sense within itself. In other words, it cannot imagine or envision that which does not exist in reality. And what is important lies in these facts.

It is deduced that Cosmic Consciousness, which is the supreme cause, possesses within itself "the object to perceive as a cause of its own consciousness." What, then, will happen to the consciousness thus arisen? When we try to make ourselves an object of our cognition, we have to begin with our object-sense, which is our object. With Cosmic Consciousness, the object of its cognition is none other than itself. Accordingly, it is understood that its object-cognition is identical with its self-cognition. This logic, which may appear contradictory, leads to an important conclusion: being conscious means that the self becomes an object of its own consciousness, and thus "at once creates its own cause and prompts the act of becoming an object of its own consciousness." To put it more concretely, it means creating an "object" of its consciousness within itself – while simultaneously "becoming its own object." Therefore, Cosmic Consciousness exists as an agreement between creation and cognition, subjectivity and objectivity.

This explains why Cosmic Consciousness is called the "supreme" cause. Given a supernatural premise, Cosmic Consciousness engenders all beings and all phenomena – which are simply manifested as a result of Cosmic Consciousness's self-cognition, or as an object of its self-consciousness. Humans born in the wilderness of the Universe are no exception. In a sense, because the Universe exists as a basis (fundamental cause) of object-sense of its consciousness, it is not a mistake to say that "God let the Universe be created in order to see Himself." This, in turn, provides an answer to the question "Why does the Universe exist?" and also gives a clear answer to the question "Through what does the Universe exist?" Let me summarise the above discussions item by item.

The necessary and sufficient conditions for Cosmic Consciousness to exist as the cause of all beings and all laws, and function as the ultimate, supreme cause include:

1) It possesses an object of its consciousness as the cause of its own consciousness within itself.

2) Accordingly, it at once engenders the cause (or basis) of its consciousness and prompts the act of becoming an object of its own consciousness. That is to say, this working itself must be the cause of its own consciousness (self-consciousness).

3) Since 2) is same as creating an object within itself in order to make an object that is an object of cognition for its own consciousness as the cause of its own self-perception, consciousness is an act of itself becoming an object, manifesting itself as a phenomenon.

In brief, with Cosmic Consciousness: a) Object-cognition is identical with self-cognition; b) Its self-cognition is nothing but the agreement of "creativity" and "cognition"; and c) As a result, "subjectivity" and "objectivity" make a universal agreement within its cognition. In other words, consciousness that sees is also consciousness that creates; and consciousness that contemplates is consciousness that knows.

The eye with which I see is the eye that creates what I want to see; the mind with which I think is the mind that knows.

A further detailed inquiry into this issue will complete this book's thesis, leading to the understanding that Cosmic Consciousness is not only the act of knowing itself, but also the most fundamental energy that creates things; that its act of knowing is not only the "will" but also a "blueprint" for the creation of things; that Cosmic Consciousness itself is not only the "principle of life" but the "principle of ego." It will become evident that the Universe is an immediate manifestation of these principles; that all beings owe their basis (or cause) of existence to these principles, i.e., Cosmic Consciousness. Not only are humans an immediate realisation of Cosmic Consciousness; but the very existence of humans proves the existence of Cosmic Consciousness. Many people have a profound knowledge of it, but our consciousness must be engendered by Cosmic Consciousness itself.

Cosmic Consciousness is at once the "principle of existence" and the "principle of life/ego," because of the following characteristics, which are respectively deduced from the above three conditions 1), 2), 3).

1)' It is the act of objectifying (actualising) the sense that I am alive (self-consciousness of life), and at the same time the awareness that I am alive.

2)' It is the act of objectifying (actualising) the sense that I exist (self-consciousness of being), and at the same time the awareness that I exist.

3)' It is the act of objectifying (actualising) the sense that I understand (self-consciousness of knowledge), and at the same time the awareness that I understand.

These merely give a concrete explanation of Cosmic Consciousness. At any rate, accordingly, the conclusion is drawn that: a)' Cosmic Consciousness is the omniscient and omnipotent consciousness; b)' It is the act of objectifying the omniscient and omnipotent consciousness; and c)' All that are objectified are thus objects of its cognition. This deepens our understanding that all beings and all phenomena of the Universe, which are objects of Cosmic Consciousness's cognition, are the objectification (actualisation) of its self-cognition. To paraphrase, the above 1)'-3)' are "actualised" in the form of the Universe.

Humans are the most immediate realisation of all, because my consciousness to think so results from the object-cognition (i.e., self-cognition) of Cosmic Consciousness. Therefore, we have an actual sense of the 1)'-3)'. This truth may be summarised as follows:

My mind to think of God is God's mind to think of me.

God's consciousness to create the world is concretely manifested in our consciousness to perceive things.

When we are cognisant of things, we accordingly understand that because the object thus recognised is the appearance of the object itself, we experience no "disagreement" between the "recognised image" and the "thing" that is an object of cognition. Therefore, an answer is given to the first questions that have been posed in this book: "What" makes my sense that allows me to sense (more precisely, to be cognisant of) a rose true? and "What" enables me to know it? The answer is Cosmic Consciousness, the consciousness that invokes the "common cognition" among us. As a result, Cosmic Consciousness comes to be satisfactorily postulated as the "mode of ego." That is to say, Cosmic Consciousness is the source of our ego, the cause of our common cognition.

However, it has nothing to do with whether or not we are "self-aware" of Cosmic

Consciousness. The self-awareness about Cosmic Consciousness is called the "experience of Cosmic Consciousness," which will be explained in detail in the next chapter. Since this book has by now provided a considerable degree of understanding about "consciousness"—the most important yet not so well understood issue in philosophy—I will hereafter discuss in detail the "Creation of the Universe and humans" through self-cognition of Cosmic Consciousness. At the same time, the book will offer an innovative understanding about humans' fundamental capacity and the structure of the Universe.

Section 3: Definition of "Cosmic Consciousness"

Now that the existence of Cosmic Consciousness that is an undeniable principle has been correctly deduced, I would like to define it again, based on the foregoing postulation.

> Definition 1: It is the cause of all laws and the supreme principle of the Universe.
> Definition 2: It is a consciousness common to all beings.
> Definition 3: It is the power to create things, the knowledge to know things, and the will to desire things.

Upon reading the above, some readers may find these definitions similar to "theological" or "Buddhist" views. In other words, they may appear to define God, on the one hand, and Brahman (ultra-self), on the other hand. However, in Christian theology and Western philosophy, although God is understood through the concept of the "personified," or reversely the "non-personified," God is placed under Cosmic Consciousness, because the foregoing definitions imply that Cosmic Consciousness is the "principle of personification." God thus understood is on the same level as Atman engendered by Brahman, the supreme principle of the Universe in Indian Upanishad cosmology. That is to say, even though Christian theology attempts to postulate God as the supreme principle of the Universe, God could never be supreme. The only philosophies comparable to cosmic philosophy are the Upanishads (originating around 600 B.C.E.) and Reg Veda (originating around 1500 B.C.E.). The magnificent vision of the Creation of the Universe by Cosmic Consciousness, which will be the topic of the next chapter, may also be reminiscent of the creation myth of the Upanishads. It is no accident that the two philosophies, though more than 2500 years apart, share important features in their cosmologies.

Chapter 2: Self-Cognition of Cosmic Consciousness
Section 1: The Supreme Principle of the Universe

Let us now describe how Cosmic Consciousness manifests the Universe and all beings, including humans—i.e., how the consciousness that is the supreme principle of the Universe manifests the Ego that is the "individual principle."

Given the fact that Cosmic Consciousness that is the supreme principle of the Universe is the universal principle and the universal cause of life, ego, senses, and existence, it may be said that the supreme principle itself presents no actual "individuality" (or particularity) to speak of, just as light is not bright in and of itself. That is to say, no "individual (or particular) principle" can be found in such ultimateness. Figuratively speaking, it is an "undifferentiated" principle, and thus an "undifferentiated" individual principle. Readers must remember that light is an undifferentiated spectrum: while light contains many phases of colour as its own individual principles, they may be known only when they are actually differentiated by a prism. Still, since light results from a certain principle, it already encompasses the individual principles. In contrast, the supreme principle does not contain a cause of itself; thus there exists no individual principle, no "individual principle of the supreme principle." Accordingly, it should be understood that the supreme principle is an "undifferentiated individual principle."

Granted that consciousness always involves an object; in the case of Cosmic Consciousness that is the supreme principle, it has an object of its own consciousness within itself as the cause of its own consciousness. This is because, as has already been established, it at once engenders the cause of its own consciousness and prompts the act of becoming an object of its own consciousness; and accordingly it creates an object of its own cognition within itself and "becomes its own object." In other words, precisely because the supreme principle is a "consciousness," it must first transform itself into "individual principles." Therefore, this working constitutes nothing but the sufficient condition for Cosmic Consciousness to be the supreme principle.

Its "individual principles" are principles necessary for the consciousness that is the supreme principle to "objectify (actualise)" itself. These may be understood as the principles of "wisdom," "will" and "power."

In brief, Cosmic Consciousness, through its self-cognition, first engenders the principles of individuality necessary for its own actualisation. This is the first stage of the Creation of the Universe. It may be said that the supreme principle first "differentiated" itself in order to actualize its own principles. Taking place within itself without external agents, this qualifies as "self-multiplication (or self-creation)" and "virgin conception." Its inward differentiation is reminiscent of a fertilised egg's "cell division." In other words, such a differentiation is "characteristic" of Life. Not coincidentally, to prove the mystery of such workings of consciousness, I would like to point to an actual example of "virgin conception": a paper presented by an American researcher at the American neurology society, which is said to have made a huge controversy in the world of biology, concerns the case of a sixteen-year-old female from Arkansas whose ovarian cysts were removed. During the procedure, a sign of living sperm was discovered alongside living eggs in adjacent tissues. The sperm-egg position was such that the possibility of their union to create a foetus was considered significant. The young patient was beyond doubt a virgin, a fact that pointed to the possibility of "virgin conception" in the human body. Today, such a case has come to be known as "unisexual reproduction" – no unusual phenomenon in biology. It is estimated that human babies unisexually conceived and born make up less than half of $1/80^5$ of all births.

A spectrum of light, which is a potential form of things, thus emerges in an initial field: undifferentiated consciousness, which may be compared to the eye that has not seen light, begins to see light everywhere. As the supreme principle begins its work, consciousness is awakened everywhere. In other words, the Universe as a whole begins to transform itself into a conscious entity. However, at this stage, as has been established, Cosmic Consciousness that is the supreme principle is still in the process of differentiation in order to objectify (actualise) itself into several necessary principles (principles of individuality). In other words, at this stage, Cosmic Consciousness engenders nothing in reality, having only established the mode it should take as the supreme principle. What is visible is the possibility that the "principles of individuality" engendered at this stage will manifest wisdom, will and power. Now, self-cognition of Cosmic Consciousness instantly enters the following stage.

Section 2: The Creation of the Universe
At this stage of self-cognition, Cosmic Consciousness creates an object of its own consciousness. That is to say, it becomes an object. In other words, at this moment, the Universe becomes an entity, or is "personified." It can be said that a consciousness geminating at the early stage of Creation becomes for the first time a "being." The eye which has been awakened in all areas of the Universe now becomes an "ego," that is, personality. The eye thus manifests itself, actualises itself within its gaze.

Cosmic Consciousness that has engendered the "individual principles" – because of them – manifests the cause of Laws that are to come at the next stage of Creation. For example, it manifests "power" that is the cause of senses, "knowledge" that is the cause of imagination/thought, and "will" that is the cause of creativity. Laws encompass neither known nor unknown laws of physics, which are to come after Creation. When we say the "power that is the cause of senses" is engendered, this power is "conscious energy," which must exist as the undifferentiated state, or in its potential form, of all kinds of physical energy, and is also a determining factor of the laws of physics. Also, when we say "knowledge that is the cause of imagination/thought" is engendered, this knowledge is also "conscious energy"; the same is true for the "will that is the cause of creation." All of them combined constitute a manifestation of Laws of Ego/Life. The spectrum of the Universe is assuming a whiter light. This implies that the Universe has been personified.

However, nothing that is visible to the eye has emerged. The Universe pulsates, cloaked in an ethereal consciousness in which light and darkness are yet to be separated. Perhaps, at this stage, Infinity is being manifested.

Naturally, Cosmic Consciousness that is the supreme principle must objectify (actualize)

Infinity, or "eternity," as an object of its own cognition. Infinity (eternity) is in itself an object of cognition of Cosmic Consciousness because Cosmic Consciousness is nothing but "consciousness of Infinity" and "consciousness of eternity."

Accordingly, when Infinity is manifested based on the "individual principles," "infinite groups" in terms of quantity and "infinite phases" in terms of quality are manifested (engendered). It is immediately after the first stage of Creation, wherein the supreme principle of the Universe is manifested as the individual principle of all beings, that the infinite groups and phases are manifested as "individuality" of the individual principles. The Universe can therefore encompass all spectra, all energy phases. Also, since "consciousness of Infinity (eternity)" comes to exist as Cosmic Consciousness itself, self-cognition of Cosmic Consciousness must infinitely "objectify" (actualise) the concept of Infinity as an object of its own cognition. This actualisation concretely results in "infinite space," "infinite time" (eternity), and "infinite being" (all things and all phenomena). In other words, the infinite groups and phases are manifested.

Now, at this stage, Time and Space are engendered (created) as the actualisation of the infinite groups and phases. Since Time and Space must be identical with another thing also manifested at this stage, i.e., "conscious energy," they in a sense must exist as "power" that effects laws and phenomena. Conscious energy exists as the factor that determines the laws of physics as well as a potential form of the differentiated physical energy; then, Time and Space, which are identical with it, must also be understood as the ultimately fundamental form of all energies. And because Time and Space are engendered along with the concept of Infinity that is Cosmic Consciousness, we cannot consider them separately. Therefore, Time and Space are understood as Time-Energy. That is to say, Time and Space as an object of cognition of Cosmic Consciousness are a positive form of the concept of Infinity. Energies observed in our world are variously differentiated and transformed forms of Time-Energy that is conscious energy.

However, it should be noted that while Time-Energy may objectively effect "passage" and "distance," it has no direct relationship with them (i.e., Time and Space). Although the manifestation of the infinite groups and phases means that of Time and Space, they are not manifested as "distance" or "passage" that we can "objectively" sense. In other words, within Cosmic Consciousness, no temporal sense of "passage" or no spatial sense of "distance" arises. As will be shortly examined, the way we today sense Time and Space is nothing but our "objective" sense of Time-Space-Energy, and this sense is not real at all. In fact, when we fuse with Cosmic Consciousness, we will lose the sense of passage/distance and feel that the whole thing constitutes our own consciousness itself.

Now, the Creation of the Universe will enter its third stage. The infinite groups and phases which have been manifested will function as Time-Energy (or conscious energy) and cause the manifestation of the "laws of physics" and "individual entities" at the next stage.

Section 3: The Birth of Ego and Laws

The supreme principle engenders the individual principles, which in turn manifest the infinite groups and the infinite phases. At this stage, the Universe engenders Time-Energy, which is conscious energy, and thus becomes personified. However, this merely means that the Universe "as a whole" becomes a conscious entity (personality), which is yet to be manifested "individually" or particularly. That is to say, although Laws of Life are manifested, Life itself is not manifested as an individual entity. Needless to say, the individual entity that Cosmic Consciousness that is the supreme principle manifests itself in is Ego or Soul. Since Soul is nothing but the particular or individual expression of Cosmic Consciousness that is the supreme principle, we may call it "Cosmic Consciousness that has acquired an individual expression."

Naturally, it is a logical result of the individual principles.

Moreover, as we have investigated at the second stage of Creation, since the individual principles manifest themselves in infinite groups and phases, "the Soul that is Cosmic Consciousness that has acquired an individual expression" must also be manifested in the infinite groups and phases. Therefore, the Soul must be infinite in number (quantity) and infinite in kind (quality). Consequently, the Soul is created everywhere in the Universe – that is to say, individualities of infinite kinds are created in infinite numbers as conscious entities.

As will be examined in the next chapter in the section "Experience of Cosmic Consciousness," Souls manifested by Cosmic Consciousness cannot be identical individuals. Because, if so, Cosmic Consciousness has not acquired an individual expression.

Cosmic Consciousness is "infinite consciousness" and a consciousness that actually senses that it is infinite. Since its Infinity must be infinite in kind as well as phase, when it objectifies (actualises) the "actual sense that it is infinite" within itself as an object of its own cognition, the objectified Soul must be infinite in kind. This, in and of itself, constitutes the "individual expression of Cosmic Consciousness." Therefore, even though all beings possess infinite consciousness, or what may be called Divinity, because of this very consciousness, the individualities of their Souls cannot be identical. That is to say, all Souls can individualise themselves through their "consciousness of Infinity."

To repeat, no matter what it is called, at this stage, Cosmic Consciousness becomes an "entity" in its individual groups and its individual phases (appearances). This must be understood as a state of Cosmic Consciousness that has acquired an individual expression (or become individualised). And that is an individual Soul. The spectrum of the Universe, which has appeared a mere white light, now reveals countless radiant lines (as observed in an atom's line spectrum). Now, with its various pulses and radiations, the Universe appears to work like a "mind." This is one of the phenomena that take place at the third stage of Creation. To rephrase the above in our ordinary language, "matter" is created as a living entity.

Conscious energy manifested at the second stage of Creation must hereby manifest Laws as well. As has been observed, conscious energy is also the determining factor for the laws of physics. In other words, Laws constitute a differentiated form of conscious energy, which is the undifferentiated (and thus ultimate) state of energy. Laws, a form of energy as such, effect what is generally called the laws of physics – or the order concerning various forms of existence and different modes of motion, as well as the pattern of their correlations.

The differentiation of Time-Energy manifests itself not only in Laws but also in Time and

Space. That is to say, since Time and Space may be understood as differentiated forms of conscious energy (Time-Energy), Laws and Time and Space are qualitatively identical. Since they are all differentiated forms of conscious energy, consciousness (in this case subjectivity) can freely modify Laws as well as Time and Space. Accordingly, an important conclusion is drawn that Time and Space is objectively sensed as "passage" and "distance," merely because Time and Space are "modified" by s/he who senses them and are made to take the forms of "passage" and "distance."

This is quite logical, for Time and Space are nothing but products of self-cognition of Cosmic Consciousness. If Cosmic Consciousness "actually senses" Time and Space as "passage" and "distance," then they must be manifested as such (because as has been already established, Cosmic Consciousness is a consciousness that objectifies its "actual sense" as an object of its own cognition). Still, there is no sign that Cosmic Consciousness actually sensed or senses (was/is cognisant of) Time and Space as "passage" and "distance." In fact, such cognition is contradictory to the nature of Cosmic Consciousness. Should Cosmic Consciousness objectively sense Time and Space as passage and distance, just as we do, what it senses should "limit" itself – in other words, it senses itself in a limited manner, which is contrary to the essential nature of Cosmic Consciousness.

Therefore, even if Cosmic Consciousness also senses passage and distance, they must be sensed as something "static" or "unified." This is consistent with the fact that when we "experience" Cosmic Consciousness, we feel as if we are one with the whole, as if Time and Space are suspended.

What, then, does this mean objectively and physically? For one thing, this indicates that the law of "conservation of energy" also applies to Time and Space. That is to say, were we to feel that Time were suspended, this Time is being reduced to Space, which means that this Space is "distorted" in such a way that its distance is shortened to the minimum. To rephrase it in terms of consciousness, when consciousness does not sense Time as passage, it is not cognisant of Space as distance. And since a sense of distance is lost, this sense is actualised and Space is distorted in a shortened way. This also means that Time and Space, which are differentiated forms of Time-Energy (or conscious energy), revert to Time-Energy in its undifferentiated state. Conversely, when Space is sensed as distance, Time appears as passage; Space is then distorted in an expanded way. Needless to say, these distortions – shortening and expansion – result in a closed and an open surface, respectively. When Space is completely and positively closed, Time passes at zero-speed; when Space is negatively closed, Time passes at infinite speed. This means that if consciousness distorts Space in a closed way, an object moving therein is gradually provided infinite speed in the form of Time-Energy by Space, i.e., the object is accelerated; and that when space is negatively closed, an object moving therein "releases" its own matter (Space-Potential, so to speak) in the form of Time-Energy. Therefore, as (negatively closed) Space is provided Time-Energy from the object, it begins to oscillate from the positive to the negative domain, while the object's Potential at once dissipates and inflates limitlessly. That is to say, the object vanishes.

This simply means that "distance" and "passage" are manifested as such in an objective reflection of "increase/decrease" of Time-Energy's entropy. The increase of Time's entropy is manifested as passage, and the rhythm of its decrease as passage's "discontinuous rhythm." Conversely, if Time's entropy is maintained by Space's Potential, it decreases to an eventual lull, whereby Time and Space cannot be objectively sensed as "passage" and "distance." Thus, in such a world, as Time-Space-Energy is continuously supplied, aging and death will not occur.

What should be noted in the foregoing discussion is that Time and Space themselves are given positivity (Potential) by Time-Energy and they cannot be energy in themselves. Accordingly, when provided with Potential by Time-Energy, Time in turn can provide it in the form of energy to Space (including "matter" which is a simple space); conversely, when similarly provided with Potential, Space can give it in the form of energy to Time. Therefore, the total of Time's and Space's Potential equals the amount of Time-Energy's Potential. It follows, then, that Time-Energy, which is the sum total of Time's and Space's Potential, is neither Time nor Space, but what may be called another "consciousness." In the not distant future, contemporary nuclear and quantum physics discover such a view.

Now, this explains why consciousness through which Time and Space are subjectively sensed subtly varies from person to person: a person may sense the passage of a second longer than another does.

Let us consider an example to illustrate the above theory. Suppose there are two rooms, A and B, and two groups of people, A' and B', in the respective rooms; the members of Group A' in Room A all feel, and continue to feel, that "time passes quickly," and those of Group B' in Room B, that "time passes slowly." Each room is equipped with a very precise clock (much more precise than today's technology allows). The minute and second hands of the two clocks are initially synchronized. Still, if we compare the two clocks after a while, the clock of Room A, in which Group A' continue to feel "subjectively" that time is passing quickly, is indeed "objectively" faster than its counterpart in Room B. This can actually happen – because "objectivity" and "objective senses" are engendered as objects of Cosmic Consciousness's cognition and Cosmic Consciousness's objectivity is a result of its subjectivity, which is a cause of its objectivity. Therefore, an objective phenomenon is also affected by subjectivity. If we are convinced that "time is not passing," such a conviction manifests itself as an objective fact. Please examine such phenomena in relation to Time-Energy.

I have by now established that Time and Space are differentiated forms of Time-Energy, and are thus affected by consciousness. This applies to that which is called Laws. That is to say, no Law constitutes an absolute truth. The only absolute truth is: Cosmic Consciousness is the supreme principle. There is no law that does not follow this truth; conversely, all laws (including the laws of physics) may be actually modified by consciousness.

Kajin Yamamoto, "A Philosophical Study of Cosmic Consciousness"
Published by Kasumiga-Shobu, 1974, P10-40. Translated by Reiko Tomii

Krishnamurti: I thought we should talk about the future of Man. As things are, from what one observes, the world has become tremendously dangerous. There are terrorists, wars, and national and racial divisions, some dictators who want to destroy the world and so on. Also, religiously there is tremendous separation.

David Bohm: And there is the economic crisis and the ecological crisis.

K: Problems seem to be multiplying more and more. So what is the future of Man? What is the future not only of the present generation but of the coming generations?

DB: Well, the future looks very grim.

K: Yes, if you and I were quite young, and knowing all this, what would we do? What would be our reaction? What would be our life, our way of earning a livelihood and so on?

DB: I have often thought about that. I have asked myself, "would I go into science again?" And I am not at all certain now because science does not seem to be relevant to this crisis.

K: No, on the contrary it is helping to...

DB: ... make it worse. Science might help but in fact it isn't.

K: So, what would you do? I think I would stick to what I am doing.

DB: Well, that would be easy for you.

K: For me, quite easy. You see, I don't think in terms of evolution.

DB: I was expecting we would discuss that.

K: I don't think there is psychological evolution at all.

DB: We have often discussed this, so I understand to some extent what you mean. But I think that people new to this are not going to understand.

K: Yes, we will discuss this whole question, if you will. But why are we concerned about the future? The whole future is now.

DB: Well, in some sense the whole future is now but we have to make that clear. This goes very much against the whole traditional way of thinking.

K: Yes, I know. Mankind thinks in terms of evolution, continuance, and so on.

DB: Maybe we could approach it in another way. That is, evolution seems in the present era to be the most natural way to think. So I would like to ask you: what objections do you have to thinking in terms of evolution? The word has, of course, many meanings.

K: Of course, we are talking psychologically.

DB: Yes, now the first point is: let's dispose of it physically.

K: An acorn will grow into an oak.

DB: Yes, also the species has evolved; for example, from plants to animals and to Man.

K: Yes, we have taken a million years to be what we are.

DB: You do not doubt that that has happened?

K: No, that has happened.

DB: It may continue to happen. That is a valid process.

K: That is evolution. Of course, that is a valid, natural process.

DB: It takes place in time and therefore in that region the past, present and future are important.

K: Yes, obviously. I don't know a certain language, and I need time to learn it.

DB: It also takes time to improve the brain. If the brain was small when it started out, it got steadily larger, and that took a million years.

K: Yes, and it becomes much more complex and so on. All that needs time, all that is movement in space and time.

DB: So you will admit physical time and neurophysiological time.

K: Absolutely, of course, any sane man would.

DB: Now, most people also admit psychological time, what they call mental time.

K: Yes, that is what we are talking about. Whether there is such a thing as psychological tomorrow, psychological evolution.

DB: Now, at first sight I am afraid this will sound strange. It seems I can remember yesterday, and there is tomorrow, I can anticipate.

It has happened many times, you know that days have succeeded each other. So I do have the experience of time, from yesterday to today to tomorrow – right?

K: Of course, that is simple enough.

DB: Now what is it that you are denying?

K: I deny that I will be something, become better.

DB: But there are two ways of looking at that. One way is: will I intentionally become better because I am trying? Or some people feel that evolution is a kind of natural, inevitable process, which is sweeping us along like a current, and we are perhaps becoming better or worse, or something else is happening to us.

K: Psychologically.

DB: Yes, which takes time but which may not be the result of my trying to become better. It may or may not be, some people may think one way, some another. But are you denying that there is a kind of natural psychological evolution like the natural biological evolution?

K: I am denying that, yes.

DB: Well, why do you deny it?

K: First of all, what is the psyche, the "me", the ego, and so on, what is it?

DB: Well, the word "psyche" has many meanings. It may mean the mind, for example. Do you mean that the ego is the same thing?

K: The ego, I am talking of the ego, the "me".

DB: Yes, now some people think of evolution as a process in which the "me" will be transcended, that it will rise to a higher level. So there are two questions. One is: will the "me" ever improve? And the other question is: supposing we want to get beyond the "me" can that be done in time?

K: That cannot be done in time.

DB: Yes, now we have to make it clear why not.

K: I will, we will go into it. What is the "me"? If the word "psyche" has such different meanings, the "me" is the whole movement which thought has brought about.

DB: Why do you say that?

K: The "me" is the consciousness, my consciousness, the "me" is my name, form and all the various experiences that I have had, remembrances and so on. The whole struture of the "me" is put together by thought.

DB: Well, that again would be something which some people might find hard to accept.

K: Of course, we are discussing it.

DB: Let us try to bring it out. Because the first experience, the first feeling I have about the "me" is that it is there independently and that the "me" is thinking.

K: Is the "me" independent of my thinking?

DB: Well, my own first feeling is that the "me" is there independent of my thinking, and it is the "me" that is thinking.

K: Yes.

DB: Just as I am here and can move my arm or head, I can think. Now is that an illusion?

K: No, because when I move my arm, there is an intention to grasp or pick up something, which means that first it is the movement of thought. That makes the arm move and so on. My contention – and I am open to this being challenged – is that thought is the basis of all this.

DB: Yes, your contention is that the whole sense of the "me" and what it is doing is coming out of thought. What you mean by thought, though, is not merely intellectual.

K: No, of course not. Thought is the whole movement of experience, knowledge, and memory. It is this movement.

DB: It sounds to me as if you mean the consciousness as a whole.

K: As a whole, that's right.

DB: And you are saying that this movement is the "me" – right?

K: The whole content of that consciousness is the "me". The "me" is not different from my consciousness.

DB: Yes, well, I think one could say that I am my consciousness, for if I am not conscious I am not here. Now, is consciousness nothing but what you have just described, which includes thought, feeling, intention?

K: … intention, aspirations …

DB: ... memories …

K: ... memories, beliefs, dogmas, the rituals that are performed, the whole of that, like a computer that has been programmed.

DB: Yes, everybody would agree that certainly is in consciousness, but many people would feel that there is more to it, that consciousness may go beyond that.

K: Let's go into it. The content of our consciousness makes up the consciousness.

DB: I think that requires some clarification. The ordinary use of the word "content" is quite different. If you say that the content of a glass is water, the glass is one thing and the water is another. The glass contains the water, so the word "content" would suggest that something contains it.

K: All right, consciousness is made up of all that it has remembered, beliefs, dogmas, rituals, nationalities, fears, pleasures, sorrow.

DB: Yes, now if all that were absent would there be no consciousness?

K: Not as we know it.

DB: But there would still be a kind of consciousness?

K: A totally different kind.

DB: Well, then I think you really mean to say that consciousness, as we know it, is made up ...

K: ... is the result of the multiple activities of thought. Thought has put my consciousness together – the reactions, the responses, the memories, the extraordinary complex intricacies, subtleties – all that is, makes up, consciousness.

DB: As we know it.

K: As we know it. The question is whether that consciousness has a future.

DB: Does it have a past?

K: Of course, remembrance.

DB: Remembrance, yes. Why do you say it has no future then?

K: If it has a future it will be exactly the same kind of thing. The same activities, same thoughts, modified, but the pattern will be repeated over and over again.

DB: So are you saying that thought can only repeat?

K: Yes.

DB: But there is a feeling that thought can develop new ideas, for example.

K: But thought is limited because knowledge is limited, if you admit that knowledge will always be limited.

DB: Now, why do you say knowledge is always limited?

K: Because you as a scientist are experimenting, adding, searching. You are adding, and after you some other person will add more. So knowledge, which is born of experience, is limited.

DB: Some people have argued that it isn't. They would hope to obtain perfect or absolute knowledge of the laws of Nature.

K: The laws of Nature are not the laws of human being.

DB: Well, do you want to restrict the discussion then to knowledge about the human being?

K: Of course, that's all we can talk about.

DB: All right. So are we saying that Man cannot obtain unlimited knowledge of the psyche? Is that what you are saying? There is always more that is unknown.

K: Yes, there is always more that is unknown. So once we admit that knowledge is limited then thought is limited.

DB: Yes, thought depends on knowledge and knowledge does not cover everything. Therefore thought will not be able to handle everything that happens.

K: That's right. But that is what the politicians and all the other people are trying to do. They think that thought can solve every problem.

DB: You can see in the case of politicians that knowledge is very limited. And when you lack adequate knowledge of what you are dealing with you create confusion.

K: So then as thought is limited, our consciousness, which has been put together by thought, is limited.

DB: Now, can you make that clear? That means we can only stay in the same circle.

K: The same circle.

DB: You see, if you compare with science, people might argue that although my knowledge is limited I am constantly discovering.

K: What you discover is added on, but is still limited.

DB: It is still limited. That's the point. I think one of the ideas behind the scientific approach is that although knowledge is limited I can discover and keep up with the actuality.

K: But that is also limited.

DB: My discoveries are limited and there is always the unknown that I have not discovered.

K: That is what I am saying. The unknown, the limitless, cannot be captured by thought because thought in itself is limited. So do you and I agree to that, not only agree but see it is a fact?

DB: Well, perhaps we could bring it out still more. That is, thought is limited, even though there is a very strong predisposition, feeling, tendency, to feel that thought can do anything.

K: But it can't. See what it has done in the world!

DB: Well, I agree that is has done some terrible things but that doesn't prove that it is always wrong. You see, maybe you could always blame that on people who have used it wrongly.

K: I know, that is a good old trick! But thought in *itself* is limited, therefore whatever it does is limited.

DB: And you are saying it is limited in a very serious way.

K: That's right, in a very, very serious way.

DB: Well, could we bring that out, and say what that way is?

K: That way is what is happening in the world. The totalitarian ideals are the invention of thought.

DB: Yes, we could say that the very word "totalitarian" means they wanted to cover the totality but they couldn't – and the thing collapsed.

K: It is collapsing.

DB: But then there are those who say they are not totalitarians.

K: But the thinking of the democrats, the republicans and the idealists and so on is also limited.

DB: Yes, limited in a way that is …

K: … very destructive.

DB: ... that is very serious and destructive. Now in what way could we bring that out? You see, I could say, "OK, my thought is limited but this may not be all that serious". Why is it so important?

K: That is fairly simple: because whatever action is born of limited thought must inevitably breed conflict. Dividing humanity geographically into nationalities and dividing humanity religiously and so on has created havoc in the world.

DB: Yes, let's connect that with the limitation of thought. That is, my knowledge is limited. Now how does that lead me to divide the world?

K: Aren't we seeking security? We thought there was security in the family, security in the tribe, security in nationalism. So we thought that there was security in division.

DB: Yes, that seems to be how it has come out: take the tribe, for example; one may feel insecure and then say, "with the tribe I am secure". That is a conclusion. And I think I know enough to be sure that is so but I don't. Other things happen that I don't know of which make that very insecure. Other tribes come along.

K: No, the very division itself creates insecurity.

DB: It helps to create it but I am trying to say that I don't know enough to know that – I don't see that.

K: One doesn't see it because one has not looked at the world as a whole.

DB: Well, the thought that aims at security attempts to know everything important. As soon as it knows everything important it says, "this will bring security" – yet not only are there a lot of things it doesn't know but one thing it doesn't know is that this very thought is itself divisive. It's going to be divisive, because I define an area that is secure, divided from another area.

K: It is divisive because in itself it is limited. Anything that is limited must inevitably create conflict.

DB: Well, you mean any thought that is …

K: If I say I am an individual, it is limited. I am concerned with myself, that is very limited.

DB: Yes, we have to get this clear. You see, if I say this is a table, which is limited, it creates no conflict – right?

K: No, there is no conflict there.

DB: Now when I say this is "me", that creates conflict.

K: The "me" is a divisive entity.

DB: Let's see more clearly why.

K: Because it is separative, it is concerned with itself; and the "me" identifying with the greater, the nation, is still divisive.

DB: Yes, well, I define myself in the interest of security so that I know what I am as opposed to what you are and I protect myself. Now this creates a division between me and you.

K: We and they and so on.

DB: We and they. Now that comes from my limited thought, because I don't understand that we are really closely related and connected.

K: We are human beings.

DB: Yes, we are all human beings.

K: All human beings have more or less the same problems.

DB: But I haven't understood that. My knowledge is limited, I think that we *can* make a distinction and protect ourselves and me and not the others. But in the very act of doing that I create instability, insecurity.

K: That's right, you create insecurity. So if we see that, not merely intellectually or verbally, but actually feel it, that we are the rest of humanity, then the responsibility becomes immense.

DB: Well, how can you do anything about that responsibility?

K: Then I either contribute to the whole mess, or keep out of it. That is, to be at peace, to have order in oneself. I will come to that, I am going too fast.

DB: You see, I think we have touched upon an important point. We say the whole of humanity, of mankind, is one, and therefore to create division there is …

K: … dangerous.

DB: Yes, whereas to create division between me and the table is not dangerous because in some sense we are not one. Now mankind doesn't realize that it is all one.

K: Why, why?

DB: Well, let's go into that. This is a crucial point. It is clear it doesn't, because there are so many divisions, and not only between nations and religions but between one person and another.

K: Why is there this division?

DB: Well, the first thing, at least in the modern era, is the belief that every human being is an individual. This may not have been so strong in the past.

K: That is what I question. I question altogether whether we are individuals.

DB: That is a big question because …

K: Of course. We said just now that the consciousness which is 'me' is similar to that of all other human beings. They all suffer, they all have fears, they are all insecure, they have their own particular gods and rituals, all put together by thought.

DB: Yes, well, I think this calls for some clarification. There are two questions here. One is, not everybody feels that he is similar – most people feel they have some unique distinction.

K: What do you mean by "unique distinction"? Distinction in doing something?

DB: There may be many things. For example, one nation may feel that it is able to do some things better than another, one person has some special things he does, or a particular quality.

K: Of course, you are more intellectual than I am. Somebody else is better in this or that.

DB: He may take pride in his own special abilities or advantages.

K: But when you put that away we are basically the same.

DB: You are saying that these things you have just described are …

K: … superficial.

DB: Now, what are the things that are basic?

K: Fear, sorrow, pain, anxiety, loneliness, all the human travail.

DB: But many people might feel that the highest achievements of Man are the basic things.

K: What have we achieved?

DB: For one thing people may feel proud of the achievements of Man in science, art, culture and technology.

K: We have achievements in all those directions, certainly we have vast technology, communication, travel, medicines, surgery …

DB: It is really remarkable in many ways.

K: There is no question about that. But what have we achieved psychologically?

DB: You are saying that none of these achievements has affected us psychologically?

K: Yes, that's right.

DB: And the psychological question is more important than any of the others because if the psychological question is not cleared up the rest is dangerous.

K: If we are limited psychologically, then whatever we do will be limited, and the technology will then be used by our limited psyche.

DB: Yes, the master is this limited psyche and not the rational structure of technnology, and in fact technology then becomes a dangerous …

K: … instrument.

DB: So that is one point: that the psyche is at the core of it all, and if the psyche is not in order then the rest is useless.

K: If the house is in order …

DB: Then the second question is this: although we are saying that there are certain basic disorders in the psyche, or a lack of order which is common to us all, and that we may all have a potential for something else, are we really all one? Even though we are all similar, that doesn't say that we are all the same, that we are all one.

K: We said that in our consciousness we all have basically the same ground on which we stand.

DB: Yes, but the fact that human bodies are similar doesn't prove they are all the same.

K: Of course not, your body is different from mine.

DB: Yes, we are in different places, different entities and so on. But I think you are trying to say that consciousness is not an entity which is individual …

K: That's right.

DB: … the body is an entity that has a certain individuality.

K: That all seems so clear.

DB: It may be clear, but I think …

K: Your body is different from mine, I have a different name from you.

DB: Well, we are different – though of similar material, it is different, we can't exchange bodies because the proteins in one body may not agree with those in the other. Now many people feel that way about the mind, saying that there is a chemistry between people which may agree or disagree.

K: But if you actually go deeper into the question, consciousness is shared by all human beings.

DB: Yes, but the feeling is that the consciousness is individual and that it is communicated as it were …

K: I think that is an illusion because we are sticking to something that is not true.

DB: Well, do you want to say that there is one consciousness of mankind?

K: It is all one.

DB: It is all one. That is important because whether it is many or one is a crucial question.

K: Yes.

DB: Now, it could be there are many who are then communicating and building up the larger unit. Or do you think that from the very beginning it is all one?

K: From the very beginning it is all one.

DB: And the sense of separateness is an illusion – right?

K: That is what I am saying over and over again. That seems so logical, sane: the other is insane.

DB: Now, people don't feel, at least not immediately, that the notion of separate existence is insane, because one extrapolates from the body to the mind, one says it is quite sensible to say my body is separate from yours, and inside my body is my mind. Now are you saying that the mind is not inside the body?

K: That is quite a different question. Now just a minute, let's finish with the other first. If each one of us thinks that we are separate individuals psychically, what we have done in the world is a colossal mess.

DB: Well, if we think we are separate when we are not separate then it clearly will be a colossal mess.

K: That is what is happening. Each one thinks he has to do what he wants to do, fulfil himself. So he is struggling in his separateness to achieve peace, to achieve security, a secunty and peace which is totally denied by that.

DB: Well, the reason it is denied is because there is no separation. You see if there were really separation it would be a rational thing to try to do. But if we are trying to separate what is inseparable the result will be chaos.

K: That's right.

DB: Now that is clear but I think that it will not be clear to people immediately that the consciousness of mankind is one inseparable whole.

K: Yes, sir, an inseparable whole, absolutely right.

DB: Many questions will arise if you once even consider the notion, but I don't know if we have gone far enough into this yet. One question is: why do we think we are separate?

K: Why do I think I am separate? That is my conditioning.

DB: Yes, but how did we ever adopt such a foolish conditioning?

K: From childhood this is mine, this is *my* toy, not *yours*.

DB: But the first feeling you get is to say it is mine because I feel I am separate. Now, it isn't clear how the mind which was one came to this illusion that it is all broken up into many pieces.

K: I think it is again the activity of thought. Thought in its very nature is divisive, fragmentary, and therefore I am a fragment.

DB: Thought will create a sense of fragments. You can see, for example, that once we decide to set up a nation we will be separate, think we are separate from another nation, and from that all sorts of things, consequences, follow that make the whole thing seem independently real. We all have a separate language and a separate flag and a separate this and that, and we set up a boundary. And after a while we see so much evidence of separation that we forget how it started and say that was always how it was and we are merely proceeding from what was always there.

K: Of course. That's why, I feel if once we grasp the nature of thought, the structure of thought, how thought operates, what is the source of thought, and therefore see it is always limited, if we really see that then …

DB: Now, what is the source of thought, is it memory?

K: Memory, the remembrance of things past, which is knowledge, and knowledge is the outcome of experience and experience is always limited.

DB: But thought also includes, of course, the attempt to go forward, to use logic, to take into account discoveries and insights.

K: And, as we were saying some time ago, thought is time.

DB: Yes, all right, thought is time. That requires more discussion too, because you see the first experience is to say that time is there first, and thought is taking place in time.

K: Ah, no.

DB: For example, if we say that movement is taking place, the body is moving, and this requires time.

K: To go from here to there needs time, to learn a language needs time, to paint a picture takes time.

DB: To grow a plant needs time. We also say to think takes time.

K: So we think in terms of time.

DB: You see the first point that one would tend to look at is to say that just as everything takes time, to think takes time. And you are saying something else, which is: thought is time.

K: Thought is time.

DB: That is, psychically speaking, psychologically speaking. Now, how do we understand that? That thought is time. You see it is not obvious.

K: Would you say that thought is movement and time is movement?

DB: You see, time is a mysterious thing, people have argued about it. We could say that time requires movement. I could understand that we cannot have time without movement.

K: Time is movement, time is not separate from movement.

DB: Now, I don't say it is separate from movement, but to say time is movement, you see if we said time and movement are one …

K: Yes, we are saying that.

DB: Yes, they cannot be separated. That seems fairly clear. Now there is physical movement which means physical time – right?

K: Physical time, hot and cold, and also dark and light, sunset and sunrise, all that …

DB: The seasons, yes. Now then we have the movement of thought. Now that brings in the question of the nature of thought. You see, is thought nothing but a movement in the nervous system, in the brain? Would you say that?

K: Yes.

DB: Some people have said it includes the movement of the nervous system but there might be something beyond.

K: What is time, actually? Time is hope.

DB: Psychologically speaking.

K: Psychologically, I am talking entirely psychologically for the moment. Hope is time, becoming is time, achieving is time. Now take the question of becoming: I want to become something psychologically. I want to become non-violent, take that for example. That is altogether a fallacy.

DB: Well, we understand it is a fallacy but the reason it is one is that there is no time of that kind. Is that it?

K: Yes. Human beings are violent: and Tolstoy and people in India, have been talking a great deal of non-violence. The fact is we are violent and the non-violence is not real. But we want to become that.

DB: Yes, but again it is an extension of the kind of thought that we have with regard to material things. If you see a desert, it is real and you say the garden is not real, but in your mind is the garden that will come about when you put water there. So we say we can plan for the future when the desert will become fertile. Now we have to be careful: we say we are violent but we cannot by similar planning become non-violent. Now why is that?

K: Why? Because the non-violent state cannot exist when there is violence. That's an ideal.

DB: Well, one has to make it clearer because in the same sense the fertile state and the desert don't exist together either. You see, I think that you are saying that, in the case of the mind when you are violent, non-violence has no meaning.

K: That is the only state, not the other.

DB: That is all there is, the movement towards the other is illusory.

K: Yes, all ideals are psychologically illusory. The ideal of building a marvellous bridge is not illusory. You can plan a bridge but to have psychological ideals …

DB: Yes, if you are violent and continue to be violent while you are trying to be non-violent …

K: … it has no meaning and yet that has become such an important thing. So I question both becoming "what is" and becoming away from "what is."

DB: "What should be", yes. Well, if you say there can be no sense to becoming in the way of self-improvement, that's …

K: Oh, self-improvement is something so utterly ugly. We are saying that the source of all this is a movement of thought as time. Once we have made time important psychologically all the ideals, such as non-violence, achieving some superstate and so on, become utterly illusory.

DB: Yes, when you talk of the movement of thought as time, it seems to me that that time is illusory.

K: Yes.

DB: We sense it as time but it is not a real kind of time.

K: That is why we asked: what is time? I need time to go from here to there. I need time if I want to learn engineering, I must study it, that takes time. That same movement is carried over into the psyche. We say, I need time to be good, I need time to be enlightened.

DB: Yes, that will always create a conflict. One part of you and another. So that movement in which you say, I need time, also creates a division in the psyche. Between the observer and the observed.

K: Yes, that's right. We are saying that the observer is the observed.

DB: And psychologically, therefore, there is no time.

K: That's right. The thinker is the thought, there is no thinker separate from thought.

DB: All that you are saying, you know, seems very reasonable, but I think that it goes so strongly against the tradition we are used to that it will be extraordinarily hard, generally speaking, for people to really understand …

K: Of course, most people want a comfortable way of living: "let me carry on as I am, for God's sake, leave me alone."

DB: Yes, that is the result of so much conflict that people are wary.

K: But conflict escaped from or unresolved still exists, whether you like it or not. So this is the whole point: is it possible to live a life without conflict?

DB: Yes, that is all implicit in what has been said. The source of conflict is thought or knowledge, or the past.

K: That's right. So then one asks: is it possible to transcend thought? Or is it possible to end knowledge? I am putting it psychologically, not …

DB: Yes, knowledge of material objects and things like that, scientific knowledge, will continue.

K: Absolutely, that must continue.

DB: But what you call self-knowledge is what you are asking to end, isn't it?

K: Yes.

DB: On the other hand people have said, even you have said, self-knowledge is very important.

K: Self-knowledge is important but if I take time to understand myself, that is, if I say I will understand myself eventually by examination, analysis, by watching my whole relationship with others and so on, all that involves time. And I am saying there is another way of looking at the whole thing without time: which is, when the observer is the observed. In that observation there is no time.

DB: Could we go into that further? I mean, you say, for example, that there is no time but you still feel that you can remember an hour ago that you were somewhere else. Now in what sense can we say that there is no time?

K: Time is division, as thought is division. That is why thought is time.

DB: Time is a series of divisions of past, present, future.

K: Thought is divisive in the same way. So time is thought. Or thought is time.

DB: Yes, well, it doesn't exactly follow from what you said.

K: Let's go into it.

DB: You see, at first sight one would think that thought makes divisions of all kinds, with the ruler and with all kinds of things, and also divides up intervals of time, past, present and future. Now it doesn't follow just from that that thought is time.

K: Look, we said time is movement. Thought is also a series of movements. So both are movements.

DB: Yes, all right. Thought is a movement, we suppose, of the nervous system and …

K: You see, it is a movement of becoming. I am speaking psychologically.

DB: But whenever you think, something is also moving in the blood, in the nerves and so on. Now when we talk of a psychological movement, do you mean just a change of content? What is the movement, what is moving?

K: Look, I am this, and I am attempting to become something else psychologically.

DB: So that movement is in the content of your thought?

K: Yes.

DB: So if you say, "I am this and I am attempting to become that", then I am in movement. At least I feel I am in movement.

K: Say, for instance, I am greedy. Greed is a movement.

DB: What kind of a movement is it?

K: To get what I want, to get more. It is a movement.

DB: All right.

K: And I find that movement painful, suppose. Then I try not to be greedy. The attempt not to be greedy is a movement of time, is becoming.

DB: Yes, but even the greed was becoming.

K: Of course. So is it possible, this is the real question, is it possible not to become? Psychologically, speaking.

DB: Well, it seems that this would require that you should not be anything psychologically. That is, as soon as you define yourself in any way then ...

K: No, we will define it in a minute or two.

DB: I meant, if I define myself as greedy, or say I am greedy or I am this, or I am that, then either I will want to become something else or to remain what I am — right?

K: Now can I remain what I am? Can I remain not with non-greed but with greed. And greed is not different from me, greed is me.

DB: Yes. That will require clarification – the ordinary way of thinking is that I am here and I could either be greedy or not greedy.

K: Of course.

DB: As these are attributes which I may or may not have.

K: But the attributes *are* me.

DB: Yes, now again that goes very much against our common language and experience.

K: Of course.

DB: But instead we are saying that I am my attributes, which suggests that the thought of attribution creates the "me", right? The sense of "me".

K: All the qualities, the attributes, the virtues, the judgements, the conclusions and opinions are "me".

DB: Well, it seems to me that this would have to be perceived immediately as obvious.

K: That is the whole question. To perceive the totality of this movement instantly. Then we come to the point of perception: whether it is possible to perceive – it sounds a little odd, and perhaps a little crazy, but it is not – is it possible to perceive without all the movement of memory? To perceive something directly without the word, without the reaction, without the memories entering into perception?

DB: That is a very big question because memory has constantly entered perception. It would raise the question of what is going to stop memory from entering perception?

K: Nothing can stop it. But if we see that the activity of memory is limited, in the very perception of that limitation we have moved out of it into another dimension.

DB: Well, it seems to me that you have to perceive the whole of the limitation of memory.

K: Yes, not one part.

DB: You can see in general that memory is limited but there are many ways in which this is not obvious. For example, many of our reactions that are not obvious may be memory but we don't experience them as such. Suppose, say, I experience "me" as being there presently and not as memory. That is the common experience. Suppose I want to become less greedy: I experience greed and I experience the urge to become as an actuality; it may be the result of memory but I say this "me" is the one who remembers, not the other way around, not that memory creates "me".

K: All this really comes down to whether humanity can live without conflict? It basically comes down to that. Can we have peace on this Earth? The activities of thought never bring it about.

DB: Yes, it seems clear from what has been said that the activity of thought cannot bring about peace; it inherently, psychologically, brings about conflict.

K: If we once really see that, our whole activity would be totally different.

DB: But are you saying then that there is an activity which is not thought, which is beyond thought? And which is not only beyond thought but which does not require the cooperation of thought? That it is possible for this to go on when thought is absent?

K: That is the real point. We have often discussed this, whether there is anything beyond thought. Not something holy, sacred – I am not talking of that. We are asking: is there an activity that is not touched by thought? We are saying there is. And that activity is the highest form of intelligence.

DB: Yes, now we have brought in intelligence.

K: I know, I purposely brought it in! So intelligence is not the activity of cunning thought.

DB: Well, intelligence can use thought, as you have often said.

K: Intelligence can use thought.

DB: Thought can be the action of intelligence – would you put it that way?

K: Yes.

DB: Or it could be the action of memory?

K: That's it. Or it is the action born of memory, and memory being limited, thought is therefore limited, and has its own activity which then brings about conflict.

DB: I think this would connect up with what people are saying about computers. Every computer must eventually depend on some kind of memory, which is put in, programmed. And that must be limited – right?

K: Of course.

DB: Therefore when we operate from memory we are not very different from a computer; the other way around perhaps, the computer is not very different from us!

K: I would say a Hindu has been programmed for the last five thousand years to be a Hindu, or in this country you have been programmed to be British or a Catholic or a Protestant. So we are all programmed to a certain extent.

DB: Yes, now you are bringing in the notion of an intelligence that is free of the programme, it is creative perhaps.

K: That's right. That intelligence has nothing to do with memory and knowledge.

DB: It may act in memory and knowledge but it is has nothing to do with it.

K: It can act through memory, etc. That's right. Now, how do you find out whether this has any reality, and is not just imagination and romantic nonsense, how do you find out? To come to that one has to go into the whole question of suffering, whether there is an ending to suffering. As long as suffering and fear and the pursuit of pleasure exist there cannot be love.

DB: Yes, well there are many questions there. The first point is that suffering, pleasure, fear, anger, violence and greed are all the response of memory. They are nothing to do with intelligence.

K: Yes, they are all part of thought and memory.

DB: As long as they are going on it seems to me that intelligence cannot operate in or through thought.

K: That's right, so there must be freedom from suffering.

DB: Well, that is a very key point.

K: That is really a very serious and deep question: whether it is possible to end suffering, which is the ending of "me".

DB: Yes, again, it may seem repetitious but the feeling is that "I" am there and "I" either suffer or dont, "I" either enjoy things or don't. Now I think you are saying that suffering arises from thought, it is thought.

K: Through identification, attachment.

DB: So what is it that suffers? It seems to me that memory may produce pleasure and then when it doesn't work it produces pain and suffering.

K: Not only that. Suffering is much more complex, isn't it? What is suffering? The meaning of the word is to have pain, to have grief, to feel utterly lost, lonely.

DB: It seems to me that it is not only pain but a kind of total, very pervasive pain.

K: Suffering is the loss of someone.

DB: Or the loss of something very important.

K: Yes, of course. Loss of my wife, of my son, brother, or whatever it is, and the desperate sense of loneliness.

DB: Or else just simply the fact that the whole world is going into such a state. It makes everything meaningless, you see.

K: What a lot of suffering all the wars have created! And this has been going on for thousands of years. That is why I am saying we are carrying on with the same pattern of the last five thousand years or more.

DB: Yes, and one can easily see that the violence and hatred of war will interfere with intelligence.

K: Obviously.

DB: But some people have felt that by going through suffering they become purified, like going through a crucible.

K: I know; that through suffering you learn, you are purified, through suffering your ego vanishes, is dissolved. It isn't. People have suffered immensely, from so many wars, with so many tears, and from the destructive nature of governments, unemployment, ignorance …

DB: … ignorance of disease, pain, everything. What is suffering really? Why does it destroy or prevent intelligence? What is actually going on?

K: Suffering is a shock – I suffer, I have pain, it is the essence of the "me".

DB: Yes, the difficulty with suffering is that it is the 'me' that is suffering, and this 'me' is really being sorry for itself in some way.

K: My suffering is different from your suffering.

DB: It isolates itself, it creates an illusion of some kind.

K: We don't see suffering is shared by all humanity.

DB: Yes, but suppose we do see it is shared by all humanity?

K: Then I begin to question what suffering is. It is not my suffering.

DB: Well, that is important. In order to understand the nature of suffering I have to drop this idea that it is my suffering because as long as I believe that I have an illusory notion of the whole thing.

K: And I can never end it.

DB: If you are dealing with an illusion you can do nothing with it. You see, we have to come back. Why is suffering the suffering of the many? At first, it seems that I feel toothache, or else I have a loss, or something has happened to me, and the other person seems perfectly happy.

K: Happy, yes. But he is suffering too in his own way.

DB: Yes, at the moment he doesn't see it but he has his problems too.

K: Suffering is common to all humanity.

DB: But the fact that it is common is not enough to make it all one.

K: It is actual.

DB: Are you saying that the suffering of mankind is all one, inseparable?

K: Yes, that is what I have been saying.

DB: As is the consciousness of Man?

K: Yes, that's right.

DB: That when anybody suffers the whole of mankind is suffering.

K: The whole point is we have suffered from the beginning of time and we haven't solved it.

DB: But what you have said is that the reason we haven't solved it is because we are treating it as personal or as in a small group, and that is an illusion. And any attempt to deal with an illusion cannot solve anything.

K: Thought cannot solve anything psychologically.

DB: Because you can say that thought itself divides. Thought is limited and is not able to see that this suffering is all one. And in that way divides it up as mine and yours.

K: That's right.

DB: And that creates illusion, which can only multiply suffering. Now, it seems to me that the statement that the suffering of mankind is one is inseparable from the statement that the consciousness of mankind is one.

K: Sir, the world is me, I am the world.

DB: You have often said that.

K: Yes, but we have divided it up into the British Earth and the French Earth and all the rest of it!

DB: Do you mean by the world, the physical world, or the world of society?

K: The world of society, the psychological world, primarily.

DB: So we say the world of society, of human beings, is one, and when I say I am that world, what does it mean?

K: The world is not different from me.

DB: The world and I are one, we are inseparable.

K: Yes. And what that requires, is real meditation, you must feel this, it is not just a verbal statement, it is an actuality. I am my brother's keeper.

DB: Many religions have said that.

K: That is just a verbal statement; they don't keep it, they don't do it in their hearts.

DB: Perhaps a few have done it but in general it is not being done.

K: I don't know if anybody has done it, we human beings haven't done it. Our religions have actually prevented it!

DB: Because of division, every religion having its own beliefs and its own organisation?

K: Of course, its own gods and its own saviours. So after all this, is that intelligence actual? You understand my question? Or is it some kind of fanciful projection, hoping that it will solve our problems? It is not to me, it is an actuality. Because the ending of suffering means love.

DB: Now before we go on, let's clear up a point about "me". You have just said "it is not to me". Now in some sense it seems that you are still defining an individual. Is that right?

K: Yes, I am using the word 'I' as a means of communication.

DB: But what does it mean? Let's say there are two people, "A" who sees the way you do and "B" who does not. That seems to create a division between "A" and "B".

K: That's right, but "B" creates the division.

DB: Why?

K: What is the relationship between the two?

DB: Well, "B" is creating the division by saying "I am a seperate person", but it may confuse "B" further when "A" says, "it's not that way to me" – right?

K: That is the whole point, isn't it, in relationship? You feel that you are not separate, and that you really have this sense of love and compassion, and I haven't got it. I haven't even perceived or gone into this question. What is your relationship to me? You have a relationship with me but I haven't any relationship with you.

DB: Yes, I think one could say that the person who hasn't seen is, psychologically, almost living in a dream world, and therefore the dream world is not related to the world of being awake.

K: That's right.

DB: But the fellow who is awake can at least perhaps awaken the other fellow.

K: You are awake, I am not. Then your relationship with me is very clear. But I have no relationship with you, I cannot. I insist on division and you don't.

DB: Yes, in some way we have to say that the consciousness of mankind has divided itself, it is all one, but it has divided itself by thought. That is why we are in this situation.

K: That is why – all the problems that humanity has now, psychologically as well as in other ways, are the result of thought. And we are pursuing the same pattern of thought, and thought will never solve any of these problems. So there is another kind of instrument, which is intelligence.

DB: That opens up an entirely different subject, and you also mentioned love and compassion as well.

K: Without love and compassion there is no intelligence. And you cannot be compassionate if you are attached to some religion, like an animal tied to a post.

DB: Well, as soon as your self is threatened then it cannot …

K: Of course. But you see, the self hides behind …

DB: … other things, such as noble ideals.

K: Yes, it has immense capacity to hide itself. So what is the future of mankind? From what one observes it is leading to destruction.

DB: That is the way it seems to be going.

K: Very gloomy, grim, dangerous and if one has children what is their future? To enter into all this and go through all the misery of it all? So education becomes extraordinarily important. But now education is merely the accumulation of knowledge.

DB: Every instrument that Man has invented, discovered or developed has been turned toward destruction.

K: Absolutely. They are destroying Nature, there are very few tigers now.

DB: Forests and agricultural land are being destroyed too.

K: Nobody seems to care.

DB: Well, most people are just immersed in their plans to save themselves but others have plans to save humanity. I think also there is a tendency toward despair implicit in what is happening now in that people don't think anything can be done.

K: Yes, and if they think something can be done they form little groups and little theories.

DB: Well, there are those who are very confident in what they are doing and those who …

K: Most Prime Ministers are very confident. But they don't really know what they are doing.

DB: But most people don't have much confidence in what they are doing.

K: I know. But if you have tremendous confidence, I may accept your confidence and go with you. So what then is the future of mankind? I wonder if anybody is concerned about it? Or is each person, or each group, concerned only with its own survival?

DB: Well, I think the first concern has almost always been with the survival of the individual or the group. That has been the history of mankind.

K: And therefore perpetual wars, perpetual insecurity.

DB: But this, as you said, is the result of thought making the mistake, on an incomplete basis, of identifying the self with the group, and so on.

K: Sir, you happen to listen to all this, you agree to all this, you see the truth of all this. Those in power will not even listen to you, they are creating more and more misery, the world is becoming more and more dangerous. What is the point of you and I agreeing and seeing something true? This is what people are asking: what is the point of you and I seeing something to be true and what effect has it?

DB: Well it seems to me if we think in terms of the effects, we are bringing in the very thing that is behind the trouble – time. That is, the first response would be we must quickly get in and do something to change the course of events.

K: Therefore form a society, foundation, organisation and all the rest of it.

DB: You see, our mistake is to feel that we must think of something, and that thought is incomplete. We don't really know what is going on, and people have made theories about it, but they don't know.

K: No, but if that is the wrong question, then as a human being, who is mankind, what is my responsibility, apart from effect and all the rest of it?

DB: Yes, we can't look toward effects. But it is the same as with "A" and "B", that "A" sees and "B" does not. Now suppose "A" sees something and most of the rest of mankind does not. Then it seems, one could say mankind is in some way dreaming, it is asleep.

K: It is caught in illusion.

DB: And the point is that, if somebody sees something, his responsibility is to help awaken the others out of the illusion.

K: That is just it. I mean this has been the problem. That is why the Buddhists have projected the idea of the Bodhisattva, who is compassionate, the essence of all compassion, and who is waiting to save humanity. It sounds nice, it is a happy feeling that there is somebody doing this. But in actuality we won't do anything that is not, both psychologically and physically, comfortable, satisfying, secure.

DB: Well, that is basically the source of the illusion.

K: How does one make others see all this? They haven't time, the energy, even the inclination, they want to be amused. How does one make "X" see this whole thing so clearly that he says, "all right, I have got it, I will work, and I am responsible", and all the rest of it. I think there is the tragedy of those who I see and those who do not.

"What Future Does Man Have" J. Kirshnamurti in conversation with David Bohm in *Questioning Krishnamurti*
Edited by David Skitt, published by Thorsons (An Imprint of Harper Collins Publishers), London, 1996, P73-98

Ikuro Adachi
Three Kinds of "Consciousness"
and "Volition"

There are three kinds of "Consciousness" and "Volition"

I use the term "EXA PIECO" to refer to the sum of what we call "Consciousness" and "Volition" in everyday language.

There are in fact three types of "Consciousness" and "Volition". Among these three kinds, the most commonly used "Consciousness" and "Volition," what we call the conscious mind (hereafter referred to as DIKAG), has the functions of thinking, acting and deciding. Actually, from birth the DIKAG mainly takes the role of generating the way of thinking on which one's actions are based.

The present Earth culture is based on the DIKAG. The culture during the past five thousand years or so has progressed mostly on the premise that in all things, it is ultimately the DIKAG that has the most important role. In that period there have been various problems, and there are various stages in the historical interpretation, but we might say it started from the time religion was at the centre and continues until now, when Earth style natural science has become the centre.

At any rate, I would like to describe the actual role of the DIKAG and the other two types of "Consciousness" and "Volition." This includes the EXA PIECO, which exists not only in humans, but in all animals, plants and minerals, and how it deals with and influences them. Now the energy of Earth itself has entered a period of drastic change and is about to alter its frequency to make a great shift across the Universe ...

Knowing the role of the conscious and subconscious minds

I mentioned above that there are three types of "Consciousness" and "Volition." One of these is the DIKAG, and another is something like the subconscious mind, to use a psychological term. I refer to it as the subconscious mind in this Earth language, but to be more accurate, in cosmic language it is called FIK.

The main responsibility of the DIKAG is to enable each individual to care for and protect its body, the human body, and to maintain, manage and operate it. For that purpose, it is its main job to always collect the current information around itself and to maintain, manage and operate its own body safely. Whether you are conscious of it or not, as long as you live as a human being, you repeat this behaviour of thinking and judging.

In contrast to the DIKAG, the main job of the FIK is to control past information. The FIK collects past information and controls it through the use of a storage device; it is in charge of most parts which are not handled by the human DIKAG. Think about how your body has been built up from birth.

As understood in modern science and medicine, at the adult stage, the approximately 82 trillion (in Earth culture it is said to be 60 trillion) cells go through the process of metabolism and are replaced every few months. It is the FIK which bears all responsibility for controlling this state. I would like to impart the information that entered into me as it is, even though it is different from the psychological explanation on Earth. Therefore, note that although I use the term subconscious mind, the meaning slightly differs from that in psychology.

The information indicates that in the case of human beings, the FIK lies close to the centre of gravity, somewhere around the belly. In fact, the specific internal organ which receives and transmits the vibrations of the FIK is the "pancreas." I think this basic function of the pancreas is not understood at all in current medical science. The FIK is responsibility for and controls the replacement of all cells in the body, unerringly placing eyes and noses where they are supposed to be. Thus, a mouth would never turn into an ear by mistake. Everything is repeatedly reproduced as scheduled, from the tips of the toes to the tips of the hair. The DIKAG has nothing to do with this control; it is the FIK which takes care of this. When we consider and explore why this can be controlled, we naturally reach a certain conclusion.

The physical sciences, which consider "Consciousness" and "Volition" to be outside their domain

There are at most about 82 trillion cells in the human body. These approximately 82 trillion cells are comprised of molecules, which in turn are comprised of atoms. The atom consists of an atomic nucleus and numerous electrons rotating around it. The atomic nucleus is comprised of mainly neutrons and protons.

In modern Earth science and physics, it is understood, at least as a general concept, that the neutron and proton in the atomic nucleus are the fundamental components of all kinds of organisms, not just human cells, and that they perform important functions. Generally, it appears to be headed in the right direction towards the understanding of Nature, but strictly speaking, there are many problems with the explanations.

In the field of natural science, which insists on objective observation at all cost, has recently proposed an elementary particle theory, which views the top quark or the quark as the most elementary particle which constitute neutrons and protons, and is putting full effort into that research. Something around this area forms the foundation of Earth science and culture. In this present culture everything is built upon this starting point. The most fundamental way of thinking, the philosophy if you will, physical science, which explores the origin from which all matter is made up, strives to ultimately understand how the Universe is structured, and in that process of searching, "culture" changes rapidly.

The problem here is that basically, naturally science has advanced with the prerequisite that we have to "understand or observe objectively." Historically, it seems that such views became central somewhere around the time of Descartes. It was asserted that Nature cannot be understood accurately if subjective views are allowed.

So issues of "Consciousness" or "Volition," which are subjective in nature, got in the way and were ignored in the exploration of natural science. They were separated off. I think that sort of dichotomy was created. We have progressed with the view that if natural science is explored by separating the spiritual and the material, then we can understand it by accumulating our explorations of the material world.

The problem is that "Consciousness" and "Volition" were separated off in order to avoid inconvenience. Dealing separately with "Consciousness" and "Volition," which are unexplainable in science, has produced another field of study, psychology. Or, although it is explained in the form of religion, it cannot be explained through science.

In short, we have progressed this far without dealing with them scientifically. As a result, fields of study such as psychology were born to explain it in terms of phenomena. Actually, aside from the DIKAG and the FIK, which I have mentioned so far, there is another "Consciousness" and another "Volition," which exist not only in humans, but in all animals, plants and minerals.

"Consciousness" and "Volition" of the EXA PIECO

Now I would like to go on to the third "Consciousness" and "Volition," but before that, let me talk briefly about the brain. The DIKAG is located inside the skull, and it is the easiest to understand, being materialised in a cellular constitution as part of the physical human body, including the cerebrum, or what we commonly refer to as the brain. Actually, usually only 5% of the cerebrum acts as the DIKAG. The cerebrum of most people on Earth today is 5% active, centred in the DIKAG. Among the brain cells inside the skull, those that communicate with the FIK, also make up about 5%. So even when the FIK and the DIKAG are in full, active communication, only 10% of the neocortex is used.

However, usually you do not really notice when you are using your FIK. Most people are centred on the DIKAG and use only 5% of the nerve cells of the cerebrum. Most of us do not use the remaining 90% or more. Also, even with ongoing research in neurophysiology and related fields, with today's science we have not yet discovered what this is for, or to what degree the brain actually performs which functions. There are many hypotheses as to why 90% of the brain is inactive, but as of now, most of this is not understood in the medical field.

We might say that the third "Consciousness" and "Volition" comprise "what is essential." This does not contain any electrons.

The DIKAG and the FIK are part of the physical body. The FIK, as part of the pancreas, transceives wave energy. It also exists in cellular form as part of the physical body. In the pancreas there is a portion that generates wave energy, playing the role of the subconscious mind, and which is materialized in reality.

"Consciousness" (neutrons) and "Volition" (protons) accompanied by electrons form atoms. Atoms collected together make up molecules, and molecules collected together form cells. Also, the approximately 82 trillion human cells are all filled with neutrons and protons.

Vibrations are transmitted and controlled from within the pancreas, which contains electrons, but because all the cells, even those in the farthest reaches, contain molecules and atoms whose atomic nuclei contain neutrons and protons, every part has "Consciousness" and "Volition," and transceives material waves, electromagnetic waves and magnetic waves, and so on. They all communicate through vibrations.

The route of transmission is along the vertebrae from the coccyx to the brain stem. Every bone, such as the cervical, thoracic and lumbar vertebrae and the sacrum, receives and sends frequencies; it seems that each plays a different role, and has its own range of frequencies. This enables control of even the remote organs and every single cell. It is said that the spinal fluid contains 10^{5000} kinds of information. Vibrations run across all cells from the spinal fluid in which the entire programming of the person's life is recorded, are stored in a memory device which is part of the cerebrum, and contact the FIK when necessary. Each part of the spinal cord is under the control of the FIK.

Recently Earth medicine has made considerable progress in its studies at the molecular level about the form of DNA. It is now well-known that the DNA plays the important role of controlling the memory devices at the molecular level. But even though it has an important function, the range of memory at the molecular level is said to be only about 10^{20} kinds, so it is not so great an amount of information that understanding DNA would reveal everything. The information indicates that there are really about $10^{5.000}$ types in all.

So there are various levels of vibration, such as those at the molecular, atomic, electronic, atomic nuclear levels, or at the level of the neutron/proton. Communication between levels is made possible through transmission using variations in each property of Undulation, namely, the frequency, length, form, width etc. of the wave. There are many properties of "Undulation": for instance, they always interfere with, synchronise with, or amplify vibrations of similar frequency, length, form and width.

By understanding Undulation and utilising its properties, it can in actuality be used to control everything.

What we are concerned with here is the state in which the neutrons and protons of "Consciousness" and "Volition" do not rotate, and only atomic nuclei without electrons rotate and accumulate.

This is the third "Consciousness" and "Volition," called the Collection of Atomic Nuclei (EXA PIECO). It does not contain any electrons and is therefore not material. It is not visible to us, but at birth, in the case of humans, it reaches out a bit beyond the outside of the skull in the form of vibrating bodies.

Perhaps in English the word "soul" comes close to describing the Collection of Atomic Nuclei (EXA PIECO), but this is still quite inaccurate. To be precise, in cosmic language it is called EXA PIECO. Figure 1 illustrates the typical Collection of Atomic Nuclei (EXA PIECO) in the case of humans.

Figure 1.

$$\text{Neutron}(n) + \text{Proton}(P) = \text{Collection of Atomic Nuclei} = \text{Part of the form of the soul (EXA PIECO)}$$

$$=$$
$$=$$

Consciousness + Volition (Love)

{ This refers to the state in wich time and space are totally harmonized and unified

● The number of atomic nuclei in the Collection of Atomic Nuclei (soul) of modern human

Approximately $10^{34} \to 10^{68} \to 10^{140} \to$ nuclei $\to$ increases further

At birth   average stage of enlightenment   (becomes bigger)

Average diameter = 22 cm (4g)

● Cross sectional form
Soul of human → 12
Soul of animals → 8
Soul of plants → 6
Soul of minerals → 6

Minimum for one sphere is $n+p=10^{32}$ nuclei

Formed through the rotation of atomic nuclei and OCTSTOP

Normal speed of rotation is 10^{15}cm/sec OCTSTOP rotates and unifies (into a sphere)

Filled with quarks

Frequency of soul=2.513x10⁵Hz
Frequency of physical body=2.513x10⁵Hz
of Earth people

{ always fixed (no matter how much the number of atomic nuclei increases)

Approx. 22cm (4g)

(two and three dimensional) cross sections are the same

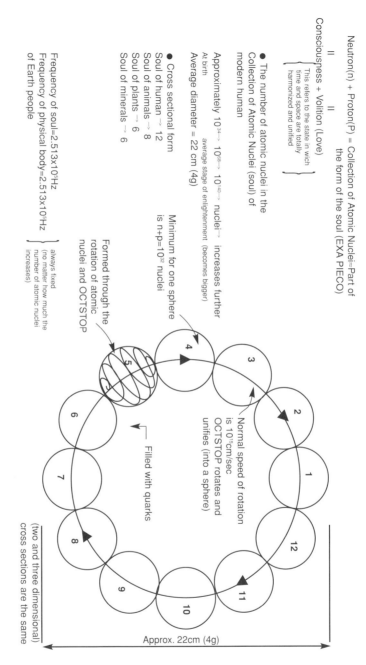

Knowing the structure and nature of the Collection of Atomic Nuclei

Let me explain this a bit further. It is called the Collection of Atomic Nuclei (EXA PIECO) since neutrons and protons, namely, "Consciousness" and "Volition," combine to form rotating atomic nuclei, which gather together to form spheres.

If we draw a cross section of that sphere, twelve smaller spheres become visible. From any angle, the main sphere has a cross section in which twelve smaller cross sections are visible; there are twelve of them whether we cut it horizontally or vertically, so that means there are a total of 62 groups of atomic nuclei collected together and rotating in spherical form. The material which unifies the neutron, called OCTSTOP, the same one mentioned above, rotates inside the sphere at tremendous speed (average 10^{18} cm per sec) preventing the nuclei from separating. There are no accompanying electrons, and that is why it is not materialised. In the case of Earth humans, the physical human body, which contains a total of approximately 82 trillion cells, has a frequency of 2.513×10^5 Hz. The Collection of Atomic Nuclei (EXA PIECO) synchronises and unifies at that same frequency of vibration. It exists in the same time and space as a oscillating body unified with the 90% of the brain which most people leave untouched and which the DIKAG or the FIK do not use.

It is not physically materialised, so when the physical body is terminated, it can separate at any time and can travel freely across time and space. This is the EXA PIECO, and the body, the physical human body, is only borrowed. In the DIPS, Collections of Atomic Nuclei (EXA PIECO) exist in all the beings in the Universe, and all of them are learning.

Ikuro Adachi, "Three Kinds of 'Consciousness' and 'Volition'", from the book *The Law of Undulation*
Published by The EVHA Creation, Yokohama, 1995, P69-79. Translated by Mayumi Mori and Victor A.H. Debuque

Stuart Hameroff, Roger Penrose
Conscious Events
as Orchestrated Space-Time Selections

Abstract: What *is* consciousness? Some philosophers have contended that "qualia", or an experiential medium from which consciousness is derived, exists as a fundamental component of reality. Whitehead, for example, described the universe as being comprised of "occasions of experience". To examine this possibility scientifically, the very nature of physical reality must be re-examined. We must come to terms with the physics of space-time – as is described by Einstein's general theory of relativity – and its relation to the fundamental theory of matter – as described by quantum theory. This leads us to employ a new physics of *objective reduction*: "**OR**" which appeals to a form of "quantum gravity" to provide a useful description of fundamental processes at the quantum/classical borderline (Penrose, 1994; 1996). Within the **OR** scheme, we consider that consciousness occurs if an appropriately organized system is able to develop and maintain quantum coherent superposition until a specific "objective" criterion (a threshold related to quantum gravity) is reached: the coherent system then self-reduces (objective reduction: **OR**). We contend that this type of objective self-collapse introduces non-computability, an essential feature of consciousness. **OR** is taken as an instantaneous event – the climax of a self-organizing process in fundamental space-time – and a candidate for a conscious Whitehead-like "occasion" of experience. How could an **OR** process occur in the brain, be coupled to neural activities, and account for other features of consciousness? We nominate an **OR** process with the requisite characteristics to be occurring in cytoskeletal microtubules within the brain's neurons (Penrose and Hameroff, 1995, Hameroff and Penrose, 1995; 1996).

In this model, quantum-superposed states develop in microtubule subunit proteins ("tubulins"), remain coherent, and recruit more superposed tubulins until a mass-time-energy threshold (related to quantum gravity) is reached. At that stage, self-collapse, or objective reduction (**OR**) abruptly occurs. We equate the pre-reduction, coherent superposition ("quantum computing") phase with pre-conscious processes, and each instantaneous (and non-computable) **OR**, or self-collapse, with a discrete conscious event. Sequences of **OR** events give rise to a "stream" of consciousness. Microtubule-associated proteins can "tune" the quantum oscillations of the coherent superposed states; the **OR** is thus self-organized, or "orchestrated" ("**Orch OR**"). Each **Orch OR** event selects (non-computably) microtubule subunit states which regulate synaptic/neural functions using classical signalling.

The quantum gravity threshold for self-collapse is relevant to consciousness, according to our arguments, because macroscopic superposed quantum states each have their own space-time geometries (Penrose, 1994; 1996). These geometries are also superposed, and in some way "separated", but when sufficiently separated, the superposition of space-time geometries becomes significantly unstable, and reduce to a single universe sate. Quantum gravity determines the scale of the instability; we contend that the actual choice of state made by Nature is non-computable. Thus each **Orch OR** event is a self-selection of space-time geometry, coupled to the brain through microtubules and other biomolecules.

If conscious experience is intimately connected with the very physics underlying space-time structure, then **Orch OR** in microtubules indeed provides us with a completely new and uniquely promising perspective on the hard problem of consciousness.

Introduction: Self-Selection in an Experiential Medium?

The "hard problem" of incorporating the phenomenon of consciousness into a scientific world-view involves finding scientific explanations of qualia, or the subjective experience of mental states (Chalmers, 1995; 1996). On this, reductionist science is still at sea. Why do we have an inner life, and what exactly is it?

One set of philosophical positions, addressing the hard problem, views consciousness as a fundamental component of physical reality. For example an extreme view – "panpsychism"– is that consciousness is a quality of all matter: atoms and their subatomic components having elements of consciousness (e.g. Spinoza, 1677; Rensch, 1960). "Mentalists" such as Leibnitz and Whitehead (e.g. 1929) contended that systems ordinarily considered to be physical are constructed in some sense from mental entities. Bertrand Russel (1954) described "neutral monism" in which a common underlying entity, neither physical nor mental, gave rise to both. Recently Stubenberg (1996) has claimed that qualia are that common entity. In monistic idealism, matter and mind arise from consciousness – the fundamental constituent of reality (e.g. Goswami, 1993). Wheeler (1990) has suggested that information is fundamental to the physics of the universe. From this, Chalmers (1995; 1996) proposes a double-aspect theory in which information has both physical and experiential aspects.

Among these positions, the philosophy of Alfred North Whitehead (1929; 1933) may be most directly applicable. Whitehead describes the ultimate concrete entities in the cosmos as being actual "occasions of experience", each bearing a quality akin to "feeling". Whitehead construes "experience" broadly – in a manner consistent with panpsychism – so that even 'temporal events in the career of an electron have a kind of "protomentality". Whitehead's view may be considered to differ from panpsychism, however, in that his discrete "occasions of experience" can be taken to be related to "quantum events" (Shimony, 1993). In the standard descriptions of quantum mechanics, randomness occurs in the events described as quantum state reductions – these being events which appear to take place when a quantum-level process gets magnified to a macroscopic scale.

Quantum state reduction (here denoted by the letter **R**; cf. Penrose 1989, 1994) is the random procedure that is adopted by physicists in their descriptions of the quantum measurement process. It is still a highly controversial matter whether **R** is to be taken as a "real" physical process, or whether it is some kind of illusion and not to be regarded as a fundamental ingredient of the behaviour of Nature. Our position is to take **R** to be indeed real – or, rather to regard it as a close appoximation to an objectively real process **OR** (objective reduction), which is to be a non-computable process instead of merely a random one (see Penrose 1989; 1994). In almost all physical situations, **OR** would come about in situations in which the random effects of the environment dominate, so **OR** would be virtually indistinguishable from the random **R** procedure that is normally adopted by quantum theorists. However, when the quantum system under consideration remains coherent and well isolated from its environment, then it becomes possible for its state to collapse spontaneously, in accordance with the **OR** scheme we adopt, and to behave in non-computable rather than random ways. Moreover, this **OR** scheme intimately involves the geometry of the physical universe at its deepest levels.

Our viewpoint is to regard experiential phenomena as also inseparable from the physical universe, and in fact to be deeply connected with the very laws which govern the physical universe. The connection is so deep, however, that we perceive only glimmerings of it in our present day physics. One of these glimmerings, we contend, is a necessary non-computability in conscious thought processes; and we argue that this non-computability must also be inherent in the phenomenon of quantum state *self*-reduction – the "objective reduction" (**OR**) referred to above. This is the main thread of argument in *Shadows of the Mind* (Penrose, 1994). The argument that conscious thought, whatever other attributes it may also have, is non-computable (as follows most powerfully from certain deductions from Gödel's incompleteness theorem) grabs hold of one tiny but extremely valuable point. This means that at least some conscious states cannot be derived from previous states by an algorithmic process – a property which distinguishes human (and other animal) minds from computers. Noncomputability *per se* does not directly address the "hard problem" of the nature of experience, but it is a clue to the kind of physical activity that lies behind it. This points to **OR**, an underlying physical action of a completely different character from that which would appear to underlie nonconscious activity. Following this clue with sensitivity and patience should ultimately lead to real progress towards understanding mental phenomena in their inward manifestations as well as outward.

In the **OR** description, consciousness takes place if an organized quantum system is able to isolate and sustain coherent superpositions until its quantum gravity threshold for space-time separation is met; it then *self*-reduces (non-computably). For consciousness to occur, *self*-reduction is essential, as opposed to the reduction being triggered by the system's random environment. (In the latter case, the reduction would itself be effectively random and would lack useful non-computability, being unsuitable for direct involvement in consciousness.) We take the *self*-reduction to be an instantaneous event – the climax of a *self*-organizing process fundamental to the structuring of space-time – and apparently consistent with a Whitehead "occasion of experience".

As **OR** could, in principle, occur ubiquitously within many types of inanimate media, it may seem to imply a form of "panpsychism" (in which individual electrons, for example, possess an experiential quality). However according to the principles of **OR** (as expounded in Penrose, 1994; 1996), a single superposed electron would spontaneously reduce its state (assuming it could maintain isolation) only once in a period longer than the present age of the universe. Only large collections of particles acting coherently in a single macroscopic quantum state could possibly sustain isolation and support coherent superposition in a timeframe brief enough to be relevant to our consciousness. Thus, only very special circumstances could support consciousness:

1) High degree of coherence of a quantum state – a collective mass of particles in

superposition for a time period long enough to reach threshold, and brief enough to be useful in thought processes.

2) Ability for the **OR** process to be at least transiently isolated from a "noisy" environment until the spontaneous state reduction takes place. This isolation is required so that reduction is not simply random. Mass movement in the environment which entangles with the quantum state would effect a random (not non-computable) reduction.

3) Cascades of **OR**s to give a "stream" of consciousness, huge numbers of **OR** events taking place during the course of a lifetime.

By reaching the quantum gravity threshold, each **OR** event has a fundamental bearing on space-time geometry. One could say that a cascade of **OR** events charts an actual course of physical space-time geometry selections.

It may seem surprising that quantum gravity effects could plausibly have relevance at the physical scales relevant to brain processes. For quantum gravity is normally viewed as having only absurdly tiny influences at ordinary dimensions. However, we shall show later that this is not the case, and the scales determined by basic quantum gravity principles are indeed those that are relevant for conscious brain processes.

We must ask how such an **OR** process could actually occur in the brain? How could it be coupled to neural activities at a high rate of information exchange; how could it account for preconscious to conscious transitions, have spatial and temporal binding, and both simultaneity and time flow?

We here nominate an **OR** process with the requisite characteristics to be occuring in cytoskeletal microtubules within the brain's neurons. In our model, microtubule-associated proteins "tune" the quantum oscillations leading to **OR**; we thus term the process "orchestrated objective reduction" (**Orch OR**).

Space-time: Quantum Theory and Einstein's Gravity

Quantum theory describes the extraordinary behaviour of the matter and energy which comprise our universe at a fundamental level. At the root of quantum theory is the wave/particle duality of atoms, molecules, and their constituent particles. A quantum system such as an atom or subatomic particle which remains isolated from its environment behaves as a "wave of possibilities" and exists in a coherent complex-number valued "superposition" of many possible states. The behaviour of such wave-like, quantum-level objects can be satisfactorily described in terms of a state vector which evolves deterministically according to the Schrödinger equation (unitary evolution), denoted by **U**.

Somehow, quantum microlevel superpositions lead to unsuperposed stable structures in our macro-world. In a transition known as wave function collapse, or state reduction (**R**), the quantum wave of alternative possibilities reduces to a single macroscopic reality – an "eigenstate" of some appropriate operator. (This would be just one out of many possible alternative eigenstates relevant to the quantum operator.) This process is invoked in the description of a macroscopic measurement, when effects are magnified from the small, quantum scale to the large, classical scale.

According to conventional quantum theory (as part of the standard "Copenhagen interpretation"), each choice of eigenstate is entirely random, weighted according to a probability value that can be calculated from the previous state according to the precise procedures of the quantum formalism. This probabilistic ingredient was a feature with which Einstein, among others, expressed displeasure: "You believe in a God who plays dice, and I in complete law and order." Penrose (1989; 1994) has contended that, at a deeper level of description, the choices may more accurately arise as the result of some presently unknown "non-computational" mathematical/physical (i.e. "Platonic realm") theory, that is they cannot be deduced algorithmically. Penrose argues that such non-computablilty is essential to consciousness, because (at least some) conscious mental activity is unattainable by computers.

It can be argued that present-day physics has no clear explanation for the cause and occurence of wave function collapse **R**. Experimental and theoretical evidence through the 1930's led quantum physicists (such as Schrödinger, Heisenberg, Dirac, von Neumann, and others) to postulate that quantum-coherent superpositions persist indefinitely in time, and would, in principle be maintained from the micro to macro levels. Or perhaps they would persist until conscious observation collapses, or reduces, the wave function (subjective reduction, or "**SR**"). Accordingly, even macroscopic objects, if unobserved, could remain superposed. To illustrate the apparent absurdity of this notion, Erwin Schrödinger (e.g. 1935) described his now-famous "cat in a box" being simultaneously *both* dead and alive until the box was opened and the cat observed.

As a counter to this unsettling prospect, various new physical schemes for collapse according to objective criteria (objective reduction – "**OR**") have recently been proposed. According to such a scheme, the growth and persistence of superposed states could reach a critical threshold, at which collapse, or **OR** rapidly occurs (e.g. Pearle, 1989; Ghirardi *et al.*, 1986). Some of these schemes are based specifically on gravitational effects mediating **OR** (e.g. Károlyházy, 1966; Károlyházy *et al.*, 1986; Diósi, 1989; Ghirardi *et al.*, 1990; Penrose, 1989; 1994; Pearle and Squires, 1995; Percival, 1995). Table 1 categorizes types of reduction.

Context	Cause of Collapse (Reduction)	Description	Acronym
Quantum coherent superposition	No collapse	Evolution of wave function (Schrödinger equation)	U
Conventional quantum theory (Copenhagen interpretation)	Environmental entanglement, Measurement, Conscious observation	Reduction : Subjective reduction	R SR
New physics (Penrose, 1994)	Self-collapse – quantum gravity induced (Penrose, Diosi, etc.)	Objective reduction	OR
Consciousness (present paper)	Self-collapse, quantum gravity threshold in microtubules orchestrated by MAPs etc.	Orchestrated objective reduction	Orch OR

Table 1: Description of wave function collapse

The physical phenomenon of gravity, described to a high degree of accuracy by Isaac Newton's mathematics in 1687, has played a key role in scientific understanding. However, in 1915, Einstein created a major revolution in our scientific world-view. According to Einstein's theory, gravity plays a unique role in physics for several reasons (cf. Penrose, 1994). Most particularly, these are:

1) Gravity is the only physical quality which influences causal relationships between space-time events.

2) Gravitational force has no local reality, as it can be eliminated by a change in space-time coordinates; instead, gravitational tidal effects provide a *curvature* for the very *space-time* in which all other particles and forces are contained.

It follows from this that gravity cannot be regarded as some kind of "emergent phenomenon", secondary to other physical effects, but must be a "fundamental component" of physical reality.

There are strong arguments (e.g. Penrose, 1987; 1996) to suggest that the appropriate union of general relativity (Einstein's theory of gravity) with quantum mechanics – a union often referred to as "quantum gravity" – will lead to a significant change in *both* quantum theory and general relativity, and, when the correct theory is found, will yield a profoundly *new* understanding of physical reality. And although gravitational *forces* between objects are exceedingly weak (feebler than, for example, electrical forces by some 40 orders of magnitude), there are significant reasons for believing that gravity has a fundamental influence on the behaviour of quantum systems as they evolve from the micro to the macrolevels. The appropriate union of quantum gravity with biology, or at least with advanced biological nervous systems, may yield a profoundly new understanding of consciousness.

Curved Space-time Superpositions and Objective Reduction ('OR')

According to modern accepted physical pictures, reality is rooted in 3-dimensional space and a 1-dimensional time, combined together into a 4-dimensional space-time. This space-time is slightly curved, in accordance with Einstein's general theory of relativity, in a way which encodes the gravitational fields of all distributions of mass density. Each mass density effects a space-time curvature, albeit tiny.

This is the standard picture according to *classical* physics. On the other hand, when *quantum* systems have been considered by physicists, this mass-induced tiny curvature in the structure of space-time has been almost invariably ignored, gravitational effects having been assumed to be totally insignificant for normal problems in which quantum theory is important. Surprising as it may seem, however, such tiny differences in space-time structure *can* have large effects: for they entail subtle but fundamental influences on the very rules of quantum mechanics.

Superposed quantum states for which the respective mass distributions differ significantly from one another will have space-time geometries which correspondingly differ. Thus, according to standard quantum theory, the superposed state would have to involve a quantum superposition of these differing space-times. In the absence of a coherent theory of quantum gravity there is no accepted way of handling such a superposition. Indeed, the basic principles of Einstein's general relativity begin to come into profound conflict with those of quantum mechanics (cf. Penrose, 1996). Nevertheless, various tentative procedures have been put forward in attempts to describe such a superposition. Of particular relevance to our present proposals are the suggestions of certain authors (e.g. Károlyházy, 1966; 1974; Károlyházy *et al.*, 1986; Kibble, 1981; Diósi, 1989; Ghirardi *et al.*, 1990; Pearle and Squires, 1995; Percival 1995; Penrose, 1993; 1994; 1996) that it is at this point that an objective quantum state reduction (**OR**) ought to occur, and the rate or timescale of this process can be calculated from basic quantum gravity considerations. These particular proposals differ in certain detailed respects, and for definiteness we shall follow the specific suggestions made in Penrose (1994; 1996). Accordingly, the quantum superposition of significantly differing space-times is unstable, with a life-time given by that timescale. Such a superposed state will decay – or "reduce" – into a single universe state, which is one or the other of the space-time geometries involved in that superposition.

Whereas such an **OR** action is not a generally recognized part of the normal quantum-mechanical procedures, there is no plausible or clearcut alternative that standard quantum theory has to offer. This **OR** procedure avoids the need for "multiple universes" (cf. Everett, 1957; Wheeler, 1957, for example). There is no agreement, among quantum gravity experts, about how else to address this problem. For the purposes of the present article, it will be assumed that a gravitationally induced **OR** action is indeed the correct resolution of this fundamental conundrum.

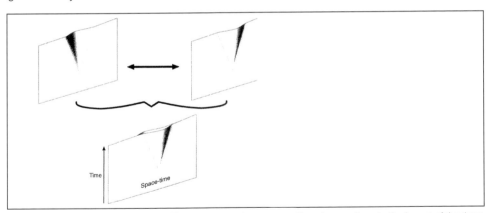

Figure 1. Quantum coherent superposition represented as a separation of space-time. In the lowest of the three diagrams, a bifurcating space-time is depicted as the union ("glued together version"), of the two alternative space-time histories that are depicted at the top of the Figure. The bifurcating space-time diagram illustrates two alternative mass distributions actually in quantum superposition, whereas the top two diagrams illustrate the two individual alternatives which take part in the superposition (adapted from Penrose, 1994, p. 338).

Figure 1 (adapted from Penrose, 1994, p. 338) schematically illustrates the way in which space time structure can be affected when two macroscopically different mass distributions take part in a quantum superposition. Each mass distribution gives rise to a separate space-time, the two differing slightly in their curvatures. So long as the two distributions remain in quantum superposition, we must consider that the two space-times remain in superposition. Since, according to the principles of general relativity, there is no natural way to identify the points of one space-time with corresponding points of the other, we have to consider the two as separated from one another in some sense, resulting in a kind of "blister" where the space-time bifurcates.

A bifurcating space-time is depicted in the lowest of the three diagrams, this being the union ("glued together version") of the two alternative space-time histories that are depicted at the top of Figure 1. The initial part of each space-time is at the lower end of each individual space-time diagram. The bottom space-time diagram (the bifurcating one) illustrates two alternative mass distributions actually in quantum superposition, whereas the top two illustrate the two individual alternatives which take part in the superposition. The combined space-time describes a superposition in which the alternative locations of a mass move gradually away from each other as we proceed in the upward direction in the diagram. Quantum mechanically (i.e. so long as **OR** has not taken place), we must think of the "physical reality" of this situation as being illustrated as an actual superposition of these two slightly differing space-time manifolds, as indicated in the bottom diagram. As soon as **OR** has occurred, one of the two individual space-times takes over, as depicted as one of the two sheets of the bifurcation. For clarity only, the bifurcating parts of these two sheets are illustrated as being one convex and the other concave. Of course there is additional artistic licence involved in drawing the space-time sheets as 2-dimensional, whereas tha actual space-time constituents are 4-dimensional. Moreover, there is no significance to be attached to the imagined "3-dimensional space" within which the space-time sheets seem to be residing. There is no "actual" higher dimensional space there, the "intrinsic geometry" of the bifurcating space-time being all that has physical significance. When the "separation" of the two space-time sheets reaches a critical amount, one of the two sheets "dies" – in accordance with the **OR** criterion – the other being the one that persists in physical reality. The quantum state thus reduces (**OR**), by choosing between either the "concave" or "convex" space-time of Figure 1.

It should be made clear that this measure of separation is only very schematically illustrated as the "distance" between the two sheets in the lower diagram in Figure 1. As remarked above, there is no physically existing "ambient higher-dimensional space" inside which the two sheets reside. The degree of separation between the space-time sheets is a more abstract mathematical thing; it would be more appropriately described in terms of a *symplectic measure* on the space of 4-dimensional metrics (cf. Penrose, 1993) – but the details (and difficulties) of this will not be important for us here. It may be noted, however, that this separation is a space-time separation, not just a spatial one. Thus the *time* of separation contributes as well as the spatial displacement. Roughly speaking, it is the product of the temporal separation T with the spatial separation S that measures the overall degree of separation, and **OR** takes place when this overall separation reaches the critical amount.

[This critical amount would be of the order of unity, in absolute units, for which the Planck-Dirac constant h (= h/2π), the gravitational constant G, and the velocity of light c, all take the value unity; cf. Penrose, 1994, pp. 337-9.] Thus for small S, the lifetime T of the superposed state will be large; on the other hand, if S is large, then T will be small. To calculate S, we compute (in the Newtonian limit of weak gravitational fields) the gravitational self-energy E of the difference between the mass distributions of the two superposed states. (That is, one mass distribution counts positively and the other, negatively; see Penrose, 1994; 1996.) The quantity S is then given in absolute units, by:

$$S = E$$

Thus, restoring standard units,

$$T = h\,E^{-1}$$

Schematically, since S represents three dimensions of displacement rather than the one dimension involved in T, we can imagine that this displacement is shared equally between each of these three dimensions of space – and this is what has been depicted in Figure 3 (below). However, it should be emphasized that this is for pictorial purposes only, the appropriate rule being the one given above. These two equations relate the mass distribution, time of coherence, and space-time separation for a given **OR** event. If, as some philosophers contend, experience is contained in space-time, **OR** events are *self*-organizing processes in that experiential medium, and a candidate for consciousness.

But where in the brain, and how, could coherent superposition and **OR** occur? A number of sites and various types of quantum interactions have been proposed. We strongly favour microtubules as an important ingredient; however various organelles and biomolecular structures including clathrins, myelin (glial cells), presynaptic vesicular grids (Beck and Eccles, 1992) and neural membrane proteins (Marshall, 1989) might also participate.

Microtubules

Properties of brain structures suitable for quantum coherent superposition, **OR** and relevant to consciousness might include: 1) high prevalence, 2) functional importance (for example regulating neural connectivity and synaptic function), 3) periodic, crystal-like lattice dipole structure with longrange order, 4) ability to be transiently isolated from external interaction/observation, 5) functionally coupled to quantum-level events, 6) hollow, cylindrical (possible wave-guide), and 7) suitable for information processing. Membranes, membrane proteins, synapses, DNA and other types of structures have some, but not all, of these characteristics. Cytoskeletal microtubules appear to qualify in all respects.

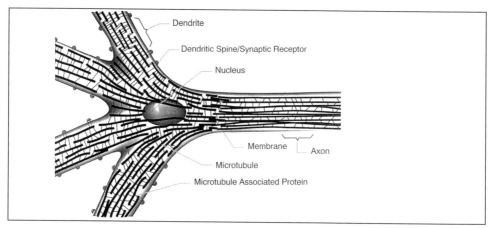

Figure 2. Schematic of central region of neuron (distal axon and dendrites not shown), showing parallel arrayed microtubules interconnected by MAPs. Microtubules in axons are lengthy and continuous, whereas in dendrites they are interrupted and of mixed polarity. Linking proteins connect microtubules to membrane proteins including receptors on dendritic spines.

Interiors of living cells, including the brain's neurons, are spatially and dynamically organized by *self*-assembling protein networks: the cytoskeleton. Within neurons, the cytoskeleton establishes neuronal form, and maintains and regulates synaptic connections. Its major components are microtubules, hollow cylindrical polymers of individual proteins known as tubulin. Microtubules ("MTs") are interconnected by linking proteins (microtubule-associated proteins: "MAPs") to other microtubules and cell structures to form cytoskeletal lattice networks (Figure 2).

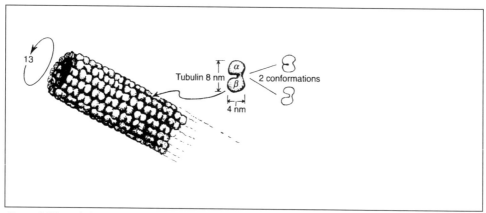

Figure 3. Microtubule structure: a hollow tube of 25 nanometers diameter, consisting of 13 columns of tubulin dimers. Each tubulin molecule is capable of (at least), two conformations. (Reprinted with permission from Penrose, 1994, p. 359.)

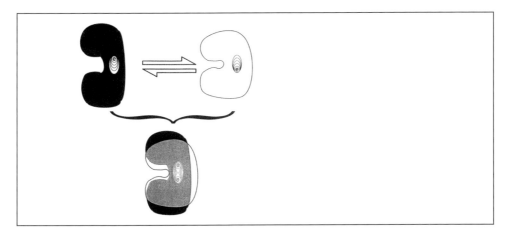

Figure 4. Top: two states of tubulin in which a *single* quantum event (electron localization), within a central hydrophobic pocket is coupled to a *global* protein conformation. Switching between the two states can occur on the order of nanoseconds to picoseconds. Bottom: Tubulin in quantum coherent superposition.

MTs are hollow cylinders 25 nanometers (nm) in diameter whose lengths vary and may be quite long within some nerve axons. MT cylinder walls are comprised of 13 longitudinal protofilaments which are each a series of subunit proteins known as tubulin (Figure 3). Each tubulin subunit is a polar, 8 nm dimer which consists of two slightly different 4 nm monomers (α and β tubulin – Figure 4). Tubulin dimers are dipoles, with surplus negative charges localized toward monomers (DeBrabander, 1982), and within MTs are arranged in a hexagonal lattice which is slightly twisted, resulting in helical pathways which repeat every 3, 5, 8 and other numbers of rows. Traditionally viewed as the cell's "bonelike" scaffolding, microtubules and other cytoskeletal structures also appear to fill communicative and information processing roles. Numerous types of studies link the cytoskeleton to cognitive processes (for review, cf. Hameroff and Penrose, 1996). Theoretical models and simulations suggest how conformational states of tubulins within microtubule lattices can interact with neighbouring tubulins to represent, propagate and process information as in molecular-level "cellular automata", or "spinglass" type computing systems (Figure 5; e.g. Hameroff and Watt, 1982; Rasmussen *et al.*, 1990; Tuszynski *et al.*, 1995). In Hameroff and Penrose (1996, and in summary from Penrose and Hameroff, 1995), we present a model linking microtubules to consciousness, using quantum theory as viewed in the particular "realistic" way referred to above, and as described in *Shadows of the Mind* (Penrose, 1994). In our model, quantum coherence emerges, and is isolated, in brain microtubules until the differences in mass-energy distribution among superposed tubulin states reach the above threshold of instability, related to quantum gravity (Figure 6). The resultant *self*-collapse (OR), considered to be a time-irreversible process, creates an instantaneous "now" event in our model. Sequences of such events create a flow of time and consciousness (Figures 7 and 8).

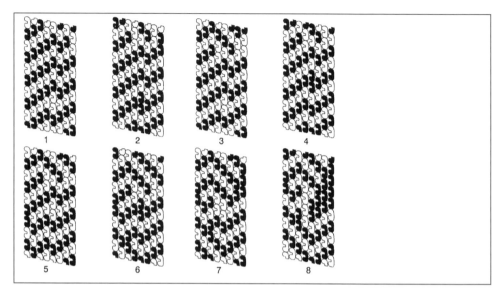

Figure 5. Microtubule automaton simulation (from Rasmussen *et al.*, 1990). Black and white tubulins correspond to states shown in Figure 2. Eight nanosecond time steps of a segment of one microtubule are shown in "classical computing" mode in which patterns move, evolve, interact and lead to emergence of new patterns.

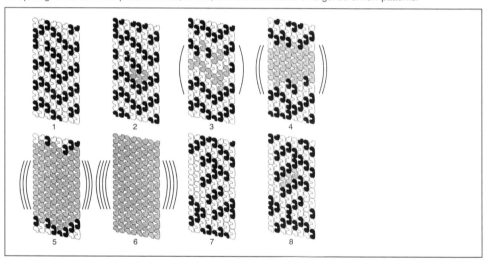

Figure 6. Microtubule automaton sequence simulation in which classical computing (step 1), leads to emergence of quantum coherent superposition (steps 2-6), in certain (grey) tubulins due to pattern resonance. Step 6 (in coherence with other microtubule tubulins) meets critical threshold related to quantum gravity for self-collapse (**Orch OR**). Consciousness (**Orch OR**) occurs in the step 6 to 7 transition. Step 7 represents the eigenstate of mass distribution of the collapse which evolves by classical computing automata to regulate neural function. Quantum coherence begins to re-emerge in step 8.

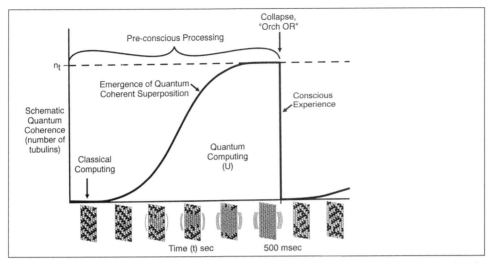

Figure 7. Schematic graph of proposed quantum coherence (number of tubulins), emerging vs time in microtubules. 500 milliseconds is time for pre-conscious processing (e.g. Libet *et al.*, 1979). Area under curve connects mass-energy differences with collapse time in accordance with gravitational **OR**. This degree of coherent superposition of differing space-time geometries leads to abrupt quantum –> classical reduction ("self-collapse" or "orchestrated objective reduction: **Orch OR**").

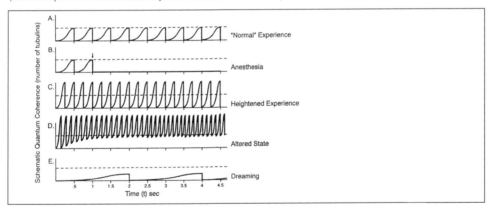

Figure 8. Quantum coherence in microtubules schematically graphed on longer time scale for five different states related to consciousness. Area under each curve equivalent in all cases. A. Normal experience: as in Figure 8. B. Anaesthesia: anaesthetics bind in hydrophobic pockets and prevent quantum delocalizability and coherent superposition (e.g. Louria and Hameroff, 1996). C. Heightened Experience: increased sensory experience input (for example), increases rate of emergence of quantum coherent superposition. **Orch OR** threshold is reached faster (e.g. 250 msec), and **Orch OR** frequency is doubled. D. Altered State: even greater rate of emergence of quantum coherence due to sensory input and other factors promoting quantum state (e.g. meditation, psychedelic drug, etc.). Predisposition to quantum state results in baseline shift and only partial collapse so that conscious experience merges with normally sub-conscious quantum computing mode. E. Dreaming: prolonged quantum coherence time. (Highly schematic)

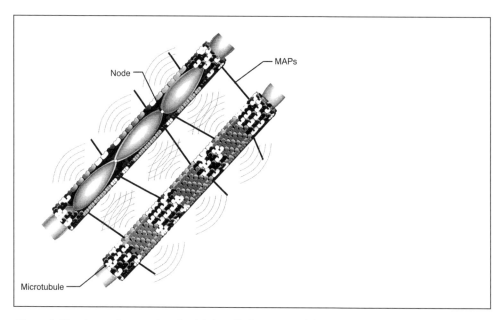

Figure 9. Quantum coherence in microtubules. Having emerged from resonance in classical automaton patterns, quantum coherence non-locally links superpositioned tubulins (grey), within and among microtubules. Upper microtubule cutaway view shows coherent photons generated by quantum ordering of water on tubulin surfaces, propagating in microtubule waveguide. MAP (microtubule-associated protein), attachments breach isolation and prevent quantum coherence; MAP attachment sites thus act as "nodes" which tune and orchestrate quantum oscillations and set possibilities and probabilities for collapse outcomes ("orchestrated objective reduction": **Orch OR**).

We envisage that attachments of MAPs on microtubules "tune" quantum oscillations, and "orchestrate" possible collapse outcomes (Figure 9). Thus we term the particular *self*-organizing **OR** occuring in MAP-connected microtubules, and relevant to consciousness, orchestrated objective reduction ("**Orch OR**"). **Orch OR** events are thus *self*-selecting processes in fundamental space-time geometry. If experience is truly a component of fundamental space-time, **Orch OR** may indeed begin to to address the "hard problem" of consciousness.

Summary of the "Orch OR" Model for Consciousness

The full details of this model are given in Hameroff and Penrose (1996). The picture we are putting forth involves the following ingredients:
(1) Aspects of quantum theory (e.g. quantum coherence) and of the suggested physical phenomenon of quantum wave function "*self*-collapse" (objective reduction: **OR** – Penrose,

1994; 1996) are essential for consciousness, and occur in cytoskeletal microtubules (MTs) and other structures within each of the brain's neurons.

(2) Conformational states of MT subunits (tubulins) are coupled to internal quantum events, and cooperatively interact with other tubulins in both classical and quantum computation (Hameroff *et al.*, 1992; Rasmussen *et al.*, 1990 – Figures 4, 5, and 6).

(3) Quantum coherence occurs among tubulins in MTs, pumped by thermal and biochemical energies (perhaps in the manner proposed by Fröhlich, 1968; 1970; 1975). Evidence for some kind of coherent excitation in proteins has recently been reported by Vos *et al.* (1993).

It is also considered that water at MT surfaces is "ordered" – dynamically coupled to the protein surface. Water ordering within the hollow MT core (acting something like a quantum waveguide) may result in quantum coherent photons (as suggested by the phenomena of "super-radiance" and "*self*-induced transparency" – Jibu *et al.*, 1994; 1995). We require that coherence be sustained (protected from environmental interaction) for up to hundreds of milliseconds by isolation (a) within hollow MT cores, (b) within tubulin hydrophobic pockets, (c) by coherently ordered water, (d) sol-gel layering (Hameroff and Penrose, 1996). Feasibility of quantum coherence in the seemingly noisy, chaotic cell environment is supported by the observation that quantum spins from biochemical radical pairs which become separated retain their correlation in cytoplasm (Walleczek, 1995).

(4) During preconscious processing, quantum coherent superposition/computation occurs in MT tubulins and continues until the mass-distribution difference among the separated states of tubulins reaches a threshold related to quantum gravity. Self-collapse (**OR**) then occurs (Figures 6 & 7).

(5) The **OR** *self*-collapse process results in classical "outcome states" of MT tubulins which then implement neurophysiological functions. According to certain ideas for **OR** (Penrose, 1994), the outcome states are "non-computable"; that is they cannot be determined algorithmically from the tubulin states at the beginning of the quantum computation.

(6) Possibilities and probabilities for post**OR** tubulin states are influenced by factors including initial tubulin states, and attachments of microtubule-associated proteins (MAPs) acting as "nodes" wich tune and "orchestrate" the quantum oscillations (Figure 9). We thus term the *self*-tuning **OR** process in microtubules "orchestrated objective reduction" – **Orch OR** .

(7) According to the arguments for **OR** put forth in Penrose (1994), superposed states each have their own space-time geometries. When the degree of coherent mass-energy difference leads to sufficient separation of space-time geometry, the system must choose and decay (reduce, collapse) to a single universe state. Thus **Orch OR** involves *self*-selections in fundamental space-time geometry (Figures 10 & 11).

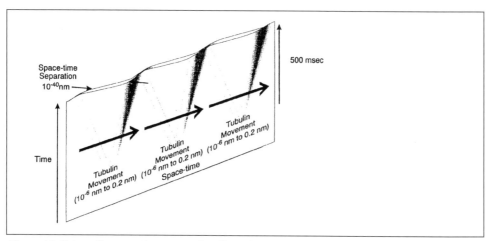

Figure 10. Schematic space-time separation illustration of three superposed tubulins. The space-time differences are very tiny in ordinary terms (10^{-40} nm), but relatively large mass movements (e.g. hundreds of tubulin conformations, each moving from 10^{-6} nm to 0.2 nm), indeed have precisely such very tiny effects on the space-time curvature.

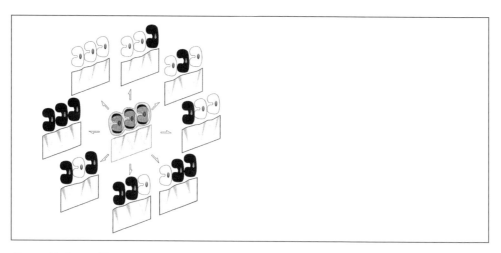

Figure 11. Centre: Three superposed tubulins (e.g. Figure 4), with corresponding schematic space-time separation illustrations (Figures 1 and 10). Surrounding the superposed tubulins are the eight possible post-reduction "eigenstates" for tubulin conformation, and corresponding space-time geometry.

(8) To quantify the **Orch OR** process, in the case of a pair of roughly equally superposed states, each of which has a reasonably well-defined mass distribution, we calculate the gravitational *self*-energy E of the difference between these two mass distributions, and then obtain the approximate lifetime T for the superposition to decay into one state or the other by the formula

$T = h / E$. Here, h is Planck's constant over 2π. We call T the coherence time for the superposition (how long the coherence is sustained). If we assume a coherence time $T = 500$ msec (shown by Libet *et al.*, 1979, and others to be a relevant time for preconscious processing), we calculate E, and determine the number of MT tubulins whose coherent superposition for 500 msec will elicit **Orch OR**. This turns out to be about 10^9 tubulins.

(9) A typical brain neuron has roughly 10^7 tubulins (Yu and Baas, 1994). If, say, 10 % of tubulins within each neuron are involved in the quantum coherent state, then roughly 10^3 (one thousand) neurons would be required to sustain coherence for 500 msec, at which time the quantum gravity threshold is reached and **Orch OR** then occurs.

(10) We consider each *self*-organized **Orch OR** as a single conscious event; cascades of such events would constitute a "stream" of consciousness. If we assume some form of excitatory input (e.g. you are threatened, or enchanted) in which quantum coherence emerges faster, then, for example, 10^{10} coherent tubulins could **Orch OR** after 50 msec, or 10^{11} after 5 msec (e.g. Figure 8c). Turning to see a bengal tiger in your face might perhaps elicit 10^{12} in 0.5 msec, or more tubulins, faster. A slow emergence of coherence (your forgotten phone bill) may require longer times. A single electron would require more than the age of the universe.

(11) Quantum states are non-local (because of quantum entanglement – or "Einstein-Podolsky-Rosen" (EPR) effects), so that the entire non-localized state reduces all at once. This can happen if the mass movement that induces collapse takes place in a small region encompassed by the state, or if it takes place uniformly over a large region. Thus, each instantaneous **Orch OR** could "bind" various superpositions which may have evolved in separated spatial distributions and even over different time scales, but whose net displacement *self*-energy reaches threshold at a particular moment. Information is bound into an instantaneous event (a "conscious now"). Cascades of **Orch ORs** could then represent our familiar "stream of consciousness", and create a "forward" flow of time (Aharonov and Vaidman, 1990; Elitzur, 1996; Tollaksen, 1996).

It may be interesting to compare our considerations with subjective viewpoints that have been expressed with regard to the nature of the progression of conscious experience. For example, support for consciousness consisting of sequences of individual, discrete events is found in Buddhism; trained meditators describe distinct "flickerings" in their experience of reality (Tart, 1995). Buddhist texts portray consciousness as "momentary collections of mental phenomena", and as "distinct, unconnected and impermanent moments which perish as soon as they arise". Each conscious moment successively becomes, exists, and disappears – its existence is instantaneous, with no duration in time, as a point has no length. Our normal perceptions, of course, are seemingly continuous, presumably as we perceive "movies" as continuous despite their actual makeup being a series of frames. Some Buddhist writings even quantify the frequency of conscious moments. For example the Sarvaastivaadins (von Rospatt, 1995) described 6,480,000 "moments" in 24 hours (an average of one "moment" per

13.3 msec), while other Buddhist writings describe one moment per 0.13 msec (Conze, 1988), and some Chinese Buddhism as one "thought" per 20 msec. These accounts, including variations in frequency, seem to be consistent with our proposed **Orch OR** events. For example a 13.3 msec preconscious interval would correspond with an **Orch OR** involving 4×10^{10} coherent tubulins, a 0.13 msec interval would correspond with 4×10^{12} coherent tubulins, and a 20 msec interval with 2.5×10^{10} coherent tubulins. Thus Buddhist "moments of experience", Whitehead "occasions of experience", and our proposed **Orch OR** events seem to correspond tolerably well with one another.

The **Orch OR** model thus appears to accommodate some important features of consciousness:

1) control/regulation of neural action
2) pre-conscious to conscious transition
3) non-computability
4) causality
5) binding of various (time scale and spatial) superpositions into instantaneous "now"
6) a "flow" of time, and
7) a connection to fundamental space-time geometry in which experience may be based.

Conclusion: What Is It Like To Be a Worm?

The **Orch OR** model has the implication that an organism able to sustain quantum coherence among, for example, 10^9 tubulins for 500 msec might be capable of having conscious experience. More tubulins coherent for a briefer period, or fewer for a longer period ($E = h/T$) will also have conscious events. Human brains appear capable of, for example, 10^{12} tubulin, 0.5 msec "bengal tiger experiences", but what about simpler organisms?

From an evolutionary standpoint, introduction of a dynamically functional cytoskeleton (perhaps symbiotically from spirochetes, e.g. Margulis, 1975) greatly enhanced eukaryotic cells by providing cell movement, internal organization, separation of chromosomes and numerous others functions. As cells became more specialized with extensions like axopods and eventually neural processes, increasingly larger cytoskeletal arrays providing transport and motility may have developed quantum coherence via the Fröhlich mechanism as a by-product of their functional coordination.

Another possible scenario for emergence of quantum coherence leading to **Orch OR** and conscious events is "cellular vision". Albrecht-Buehler (1992) has observed that single cells utilize their cytoskeletons in "cellular vision" – detection, orientation and directional response to beams of red/infrared light. Jibu *et al.* (1995) argue that this process requires quantum coherence in microtubules and ordered water, and Hagan (1995) suggests the quantum effects/cellular vision provided an evolutionary advantage for cytoskeletal arrays capable of quantum coherence. For whatever reason quantum coherence emerged, one could then suppose that, one day, an organism achieved sufficient microtubule quantum coherence to elicit **Orch OR**, and had a "conscious" experience.

At what level of evolutionary development might this primitive consciousness have emerged? A single cell organism like *Paramecium* is extremely clever, and utilizes its cytoskeleton extensively. Could a paramecium be conscious? Assuming a single paramecium contains, like each neuronal cell, 10^7 tubulins, then for a paramecium to elicit **Orch OR**, 100 % of its tubulins would need to remain in quantum coherent superposition for nearly a minute. This seems unlikely.

Consider the nematode worm *C elegans*. It's 302 neuron nervous system is completely mapped. Could *C elegans* support **Orch OR**? With 3×10^9 tubulins, *C elegans* would require roughly one third of its tubulins to sustain quantum coherent superposition for 500 msec. This seems unlikely, but not altogether impossible. If not *C elegans*, then perhaps *Aplysia* with a thousand neurons, or some higher organism. **Orch OR** provides a theoretical framework to entertain such possibilities.

Would a primitive **Orch OR** experience be anything like ours? If *C elegans* were able to *self*-collapse, what would it be like to be a worm? (cf. Nagel, 1974). A single, 10^9 tubulin, 500 msec **Orch OR** in *C elegans* should be equal in gravitational *self*-energy terms (and thus perhaps, experiential intensity) to one of your "everyday experiences". A major difference is that we would have many **Orch OR** events sequentially (up to, say, 50 per second) whereas **C elegans** could generate, at most, 2 per second. *C elegans* would also presumably lack extensive memory and associations, and have poor sensory data, but nonetheless, by our criteria a 10^9 tubulin, 500 msec **Orch OR** in *C elegans* could be a conscious experience: a mere smudge of known reality, the next space-time move.

Consciousness has an important place in the universe. **Orch OR** in microtubules is a model depicting consciousness as sequences of non-computable *self*-selections in fundamental space time geometry. If experience is a quality of space-time, then **Orch OR** indeed begins to address the 'hard problem' of consciousness in a serious way.

References

Aharonov, Y. and Vaidman, L. (1990), "Properties of a quantum system during the time interval between two measurements", *Phys. Rev. A*, 41, p. 11.

Albrecht-Buehler, G. (1992), "Rudimentary form of 'cellular vision'", *Cell. Biol.* 89, pp. 8288-92.

Beck, F. and Eccles, J.C. (1992), "Quantum aspects of brain activity and the role of consciousness", *Proc. Natl. Acad. Sci. USA*, 89 (23), pp. 11357-61.

Chalmers, D. (1995), "Facing up to the problem of consciousness", *Journal of Consciousness Studies*, 2 (3). pp. 200-19. Reprinted in Hameroff *et al.* (1996).

Chalmers, D. (1996), *The Conscious Mind* (New York: Oxford University Press).

Conze, E. (1988), *Buddhist Thought in India*, Louis de La Vallée Poussin (trans.). Abhidharmako'sabhaa.syam; English translation by Leo M. Pruden, 4 vols (Berkeley), pp. 85-90.

DeBrabander, M. (1982), "A model for the microtubule organizing activity of the centrosomes and kinetochores in mammalian cells", *Cell Biol. Intern. Rep.,* 6, pp. 901-15.

Diósi, L. (1989), "Models for universal reduction of macroscopic quantum fluctuations", *Phys. Rev. A*, 40, pp. 1165-74.

Elitzur, A. (1996), "Time and consciousness: The uneasy bearing of relativity theory on the mind-body problem", in Hameroff *et al.* (1996).

Everett, H. (1957), "Relative state formulation of quantum mechanics", *Rev Mod. Physics*, 29, pp. 454-62. Reprinted in *Quantum Theory and Measurement,* ed. J.A. Wheeler and W.H. Zurek (Princeton: Princeton University Press, 1983).

Fröhlich, H. (1968), "Long-range coherence and energy storage in biological systems", *Int. J. Quantum Chem.*, 2, pp. 641-9.

Fröhlich, H. (1970), "Long-range coherence and the actions of enzymes", *Nature*, 228, p. 1093.

Fröhlich, H. (1975), "The extraordinary dielectric properties of biological materials and the action of enzymes", *Proc. Natl. Acad. Sci.*, 72, pp. 4211-15.

Ghirardi, G.C., Grassi, R. and Rimini, A. (1990), "Continuous-spontaneous reduction model involving gravity", *Phys. Rev. A*, 42, pp. 1057-64.

Ghirardi, G.C., Rimini, A. and Weber, T. (1986), "Unified dynamics for microscopic and macroscopic systems", *Phys. Rev. D,* 34, p. 470.

Goswami, A. (1993), *The Self-Aware Universe: How Consciousness Creates the Material World* (New York: Tarcher/Putman).

Hagan, S. (1995), Personal communication.

Hameroff, S.R., Dayhoff, J.E., Lahoz-Beltra, R., Samsonovitch, A. and Rasmussen, S. (1992), "Conformational automata in the cytoskeleton: models for molecular computation" *IEEE Computer* (October Special Issue on Molecular Computing), pp. 30-9.

Hameroff, S.R., Kaszniak, A. and Scott, A.C. (eds. 1996), *Toward a Science of Consciousness – The First Tucson Discussions and Debates* (Cambridge, MA: MIT Press).

Hameroff, S.R. and Penrose, R. (1995), "Orchestrated reduction of quantum coherence in brain microtubules: A model for consciousness", *Neural Network World*, 5 (5), pp. 793-804.

Hameroff, S.R. and Penrose, R. (1996), "Orchestrated reduction of quantum coherence in brain microtubules: A model for consciousness", in Hameroff *et al.* (1996).

Hameroff, S.R. and Watt, R.C. (1982), "Information processing in microtubules", *J. Theor. Biol.*, 98, pp. 549-61.

Jibu, M., Hagan, S., Hameroff, S.R., Pribram, H.K. and Yasue, K. (1994), "Quantum optical coherence in cytoskeletal microtubules: implications for brain function", *BioSystems*, 32, pp. 195-209.

Jibu, M., Yasue, K. and Hagan, S. (1995), "Water laser as cellular 'vision'", submitted.

Károlyházy, F., Frenkel, A. and Lukacs, B. (1986), "On the possible role of gravity on the reduction of wave function" in *Quantum Concepts in Space and Time*, ed. R. Penrose and C.J. Isham (Oxford: Oxford University Press).

Károlyházy, F. (1966), "Gravitation and quantum mechanics of macroscopic bodies", *Nuovo Cim. A*, 42, p. 390.

Károlyházy, F. (1974), "Gravitation and quantum mechanics of macroscopic bodies", *Magyar Fizikai Polyoirat*, 12, p. 24.

Kibble, T.W.B. (1981), "Is a semi-classical theory of gravity viable?", in *Quantum Gravity 2: A Second Oxford Symposium*, ed. C.J. Isham, R. Penrose and D.W. Sciama (Oxford: Oxford University Press).

Libet, B., Wright, E.W. Jr., Feinstein, B. and Pearl, D.K. (1979), "Subjective referral of the timing for a conscious sensory experience", *Brain*, 102, pp. 193-224.

Louria, D. and Hameroff, S.R. (1996), "Computer simulation of anesthetic binding in protein hydrophobic pockets", in Hameroff *et al.* (1996).

Marshall, I.N. (1989), "Consciousness and Bose-Einstein condensates", *New Ideas in Psychology*, 7, pp. 73-83.

Margulis, L. (1975), *Origin of Eukaryotic Cells* (New Haven: Yale University Press).

Nagel, T. (1974), "What is it like to be a bat?", *The Philosophical Review*, 83, pp. 435-50. Reprinted in *The Mlnd's I. Fantasies and Reflections on Self and Soul,* ed. D.R. Hofstadter and D.C. Dennett (New York: Basic Books, 1981).

Pearle, P. (1989), "Combining stochastic dynamical sate vector with spontaneous localization", *Phys. Rev. D*, 13, pp. 857-68.

Pearle, P. and Squires, E. (1995), "Gravity, energy, conservation and parameter values in collapse models", *Durham University preprint*, DTP/95/13.

Penrose, R. (1987), "Newton, quantum theory and reality", in *300 Years of Gravity*, ed. S.W. Hawking and W. Israel (Cambridge: Cambridge University Press).

Penrose, R. (1989), *The Emperor's New Mind*, (Oxford: Oxford University Press).

Penrose, R. (1993), "Gravity and quantum mechanics" in *General Relativity and Gravitation. Proceedings of the Thirteenth International Conference on General Relativity and Gravitation held at Cordoba. Argentina*

28 June – 4 July 1992, Part 1: Plenary Lectures, ed. R.J. Gleiser, C.N. Kozameh and O.M. Moreschi (Bristol: Institute of Physics Publications).

Penrose, R. (1994), *Shadows of the MInd* (Oxford: Oxford University Press).

Penrose, R. and Hameroff, S.R., "What gaps? Reply to Grush and Churchland", *Journal of Consciousness Studies,* 2 (2), pp. 99-112.

Penrose, R. (1996), "On gravity's role in quantum sate reduction", *Gen. Rel. Grav.* to appear May 1996.

Percival, I.C. (1995), "Quantum space-time fluctuations and primary state diffusion", *Proc. Roy. Soc. Lond. A,* 451, pp. 503-13.

Rasmussen, S., Karampurwala, H., Vaidyanath, R., Jensen, K.S. and Hameroff, S.R. (1990), "Computational connectionism within neurons: A model of cyclosketal automata subserving neural networks", *Physica D,* 42, pp. 428-49.

Rensch, B. (1960), *Evolution Above the Species Level* (New York: Columbia University Press).

Russell, B. (1954), *The Analysis of Matter* (New York: Dover).

Schrödinger, E. (1935), "Die gegenwarten Situation in der Quantenmechanik", *Naturwissenschaften,* 23, pp. 807-12, 823-8, 844-9. (Translation by J.T. Trimmer, 1980, in *Proc. Amer. Phil. Soc.,* 124, pp. 323-38.) In *Quantum Theory and Measurement,* ed. J.A. Wheeler and W.H. Zurek (Princeton: Princeton University Press, 1983).

Shimony, A. (1993), *Search for a Naturalistic World View – Volume II. Natural Science and Metaphysics,* (Cambridge: Cambridge University Press).

Spinoza, B. (1677), *Ethica in Opera quotque reperta sunt,* 3rd edition, ed. J. van Vloten and J.P.N. Land (Netherlands: Den Haag).

Stubenberg, L. (1996), "The place of qualia in the world of science", in Hameroff *et al.* (1996).

Tart, C.T. (1995), Personal communication and information gathered from "Buddha-I newsnet".

Tollaksen, J. (1996), "New insights from quantum theory on time, consciousness, and reality", in Hameroff *et al.* (1996).

Tusznyski, J., Hameroff, S.R., Sataric, M.V., Trpisová, B. and Nip, M.L.A. (1995), "Ferroelectric behavior in microtubule dipole lattices: implications for information processing, signalling and assembly/disassembly", *J. Theor. Biol.,* 174, pp. 371-80.

von Rospatt, A. (1995), *The Buddhist Doctrine of Momentariness: A survey of the origins and early phase of his doctrine up to Vasubandhu* (Stuttgart: Franz Steiner Verlag).

Vos, M.H., Rappaport, J., Lambry, J.Ch., Breton, J. and Martin, J.L. (1993), "Visualization of coherent nuclear motion in a membrane protein by femtosecond laser spectroscopy", *Nature,* 363, pp. 320-5.

Walleczek, J. (1995), "Magnetokinetic effects on radical pairs: a possible paradigm for understanding sub-kT magnetic field interactions with biological systems", in *Biological Effects of Environmental Electromagnetic Fields* (Advances in Chemistry, No. 250), ed. M. Blank (Washington, DC: American Chemical Society Books, in press).

Wheeler, J.A. (1957), "Assessment of Everett's 'relative state' formulation of quantum theory", *Revs. Mod. Phys.,* 29, pp. 463-5.

Wheeler, J.A. (1990), "Information, physics, quantum: The search for links", in *Complexity, Entropy and the Physics of Information,* ed. W. Zurek (Addison-Wesley).

Whitehead, A.N. (1929), *Science and the Modern World* (New York: Macmillan).

Whitehead, A.N. (1933), *Process and Reality* (New York: Macmillan).

Yu, W. and Baas, P.W. (1994), "Changes in microtubule number and lengh during axon differentiation", *J. Neuroscience,* 14, pp. 2818-29.

S.R. Hameroff & R. Penrose, "Conscious Events as Orchastrated Space-Time Selections", from *The Journal of Consciousness Studies 3.* No 1, 1996, P36-53

CONSCIOUSNESS . MEDITATION . WATCHER ON THE HILLS

ONE MILLION YEARS

I

ON KAWARA

For all those who have lived and died

```
                                                                                           998031 BC
998030 BC  998029 BC  998028 BC  998027 BC  998026 BC  998025 BC  998024 BC  998023 BC  998022 BC  998021 BC
998020 BC  998019 BC  998018 BC  998017 BC  998016 BC  998015 BC  998014 BC  998013 BC  998012 BC  998011 BC
998010 BC  998009 BC  998008 BC  998007 BC  998006 BC  998005 BC  998004 BC  998003 BC  998002 BC  998001 BC
```

998000 BC 997999 BC 997998 BC 997997 BC 997996 BC 997995 BC 997994 BC 997993 BC 997992 BC 997991 BC
997990 BC 997989 BC 997988 BC 997987 BC 997986 BC 997985 BC 997984 BC 997983 BC 997982 BC 997981 BC
997980 BC 997979 BC 997978 BC 997977 BC 997976 BC 997975 BC 997974 BC 997973 BC 997972 BC 997971 BC
997970 BC 997969 BC 997968 BC 997967 BC 997966 BC 997965 BC 997964 BC 997963 BC 997962 BC 997961 BC
997960 BC 997959 BC 997958 BC 997957 BC 997956 BC 997955 BC 997954 BC 997953 BC 997952 BC 997951 BC
997950 BC 997949 BC 997948 BC 997947 BC 997946 BC 997945 BC 997944 BC 997943 BC 997942 BC 997941 BC
997940 BC 997939 BC 997938 BC 997937 BC 997936 BC 997935 BC 997934 BC 997933 BC 997932 BC 997931 BC
997930 BC 997929 BC 997928 BC 997927 BC 997926 BC 997925 BC 997924 BC 997923 BC 997922 BC 997921 BC
997920 BC 997919 BC 997918 BC 997917 BC 997916 BC 997915 BC 997914 BC 997913 BC 997912 BC 997911 BC
997910 BC 997909 BC 997908 BC 997907 BC 997906 BC 997905 BC 997904 BC 997903 BC 997902 BC 997901 BC

997900 BC 997899 BC 997898 BC 997897 BC 997896 BC 997895 BC 997894 BC 997893 BC 997892 BC 997891 BC
997890 BC 997889 BC 997888 BC 997887 BC 997886 BC 997885 BC 997884 BC 997883 BC 997882 BC 997881 BC
997880 BC 997879 BC 997878 BC 997877 BC 997876 BC 997875 BC 997874 BC 997873 BC 997872 BC 997871 BC
997870 BC 997869 BC 997868 BC 997867 BC 997866 BC 997865 BC 997864 BC 997863 BC 997862 BC 997861 BC
997860 BC 997859 BC 997858 BC 997857 BC 997856 BC 997855 BC 997854 BC 997853 BC 997852 BC 997851 BC
997850 BC 997849 BC 997848 BC 997847 BC 997846 BC 997845 BC 997844 BC 997843 BC 997842 BC 997841 BC
997840 BC 997839 BC 997838 BC 997837 BC 997836 BC 997835 BC 997834 BC 997833 BC 997832 BC 997831 BC
997830 BC 997829 BC 997828 BC 997827 BC 997826 BC 997825 BC 997824 BC 997823 BC 997822 BC 997821 BC
997820 BC 997819 BC 997818 BC 997817 BC 997816 BC 997815 BC 997814 BC 997813 BC 997812 BC 997811 BC
997810 BC 997809 BC 997808 BC 997807 BC 997806 BC 997805 BC 997804 BC 997803 BC 997802 BC 997801 BC

997800 BC 997799 BC 997798 BC 997797 BC 997796 BC 997795 BC 997794 BC 997793 BC 997792 BC 997791 BC
997790 BC 997789 BC 997788 BC 997787 BC 997786 BC 997785 BC 997784 BC 997783 BC 997782 BC 997781 BC
997780 BC 997779 BC 997778 BC 997777 BC 997776 BC 997775 BC 997774 BC 997773 BC 997772 BC 997771 BC
997770 BC 997769 BC 997768 BC 997767 BC 997766 BC 997765 BC 997764 BC 997763 BC 997762 BC 997761 BC
997760 BC 997759 BC 997758 BC 997757 BC 997756 BC 997755 BC 997754 BC 997753 BC 997752 BC 997751 BC
997750 BC 997749 BC 997748 BC 997747 BC 997746 BC 997745 BC 997744 BC 997743 BC 997742 BC 997741 BC
997740 BC 997739 BC 997738 BC 997737 BC 997736 BC 997735 BC 997734 BC 997733 BC 997732 BC 997731 BC
997730 BC 997729 BC 997728 BC 997727 BC 997726 BC 997725 BC 997724 BC 997723 BC 997722 BC 997721 BC
997720 BC 997719 BC 997718 BC 997717 BC 997716 BC 997715 BC 997714 BC 997713 BC 997712 BC 997711 BC
997710 BC 997709 BC 997708 BC 997707 BC 997706 BC 997705 BC 997704 BC 997703 BC 997702 BC 997701 BC

997700 BC 997699 BC 997698 BC 997697 BC 997696 BC 997695 BC 997694 BC 997693 BC 997692 BC 997691 BC
997690 BC 997689 BC 997688 BC 997687 BC 997686 BC 997685 BC 997684 BC 997683 BC 997682 BC 997681 BC
997680 BC 997679 BC 997678 BC 997677 BC 997676 BC 997675 BC 997674 BC 997673 BC 997672 BC 997671 BC
997670 BC 997669 BC 997668 BC 997667 BC 997666 BC 997665 BC 997664 BC 997663 BC 997662 BC 997661 BC
997660 BC 997659 BC 997658 BC 997657 BC 997656 BC 997655 BC 997654 BC 997653 BC 997652 BC 997651 BC
997650 BC 997649 BC 997648 BC 997647 BC 997646 BC 997645 BC 997644 BC 997643 BC 997642 BC 997641 BC
997640 BC 997639 BC 997638 BC 997637 BC 997636 BC 997635 BC 997634 BC 997633 BC 997632 BC 997631 BC
997630 BC 997629 BC 997628 BC 997627 BC 997626 BC 997625 BC 997624 BC 997623 BC 997622 BC 997621 BC
997620 BC 997619 BC 997618 BC 997617 BC 997616 BC 997615 BC 997614 BC 997613 BC 997612 BC 997611 BC
997610 BC 997609 BC 997608 BC 997607 BC 997606 BC 997605 BC 997604 BC 997603 BC 997602 BC 997601 BC

997600 BC 997599 BC 997598 BC 997597 BC 997596 BC 997595 BC 997594 BC 997593 BC 997592 BC 997591 BC
997590 BC 997589 BC 997588 BC 997587 BC 997586 BC 997585 BC 997584 BC 997583 BC 997582 BC 997581 BC
997580 BC 997579 BC 997578 BC 997577 BC 997576 BC 997575 BC 997574 BC 997573 BC 997572 BC 997571 BC
997570 BC 997569 BC 997568 BC 997567 BC 997566 BC 997565 BC 997564 BC 997563 BC 997562 BC 997561 BC
997560 BC 997559 BC 997558 BC 997557 BC 997556 BC 997555 BC 997554 BC 997553 BC 997552 BC 997551 BC
997550 BC 997549 BC 997548 BC 997547 BC 997546 BC 997545 BC 997544 BC 997543 BC 997542 BC 997541 BC
997540 BC 997539 BC 997538 BC 997537 BC 997536 BC 997535 BC 997534 BC 997533 BC 997532 BC 997531 BC
997530 BC 997529 BC 997528 BC 997527 BC 997526 BC 997525 BC 997524 BC 997523 BC 997522 BC 997521 BC
997520 BC 997519 BC 997518 BC 997517 BC 997516 BC 997515 BC 997514 BC 997513 BC 997512 BC 997511 BC
997510 BC 997509 BC 997508 BC 997507 BC 997506 BC 997505 BC 997504 BC 997503 BC 997502 BC 997501 BC

997500 BC 997499 BC 997498 BC 997497 BC 997496 BC 997495 BC 997494 BC 997493 BC 997492 BC 997491 BC
997490 BC 997489 BC 997488 BC 997487 BC 997486 BC 997485 BC 997484 BC 997483 BC 997482 BC 997481 BC
997480 BC 997479 BC 997478 BC 997477 BC 997476 BC 997475 BC 997474 BC 997473 BC 997472 BC 997471 BC
997470 BC 997469 BC 997468 BC 997467 BC 997466 BC 997465 BC 997464 BC 997463 BC 997462 BC 997461 BC
997460 BC 997459 BC 997458 BC 997457 BC 997456 BC 997455 BC 997454 BC 997453 BC 997452 BC 997451 BC
997450 BC 997449 BC 997448 BC 997447 BC 997446 BC 997445 BC 997444 BC 997443 BC 997442 BC 997441 BC
997440 BC 997439 BC 997438 BC 997437 BC 997436 BC 997435 BC 997434 BC 997433 BC 997432 BC 997431 BC
997430 BC 997429 BC 997428 BC 997427 BC 997426 BC 997425 BC 997424 BC 997423 BC 997422 BC 997421 BC
997420 BC 997419 BC 997418 BC 997417 BC 997416 BC 997415 BC 997414 BC 997413 BC 997412 BC 997411 BC
997410 BC 997409 BC 997408 BC 997407 BC 997406 BC 997405 BC 997404 BC 997403 BC 997402 BC 997401 BC

997400 BC 997399 BC 997398 BC 997397 BC 997396 BC 997395 BC 997394 BC 997393 BC 997392 BC 997391 BC
997390 BC 997389 BC 997388 BC 997387 BC 997386 BC 997385 BC 997384 BC 997383 BC 997382 BC 997381 BC
997380 BC 997379 BC 997378 BC 997377 BC 997376 BC 997375 BC 997374 BC 997373 BC 997372 BC 997371 BC
997370 BC 997369 BC 997368 BC 997367 BC 997366 BC 997365 BC 997364 BC 997363 BC 997362 BC 997361 BC
997360 BC 997359 BC 997358 BC 997357 BC 997356 BC 997355 BC 997354 BC 997353 BC 997352 BC 997351 BC
997350 BC 997349 BC 997348 BC 997347 BC 997346 BC 997345 BC 997344 BC 997343 BC 997342 BC 997341 BC
997340 BC 997339 BC 997338 BC 997337 BC 997336 BC 997335 BC 997334 BC 997333 BC 997332 BC 997331 BC
997330 BC 997329 BC 997328 BC 997327 BC 997326 BC 997325 BC 997324 BC 997323 BC 997322 BC 997321 BC
997320 BC 997319 BC 997318 BC 997317 BC 997316 BC 997315 BC 997314 BC 997313 BC 997312 BC 997311 BC
997310 BC 997309 BC 997308 BC 997307 BC 997306 BC 997305 BC 997304 BC 997303 BC 997302 BC 997301 BC

997300 BC 997299 BC 997298 BC 997297 BC 997296 BC 997295 BC 997294 BC 997293 BC 997292 BC 997291 BC
997290 BC 997289 BC 997288 BC 997287 BC 997286 BC 997285 BC 997284 BC 997283 BC 997282 BC 997281 BC
997280 BC 997279 BC 997278 BC 997277 BC 997276 BC 997275 BC 997274 BC 997273 BC 997272 BC 997271 BC
997270 BC 997269 BC 997268 BC 997267 BC 997266 BC 997265 BC 997264 BC 997263 BC 997262 BC 997261 BC
997260 BC 997259 BC 997258 BC 997257 BC 997256 BC 997255 BC 997254 BC 997253 BC 997252 BC 997251 BC
997250 BC 997249 BC 997248 BC 997247 BC 997246 BC 997245 BC 997244 BC 997243 BC 997242 BC 997241 BC
997240 BC 997239 BC 997238 BC 997237 BC 997236 BC 997235 BC 997234 BC 997233 BC 997232 BC 997231 BC
997230 BC 997229 BC 997228 BC 997227 BC 997226 BC 997225 BC 997224 BC 997223 BC 997222 BC 997221 BC
997220 BC 997219 BC 997218 BC 997217 BC 997216 BC 997215 BC 997214 BC 997213 BC 997212 BC 997211 BC
997210 BC 997209 BC 997208 BC 997207 BC 997206 BC 997205 BC 997204 BC 997203 BC 997202 BC 997201 BC

997200 BC 997199 BC 997198 BC 997197 BC 997196 BC 997195 BC 997194 BC 997193 BC 997192 BC 997191 BC
997190 BC 997189 BC 997188 BC 997187 BC 997186 BC 997185 BC 997184 BC 997183 BC 997182 BC 997181 BC
997180 BC 997179 BC 997178 BC 997177 BC 997176 BC 997175 BC 997174 BC 997173 BC 997172 BC 997171 BC
997170 BC 997169 BC 997168 BC 997167 BC 997166 BC 997165 BC 997164 BC 997163 BC 997162 BC 997161 BC
997160 BC 997159 BC 997158 BC 997157 BC 997156 BC 997155 BC 997154 BC 997153 BC 997152 BC 997151 BC
997150 BC 997149 BC 997148 BC 997147 BC 997146 BC 997145 BC 997144 BC 997143 BC 997142 BC 997141 BC
997140 BC 997139 BC 997138 BC 997137 BC 997136 BC 997135 BC 997134 BC 997133 BC 997132 BC 997131 BC
997130 BC 997129 BC 997128 BC 997127 BC 997126 BC 997125 BC 997124 BC 997123 BC 997122 BC 997121 BC
997120 BC 997119 BC 997118 BC 997117 BC 997116 BC 997115 BC 997114 BC 997113 BC 997112 BC 997111 BC
997110 BC 997109 BC 997108 BC 997107 BC 997106 BC 997105 BC 997104 BC 997103 BC 997102 BC 997101 BC

997100 BC 997099 BC 997098 BC 997097 BC 997096 BC 997095 BC 997094 BC 997093 BC 997092 BC 997091 BC
997090 BC 997089 BC 997088 BC 997087 BC 997086 BC 997085 BC 997084 BC 997083 BC 997082 BC 997081 BC
997080 BC 997079 BC 997078 BC 997077 BC 997076 BC 997075 BC 997074 BC 997073 BC 997072 BC 997071 BC
997070 BC 997069 BC 997068 BC 997067 BC 997066 BC 997065 BC 997064 BC 997063 BC 997062 BC 997061 BC
997060 BC 997059 BC 997058 BC 997057 BC 997056 BC 997055 BC 997054 BC 997053 BC 997052 BC 997051 BC
997050 BC 997049 BC 997048 BC 997047 BC 997046 BC 997045 BC 997044 BC 997043 BC 997042 BC 997041 BC
997040 BC 997039 BC 997038 BC 997037 BC 997036 BC 997035 BC 997034 BC 997033 BC 997032 BC 997031 BC
997030 BC 997029 BC 997028 BC 997027 BC 997026 BC 997025 BC 997024 BC 997023 BC 997022 BC 997021 BC
997020 BC 997019 BC 997018 BC 997017 BC 997016 BC 997015 BC 997014 BC 997013 BC 997012 BC 997011 BC
997010 BC 997009 BC 997008 BC 997007 BC 997006 BC 997005 BC 997004 BC 997003 BC 997002 BC 997001 BC

—3—

91

```
997000 BC  996999 BC  996998 BC  996997 BC  996996 BC  996995 BC  996994 BC  996993 BC  996992 BC  996991 BC
996990 BC  996989 BC  996988 BC  996987 BC  996986 BC  996985 BC  996984 BC  996983 BC  996982 BC  996981 BC
996980 BC  996979 BC  996978 BC  996977 BC  996976 BC  996975 BC  996974 BC  996973 BC  996972 BC  996971 BC
996970 BC  996969 BC  996968 BC  996967 BC  996966 BC  996965 BC  996964 BC  996963 BC  996962 BC  996961 BC
996960 BC  996959 BC  996958 BC  996957 BC  996956 BC  996955 BC  996954 BC  996953 BC  996952 BC  996951 BC
996950 BC  996949 BC  996948 BC  996947 BC  996946 BC  996945 BC  996944 BC  996943 BC  996942 BC  996941 BC
996940 BC  996939 BC  996938 BC  996937 BC  996936 BC  996935 BC  996934 BC  996933 BC  996932 BC  996931 BC
996930 BC  996929 BC  996928 BC  996927 BC  996926 BC  996925 BC  996924 BC  996923 BC  996922 BC  996921 BC
996920 BC  996919 BC  996918 BC  996917 BC  996916 BC  996915 BC  996914 BC  996913 BC  996912 BC  996911 BC
996910 BC  996909 BC  996908 BC  996907 BC  996906 BC  996905 BC  996904 BC  996903 BC  996902 BC  996901 BC

996900 BC  996899 BC  996898 BC  996897 BC  996896 BC  996895 BC  996894 BC  996893 BC  996892 BC  996891 BC
996890 BC  996889 BC  996888 BC  996887 BC  996886 BC  996885 BC  996884 BC  996883 BC  996882 BC  996881 BC
996880 BC  996879 BC  996878 BC  996877 BC  996876 BC  996875 BC  996874 BC  996873 BC  996872 BC  996871 BC
996870 BC  996869 BC  996868 BC  996867 BC  996866 BC  996865 BC  996864 BC  996863 BC  996862 BC  996861 BC
996860 BC  996859 BC  996858 BC  996857 BC  996856 BC  996855 BC  996854 BC  996853 BC  996852 BC  996851 BC
996850 BC  996849 BC  996848 BC  996847 BC  996846 BC  996845 BC  996844 BC  996843 BC  996842 BC  996841 BC
996840 BC  996839 BC  996838 BC  996837 BC  996836 BC  996835 BC  996834 BC  996833 BC  996832 BC  996831 BC
996830 BC  996829 BC  996828 BC  996827 BC  996826 BC  996825 BC  996824 BC  996823 BC  996822 BC  996821 BC
996820 BC  996819 BC  996818 BC  996817 BC  996816 BC  996815 BC  996814 BC  996813 BC  996812 BC  996811 BC
996810 BC  996809 BC  996808 BC  996807 BC  996806 BC  996805 BC  996804 BC  996803 BC  996802 BC  996801 BC

996800 BC  996799 BC  996798 BC  996797 BC  996796 BC  996795 BC  996794 BC  996793 BC  996792 BC  996791 BC
996790 BC  996789 BC  996788 BC  996787 BC  996786 BC  996785 BC  996784 BC  996783 BC  996782 BC  996781 BC
996780 BC  996779 BC  996778 BC  996777 BC  996776 BC  996775 BC  996774 BC  996773 BC  996772 BC  996771 BC
996770 BC  996769 BC  996768 BC  996767 BC  996766 BC  996765 BC  996764 BC  996763 BC  996762 BC  996761 BC
996760 BC  996759 BC  996758 BC  996757 BC  996756 BC  996755 BC  996754 BC  996753 BC  996752 BC  996751 BC
996750 BC  996749 BC  996748 BC  996747 BC  996746 BC  996745 BC  996744 BC  996743 BC  996742 BC  996741 BC
996740 BC  996739 BC  996738 BC  996737 BC  996736 BC  996735 BC  996734 BC  996733 BC  996732 BC  996731 BC
996730 BC  996729 BC  996728 BC  996727 BC  996726 BC  996725 BC  996724 BC  996723 BC  996722 BC  996721 BC
996720 BC  996719 BC  996718 BC  996717 BC  996716 BC  996715 BC  996714 BC  996713 BC  996712 BC  996711 BC
996710 BC  996709 BC  996708 BC  996707 BC  996706 BC  996705 BC  996704 BC  996703 BC  996702 BC  996701 BC

996700 BC  996699 BC  996698 BC  996697 BC  996696 BC  996695 BC  996694 BC  996693 BC  996692 BC  996691 BC
996690 BC  996689 BC  996688 BC  996687 BC  996686 BC  996685 BC  996684 BC  996683 BC  996682 BC  996681 BC
996680 BC  996679 BC  996678 BC  996677 BC  996676 BC  996675 BC  996674 BC  996673 BC  996672 BC  996671 BC
996670 BC  996669 BC  996668 BC  996667 BC  996666 BC  996665 BC  996664 BC  996663 BC  996662 BC  996661 BC
996660 BC  996659 BC  996658 BC  996657 BC  996656 BC  996655 BC  996654 BC  996653 BC  996652 BC  996651 BC
996650 BC  996649 BC  996648 BC  996647 BC  996646 BC  996645 BC  996644 BC  996643 BC  996642 BC  996641 BC
996640 BC  996639 BC  996638 BC  996637 BC  996636 BC  996635 BC  996634 BC  996633 BC  996632 BC  996631 BC
996630 BC  996629 BC  996628 BC  996627 BC  996626 BC  996625 BC  996624 BC  996623 BC  996622 BC  996621 BC
996620 BC  996619 BC  996618 BC  996617 BC  996616 BC  996615 BC  996614 BC  996613 BC  996612 BC  996611 BC
996610 BC  996609 BC  996608 BC  996607 BC  996606 BC  996605 BC  996604 BC  996603 BC  996602 BC  996601 BC

996600 BC  996599 BC  996598 BC  996597 BC  996596 BC  996595 BC  996594 BC  996593 BC  996592 BC  996591 BC
996590 BC  996589 BC  996588 BC  996587 BC  996586 BC  996585 BC  996584 BC  996583 BC  996582 BC  996581 BC
996580 BC  996579 BC  996578 BC  996577 BC  996576 BC  996575 BC  996574 BC  996573 BC  996572 BC  996571 BC
996570 BC  996569 BC  996568 BC  996567 BC  996566 BC  996565 BC  996564 BC  996563 BC  996562 BC  996561 BC
996560 BC  996559 BC  996558 BC  996557 BC  996556 BC  996555 BC  996554 BC  996553 BC  996552 BC  996551 BC
996550 BC  996549 BC  996548 BC  996547 BC  996546 BC  996545 BC  996544 BC  996543 BC  996542 BC  996541 BC
996540 BC  996539 BC  996538 BC  996537 BC  996536 BC  996535 BC  996534 BC  996533 BC  996532 BC  996531 BC
996530 BC  996529 BC  996528 BC  996527 BC  996526 BC  996525 BC  996524 BC  996523 BC  996522 BC  996521 BC
996520 BC  996519 BC  996518 BC  996517 BC  996516 BC  996515 BC  996514 BC  996513 BC  996512 BC  996511 BC
996510 BC  996509 BC  996508 BC  996507 BC  996506 BC  996505 BC  996504 BC  996503 BC  996502 BC  996501 BC
```

— 4 —

```
996500 BC  996499 BC  996498 BC  996497 BC  996496 BC  996495 BC  996494 BC  996493 BC  996492 BC  996491 BC
996490 BC  996489 BC  996488 BC  996487 BC  996486 BC  996485 BC  996484 BC  996483 BC  996482 BC  996481 BC
996480 BC  996479 BC  996478 BC  996477 BC  996476 BC  996475 BC  996474 BC  996473 BC  996472 BC  996471 BC
996470 BC  996469 BC  996468 BC  996467 BC  996466 BC  996465 BC  996464 BC  996463 BC  996462 BC  996461 BC
996460 BC  996459 BC  996458 BC  996457 BC  996456 BC  996455 BC  996454 BC  996453 BC  996452 BC  996451 BC
996450 BC  996449 BC  996448 BC  996447 BC  996446 BC  996445 BC  996444 BC  996443 BC  996442 BC  996441 BC
996440 BC  996439 BC  996438 BC  996437 BC  996436 BC  996435 BC  996434 BC  996433 BC  996432 BC  996431 BC
996430 BC  996429 BC  996428 BC  996427 BC  996426 BC  996425 BC  996424 BC  996423 BC  996422 BC  996421 BC
996420 BC  996419 BC  996418 BC  996417 BC  996416 BC  996415 BC  996414 BC  996413 BC  996412 BC  996411 BC
996410 BC  996409 BC  996408 BC  996407 BC  996406 BC  996405 BC  996404 BC  996403 BC  996402 BC  996401 BC

996400 BC  996399 BC  996398 BC  996397 BC  996396 BC  996395 BC  996394 BC  996393 BC  996392 BC  996391 BC
996390 BC  996389 BC  996388 BC  996387 BC  996386 BC  996385 BC  996384 BC  996383 BC  996382 BC  996381 BC
996380 BC  996379 BC  996378 BC  996377 BC  996376 BC  996375 BC  996374 BC  996373 BC  996372 BC  996371 BC
996370 BC  996369 BC  996368 BC  996367 BC  996366 BC  996365 BC  996364 BC  996363 BC  996362 BC  996361 BC
996360 BC  996359 BC  996358 BC  996357 BC  996356 BC  996355 BC  996354 BC  996353 BC  996352 BC  996351 BC
996350 BC  996349 BC  996348 BC  996347 BC  996346 BC  996345 BC  996344 BC  996343 BC  996342 BC  996341 BC
996340 BC  996339 BC  996338 BC  996337 BC  996336 BC  996335 BC  996334 BC  996333 BC  996332 BC  996331 BC
996330 BC  996329 BC  996328 BC  996327 BC  996326 BC  996325 BC  996324 BC  996323 BC  996322 BC  996321 BC
996320 BC  996319 BC  996318 BC  996317 BC  996316 BC  996315 BC  996314 BC  996313 BC  996312 BC  996311 BC
996310 BC  996309 BC  996308 BC  996307 BC  996306 BC  996305 BC  996304 BC  996303 BC  996302 BC  996301 BC

996300 BC  996299 BC  996298 BC  996297 BC  996296 BC  996295 BC  996294 BC  996293 BC  996292 BC  996291 BC
996290 BC  996289 BC  996288 BC  996287 BC  996286 BC  996285 BC  996284 BC  996283 BC  996282 BC  996281 BC
996280 BC  996279 BC  996278 BC  996277 BC  996276 BC  996275 BC  996274 BC  996273 BC  996272 BC  996271 BC
996270 BC  996269 BC  996268 BC  996267 BC  996266 BC  996265 BC  996264 BC  996263 BC  996262 BC  996261 BC
996260 BC  996259 BC  996258 BC  996257 BC  996256 BC  996255 BC  996254 BC  996253 BC  996252 BC  996251 BC
996250 BC  996249 BC  996248 BC  996247 BC  996246 BC  996245 BC  996244 BC  996243 BC  996242 BC  996241 BC
996240 BC  996239 BC  996238 BC  996237 BC  996236 BC  996235 BC  996234 BC  996233 BC  996232 BC  996231 BC
996230 BC  996229 BC  996228 BC  996227 BC  996226 BC  996225 BC  996224 BC  996223 BC  996222 BC  996221 BC
996220 BC  996219 BC  996218 BC  996217 BC  996216 BC  996215 BC  996214 BC  996213 BC  996212 BC  996211 BC
996210 BC  996209 BC  996208 BC  996207 BC  996206 BC  996205 BC  996204 BC  996203 BC  996202 BC  996201 BC

996200 BC  996199 BC  996198 BC  996197 BC  996196 BC  996195 BC  996194 BC  996193 BC  996192 BC  996191 BC
996190 BC  996189 BC  996188 BC  996187 BC  996186 BC  996185 BC  996184 BC  996183 BC  996182 BC  996181 BC
996180 BC  996179 BC  996178 BC  996177 BC  996176 BC  996175 BC  996174 BC  996173 BC  996172 BC  996171 BC
996170 BC  996169 BC  996168 BC  996167 BC  996166 BC  996165 BC  996164 BC  996163 BC  996162 BC  996161 BC
996160 BC  996159 BC  996158 BC  996157 BC  996156 BC  996155 BC  996154 BC  996153 BC  996152 BC  996151 BC
996150 BC  996149 BC  996148 BC  996147 BC  996146 BC  996145 BC  996144 BC  996143 BC  996142 BC  996141 BC
996140 BC  996139 BC  996138 BC  996137 BC  996136 BC  996135 BC  996134 BC  996133 BC  996132 BC  996131 BC
996130 BC  996129 BC  996128 BC  996127 BC  996126 BC  996125 BC  996124 BC  996123 BC  996122 BC  996121 BC
996120 BC  996119 BC  996118 BC  996117 BC  996116 BC  996115 BC  996114 BC  996113 BC  996112 BC  996111 BC
996110 BC  996109 BC  996108 BC  996107 BC  996106 BC  996105 BC  996104 BC  996103 BC  996102 BC  996101 BC

996100 BC  996099 BC  996098 BC  996097 BC  996096 BC  996095 BC  996094 BC  996093 BC  996092 BC  996091 BC
996090 BC  996089 BC  996088 BC  996087 BC  996086 BC  996085 BC  996084 BC  996083 BC  996082 BC  996081 BC
996080 BC  996079 BC  996078 BC  996077 BC  996076 BC  996075 BC  996074 BC  996073 BC  996072 BC  996071 BC
996070 BC  996069 BC  996068 BC  996067 BC  996066 BC  996065 BC  996064 BC  996063 BC  996062 BC  996061 BC
996060 BC  996059 BC  996058 BC  996057 BC  996056 BC  996055 BC  996054 BC  996053 BC  996052 BC  996051 BC
996050 BC  996049 BC  996048 BC  996047 BC  996046 BC  996045 BC  996044 BC  996043 BC  996042 BC  996041 BC
996040 BC  996039 BC  996038 BC  996037 BC  996036 BC  996035 BC  996034 BC  996033 BC  996032 BC  996031 BC
996030 BC  996029 BC  996028 BC  996027 BC  996026 BC  996025 BC  996024 BC  996023 BC  996022 BC  996021 BC
996020 BC  996019 BC  996018 BC  996017 BC  996016 BC  996015 BC  996014 BC  996013 BC  996012 BC  996011 BC
996010 BC  996009 BC  996008 BC  996007 BC  996006 BC  996005 BC  996004 BC  996003 BC  996002 BC  996001 BC
```

— 5 —

995000 BC 995999 BC 995998 BC 995997 BC 995996 BC 995995 BC 995994 BC 995993 BC 995992 BC 995991 BC
995990 BC 995989 BC 995988 BC 995987 BC 995986 BC 995985 BC 995984 BC 995983 BC 995982 BC 995981 BC
995980 BC 995979 BC 995978 BC 995977 BC 995976 BC 995975 BC 995974 BC 995973 BC 995972 BC 995971 BC
995970 BC 995969 BC 995968 BC 995967 BC 995966 BC 995965 BC 995964 BC 995963 BC 995962 BC 995961 BC
995960 BC 995959 BC 995958 BC 995957 BC 995956 BC 995955 BC 995954 BC 995953 BC 995952 BC 995951 BC
995950 BC 995949 BC 995948 BC 995947 BC 995946 BC 995945 BC 995944 BC 995943 BC 995942 BC 995941 BC
995940 BC 995939 BC 995938 BC 995937 BC 995936 BC 995935 BC 995934 BC 995933 BC 995932 BC 995931 BC
995930 BC 995929 BC 995928 BC 995927 BC 995926 BC 995925 BC 995924 BC 995923 BC 995922 BC 995921 BC
995920 BC 995919 BC 995918 BC 995917 BC 995916 BC 995915 BC 995914 BC 995913 BC 995912 BC 995911 BC
995910 BC 995909 BC 995908 BC 995907 BC 995906 BC 995905 BC 995904 BC 995903 BC 995902 BC 995901 BC

995900 BC 995899 BC 995898 BC 995897 BC 995896 BC 995895 BC 995894 BC 995893 BC 995892 BC 995891 BC
995890 BC 995889 BC 995888 BC 995887 BC 995886 BC 995885 BC 995884 BC 995883 BC 995882 BC 995881 BC
995880 BC 995879 BC 995878 BC 995877 BC 995876 BC 995875 BC 995874 BC 995873 BC 995872 BC 995871 BC
995870 BC 995869 BC 995868 BC 995867 BC 995866 BC 995865 BC 995864 BC 995863 BC 995862 BC 995861 BC
995860 BC 995859 BC 995858 BC 995857 BC 995856 BC 995855 BC 995854 BC 995853 BC 995852 BC 995851 BC
995850 BC 995849 BC 995848 BC 995847 BC 995846 BC 995845 BC 995844 BC 995843 BC 995842 BC 995841 BC
995840 BC 995839 BC 995838 BC 995837 BC 995836 BC 995835 BC 995834 BC 995833 BC 995832 BC 995831 BC
995830 BC 995829 BC 995828 BC 995827 BC 995826 BC 995825 BC 995824 BC 995823 BC 995822 BC 995821 BC
995820 BC 995819 BC 995818 BC 995817 BC 995816 BC 995815 BC 995814 BC 995813 BC 995812 BC 995811 BC
995810 BC 995809 BC 995808 BC 995807 BC 995806 BC 995805 BC 995804 BC 995803 BC 995802 BC 995801 BC

995800 BC 995799 BC 995798 BC 995797 BC 995796 BC 995795 BC 995794 BC 995793 BC 995792 BC 995791 BC
995790 BC 995789 BC 995788 BC 995787 BC 995786 BC 995785 BC 995784 BC 995783 BC 995782 BC 995781 BC
995780 BC 995779 BC 995778 BC 995777 BC 995776 BC 995775 BC 995774 BC 995773 BC 995772 BC 995771 BC
995770 BC 995769 BC 995768 BC 995767 BC 995766 BC 995765 BC 995764 BC 995763 BC 995762 BC 995761 BC
995760 BC 995759 BC 995758 BC 995757 BC 995756 BC 995755 BC 995754 BC 995753 BC 995752 BC 995751 BC
995750 BC 995749 BC 995748 BC 995747 BC 995746 BC 995745 BC 995744 BC 995743 BC 995742 BC 995741 BC
995740 BC 995739 BC 995738 BC 995737 BC 995736 BC 995735 BC 995734 BC 995733 BC 995732 BC 995731 BC
995730 BC 995729 BC 995728 BC 995727 BC 995726 BC 995725 BC 995724 BC 995723 BC 995722 BC 995721 BC
995720 BC 995719 BC 995718 BC 995717 BC 995716 BC 995715 BC 995714 BC 995713 BC 995712 BC 995711 BC
995710 BC 995709 BC 995708 BC 995707 BC 995706 BC 995705 BC 995704 BC 995703 BC 995702 BC 995701 BC

995700 BC 995699 BC 995698 BC 995697 BC 995696 BC 995695 BC 995694 BC 995693 BC 995692 BC 995691 BC
995690 BC 995689 BC 995688 BC 995687 BC 995686 BC 995685 BC 995684 BC 995683 BC 995682 BC 995681 BC
995680 BC 995679 BC 995678 BC 995677 BC 995676 BC 995675 BC 995674 BC 995673 BC 995672 BC 995671 BC
995670 BC 995669 BC 995668 BC 995667 BC 995666 BC 995665 BC 995664 BC 995663 BC 995662 BC 995661 BC
995660 BC 995659 BC 995658 BC 995657 BC 995656 BC 995655 BC 995654 BC 995653 BC 995652 BC 995651 BC
995650 BC 995649 BC 995648 BC 995647 BC 995646 BC 995645 BC 995644 BC 995643 BC 995642 BC 995641 BC
995640 BC 995639 BC 995638 BC 995637 BC 995636 BC 995635 BC 995634 BC 995633 BC 995632 BC 995631 BC
995630 BC 995629 BC 995628 BC 995627 BC 995626 BC 995625 BC 995624 BC 995623 BC 995622 BC 995621 BC
995620 BC 995619 BC 995618 BC 995617 BC 995616 BC 995615 BC 995614 BC 995613 BC 995612 BC 995611 BC
995610 BC 995609 BC 995608 BC 995607 BC 995606 BC 995605 BC 995604 BC 995603 BC 995602 BC 995601 BC

995600 BC 995599 BC 995598 BC 995597 BC 995596 BC 995595 BC 995594 BC 995593 BC 995592 BC 995591 BC
995590 BC 995589 BC 995588 BC 995587 BC 995586 BC 995585 BC 995584 BC 995583 BC 995582 BC 995581 BC
995580 BC 995579 BC 995578 BC 995577 BC 995576 BC 995575 BC 995574 BC 995573 BC 995572 BC 995571 BC
995570 BC 995569 BC 995568 BC 995567 BC 995566 BC 995565 BC 995564 BC 995563 BC 995562 BC 995561 BC
995560 BC 995559 BC 995558 BC 995557 BC 995556 BC 995555 BC 995554 BC 995553 BC 995552 BC 995551 BC
995550 BC 995549 BC 995548 BC 995547 BC 995546 BC 995545 BC 995544 BC 995543 BC 995542 BC 995541 BC
995540 BC 995539 BC 995538 BC 995537 BC 995536 BC 995535 BC 995534 BC 995533 BC 995532 BC 995531 BC
995530 BC 995529 BC 995528 BC 995527 BC 995526 BC 995525 BC 995524 BC 995523 BC 995522 BC 995521 BC
995520 BC 995519 BC 995518 BC 995517 BC 995516 BC 995515 BC 995514 BC 995513 BC 995512 BC 995511 BC
995510 BC 995509 BC 995508 BC 995507 BC 995506 BC 995505 BC 995504 BC 995503 BC 995502 BC 995501 BC

995500 BC	995499 BC	995498 BC	995497 BC	995496 BC	995495 BC	995494 BC	995493 BC	995492 BC	995491 BC
995490 BC	995489 BC	995488 BC	995487 BC	995486 BC	995485 BC	995484 BC	995483 BC	995482 BC	995481 BC
995480 BC	995479 BC	995478 BC	995477 BC	995476 BC	995475 BC	995474 BC	995473 BC	995472 BC	995471 BC
995470 BC	995469 BC	995468 BC	995467 BC	995466 BC	995465 BC	995464 BC	995463 BC	995462 BC	995461 BC
995460 BC	995459 BC	995458 BC	995457 BC	995456 BC	995455 BC	995454 BC	995453 BC	995452 BC	995451 BC
995450 BC	995449 BC	995448 BC	995447 BC	995446 BC	995445 BC	995444 BC	995443 BC	995442 BC	995441 BC
995440 BC	995439 BC	995438 BC	995437 BC	995436 BC	995435 BC	995434 BC	995433 BC	995432 BC	995431 BC
995430 BC	995429 BC	995428 BC	995427 BC	995426 BC	995425 BC	995424 BC	995423 BC	995422 BC	995421 BC
995420 BC	995419 BC	995418 BC	995417 BC	995416 BC	995415 BC	995414 BC	995413 BC	995412 BC	995411 BC
995410 BC	995409 BC	995408 BC	995407 BC	995406 BC	995405 BC	995404 BC	995403 BC	995402 BC	995401 BC
995400 BC	995399 BC	995398 BC	995397 BC	995396 BC	995395 BC	995394 BC	995393 BC	995392 BC	995391 BC
995390 BC	995389 BC	995388 BC	995387 BC	995386 BC	995385 BC	995384 BC	995383 BC	995382 BC	995381 BC
995380 BC	995379 BC	995378 BC	995377 BC	995376 BC	995375 BC	995374 BC	995373 BC	995372 BC	995371 BC
995370 BC	995369 BC	995368 BC	995367 BC	995366 BC	995365 BC	995364 BC	995363 BC	995362 BC	995361 BC
995360 BC	995359 BC	995358 BC	995357 BC	995356 BC	995355 BC	995354 BC	995353 BC	995352 BC	995351 BC
995350 BC	995349 BC	995348 BC	995347 BC	995346 BC	995345 BC	995344 BC	995343 BC	995342 BC	995341 BC
995340 BC	995339 BC	995338 BC	995337 BC	995336 BC	995335 BC	995334 BC	995333 BC	995332 BC	995331 BC
995330 BC	995329 BC	995328 BC	995327 BC	995326 BC	995325 BC	995324 BC	995323 BC	995322 BC	995321 BC
995320 BC	995319 BC	995318 BC	995317 BC	995316 BC	995315 BC	995314 BC	995313 BC	995312 BC	995311 BC
995310 BC	995309 BC	995308 BC	995307 BC	995306 BC	995305 BC	995304 BC	995303 BC	995302 BC	995301 BC
995300 BC	995299 BC	995298 BC	995297 BC	995296 BC	995295 BC	995294 BC	995293 BC	995292 BC	995291 BC
995290 BC	995289 BC	995288 BC	995287 BC	995286 BC	995285 BC	995284 BC	995283 BC	995282 BC	995281 BC
995280 BC	995279 BC	995278 BC	995277 BC	995276 BC	995275 BC	995274 BC	995273 BC	995272 BC	995271 BC
995270 BC	995269 BC	995268 BC	995267 BC	995266 BC	995265 BC	995264 BC	995263 BC	995262 BC	995261 BC
995260 BC	995259 BC	995258 BC	995257 BC	995256 BC	995255 BC	995254 BC	995253 BC	995252 BC	995251 BC
995250 BC	995249 BC	995248 BC	995247 BC	995246 BC	995245 BC	995244 BC	995243 BC	995242 BC	995241 BC
995240 BC	995239 BC	995238 BC	995237 BC	995236 BC	995235 BC	995234 BC	995233 BC	995232 BC	995231 BC
995230 BC	995229 BC	995228 BC	995227 BC	995226 BC	995225 BC	995224 BC	995223 BC	995222 BC	995221 BC
995220 BC	995219 BC	995218 BC	995217 BC	995216 BC	995215 BC	995214 BC	995213 BC	995212 BC	995211 BC
995210 BC	995209 BC	995208 BC	995207 BC	995206 BC	995205 BC	995204 BC	995203 BC	995202 BC	995201 BC
995200 BC	995199 BC	995198 BC	995197 BC	995196 BC	995195 BC	995194 BC	995193 BC	995192 BC	995191 BC
995190 BC	995189 BC	995188 BC	995187 BC	995186 BC	995185 BC	995184 BC	995183 BC	995182 BC	995181 BC
995180 BC	995179 BC	995178 BC	995177 BC	995176 BC	995175 BC	995174 BC	995173 BC	995172 BC	995171 BC
995170 BC	995169 BC	995168 BC	995167 BC	995166 BC	995165 BC	995164 BC	995163 BC	995162 BC	995161 BC
995160 BC	995159 BC	995158 BC	995157 BC	995156 BC	995155 BC	995154 BC	995153 BC	995152 BC	995151 BC
995150 BC	995149 BC	995148 BC	995147 BC	995146 BC	995145 BC	995144 BC	995143 BC	995142 BC	995141 BC
995140 BC	995139 BC	995138 BC	995137 BC	995136 BC	995135 BC	995134 BC	995133 BC	995132 BC	995131 BC
995130 BC	995129 BC	995128 BC	995127 BC	995126 BC	995125 BC	995124 BC	995123 BC	995122 BC	995121 BC
995120 BC	995119 BC	995118 BC	995117 BC	995116 BC	995115 BC	995114 BC	995113 BC	995112 BC	995111 BC
995110 BC	995109 BC	995108 BC	995107 BC	995106 BC	995105 BC	995104 BC	995103 BC	995102 BC	995101 BC
995100 BC	995099 BC	995098 BC	995097 BC	995096 BC	995095 BC	995094 BC	995093 BC	995092 BC	995091 BC
995090 BC	995089 BC	995088 BC	995087 BC	995086 BC	995085 BC	995084 BC	995083 BC	995082 BC	995081 BC
995080 BC	995079 BC	995078 BC	995077 BC	995076 BC	995075 BC	995074 BC	995073 BC	995072 BC	995071 BC
995070 BC	995069 BC	995068 BC	995067 BC	995066 BC	995065 BC	995064 BC	995063 BC	995062 BC	995061 BC
995060 BC	995059 BC	995058 BC	995057 BC	995056 BC	995055 BC	995054 BC	995053 BC	995052 BC	995051 BC
995050 BC	995049 BC	995048 BC	995047 BC	995046 BC	995045 BC	995044 BC	995043 BC	995042 BC	995041 BC
995040 BC	995039 BC	995038 BC	995037 BC	995036 BC	995035 BC	995034 BC	995033 BC	995032 BC	995031 BC
995030 BC	995029 BC	995028 BC	995027 BC	995026 BC	995025 BC	995024 BC	995023 BC	995022 BC	995021 BC
995020 BC	995019 BC	995018 BC	995017 BC	995016 BC	995015 BC	995014 BC	995013 BC	995012 BC	995011 BC
995010 BC	995009 BC	995008 BC	995007 BC	995006 BC	995005 BC	995004 BC	995003 BC	995002 BC	995001 BC

995000 BC 994999 BC 994998 BC 994997 BC 994996 BC 994995 BC 994994 BC 994993 BC 994992 BC 994991 BC
994990 BC 994989 BC 994988 BC 994987 BC 994986 BC 994985 BC 994984 BC 994983 BC 994982 BC 994981 BC
994980 BC 994979 BC 994978 BC 994977 BC 994976 BC 994975 BC 994974 BC 994973 BC 994972 BC 994971 BC
994970 BC 994969 BC 994968 BC 994967 BC 994966 BC 994965 BC 994964 BC 994963 BC 994962 BC 994961 BC
994960 BC 994959 BC 994958 BC 994957 BC 994956 BC 994955 BC 994954 BC 994953 BC 994952 BC 994951 BC
994950 BC 994949 BC 994948 BC 994947 BC 994946 BC 994945 BC 994944 BC 994943 BC 994942 BC 994941 BC
994940 BC 994939 BC 994938 BC 994937 BC 994936 BC 994935 BC 994934 BC 994933 BC 994932 BC 994931 BC
994930 BC 994929 BC 994928 BC 994927 BC 994926 BC 994925 BC 994924 BC 994923 BC 994922 BC 994921 BC
994920 BC 994919 BC 994918 BC 994917 BC 994916 BC 994915 BC 994914 BC 994913 BC 994912 BC 994911 BC
994910 BC 994909 BC 994908 BC 994907 BC 994906 BC 994905 BC 994904 BC 994903 BC 994902 BC 994901 BC

994900 BC 994899 BC 994898 BC 994897 BC 994896 BC 994895 BC 994894 BC 994893 BC 994892 BC 994891 BC
994890 BC 994889 BC 994888 BC 994887 BC 994886 BC 994885 BC 994884 BC 994883 BC 994882 BC 994881 BC
994880 BC 994879 BC 994878 BC 994877 BC 994876 BC 994875 BC 994874 BC 994873 BC 994872 BC 994871 BC
994870 BC 994869 BC 994868 BC 994867 BC 994866 BC 994865 BC 994864 BC 994863 BC 994862 BC 994861 BC
994860 BC 994859 BC 994858 BC 994857 BC 994856 BC 994855 BC 994854 BC 994853 BC 994852 BC 994851 BC
994850 BC 994849 BC 994848 BC 994847 BC 994846 BC 994845 BC 994844 BC 994843 BC 994842 BC 994841 BC
994840 BC 994839 BC 994838 BC 994837 BC 994836 BC 994835 BC 994834 BC 994833 BC 994832 BC 994831 BC
994830 BC 994829 BC 994828 BC 994827 BC 994826 BC 994825 BC 994824 BC 994823 BC 994822 BC 994821 BC
994820 BC 994819 BC 994818 BC 994817 BC 994816 BC 994815 BC 994814 BC 994813 BC 994812 BC 994811 BC
994810 BC 994809 BC 994808 BC 994807 BC 994806 BC 994805 BC 994804 BC 994803 BC 994802 BC 994801 BC

994800 BC 994799 BC 994798 BC 994797 BC 994796 BC 994795 BC 994794 BC 994793 BC 994792 BC 994791 BC
994790 BC 994789 BC 994788 BC 994787 BC 994786 BC 994785 BC 994784 BC 994783 BC 994782 BC 994781 BC
994780 BC 994779 BC 994778 BC 994777 BC 994776 BC 994775 BC 994774 BC 994773 BC 994772 BC 994771 BC
994770 BC 994769 BC 994768 BC 994767 BC 994766 BC 994765 BC 994764 BC 994763 BC 994762 BC 994761 BC
994760 BC 994759 BC 994758 BC 994757 BC 994756 BC 994755 BC 994754 BC 994753 BC 994752 BC 994751 BC
994750 BC 994749 BC 994748 BC 994747 BC 994746 BC 994745 BC 994744 BC 994743 BC 994742 BC 994741 BC
994740 BC 994739 BC 994738 BC 994737 BC 994736 BC 994735 BC 994734 BC 994733 BC 994732 BC 994731 BC
994730 BC 994729 BC 994728 BC 994727 BC 994726 BC 994725 BC 994724 BC 994723 BC 994722 BC 994721 BC
994720 BC 994719 BC 994718 BC 994717 BC 994716 BC 994715 BC 994714 BC 994713 BC 994712 BC 994711 BC
994710 BC 994709 BC 994708 BC 994707 BC 994706 BC 994705 BC 994704 BC 994703 BC 994702 BC 994701 BC

994700 BC 994699 BC 994698 BC 994697 BC 994696 BC 994695 BC 994694 BC 994693 BC 994692 BC 994691 BC
994690 BC 994689 BC 994688 BC 994687 BC 994686 BC 994685 BC 994684 BC 994683 BC 994682 BC 994681 BC
994680 BC 994679 BC 994678 BC 994677 BC 994676 BC 994675 BC 994674 BC 994673 BC 994672 BC 994671 BC
994670 BC 994669 BC 994668 BC 994667 BC 994666 BC 994665 BC 994664 BC 994663 BC 994662 BC 994661 BC
994660 BC 994659 BC 994658 BC 994657 BC 994656 BC 994655 BC 994654 BC 994653 BC 994652 BC 994651 BC
994650 BC 994649 BC 994648 BC 994647 BC 994646 BC 994645 BC 994644 BC 994643 BC 994642 BC 994641 BC
994640 BC 994639 BC 994638 BC 994637 BC 994636 BC 994635 BC 994634 BC 994633 BC 994632 BC 994631 BC
994630 BC 994629 BC 994628 BC 994627 BC 994626 BC 994625 BC 994624 BC 994623 BC 994622 BC 994621 BC
994620 BC 994619 BC 994618 BC 994617 BC 994616 BC 994615 BC 994614 BC 994613 BC 994612 BC 994611 BC
994610 BC 994609 BC 994608 BC 994607 BC 994606 BC 994605 BC 994604 BC 994603 BC 994602 BC 994601 BC

994600 BC 994599 BC 994598 BC 994597 BC 994596 BC 994595 BC 994594 BC 994593 BC 994592 BC 994591 BC
994590 BC 994589 BC 994588 BC 994587 BC 994586 BC 994585 BC 994584 BC 994583 BC 994582 BC 994581 BC
994580 BC 994579 BC 994578 BC 994577 BC 994576 BC 994575 BC 994574 BC 994573 BC 994572 BC 994571 BC
994570 BC 994569 BC 994568 BC 994567 BC 994566 BC 994565 BC 994564 BC 994563 BC 994562 BC 994561 BC
994560 BC 994559 BC 994558 BC 994557 BC 994556 BC 994555 BC 994554 BC 994553 BC 994552 BC 994551 BC
994550 BC 994549 BC 994548 BC 994547 BC 994546 BC 994545 BC 994544 BC 994543 BC 994542 BC 994541 BC
994540 BC 994539 BC 994538 BC 994537 BC 994536 BC 994535 BC 994534 BC 994533 BC 994532 BC 994531 BC
994530 BC 994529 BC 994528 BC 994527 BC 994526 BC 994525 BC 994524 BC 994523 BC 994522 BC 994521 BC
994520 BC 994519 BC 994518 BC 994517 BC 994516 BC 994515 BC 994514 BC 994513 BC 994512 BC 994511 BC
994510 BC 994509 BC 994508 BC 994507 BC 994506 BC 994505 BC 994504 BC 994503 BC 994502 BC 994501 BC

994500 BC 994499 BC 994498 BC 994497 BC 994496 BC 994495 BC 994494 BC 994493 BC 994492 BC 994491 BC
994490 BC 994489 BC 994488 BC 994487 BC 994486 BC 994485 BC 994484 BC 994483 BC 994482 BC 994481 BC
994480 BC 994479 BC 994478 BC 994477 BC 994476 BC 994475 BC 994474 BC 994473 BC 994472 BC 994471 BC
994470 BC 994469 BC 994468 BC 994467 BC 994466 BC 994465 BC 994464 BC 994463 BC 994462 BC 994461 BC
994460 BC 994459 BC 994458 BC 994457 BC 994456 BC 994455 BC 994454 BC 994453 BC 994452 BC 994451 BC
994450 BC 994449 BC 994448 BC 994447 BC 994446 BC 994445 BC 994444 BC 994443 BC 994442 BC 994441 BC
994440 BC 994439 BC 994438 BC 994437 BC 994436 BC 994435 BC 994434 BC 994433 BC 994432 BC 994431 BC
994430 BC 994429 BC 994428 BC 994427 BC 994426 BC 994425 BC 994424 BC 994423 BC 994422 BC 994421 BC
994420 BC 994419 BC 994418 BC 994417 BC 994416 BC 994415 BC 994414 BC 994413 BC 994412 BC 994411 BC
994410 BC 994409 BC 994408 BC 994407 BC 994406 BC 994405 BC 994404 BC 994403 BC 994402 BC 994401 BC

994400 BC 994399 BC 994398 BC 994397 BC 994396 BC 994395 BC 994394 BC 994393 BC 994392 BC 994391 BC
994390 BC 994389 BC 994388 BC 994387 BC 994386 BC 994385 BC 994384 BC 994383 BC 994382 BC 994381 BC
994380 BC 994379 BC 994378 BC 994377 BC 994376 BC 994375 BC 994374 BC 994373 BC 994372 BC 994371 BC
994370 BC 994369 BC 994368 BC 994367 BC 994366 BC 994365 BC 994364 BC 994363 BC 994362 BC 994361 BC
994360 BC 994359 BC 994358 BC 994357 BC 994356 BC 994355 BC 994354 BC 994353 BC 994352 BC 994351 BC
994350 BC 994349 BC 994348 BC 994347 BC 994346 BC 994345 BC 994344 BC 994343 BC 994342 BC 994341 BC
994340 BC 994339 BC 994338 BC 994337 BC 994336 BC 994335 BC 994334 BC 994333 BC 994332 BC 994331 BC
994330 BC 994329 BC 994328 BC 994327 BC 994326 BC 994325 BC 994324 BC 994323 BC 994322 BC 994321 BC
994320 BC 994319 BC 994318 BC 994317 BC 994316 BC 994315 BC 994314 BC 994313 BC 994312 BC 994311 BC
994310 BC 994309 BC 994308 BC 994307 BC 994306 BC 994305 BC 994304 BC 994303 BC 994302 BC 994301 BC

994300 BC 994299 BC 994298 BC 994297 BC 994296 BC 994295 BC 994294 BC 994293 BC 994292 BC 994291 BC
994290 BC 994289 BC 994288 BC 994287 BC 994286 BC 994285 BC 994284 BC 994283 BC 994282 BC 994281 BC
994280 BC 994279 BC 994278 BC 994277 BC 994276 BC 994275 BC 994274 BC 994273 BC 994272 BC 994271 BC
994270 BC 994269 BC 994268 BC 994267 BC 994266 BC 994265 BC 994264 BC 994263 BC 994262 BC 994261 BC
994260 BC 994259 BC 994258 BC 994257 BC 994256 BC 994255 BC 994254 BC 994253 BC 994252 BC 994251 BC
994250 BC 994249 BC 994248 BC 994247 BC 994246 BC 994245 BC 994244 BC 994243 BC 994242 BC 994241 BC
994240 BC 994239 BC 994238 BC 994237 BC 994236 BC 994235 BC 994234 BC 994233 BC 994232 BC 994231 BC
994230 BC 994229 BC 994228 BC 994227 BC 994226 BC 994225 BC 994224 BC 994223 BC 994222 BC 994221 BC
994220 BC 994219 BC 994218 BC 994217 BC 994216 BC 994215 BC 994214 BC 994213 BC 994212 BC 994211 BC
994210 BC 994209 BC 994208 BC 994207 BC 994206 BC 994205 BC 994204 BC 994203 BC 994202 BC 994201 BC

994200 BC 994199 BC 994198 BC 994197 BC 994196 BC 994195 BC 994194 BC 994193 BC 994192 BC 994191 BC
994190 BC 994189 BC 994188 BC 994187 BC 994186 BC 994185 BC 994184 BC 994183 BC 994182 BC 994181 BC
994180 BC 994179 BC 994178 BC 994177 BC 994176 BC 994175 BC 994174 BC 994173 BC 994172 BC 994171 BC
994170 BC 994169 BC 994168 BC 994167 BC 994166 BC 994165 BC 994164 BC 994163 BC 994162 BC 994161 BC
994160 BC 994159 BC 994158 BC 994157 BC 994156 BC 994155 BC 994154 BC 994153 BC 994152 BC 994151 BC
994150 BC 994149 BC 994148 BC 994147 BC 994146 BC 994145 BC 994144 BC 994143 BC 994142 BC 994141 BC
994140 BC 994139 BC 994138 BC 994137 BC 994136 BC 994135 BC 994134 BC 994133 BC 994132 BC 994131 BC
994130 BC 994129 BC 994128 BC 994127 BC 994126 BC 994125 BC 994124 BC 994123 BC 994122 BC 994121 BC
994120 BC 994119 BC 994118 BC 994117 BC 994116 BC 994115 BC 994114 BC 994113 BC 994112 BC 994111 BC
994110 BC 994109 BC 994108 BC 994107 BC 994106 BC 994105 BC 994104 BC 994103 BC 994102 BC 994101 BC

994100 BC 994099 BC 994098 BC 994097 BC 994096 BC 994095 BC 994094 BC 994093 BC 994092 BC 994091 BC
994090 BC 994089 BC 994088 BC 994087 BC 994086 BC 994085 BC 994084 BC 994083 BC 994082 BC 994081 BC
994080 BC 994079 BC 994078 BC 994077 BC 994076 BC 994075 BC 994074 BC 994073 BC 994072 BC 994071 BC
994070 BC 994069 BC 994068 BC 994067 BC 994066 BC 994065 BC 994064 BC 994063 BC 994062 BC 994061 BC
994060 BC 994059 BC 994058 BC 994057 BC 994056 BC 994055 BC 994054 BC 994053 BC 994052 BC 994051 BC
994050 BC 994049 BC 994048 BC 994047 BC 994046 BC 994045 BC 994044 BC 994043 BC 994042 BC 994041 BC
994040 BC 994039 BC 994038 BC 994037 BC 994036 BC 994035 BC 994034 BC 994033 BC 994032 BC 994031 BC
994030 BC 994029 BC 994028 BC 994027 BC 994026 BC 994025 BC 994024 BC 994023 BC 994022 BC 994021 BC
994020 BC 994019 BC 994018 BC 994017 BC 994016 BC 994015 BC 994014 BC 994013 BC 994012 BC 994011 BC
994010 BC 994009 BC 994008 BC 994007 BC 994006 BC 994005 BC 994004 BC 994003 BC 994002 BC 994001 BC

— 9 —

994000 BC 993999 BC 993998 BC 993997 BC 993996 BC 993995 BC 993994 BC 993993 BC 993992 BC 993991 BC
993990 BC 993989 BC 993988 BC 993987 BC 993986 BC 993985 BC 993984 BC 993983 BC 993982 BC 993981 BC
993980 BC 993979 BC 993978 BC 993977 BC 993976 BC 993975 BC 993974 BC 993973 BC 993972 BC 993971 BC
993970 BC 993969 BC 993968 BC 993967 BC 993966 BC 993965 BC 993964 BC 993963 BC 993962 BC 993961 BC
993960 BC 993959 BC 993958 BC 993957 BC 993956 BC 993955 BC 993954 BC 993953 BC 993952 BC 993951 BC
993950 BC 993949 BC 993948 BC 993947 BC 993946 BC 993945 BC 993944 BC 993943 BC 993942 BC 993941 BC
993940 BC 993939 BC 993938 BC 993937 BC 993936 BC 993935 BC 993934 BC 993933 BC 993932 BC 993931 BC
993930 BC 993929 BC 993928 BC 993927 BC 993926 BC 993925 BC 993924 BC 993923 BC 993922 BC 993921 BC
993920 BC 993919 BC 993918 BC 993917 BC 993916 BC 993915 BC 993914 BC 993913 BC 993912 BC 993911 BC
993910 BC 993909 BC 993908 BC 993907 BC 993906 BC 993905 BC 993904 BC 993903 BC 993902 BC 993901 BC

993900 BC 993899 BC 993898 BC 993897 BC 993896 BC 993895 BC 993894 BC 993893 BC 993892 BC 993891 BC
993890 BC 993889 BC 993888 BC 993887 BC 993886 BC 993885 BC 993884 BC 993883 BC 993882 BC 993881 BC
993880 BC 993879 BC 993878 BC 993877 BC 993876 BC 993875 BC 993874 BC 993873 BC 993872 BC 993871 BC
993870 BC 993869 BC 993868 BC 993867 BC 993866 BC 993865 BC 993864 BC 993863 BC 993862 BC 993861 BC
993860 BC 993859 BC 993858 BC 993857 BC 993856 BC 993855 BC 993854 BC 993853 BC 993852 BC 993851 BC
993850 BC 993849 BC 993848 BC 993847 BC 993846 BC 993845 BC 993844 BC 993843 BC 993842 BC 993841 BC
993840 BC 993839 BC 993838 BC 993837 BC 993836 BC 993835 BC 993834 BC 993833 BC 993832 BC 993831 BC
993830 BC 993829 BC 993828 BC 993827 BC 993826 BC 993825 BC 993824 BC 993823 BC 993822 BC 993821 BC
993820 BC 993819 BC 993818 BC 993817 BC 993816 BC 993815 BC 993814 BC 993813 BC 993812 BC 993811 BC
993810 BC 993809 BC 993808 BC 993807 BC 993806 BC 993805 BC 993804 BC 993803 BC 993802 BC 993801 BC

993800 BC 993799 BC 993798 BC 993797 BC 993796 BC 993795 BC 993794 BC 993793 BC 993792 BC 993791 BC
993790 BC 993789 BC 993788 BC 993787 BC 993786 BC 993785 BC 993784 BC 993783 BC 993782 BC 993781 BC
993780 BC 993779 BC 993778 BC 993777 BC 993776 BC 993775 BC 993774 BC 993773 BC 993772 BC 993771 BC
993770 BC 993769 BC 993768 BC 993767 BC 993766 BC 993765 BC 993764 BC 993763 BC 993762 BC 993761 BC
993760 BC 993759 BC 993758 BC 993757 BC 993756 BC 993755 BC 993754 BC 993753 BC 993752 BC 993751 BC
993750 BC 993749 BC 993748 BC 993747 BC 993746 BC 993745 BC 993744 BC 993743 BC 993742 BC 993741 BC
993740 BC 993739 BC 993738 BC 993737 BC 993736 BC 993735 BC 993734 BC 993733 BC 993732 BC 993731 BC
993730 BC 993729 BC 993728 BC 993727 BC 993726 BC 993725 BC 993724 BC 993723 BC 993722 BC 993721 BC
993720 BC 993719 BC 993718 BC 993717 BC 993716 BC 993715 BC 993714 BC 993713 BC 993712 BC 993711 BC
993710 BC 993709 BC 993708 BC 993707 BC 993706 BC 993705 BC 993704 BC 993703 BC 993702 BC 993701 BC

993700 BC 993699 BC 993698 BC 993697 BC 993696 BC 993695 BC 993694 BC 993693 BC 993692 BC 993691 BC
993690 BC 993689 BC 993688 BC 993687 BC 993686 BC 993685 BC 993684 BC 993683 BC 993682 BC 993681 BC
993680 BC 993679 BC 993678 BC 993677 BC 993676 BC 993675 BC 993674 BC 993673 BC 993672 BC 993671 BC
993670 BC 993669 BC 993668 BC 993667 BC 993666 BC 993665 BC 993664 BC 993663 BC 993662 BC 993661 BC
993660 BC 993659 BC 993658 BC 993657 BC 993656 BC 993655 BC 993654 BC 993653 BC 993652 BC 993651 BC
993650 BC 993649 BC 993648 BC 993647 BC 993646 BC 993645 BC 993644 BC 993643 BC 993642 BC 993641 BC
993640 BC 993639 BC 993638 BC 993637 BC 993636 BC 993635 BC 993634 BC 993633 BC 993632 BC 993631 BC
993630 BC 993629 BC 993628 BC 993627 BC 993626 BC 993625 BC 993624 BC 993623 BC 993622 BC 993621 BC
993620 BC 993619 BC 993618 BC 993617 BC 993616 BC 993615 BC 993614 BC 993613 BC 993612 BC 993611 BC
993610 BC 993609 BC 993608 BC 993607 BC 993606 BC 993605 BC 993604 BC 993603 BC 993602 BC 993601 BC

993600 BC 993599 BC 993598 BC 993597 BC 993596 BC 993595 BC 993594 BC 993593 BC 993592 BC 993591 BC
993590 BC 993589 BC 993588 BC 993587 BC 993586 BC 993585 BC 993584 BC 993583 BC 993582 BC 993581 BC
993580 BC 993579 BC 993578 BC 993577 BC 993576 BC 993575 BC 993574 BC 993573 BC 993572 BC 993571 BC
993570 BC 993569 BC 993568 BC 993567 BC 993566 BC 993565 BC 993564 BC 993563 BC 993562 BC 993561 BC
993560 BC 993559 BC 993558 BC 993557 BC 993556 BC 993555 BC 993554 BC 993553 BC 993552 BC 993551 BC
993550 BC 993549 BC 993548 BC 993547 BC 993546 BC 993545 BC 993544 BC 993543 BC 993542 BC 993541 BC
993540 BC 993539 BC 993538 BC 993537 BC 993536 BC 993535 BC 993534 BC 993533 BC 993532 BC 993531 BC
993530 BC 993529 BC 993528 BC 993527 BC 993526 BC 993525 BC 993524 BC 993523 BC 993522 BC 993521 BC
993520 BC 993519 BC 993518 BC 993517 BC 993516 BC 993515 BC 993514 BC 993513 BC 993512 BC 993511 BC
993510 BC 993509 BC 993508 BC 993507 BC 993506 BC 993505 BC 993504 BC 993503 BC 993502 BC 993501 BC

993500 BC 993499 BC 993498 BC 993497 BC 993496 BC 993495 BC 993494 BC 993493 BC 993492 BC 993491 BC
993490 BC 993489 BC 993488 BC 993487 BC 993486 BC 993485 BC 993484 BC 993483 BC 993482 BC 993481 BC
993480 BC 993479 BC 993478 BC 993477 BC 993476 BC 993475 BC 993474 BC 993473 BC 993472 BC 993471 BC
993470 BC 993469 BC 993468 BC 993467 BC 993466 BC 993465 BC 993464 BC 993463 BC 993462 BC 993461 BC
993460 BC 993459 BC 993458 BC 993457 BC 993456 BC 993455 BC 993454 BC 993453 BC 993452 BC 993451 BC
993450 BC 993449 BC 993448 BC 993447 BC 993446 BC 993445 BC 993444 BC 993443 BC 993442 BC 993441 BC
993440 BC 993439 BC 993438 BC 993437 BC 993436 BC 993435 BC 993434 BC 993433 BC 993432 BC 993431 BC
993430 BC 993429 BC 993428 BC 993427 BC 993426 BC 993425 BC 993424 BC 993423 BC 993422 BC 993421 BC
993420 BC 993419 BC 993418 BC 993417 BC 993416 BC 993415 BC 993414 BC 993413 BC 993412 BC 993411 BC
993410 BC 993409 BC 993408 BC 993407 BC 993406 BC 993405 BC 993404 BC 993403 BC 993402 BC 993401 BC

993400 BC 993399 BC 993398 BC 993397 BC 993396 BC 993395 BC 993394 BC 993393 BC 993392 BC 993391 BC
993390 BC 993389 BC 993388 BC 993387 BC 993386 BC 993385 BC 993384 BC 993383 BC 993382 BC 993381 BC
993380 BC 993379 BC 993378 BC 993377 BC 993376 BC 993375 BC 993374 BC 993373 BC 993372 BC 993371 BC
993370 BC 993369 BC 993368 BC 993367 BC 993366 BC 993365 BC 993364 BC 993363 BC 993362 BC 993361 BC
993360 BC 993359 BC 993358 BC 993357 BC 993356 BC 993355 BC 993354 BC 993353 BC 993352 BC 993351 BC
993350 BC 993349 BC 993348 BC 993347 BC 993346 BC 993345 BC 993344 BC 993343 BC 993342 BC 993341 BC
993340 BC 993339 BC 993338 BC 993337 BC 993336 BC 993335 BC 993334 BC 993333 BC 993332 BC 993331 BC
993330 BC 993329 BC 993328 BC 993327 BC 993326 BC 993325 BC 993324 BC 993323 BC 993322 BC 993321 BC
993320 BC 993319 BC 993318 BC 993317 BC 993316 BC 993315 BC 993314 BC 993313 BC 993312 BC 993311 BC
993310 BC 993309 BC 993308 BC 993307 BC 993306 BC 993305 BC 993304 BC 993303 BC 993302 BC 993301 BC

993300 BC 993299 BC 993298 BC 993297 BC 993296 BC 993295 BC 993294 BC 993293 BC 993292 BC 993291 BC
993290 BC 993289 BC 993288 BC 993287 BC 993286 BC 993285 BC 993284 BC 993283 BC 993282 BC 993281 BC
993280 BC 993279 BC 993278 BC 993277 BC 993276 BC 993275 BC 993274 BC 993273 BC 993272 BC 993271 BC
993270 BC 993269 BC 993268 BC 993267 BC 993266 BC 993265 BC 993264 BC 993263 BC 993262 BC 993261 BC
993260 BC 993259 BC 993258 BC 993257 BC 993256 BC 993255 BC 993254 BC 993253 BC 993252 BC 993251 BC
993250 BC 993249 BC 993248 BC 993247 BC 993246 BC 993245 BC 993244 BC 993243 BC 993242 BC 993241 BC
993240 BC 993239 BC 993238 BC 993237 BC 993236 BC 993235 BC 993234 BC 993233 BC 993232 BC 993231 BC
993230 BC 993229 BC 993228 BC 993227 BC 993226 BC 993225 BC 993224 BC 993223 BC 993222 BC 993221 BC
993220 BC 993219 BC 993218 BC 993217 BC 993216 BC 993215 BC 993214 BC 993213 BC 993212 BC 993211 BC
993210 BC 993209 BC 993208 BC 993207 BC 993206 BC 993205 BC 993204 BC 993203 BC 993202 BC 993201 BC

993200 BC 993199 BC 993198 BC 993197 BC 993196 BC 993195 BC 993194 BC 993193 BC 993192 BC 993191 BC
993190 BC 993189 BC 993188 BC 993187 BC 993186 BC 993185 BC 993184 BC 993183 BC 993182 BC 993181 BC
993180 BC 993179 BC 993178 BC 993177 BC 993176 BC 993175 BC 993174 BC 993173 BC 993172 BC 993171 BC
993170 BC 993169 BC 993168 BC 993167 BC 993166 BC 993165 BC 993164 BC 993163 BC 993162 BC 993161 BC
993160 BC 993159 BC 993158 BC 993157 BC 993156 BC 993155 BC 993154 BC 993153 BC 993152 BC 993151 BC
993150 BC 993149 BC 993148 BC 993147 BC 993146 BC 993145 BC 993144 BC 993143 BC 993142 BC 993141 BC
993140 BC 993139 BC 993138 BC 993137 BC 993136 BC 993135 BC 993134 BC 993133 BC 993132 BC 993131 BC
993130 BC 993129 BC 993128 BC 993127 BC 993126 BC 993125 BC 993124 BC 993123 BC 993122 BC 993121 BC
993120 BC 993119 BC 993118 BC 993117 BC 993116 BC 993115 BC 993114 BC 993113 BC 993112 BC 993111 BC
993110 BC 993109 BC 993108 BC 993107 BC 993106 BC 993105 BC 993104 BC 993103 BC 993102 BC 993101 BC

993100 BC 993099 BC 993098 BC 993097 BC 993096 BC 993095 BC 993094 BC 993093 BC 993092 BC 993091 BC
993090 BC 993089 BC 993088 BC 993087 BC 993086 BC 993085 BC 993084 BC 993083 BC 993082 BC 993081 BC
993080 BC 993079 BC 993078 BC 993077 BC 993076 BC 993075 BC 993074 BC 993073 BC 993072 BC 993071 BC
993070 BC 993069 BC 993068 BC 993067 BC 993066 BC 993065 BC 993064 BC 993063 BC 993062 BC 993061 BC
993060 BC 993059 BC 993058 BC 993057 BC 993056 BC 993055 BC 993054 BC 993053 BC 993052 BC 993051 BC
993050 BC 993049 BC 993048 BC 993047 BC 993046 BC 993045 BC 993044 BC 993043 BC 993042 BC 993041 BC
993040 BC 993039 BC 993038 BC 993037 BC 993036 BC 993035 BC 993034 BC 993033 BC 993032 BC 993031 BC
993030 BC 993029 BC 993028 BC 993027 BC 993026 BC 993025 BC 993024 BC 993023 BC 993022 BC 993021 BC
993020 BC 993019 BC 993018 BC 993017 BC 993016 BC 993015 BC 993014 BC 993013 BC 993012 BC 993011 BC
993010 BC 993009 BC 993008 BC 993007 BC 993006 BC 993005 BC 993004 BC 993003 BC 993002 BC 993001 BC

993000 BC 992999 BC 992998 BC 992997 BC 992996 BC 992995 BC 992994 BC 992993 BC 992992 BC 992991 BC
992990 BC 992989 BC 992988 BC 992987 BC 992986 BC 992985 BC 992984 BC 992983 BC 992982 BC 992981 BC
992980 BC 992979 BC 992978 BC 992977 BC 992976 BC 992975 BC 992974 BC 992973 BC 992972 BC 992971 BC
992970 BC 992969 BC 992968 BC 992967 BC 992966 BC 992965 BC 992964 BC 992963 BC 992962 BC 992961 BC
992960 BC 992959 BC 992958 BC 992957 BC 992956 BC 992955 BC 992954 BC 992953 BC 992952 BC 992951 BC
992950 BC 992949 BC 992948 BC 992947 BC 992946 BC 992945 BC 992944 BC 992943 BC 992942 BC 992941 BC
992940 BC 992939 BC 992938 BC 992937 BC 992936 BC 992935 BC 992934 BC 992933 BC 992932 BC 992931 BC
992930 BC 992929 BC 992928 BC 992927 BC 992926 BC 992925 BC 992924 BC 992923 BC 992922 BC 992921 BC
992920 BC 992919 BC 992918 BC 992917 BC 992916 BC 992915 BC 992914 BC 992913 BC 992912 BC 992911 BC
992910 BC 992909 BC 992908 BC 992907 BC 992906 BC 992905 BC 992904 BC 992903 BC 992902 BC 992901 BC

992900 BC 992899 BC 992898 BC 992897 BC 992896 BC 992895 BC 992894 BC 992893 BC 992892 BC 992891 BC
992890 BC 992889 BC 992888 BC 992887 BC 992886 BC 992885 BC 992884 BC 992883 BC 992882 BC 992881 BC
992880 BC 992879 BC 992878 BC 992877 BC 992876 BC 992875 BC 992874 BC 992873 BC 992872 BC 992871 BC
992870 BC 992869 BC 992868 BC 992867 BC 992866 BC 992865 BC 992864 BC 992863 BC 992862 BC 992861 BC
992860 BC 992859 BC 992858 BC 992857 BC 992856 BC 992855 BC 992854 BC 992853 BC 992852 BC 992851 BC
992850 BC 992849 BC 992848 BC 992847 BC 992846 BC 992845 BC 992844 BC 992843 BC 992842 BC 992841 BC
992840 BC 992839 BC 992838 BC 992837 BC 992836 BC 992835 BC 992834 BC 992833 BC 992832 BC 992831 BC
992830 BC 992829 BC 992828 BC 992827 BC 992826 BC 992825 BC 992824 BC 992823 BC 992822 BC 992821 BC
992820 BC 992819 BC 992818 BC 992817 BC 992816 BC 992815 BC 992814 BC 992813 BC 992812 BC 992811 BC
992810 BC 992809 BC 992808 BC 992807 BC 992806 BC 992805 BC 992804 BC 992803 BC 992802 BC 992801 BC

992800 BC 992799 BC 992798 BC 992797 BC 992796 BC 992795 BC 992794 BC 992793 BC 992792 BC 992791 BC
992790 BC 992789 BC 992788 BC 992787 BC 992786 BC 992785 BC 992784 BC 992783 BC 992782 BC 992781 BC
992780 BC 992779 BC 992778 BC 992777 BC 992776 BC 992775 BC 992774 BC 992773 BC 992772 BC 992771 BC
992770 BC 992769 BC 992768 BC 992767 BC 992766 BC 992765 BC 992764 BC 992763 BC 992762 BC 992761 BC
992760 BC 992759 BC 992758 BC 992757 BC 992756 BC 992755 BC 992754 BC 992753 BC 992752 BC 992751 BC
992750 BC 992749 BC 992748 BC 992747 BC 992746 BC 992745 BC 992744 BC 992743 BC 992742 BC 992741 BC
992740 BC 992739 BC 992738 BC 992737 BC 992736 BC 992735 BC 992734 BC 992733 BC 992732 BC 992731 BC
992730 BC 992729 BC 992728 BC 992727 BC 992726 BC 992725 BC 992724 BC 992723 BC 992722 BC 992721 BC
992720 BC 992719 BC 992718 BC 992717 BC 992716 BC 992715 BC 992714 BC 992713 BC 992712 BC 992711 BC
992710 BC 992709 BC 992708 BC 992707 BC 992706 BC 992705 BC 992704 BC 992703 BC 992702 BC 992701 BC

992700 BC 992699 BC 992698 BC 992697 BC 992696 BC 992695 BC 992694 BC 992693 BC 992692 BC 992691 BC
992690 BC 992689 BC 992688 BC 992687 BC 992686 BC 992685 BC 992684 BC 992683 BC 992682 BC 992681 BC
992680 BC 992679 BC 992678 BC 992677 BC 992676 BC 992675 BC 992674 BC 992673 BC 992672 BC 992671 BC
992670 BC 992669 BC 992668 BC 992667 BC 992666 BC 992665 BC 992664 BC 992663 BC 992662 BC 992661 BC
992660 BC 992659 BC 992658 BC 992657 BC 992656 BC 992655 BC 992654 BC 992653 BC 992652 BC 992651 BC
992650 BC 992649 BC 992648 BC 992647 BC 992646 BC 992645 BC 992644 BC 992643 BC 992642 BC 992641 BC
992640 BC 992639 BC 992638 BC 992637 BC 992636 BC 992635 BC 992634 BC 992633 BC 992632 BC 992631 BC
992630 BC 992629 BC 992628 BC 992627 BC 992626 BC 992625 BC 992624 BC 992623 BC 992622 BC 992621 BC
992620 BC 992619 BC 992618 BC 992617 BC 992616 BC 992615 BC 992614 BC 992613 BC 992612 BC 992611 BC
992610 BC 992609 BC 992608 BC 992607 BC 992606 BC 992605 BC 992604 BC 992603 BC 992602 BC 992601 BC

992600 BC 992599 BC 992598 BC 992597 BC 992596 BC 992595 BC 992594 BC 992593 BC 992592 BC 992591 BC
992590 BC 992589 BC 992588 BC 992587 BC 992586 BC 992585 BC 992584 BC 992583 BC 992582 BC 992581 BC
992580 BC 992579 BC 992578 BC 992577 BC 992576 BC 992575 BC 992574 BC 992573 BC 992572 BC 992571 BC
992570 BC 992569 BC 992568 BC 992567 BC 992566 BC 992565 BC 992564 BC 992563 BC 992562 BC 992561 BC
992560 BC 992559 BC 992558 BC 992557 BC 992556 BC 992555 BC 992554 BC 992553 BC 992552 BC 992551 BC
992550 BC 992549 BC 992548 BC 992547 BC 992546 BC 992545 BC 992544 BC 992543 BC 992542 BC 992541 BC
992540 BC 992539 BC 992538 BC 992537 BC 992536 BC 992535 BC 992534 BC 992533 BC 992532 BC 992531 BC
992530 BC 992529 BC 992528 BC 992527 BC 992526 BC 992525 BC 992524 BC 992523 BC 992522 BC 992521 BC
992520 BC 992519 BC 992518 BC 992517 BC 992516 BC 992515 BC 992514 BC 992513 BC 992512 BC 992511 BC
992510 BC 992509 BC 992508 BC 992507 BC 992506 BC 992505 BC 992504 BC 992503 BC 992502 BC 992501 BC

```
992500 BC  992499 BC  992498 BC  992497 BC  992496 BC  992495 BC  992494 BC  992493 BC  992492 BC  992491 BC
992490 BC  992489 BC  992488 BC  992487 BC  992486 BC  992485 BC  992484 BC  992483 BC  992482 BC  992481 BC
992480 BC  992479 BC  992478 BC  992477 BC  992476 BC  992475 BC  992474 BC  992473 BC  992472 BC  992471 BC
992470 BC  992469 BC  992468 BC  992467 BC  992466 BC  992465 BC  992464 BC  992463 BC  992462 BC  992461 BC
992460 BC  992459 BC  992458 BC  992457 BC  992456 BC  992455 BC  992454 BC  992453 BC  992452 BC  992451 BC
992450 BC  992449 BC  992448 BC  992447 BC  992446 BC  992445 BC  992444 BC  992443 BC  992442 BC  992441 BC
992440 BC  992439 BC  992438 BC  992437 BC  992436 BC  992435 BC  992434 BC  992433 BC  992432 BC  992431 BC
992430 BC  992429 BC  992428 BC  992427 BC  992426 BC  992425 BC  992424 BC  992423 BC  992422 BC  992421 BC
992420 BC  992419 BC  992418 BC  992417 BC  992416 BC  992415 BC  992414 BC  992413 BC  992412 BC  992411 BC
992410 BC  992409 BC  992408 BC  992407 BC  992406 BC  992405 BC  992404 BC  992403 BC  992402 BC  992401 BC

992400 BC  992399 BC  992398 BC  992397 BC  992396 BC  992395 BC  992394 BC  992393 BC  992392 BC  992391 BC
992390 BC  992389 BC  992388 BC  992387 BC  992386 BC  992385 BC  992384 BC  992383 BC  992382 BC  992381 BC
992380 BC  992379 BC  992378 BC  992377 BC  992376 BC  992375 BC  992374 BC  992373 BC  992372 BC  992371 BC
992370 BC  992369 BC  992368 BC  992367 BC  992366 BC  992365 BC  992364 BC  992363 BC  992362 BC  992361 BC
992360 BC  992359 BC  992358 BC  992357 BC  992356 BC  992355 BC  992354 BC  992353 BC  992352 BC  992351 BC
992350 BC  992349 BC  992348 BC  992347 BC  992346 BC  992345 BC  992344 BC  992343 BC  992342 BC  992341 BC
992340 BC  992339 BC  992338 BC  992337 BC  992336 BC  992335 BC  992334 BC  992333 BC  992332 BC  992331 BC
992330 BC  992329 BC  992328 BC  992327 BC  992326 BC  992325 BC  992324 BC  992323 BC  992322 BC  992321 BC
992320 BC  992319 BC  992318 BC  992317 BC  992316 BC  992315 BC  992314 BC  992313 BC  992312 BC  992311 BC
992310 BC  992309 BC  992308 BC  992307 BC  992306 BC  992305 BC  992304 BC  992303 BC  992302 BC  992301 BC

992300 BC  992299 BC  992298 BC  992297 BC  992296 BC  992295 BC  992294 BC  992293 BC  992292 BC  992291 BC
992290 BC  992289 BC  992288 BC  992287 BC  992286 BC  992285 BC  992284 BC  992283 BC  992282 BC  992281 BC
992280 BC  992279 BC  992278 BC  992277 BC  992276 BC  992275 BC  992274 BC  992273 BC  992272 BC  992271 BC
992270 BC  992269 BC  992268 BC  992267 BC  992266 BC  992265 BC  992264 BC  992263 BC  992262 BC  992261 BC
992260 BC  992259 BC  992258 BC  992257 BC  992256 BC  992255 BC  992254 BC  992253 BC  992252 BC  992251 BC
992250 BC  992249 BC  992248 BC  992247 BC  992246 BC  992245 BC  992244 BC  992243 BC  992242 BC  992241 BC
992240 BC  992239 BC  992238 BC  992237 BC  992236 BC  992235 BC  992234 BC  992233 BC  992232 BC  992231 BC
992230 BC  992229 BC  992228 BC  992227 BC  992226 BC  992225 BC  992224 BC  992223 BC  992222 BC  992221 BC
992220 BC  992219 BC  992218 BC  992217 BC  992216 BC  992215 BC  992214 BC  992213 BC  992212 BC  992211 BC
992210 BC  992209 BC  992208 BC  992207 BC  992206 BC  992205 BC  992204 BC  992203 BC  992202 BC  992201 BC

992200 BC  992199 BC  992198 BC  992197 BC  992196 BC  992195 BC  992194 BC  992193 BC  992192 BC  992191 BC
992190 BC  992189 BC  992188 BC  992187 BC  992186 BC  992185 BC  992184 BC  992183 BC  992182 BC  992181 BC
992180 BC  992179 BC  992178 BC  992177 BC  992176 BC  992175 BC  992174 BC  992173 BC  992172 BC  992171 BC
992170 BC  992169 BC  992168 BC  992167 BC  992166 BC  992165 BC  992164 BC  992163 BC  992162 BC  992161 BC
992160 BC  992159 BC  992158 BC  992157 BC  992156 BC  992155 BC  992154 BC  992153 BC  992152 BC  992151 BC
992150 BC  992149 BC  992148 BC  992147 BC  992146 BC  992145 BC  992144 BC  992143 BC  992142 BC  992141 BC
992140 BC  992139 BC  992138 BC  992137 BC  992136 BC  992135 BC  992134 BC  992133 BC  992132 BC  992131 BC
992130 BC  992129 BC  992128 BC  992127 BC  992126 BC  992125 BC  992124 BC  992123 BC  992122 BC  992121 BC
992120 BC  992119 BC  992118 BC  992117 BC  992116 BC  992115 BC  992114 BC  992113 BC  992112 BC  992111 BC
992110 BC  992109 BC  992108 BC  992107 BC  992106 BC  992105 BC  992104 BC  992103 BC  992102 BC  992101 BC

992100 BC  992099 BC  992098 BC  992097 BC  992096 BC  992095 BC  992094 BC  992093 BC  992092 BC  992091 BC
992090 BC  992089 BC  992088 BC  992087 BC  992086 BC  992085 BC  992084 BC  992083 BC  992082 BC  992081 BC
992080 BC  992079 BC  992078 BC  992077 BC  992076 BC  992075 BC  992074 BC  992073 BC  992072 BC  992071 BC
992070 BC  992069 BC  992068 BC  992067 BC  992066 BC  992065 BC  992064 BC  992063 BC  992062 BC  992061 BC
992060 BC  992059 BC  992058 BC  992057 BC  992056 BC  992055 BC  992054 BC  992053 BC  992052 BC  992051 BC
992050 BC  992049 BC  992048 BC  992047 BC  992046 BC  992045 BC  992044 BC  992043 BC  992042 BC  992041 BC
992040 BC  992039 BC  992038 BC  992037 BC  992036 BC  992035 BC  992034 BC  992033 BC  992032 BC  992031 BC
992030 BC  992029 BC  992028 BC  992027 BC  992026 BC  992025 BC  992024 BC  992023 BC  992022 BC  992021 BC
992020 BC  992019 BC  992018 BC  992017 BC  992016 BC  992015 BC  992014 BC  992013 BC  992012 BC  992011 BC
992010 BC  992009 BC  992008 BC  992007 BC  992006 BC  992005 BC  992004 BC  992003 BC  992002 BC  992001 BC
```

992000 BC 991999 BC 991998 BC 991997 BC 991996 BC 991995 BC 991994 BC 991993 BC 991992 BC 991991 BC
991990 BC 991989 BC 991988 BC 991987 BC 991986 BC 991985 BC 991984 BC 991983 BC 991982 BC 991981 BC
991980 BC 991979 BC 991978 BC 991977 BC 991976 BC 991975 BC 991974 BC 991973 BC 991972 BC 991971 BC
991970 BC 991969 BC 991968 BC 991967 BC 991966 BC 991965 BC 991964 BC 991963 BC 991962 BC 991961 BC
991960 BC 991959 BC 991958 BC 991957 BC 991956 BC 991955 BC 991954 BC 991953 BC 991952 BC 991951 BC
991950 BC 991949 BC 991948 BC 991947 BC 991946 BC 991945 BC 991944 BC 991943 BC 991942 BC 991941 BC
991940 BC 991939 BC 991938 BC 991937 BC 991936 BC 991935 BC 991934 BC 991933 BC 991932 BC 991931 BC
991930 BC 991929 BC 991928 BC 991927 BC 991926 BC 991925 BC 991924 BC 991923 BC 991922 BC 991921 BC
991920 BC 991919 BC 991918 BC 991917 BC 991916 BC 991915 BC 991914 BC 991913 BC 991912 BC 991911 BC
991910 BC 991909 BC 991908 BC 991907 BC 991906 BC 991905 BC 991904 BC 991903 BC 991902 BC 991901 BC

991900 BC 991899 BC 991898 BC 991897 BC 991896 BC 991895 BC 991894 BC 991893 BC 991892 BC 991891 BC
991890 BC 991889 BC 991888 BC 991887 BC 991886 BC 991885 BC 991884 BC 991883 BC 991882 BC 991881 BC
991880 BC 991879 BC 991878 BC 991877 BC 991876 BC 991875 BC 991874 BC 991873 BC 991872 BC 991871 BC
991870 BC 991869 BC 991868 BC 991867 BC 991866 BC 991865 BC 991864 BC 991863 BC 991862 BC 991861 BC
991860 BC 991859 BC 991858 BC 991857 BC 991856 BC 991855 BC 991854 BC 991853 BC 991852 BC 991851 BC
991850 BC 991849 BC 991848 BC 991847 BC 991846 BC 991845 BC 991844 BC 991843 BC 991842 BC 991841 BC
991840 BC 991839 BC 991838 BC 991837 BC 991836 BC 991835 BC 991834 BC 991833 BC 991832 BC 991831 BC
991830 BC 991829 BC 991828 BC 991827 BC 991826 BC 991825 BC 991824 BC 991823 BC 991822 BC 991821 BC
991820 BC 991819 BC 991818 BC 991817 BC 991816 BC 991815 BC 991814 BC 991813 BC 991812 BC 991811 BC
991810 BC 991809 BC 991808 BC 991807 BC 991806 BC 991805 BC 991804 BC 991803 BC 991802 BC 991801 BC

991800 BC 991799 BC 991798 BC 991797 BC 991796 BC 991795 BC 991794 BC 991793 BC 991792 BC 991791 BC
991790 BC 991789 BC 991788 BC 991787 BC 991786 BC 991785 BC 991784 BC 991783 BC 991782 BC 991781 BC
991780 BC 991779 BC 991778 BC 991777 BC 991776 BC 991775 BC 991774 BC 991773 BC 991772 BC 991771 BC
991770 BC 991769 BC 991768 BC 991767 BC 991766 BC 991765 BC 991764 BC 991763 BC 991762 BC 991761 BC
991760 BC 991759 BC 991758 BC 991757 BC 991756 BC 991755 BC 991754 BC 991753 BC 991752 BC 991751 BC
991750 BC 991749 BC 991748 BC 991747 BC 991746 BC 991745 BC 991744 BC 991743 BC 991742 BC 991741 BC
991740 BC 991739 BC 991738 BC 991737 BC 991736 BC 991735 BC 991734 BC 991733 BC 991732 BC 991731 BC
991730 BC 991729 BC 991728 BC 991727 BC 991726 BC 991725 BC 991724 BC 991723 BC 991722 BC 991721 BC
991720 BC 991719 BC 991718 BC 991717 BC 991716 BC 991715 BC 991714 BC 991713 BC 991712 BC 991711 BC
991710 BC 991709 BC 991708 BC 991707 BC 991706 BC 991705 BC 991704 BC 991703 BC 991702 BC 991701 BC

991700 BC 991699 BC 991698 BC 991697 BC 991696 BC 991695 BC 991694 BC 991693 BC 991692 BC 991691 BC
991690 BC 991689 BC 991688 BC 991687 BC 991686 BC 991685 BC 991684 BC 991683 BC 991682 BC 991681 BC
991680 BC 991679 BC 991678 BC 991677 BC 991676 BC 991675 BC 991674 BC 991673 BC 991672 BC 991671 BC
991670 BC 991669 BC 991668 BC 991667 BC 991666 BC 991665 BC 991664 BC 991663 BC 991662 BC 991661 BC
991660 BC 991659 BC 991658 BC 991657 BC 991656 BC 991655 BC 991654 BC 991653 BC 991652 BC 991651 BC
991650 BC 991649 BC 991648 BC 991647 BC 991646 BC 991645 BC 991644 BC 991643 BC 991642 BC 991641 BC
991640 BC 991639 BC 991638 BC 991637 BC 991636 BC 991635 BC 991634 BC 991633 BC 991632 BC 991631 BC
991630 BC 991629 BC 991628 BC 991627 BC 991626 BC 991625 BC 991624 BC 991623 BC 991622 BC 991621 BC
991620 BC 991619 BC 991618 BC 991617 BC 991616 BC 991615 BC 991614 BC 991613 BC 991612 BC 991611 BC
991610 BC 991609 BC 991608 BC 991607 BC 991606 BC 991605 BC 991604 BC 991603 BC 991602 BC 991601 BC

991600 BC 991599 BC 991598 BC 991597 BC 991596 BC 991595 BC 991594 BC 991593 BC 991592 BC 991591 BC
991590 BC 991589 BC 991588 BC 991587 BC 991586 BC 991585 BC 991584 BC 991583 BC 991582 BC 991581 BC
991580 BC 991579 BC 991578 BC 991577 BC 991576 BC 991575 BC 991574 BC 991573 BC 991572 BC 991571 BC
991570 BC 991569 BC 991568 BC 991567 BC 991566 BC 991565 BC 991564 BC 991563 BC 991562 BC 991561 BC
991560 BC 991559 BC 991558 BC 991557 BC 991556 BC 991555 BC 991554 BC 991553 BC 991552 BC 991551 BC
991550 BC 991549 BC 991548 BC 991547 BC 991546 BC 991545 BC 991544 BC 991543 BC 991542 BC 991541 BC
991540 BC 991539 BC 991538 BC 991537 BC 991536 BC 991535 BC 991534 BC 991533 BC 991532 BC 991531 BC
991530 BC 991529 BC 991528 BC 991527 BC 991526 BC 991525 BC 991524 BC 991523 BC 991522 BC 991521 BC
991520 BC 991519 BC 991518 BC 991517 BC 991516 BC 991515 BC 991514 BC 991513 BC 991512 BC 991511 BC
991510 BC 991509 BC 991508 BC 991507 BC 991506 BC 991505 BC 991504 BC 991503 BC 991502 BC 991501 BC

— 14 —

991500 BC 991499 BC 991498 BC 991497 BC 991496 BC 991495 BC 991494 BC 991493 BC 991492 BC 991491 BC
991490 BC 991489 BC 991488 BC 991487 BC 991486 BC 991485 BC 991484 BC 991483 BC 991482 BC 991481 BC
991480 BC 991479 BC 991478 BC 991477 BC 991476 BC 991475 BC 991474 BC 991473 BC 991472 BC 991471 BC
991470 BC 991469 BC 991468 BC 991467 BC 991466 BC 991465 BC 991464 BC 991463 BC 991462 BC 991461 BC
991460 BC 991459 BC 991458 BC 991457 BC 991456 BC 991455 BC 991454 BC 991453 BC 991452 BC 991451 BC
991450 BC 991449 BC 991448 BC 991447 BC 991446 BC 991445 BC 991444 BC 991443 BC 991442 BC 991441 BC
991440 BC 991439 BC 991438 BC 991437 BC 991436 BC 991435 BC 991434 BC 991433 BC 991432 BC 991431 BC
991430 BC 991429 BC 991428 BC 991427 BC 991426 BC 991425 BC 991424 BC 991423 BC 991422 BC 991421 BC
991420 BC 991419 BC 991418 BC 991417 BC 991416 BC 991415 BC 991414 BC 991413 BC 991412 BC 991411 BC
991410 BC 991409 BC 991408 BC 991407 BC 991406 BC 991405 BC 991404 BC 991403 BC 991402 BC 991401 BC

991400 BC 991399 BC 991398 BC 991397 BC 991396 BC 991395 BC 991394 BC 991393 BC 991392 BC 991391 BC
991390 BC 991389 BC 991388 BC 991387 BC 991386 BC 991385 BC 991384 BC 991383 BC 991382 BC 991381 BC
991380 BC 991379 BC 991378 BC 991377 BC 991376 BC 991375 BC 991374 BC 991373 BC 991372 BC 991371 BC
991370 BC 991369 BC 991368 BC 991367 BC 991366 BC 991365 BC 991364 BC 991363 BC 991362 BC 991361 BC
991360 BC 991359 BC 991358 BC 991357 BC 991356 BC 991355 BC 991354 BC 991353 BC 991352 BC 991351 BC
991350 BC 991349 BC 991348 BC 991347 BC 991346 BC 991345 BC 991344 BC 991343 BC 991342 BC 991341 BC
991340 BC 991339 BC 991338 BC 991337 BC 991336 BC 991335 BC 991334 BC 991333 BC 991332 BC 991331 BC
991330 BC 991329 BC 991328 BC 991327 BC 991326 BC 991325 BC 991324 BC 991323 BC 991322 BC 991321 BC
991320 BC 991319 BC 991318 BC 991317 BC 991316 BC 991315 BC 991314 BC 991313 BC 991312 BC 991311 BC
991310 BC 991309 BC 991308 BC 991307 BC 991306 BC 991305 BC 991304 BC 991303 BC 991302 BC 991301 BC

991300 BC 991299 BC 991298 BC 991297 BC 991296 BC 991295 BC 991294 BC 991293 BC 991292 BC 991291 BC
991290 BC 991289 BC 991288 BC 991287 BC 991286 BC 991285 BC 991284 BC 991283 BC 991282 BC 991281 BC
991280 BC 991279 BC 991278 BC 991277 BC 991276 BC 991275 BC 991274 BC 991273 BC 991272 BC 991271 BC
991270 BC 991269 BC 991268 BC 991267 BC 991266 BC 991265 BC 991264 BC 991263 BC 991262 BC 991261 BC
991260 BC 991259 BC 991258 BC 991257 BC 991256 BC 991255 BC 991254 BC 991253 BC 991252 BC 991251 BC
991250 BC 991249 BC 991248 BC 991247 BC 991246 BC 991245 BC 991244 BC 991243 BC 991242 BC 991241 BC
991240 BC 991239 BC 991238 BC 991237 BC 991236 BC 991235 BC 991234 BC 991233 BC 991232 BC 991231 BC
991230 BC 991229 BC 991228 BC 991227 BC 991226 BC 991225 BC 991224 BC 991223 BC 991222 BC 991221 BC
991220 BC 991219 BC 991218 BC 991217 BC 991216 BC 991215 BC 991214 BC 991213 BC 991212 BC 991211 BC
991210 BC 991209 BC 991208 BC 991207 BC 991206 BC 991205 BC 991204 BC 991203 BC 991202 BC 991201 BC

991200 BC 991199 BC 991198 BC 991197 BC 991196 BC 991195 BC 991194 BC 991193 BC 991192 BC 991191 BC
991190 BC 991189 BC 991188 BC 991187 BC 991186 BC 991185 BC 991184 BC 991183 BC 991182 BC 991181 BC
991180 BC 991179 BC 991178 BC 991177 BC 991176 BC 991175 BC 991174 BC 991173 BC 991172 BC 991171 BC
991170 BC 991169 BC 991168 BC 991167 BC 991166 BC 991165 BC 991164 BC 991163 BC 991162 BC 991161 BC
991160 BC 991159 BC 991158 BC 991157 BC 991156 BC 991155 BC 991154 BC 991153 BC 991152 BC 991151 BC
991150 BC 991149 BC 991148 BC 991147 BC 991146 BC 991145 BC 991144 BC 991143 BC 991142 BC 991141 BC
991140 BC 991139 BC 991138 BC 991137 BC 991136 BC 991135 BC 991134 BC 991133 BC 991132 BC 991131 BC
991130 BC 991129 BC 991128 BC 991127 BC 991126 BC 991125 BC 991124 BC 991123 BC 991122 BC 991121 BC
991120 BC 991119 BC 991118 BC 991117 BC 991116 BC 991115 BC 991114 BC 991113 BC 991112 BC 991111 BC
991110 BC 991109 BC 991108 BC 991107 BC 991106 BC 991105 BC 991104 BC 991103 BC 991102 BC 991101 BC

991100 BC 991099 BC 991098 BC 991097 BC 991096 BC 991095 BC 991094 BC 991093 BC 991092 BC 991091 BC
991090 BC 991089 BC 991088 BC 991087 BC 991086 BC 991085 BC 991084 BC 991083 BC 991082 BC 991081 BC
991080 BC 991079 BC 991078 BC 991077 BC 991076 BC 991075 BC 991074 BC 991073 BC 991072 BC 991071 BC
991070 BC 991069 BC 991068 BC 991067 BC 991066 BC 991065 BC 991064 BC 991063 BC 991062 BC 991061 BC
991060 BC 991059 BC 991058 BC 991057 BC 991056 BC 991055 BC 991054 BC 991053 BC 991052 BC 991051 BC
991050 BC 991049 BC 991048 BC 991047 BC 991046 BC 991045 BC 991044 BC 991043 BC 991042 BC 991041 BC
991040 BC 991039 BC 991038 BC 991037 BC 991036 BC 991035 BC 991034 BC 991033 BC 991032 BC 991031 BC
991030 BC 991029 BC 991028 BC 991027 BC 991026 BC 991025 BC 991024 BC 991023 BC 991022 BC 991021 BC
991020 BC 991019 BC 991018 BC 991017 BC 991016 BC 991015 BC 991014 BC 991013 BC 991012 BC 991011 BC
991010 BC 991009 BC 991008 BC 991007 BC 991006 BC 991005 BC 991004 BC 991003 BC 991002 BC 991001 BC

990... (each followed by BC)

991000 BC 990999 BC 990998 BC 990997 BC 990996 BC 990995 BC 990994 BC 990993 BC 990992 BC 990991 BC
990990 BC 990989 BC 990988 BC 990987 BC 990986 BC 990985 BC 990984 BC 990983 BC 990982 BC 990981 BC
990980 BC 990979 BC 990978 BC 990977 BC 990976 BC 990975 BC 990974 BC 990973 BC 990972 BC 990971 BC
990970 BC 990969 BC 990968 BC 990967 BC 990966 BC 990965 BC 990964 BC 990963 BC 990962 BC 990961 BC
990960 BC 990959 BC 990958 BC 990957 BC 990956 BC 990955 BC 990954 BC 990953 BC 990952 BC 990951 BC
990950 BC 990949 BC 990948 BC 990947 BC 990946 BC 990945 BC 990944 BC 990943 BC 990942 BC 990941 BC
990940 BC 990939 BC 990938 BC 990937 BC 990936 BC 990935 BC 990934 BC 990933 BC 990932 BC 990931 BC
990930 BC 990929 BC 990928 BC 990927 BC 990926 BC 990925 BC 990924 BC 990923 BC 990922 BC 990921 BC
990920 BC 990919 BC 990918 BC 990917 BC 990916 BC 990915 BC 990914 BC 990913 BC 990912 BC 990911 BC
990910 BC 990909 BC 990908 BC 990907 BC 990906 BC 990905 BC 990904 BC 990903 BC 990902 BC 990901 BC

990900 BC 990899 BC 990898 BC 990897 BC 990896 BC 990895 BC 990894 BC 990893 BC 990892 BC 990891 BC
990890 BC 990889 BC 990888 BC 990887 BC 990886 BC 990885 BC 990884 BC 990883 BC 990882 BC 990881 BC
990880 BC 990879 BC 990878 BC 990877 BC 990876 BC 990875 BC 990874 BC 990873 BC 990872 BC 990871 BC
990870 BC 990869 BC 990868 BC 990867 BC 990866 BC 990865 BC 990864 BC 990863 BC 990862 BC 990861 BC
990860 BC 990859 BC 990858 BC 990857 BC 990856 BC 990855 BC 990854 BC 990853 BC 990852 BC 990851 BC
990850 BC 990849 BC 990848 BC 990847 BC 990846 BC 990845 BC 990844 BC 990843 BC 990842 BC 990841 BC
990840 BC 990839 BC 990838 BC 990837 BC 990836 BC 990835 BC 990834 BC 990833 BC 990832 BC 990831 BC
990830 BC 990829 BC 990828 BC 990827 BC 990826 BC 990825 BC 990824 BC 990823 BC 990822 BC 990821 BC
990820 BC 990819 BC 990818 BC 990817 BC 990816 BC 990815 BC 990814 BC 990813 BC 990812 BC 990811 BC
990810 BC 990809 BC 990808 BC 990807 BC 990806 BC 990805 BC 990804 BC 990803 BC 990802 BC 990801 BC

990800 BC 990799 BC 990798 BC 990797 BC 990796 BC 990795 BC 990794 BC 990793 BC 990792 BC 990791 BC
990790 BC 990789 BC 990788 BC 990787 BC 990786 BC 990785 BC 990784 BC 990783 BC 990782 BC 990781 BC
990780 BC 990779 BC 990778 BC 990777 BC 990776 BC 990775 BC 990774 BC 990773 BC 990772 BC 990771 BC
990770 BC 990769 BC 990768 BC 990767 BC 990766 BC 990765 BC 990764 BC 990763 BC 990762 BC 990761 BC
990760 BC 990759 BC 990758 BC 990757 BC 990756 BC 990755 BC 990754 BC 990753 BC 990752 BC 990751 BC
990750 BC 990749 BC 990748 BC 990747 BC 990746 BC 990745 BC 990744 BC 990743 BC 990742 BC 990741 BC
990740 BC 990739 BC 990738 BC 990737 BC 990736 BC 990735 BC 990734 BC 990733 BC 990732 BC 990731 BC
990730 BC 990729 BC 990728 BC 990727 BC 990726 BC 990725 BC 990724 BC 990723 BC 990722 BC 990721 BC
990720 BC 990719 BC 990718 BC 990717 BC 990716 BC 990715 BC 990714 BC 990713 BC 990712 BC 990711 BC
990710 BC 990709 BC 990708 BC 990707 BC 990706 BC 990705 BC 990704 BC 990703 BC 990702 BC 990701 BC

990700 BC 990699 BC 990698 BC 990697 BC 990696 BC 990695 BC 990694 BC 990693 BC 990692 BC 990691 BC
990690 BC 990689 BC 990688 BC 990687 BC 990686 BC 990685 BC 990684 BC 990683 BC 990682 BC 990681 BC
990680 BC 990679 BC 990678 BC 990677 BC 990676 BC 990675 BC 990674 BC 990673 BC 990672 BC 990671 BC
990670 BC 990669 BC 990668 BC 990667 BC 990666 BC 990665 BC 990664 BC 990663 BC 990662 BC 990661 BC
990660 BC 990659 BC 990658 BC 990657 BC 990656 BC 990655 BC 990654 BC 990653 BC 990652 BC 990651 BC
990650 BC 990649 BC 990648 BC 990647 BC 990646 BC 990645 BC 990644 BC 990643 BC 990642 BC 990641 BC
990640 BC 990639 BC 990638 BC 990637 BC 990636 BC 990635 BC 990634 BC 990633 BC 990632 BC 990631 BC
990630 BC 990629 BC 990628 BC 990627 BC 990626 BC 990625 BC 990624 BC 990623 BC 990622 BC 990621 BC
990620 BC 990619 BC 990618 BC 990617 BC 990616 BC 990615 BC 990614 BC 990613 BC 990612 BC 990611 BC
990610 BC 990609 BC 990608 BC 990607 BC 990606 BC 990605 BC 990604 BC 990603 BC 990602 BC 990601 BC

990600 BC 990599 BC 990598 BC 990597 BC 990596 BC 990595 BC 990594 BC 990593 BC 990592 BC 990591 BC
990590 BC 990589 BC 990588 BC 990587 BC 990586 BC 990585 BC 990584 BC 990583 BC 990582 BC 990581 BC
990580 BC 990579 BC 990578 BC 990577 BC 990576 BC 990575 BC 990574 BC 990573 BC 990572 BC 990571 BC
990570 BC 990569 BC 990568 BC 990567 BC 990566 BC 990565 BC 990564 BC 990563 BC 990562 BC 990561 BC
990560 BC 990559 BC 990558 BC 990557 BC 990556 BC 990555 BC 990554 BC 990553 BC 990552 BC 990551 BC
990550 BC 990549 BC 990548 BC 990547 BC 990546 BC 990545 BC 990544 BC 990543 BC 990542 BC 990541 BC
990540 BC 990539 BC 990538 BC 990537 BC 990536 BC 990535 BC 990534 BC 990533 BC 990532 BC 990531 BC
990530 BC 990529 BC 990528 BC 990527 BC 990526 BC 990525 BC 990524 BC 990523 BC 990522 BC 990521 BC
990520 BC 990519 BC 990518 BC 990517 BC 990516 BC 990515 BC 990514 BC 990513 BC 990512 BC 990511 BC
990510 BC 990509 BC 990508 BC 990507 BC 990506 BC 990505 BC 990504 BC 990503 BC 990502 BC 990501 BC

990500 BC 990499 BC 990498 BC 990497 BC 990496 BC 990495 BC 990494 BC 990493 BC 990492 BC 990491 BC
990490 BC 990489 BC 990488 BC 990487 BC 990486 BC 990485 BC 990484 BC 990483 BC 990482 BC 990481 BC
990480 BC 990479 BC 990478 BC 990477 BC 990476 BC 990475 BC 990474 BC 990473 BC 990472 BC 990471 BC
990470 BC 990469 BC 990468 BC 990467 BC 990466 BC 990465 BC 990464 BC 990463 BC 990462 BC 990461 BC
990460 BC 990459 BC 990458 BC 990457 BC 990456 BC 990455 BC 990454 BC 990453 BC 990452 BC 990451 BC
990450 BC 990449 BC 990448 BC 990447 BC 990446 BC 990445 BC 990444 BC 990443 BC 990442 BC 990441 BC
990440 BC 990439 BC 990438 BC 990437 BC 990436 BC 990435 BC 990434 BC 990433 BC 990432 BC 990431 BC
990430 BC 990429 BC 990428 BC 990427 BC 990426 BC 990425 BC 990424 BC 990423 BC 990422 BC 990421 BC
990420 BC 990419 BC 990418 BC 990417 BC 990416 BC 990415 BC 990414 BC 990413 BC 990412 BC 990411 BC
990410 BC 990409 BC 990408 BC 990407 BC 990406 BC 990405 BC 990404 BC 990403 BC 990402 BC 990401 BC

990400 BC 990399 BC 990398 BC 990397 BC 990396 BC 990395 BC 990394 BC 990393 BC 990392 BC 990391 BC
990390 BC 990389 BC 990388 BC 990387 BC 990386 BC 990385 BC 990384 BC 990383 BC 990382 BC 990381 BC
990380 BC 990379 BC 990378 BC 990377 BC 990376 BC 990375 BC 990374 BC 990373 BC 990372 BC 990371 BC
990370 BC 990369 BC 990368 BC 990367 BC 990366 BC 990365 BC 990364 BC 990363 BC 990362 BC 990361 BC
990360 BC 990359 BC 990358 BC 990357 BC 990356 BC 990355 BC 990354 BC 990353 BC 990352 BC 990351 BC
990350 BC 990349 BC 990348 BC 990347 BC 990346 BC 990345 BC 990344 BC 990343 BC 990342 BC 990341 BC
990340 BC 990339 BC 990338 BC 990337 BC 990336 BC 990335 BC 990334 BC 990333 BC 990332 BC 990331 BC
990330 BC 990329 BC 990328 BC 990327 BC 990326 BC 990325 BC 990324 BC 990323 BC 990322 BC 990321 BC
990320 BC 990319 BC 990318 BC 990317 BC 990316 BC 990315 BC 990314 BC 990313 BC 990312 BC 990311 BC
990310 BC 990309 BC 990308 BC 990307 BC 990306 BC 990305 BC 990304 BC 990303 BC 990302 BC 990301 BC

990300 BC 990299 BC 990298 BC 990297 BC 990296 BC 990295 BC 990294 BC 990293 BC 990292 BC 990291 BC
990290 BC 990289 BC 990288 BC 990287 BC 990286 BC 990285 BC 990284 BC 990283 BC 990282 BC 990281 BC
990280 BC 990279 BC 990278 BC 990277 BC 990276 BC 990275 BC 990274 BC 990273 BC 990272 BC 990271 BC
990270 BC 990269 BC 990268 BC 990267 BC 990266 BC 990265 BC 990264 BC 990263 BC 990262 BC 990261 BC
990260 BC 990259 BC 990258 BC 990257 BC 990256 BC 990255 BC 990254 BC 990253 BC 990252 BC 990251 BC
990250 BC 990249 BC 990248 BC 990247 BC 990246 BC 990245 BC 990244 BC 990243 BC 990242 BC 990241 BC
990240 BC 990239 BC 990238 BC 990237 BC 990236 BC 990235 BC 990234 BC 990233 BC 990232 BC 990231 BC
990230 BC 990229 BC 990228 BC 990227 BC 990226 BC 990225 BC 990224 BC 990223 BC 990222 BC 990221 BC
990220 BC 990219 BC 990218 BC 990217 BC 990216 BC 990215 BC 990214 BC 990213 BC 990212 BC 990211 BC
990210 BC 990209 BC 990208 BC 990207 BC 990206 BC 990205 BC 990204 BC 990203 BC 990202 BC 990201 BC

990200 BC 990199 BC 990198 BC 990197 BC 990196 BC 990195 BC 990194 BC 990193 BC 990192 BC 990191 BC
990190 BC 990189 BC 990188 BC 990187 BC 990186 BC 990185 BC 990184 BC 990183 BC 990182 BC 990181 BC
990180 BC 990179 BC 990178 BC 990177 BC 990176 BC 990175 BC 990174 BC 990173 BC 990172 BC 990171 BC
990170 BC 990169 BC 990168 BC 990167 BC 990166 BC 990165 BC 990164 BC 990163 BC 990162 BC 990161 BC
990160 BC 990159 BC 990158 BC 990157 BC 990156 BC 990155 BC 990154 BC 990153 BC 990152 BC 990151 BC
990150 BC 990149 BC 990148 BC 990147 BC 990146 BC 990145 BC 990144 BC 990143 BC 990142 BC 990141 BC
990140 BC 990139 BC 990138 BC 990137 BC 990136 BC 990135 BC 990134 BC 990133 BC 990132 BC 990131 BC
990130 BC 990129 BC 990128 BC 990127 BC 990126 BC 990125 BC 990124 BC 990123 BC 990122 BC 990121 BC
990120 BC 990119 BC 990118 BC 990117 BC 990116 BC 990115 BC 990114 BC 990113 BC 990112 BC 990111 BC
990110 BC 990109 BC 990108 BC 990107 BC 990106 BC 990105 BC 990104 BC 990103 BC 990102 BC 990101 BC

990100 BC 990099 BC 990098 BC 990097 BC 990096 BC 990095 BC 990094 BC 990093 BC 990092 BC 990091 BC
990090 BC 990089 BC 990088 BC 990087 BC 990086 BC 990085 BC 990084 BC 990083 BC 990082 BC 990081 BC
990080 BC 990079 BC 990078 BC 990077 BC 990076 BC 990075 BC 990074 BC 990073 BC 990072 BC 990071 BC
990070 BC 990069 BC 990068 BC 990067 BC 990066 BC 990065 BC 990064 BC 990063 BC 990062 BC 990061 BC
990060 BC 990059 BC 990058 BC 990057 BC 990056 BC 990055 BC 990054 BC 990053 BC 990052 BC 990051 BC
990050 BC 990049 BC 990048 BC 990047 BC 990046 BC 990045 BC 990044 BC 990043 BC 990042 BC 990041 BC
990040 BC 990039 BC 990038 BC 990037 BC 990036 BC 990035 BC 990034 BC 990033 BC 990032 BC 990031 BC
990030 BC 990029 BC 990028 BC 990027 BC 990026 BC 990025 BC 990024 BC 990023 BC 990022 BC 990021 BC
990020 BC 990019 BC 990018 BC 990017 BC 990016 BC 990015 BC 990014 BC 990013 BC 990012 BC 990011 BC
990010 BC 990009 BC 990008 BC 990007 BC 990006 BC 990005 BC 990004 BC 990003 BC 990002 BC 990001 BC

990000 BC 989999 BC 989998 BC 989997 BC 989996 BC 989995 BC 989994 BC 989993 BC 989992 BC 989991 BC
989990 BC 989989 BC 989988 BC 989987 BC 989986 BC 989985 BC 989984 BC 989983 BC 989982 BC 989981 BC
989980 BC 989979 BC 989978 BC 989977 BC 989976 BC 989975 BC 989974 BC 989973 BC 989972 BC 989971 BC
989970 BC 989969 BC 989968 BC 989967 BC 989966 BC 989965 BC 989964 BC 989963 BC 989962 BC 989961 BC
989960 BC 989959 BC 989958 BC 989957 BC 989956 BC 989955 BC 989954 BC 989953 BC 989952 BC 989951 BC
989950 BC 989949 BC 989948 BC 989947 BC 989946 BC 989945 BC 989944 BC 989943 BC 989942 BC 989941 BC
989940 BC 989939 BC 989938 BC 989937 BC 989936 BC 989935 BC 989934 BC 989933 BC 989932 BC 989931 BC
989930 BC 989929 BC 989928 BC 989927 BC 989926 BC 989925 BC 989924 BC 989923 BC 989922 BC 989921 BC
989920 BC 989919 BC 989918 BC 989917 BC 989916 BC 989915 BC 989914 BC 989913 BC 989912 BC 989911 BC
989910 BC 989909 BC 989908 BC 989907 BC 989906 BC 989905 BC 989904 BC 989903 BC 989902 BC 989901 BC

989900 BC 989899 BC 989898 BC 989897 BC 989896 BC 989895 BC 989894 BC 989893 BC 989892 BC 989891 BC
989890 BC 989889 BC 989888 BC 989887 BC 989886 BC 989885 BC 989884 BC 989883 BC 989882 BC 989881 BC
989880 BC 989879 BC 989878 BC 989877 BC 989876 BC 989875 BC 989874 BC 989873 BC 989872 BC 989871 BC
989870 BC 989869 BC 989868 BC 989867 BC 989866 BC 989865 BC 989864 BC 989863 BC 989862 BC 989861 BC
989860 BC 989859 BC 989858 BC 989857 BC 989856 BC 989855 BC 989854 BC 989853 BC 989852 BC 989851 BC
989850 BC 989849 BC 989848 BC 989847 BC 989846 BC 989845 BC 989844 BC 989843 BC 989842 BC 989841 BC
989840 BC 989839 BC 989838 BC 989837 BC 989836 BC 989835 BC 989834 BC 989833 BC 989832 BC 989831 BC
989830 BC 989829 BC 989828 BC 989827 BC 989826 BC 989825 BC 989824 BC 989823 BC 989822 BC 989821 BC
989820 BC 989819 BC 989818 BC 989817 BC 989816 BC 989815 BC 989814 BC 989813 BC 989812 BC 989811 BC
989810 BC 989809 BC 989808 BC 989807 BC 989806 BC 989805 BC 989804 BC 989803 BC 989802 BC 989801 BC

989800 BC 989799 BC 989798 BC 989797 BC 989796 BC 989795 BC 989794 BC 989793 BC 989792 BC 989791 BC
989790 BC 989789 BC 989788 BC 989787 BC 989786 BC 989785 BC 989784 BC 989783 BC 989782 BC 989781 BC
989780 BC 989779 BC 989778 BC 989777 BC 989776 BC 989775 BC 989774 BC 989773 BC 989772 BC 989771 BC
989770 BC 989769 BC 989768 BC 989767 BC 989766 BC 989765 BC 989764 BC 989763 BC 989762 BC 989761 BC
989760 BC 989759 BC 989758 BC 989757 BC 989756 BC 989755 BC 989754 BC 989753 BC 989752 BC 989751 BC
989750 BC 989749 BC 989748 BC 989747 BC 989746 BC 989745 BC 989744 BC 989743 BC 989742 BC 989741 BC
989740 BC 989739 BC 989738 BC 989737 BC 989736 BC 989735 BC 989734 BC 989733 BC 989732 BC 989731 BC
989730 BC 989729 BC 989728 BC 989727 BC 989726 BC 989725 BC 989724 BC 989723 BC 989722 BC 989721 BC
989720 BC 989719 BC 989718 BC 989717 BC 989716 BC 989715 BC 989714 BC 989713 BC 989712 BC 989711 BC
989710 BC 989709 BC 989708 BC 989707 BC 989706 BC 989705 BC 989704 BC 989703 BC 989702 BC 989701 BC

989700 BC 989699 BC 989698 BC 989697 BC 989696 BC 989695 BC 989694 BC 989693 BC 989692 BC 989691 BC
989690 BC 989689 BC 989688 BC 989687 BC 989686 BC 989685 BC 989684 BC 989683 BC 989682 BC 989681 BC
989680 BC 989679 BC 989678 BC 989677 BC 989676 BC 989675 BC 989674 BC 989673 BC 989672 BC 989671 BC
989670 BC 989669 BC 989668 BC 989667 BC 989666 BC 989665 BC 989664 BC 989663 BC 989662 BC 989661 BC
989660 BC 989659 BC 989658 BC 989657 BC 989656 BC 989655 BC 989654 BC 989653 BC 989652 BC 989651 BC
989650 BC 989649 BC 989648 BC 989647 BC 989646 BC 989645 BC 989644 BC 989643 BC 989642 BC 989641 BC
989640 BC 989639 BC 989638 BC 989637 BC 989636 BC 989635 BC 989634 BC 989633 BC 989632 BC 989631 BC
989630 BC 989629 BC 989628 BC 989627 BC 989626 BC 989625 BC 989624 BC 989623 BC 989622 BC 989621 BC
989620 BC 989619 BC 989618 BC 989617 BC 989616 BC 989615 BC 989614 BC 989613 BC 989612 BC 989611 BC
989610 BC 989609 BC 989608 BC 989607 BC 989606 BC 989605 BC 989604 BC 989603 BC 989602 BC 989601 BC

989600 BC 989599 BC 989598 BC 989597 BC 989596 BC 989595 BC 989594 BC 989593 BC 989592 BC 989591 BC
989590 BC 989589 BC 989588 BC 989587 BC 989586 BC 989585 BC 989584 BC 989583 BC 989582 BC 989581 BC
989580 BC 989579 BC 989578 BC 989577 BC 989576 BC 989575 BC 989574 BC 989573 BC 989572 BC 989571 BC
989570 BC 989569 BC 989568 BC 989567 BC 989566 BC 989565 BC 989564 BC 989563 BC 989562 BC 989561 BC
989560 BC 989559 BC 989558 BC 989557 BC 989556 BC 989555 BC 989554 BC 989553 BC 989552 BC 989551 BC
989550 BC 989549 BC 989548 BC 989547 BC 989546 BC 989545 BC 989544 BC 989543 BC 989542 BC 989541 BC
989540 BC 989539 BC 989538 BC 989537 BC 989536 BC 989535 BC 989534 BC 989533 BC 989532 BC 989531 BC
989530 BC 989529 BC 989528 BC 989527 BC 989526 BC 989525 BC 989524 BC 989523 BC 989522 BC 989521 BC
989520 BC 989519 BC 989518 BC 989517 BC 989516 BC 989515 BC 989514 BC 989513 BC 989512 BC 989511 BC
989510 BC 989509 BC 989508 BC 989507 BC 989506 BC 989505 BC 989504 BC 989503 BC 989502 BC 989501 BC

989500 BC 989499 BC 989498 BC 989497 BC 989496 BC 989495 BC 989494 BC 989493 BC 989492 BC 989491 BC
989490 BC 989489 BC 989488 BC 989487 BC 989486 BC 989485 BC 989484 BC 989483 BC 989482 BC 989481 BC
989480 BC 989479 BC 989478 BC 989477 BC 989476 BC 989475 BC 989474 BC 989473 BC 989472 BC 989471 BC
989470 BC 989469 BC 989468 BC 989467 BC 989466 BC 989465 BC 989464 BC 989463 BC 989462 BC 989461 BC
989460 BC 989459 BC 989458 BC 989457 BC 989456 BC 989455 BC 989454 BC 989453 BC 989452 BC 989451 BC
989450 BC 989449 BC 989448 BC 989447 BC 989446 BC 989445 BC 989444 BC 989443 BC 989442 BC 989441 BC
989440 BC 989439 BC 989438 BC 989437 BC 989436 BC 989435 BC 989434 BC 989433 BC 989432 BC 989431 BC
989430 BC 989429 BC 989428 BC 989427 BC 989426 BC 989425 BC 989424 BC 989423 BC 989422 BC 989421 BC
989420 BC 989419 BC 989418 BC 989417 BC 989416 BC 989415 BC 989414 BC 989413 BC 989412 BC 989411 BC
989410 BC 989409 BC 989408 BC 989407 BC 989406 BC 989405 BC 989404 BC 989403 BC 989402 BC 989401 BC

989400 BC 989399 BC 989398 BC 989397 BC 989396 BC 989395 BC 989394 BC 989393 BC 989392 BC 989391 BC
989390 BC 989389 BC 989388 BC 989387 BC 989386 BC 989385 BC 989384 BC 989383 BC 989382 BC 989381 BC
989380 BC 989379 BC 989378 BC 989377 BC 989376 BC 989375 BC 989374 BC 989373 BC 989372 BC 989371 BC
989370 BC 989369 BC 989368 BC 989367 BC 989366 BC 989365 BC 989364 BC 989363 BC 989362 BC 989361 BC
989360 BC 989359 BC 989358 BC 989357 BC 989356 BC 989355 BC 989354 BC 989353 BC 989352 BC 989351 BC
989350 BC 989349 BC 989348 BC 989347 BC 989346 BC 989345 BC 989344 BC 989343 BC 989342 BC 989341 BC
989340 BC 989339 BC 989338 BC 989337 BC 989336 BC 989335 BC 989334 BC 989333 BC 989332 BC 989331 BC
989330 BC 989329 BC 989328 BC 989327 BC 989326 BC 989325 BC 989324 BC 989323 BC 989322 BC 989321 BC
989320 BC 989319 BC 989318 BC 989317 BC 989316 BC 989315 BC 989314 BC 989313 BC 989312 BC 989311 BC
989310 BC 989309 BC 989308 BC 989307 BC 989306 BC 989305 BC 989304 BC 989303 BC 989302 BC 989301 BC

989300 BC 989299 BC 989298 BC 989297 BC 989296 BC 989295 BC 989294 BC 989293 BC 989292 BC 989291 BC
989290 BC 989289 BC 989288 BC 989287 BC 989286 BC 989285 BC 989284 BC 989283 BC 989282 BC 989281 BC
989280 BC 989279 BC 989278 BC 989277 BC 989276 BC 989275 BC 989274 BC 989273 BC 989272 BC 989271 BC
989270 BC 989269 BC 989268 BC 989267 BC 989266 BC 989265 BC 989264 BC 989263 BC 989262 BC 989261 BC
989260 BC 989259 BC 989258 BC 989257 BC 989256 BC 989255 BC 989254 BC 989253 BC 989252 BC 989251 BC
989250 BC 989249 BC 989248 BC 989247 BC 989246 BC 989245 BC 989244 BC 989243 BC 989242 BC 989241 BC
989240 BC 989239 BC 989238 BC 989237 BC 989236 BC 989235 BC 989234 BC 989233 BC 989232 BC 989231 BC
989230 BC 989229 BC 989228 BC 989227 BC 989226 BC 989225 BC 989224 BC 989223 BC 989222 BC 989221 BC
989220 BC 989219 BC 989218 BC 989217 BC 989216 BC 989215 BC 989214 BC 989213 BC 989212 BC 989211 BC
989210 BC 989209 BC 989208 BC 989207 BC 989206 BC 989205 BC 989204 BC 989203 BC 989202 BC 989201 BC

989200 BC 989199 BC 989198 BC 989197 BC 989196 BC 989195 BC 989194 BC 989193 BC 989192 BC 989191 BC
989190 BC 989189 BC 989188 BC 989187 BC 989186 BC 989185 BC 989184 BC 989183 BC 989182 BC 989181 BC
989180 BC 989179 BC 989178 BC 989177 BC 989176 BC 989175 BC 989174 BC 989173 BC 989172 BC 989171 BC
989170 BC 989169 BC 989168 BC 989167 BC 989166 BC 989165 BC 989164 BC 989163 BC 989162 BC 989161 BC
989160 BC 989159 BC 989158 BC 989157 BC 989156 BC 989155 BC 989154 BC 989153 BC 989152 BC 989151 BC
989150 BC 989149 BC 989148 BC 989147 BC 989146 BC 989145 BC 989144 BC 989143 BC 989142 BC 989141 BC
989140 BC 989139 BC 989138 BC 989137 BC 989136 BC 989135 BC 989134 BC 989133 BC 989132 BC 989131 BC
989130 BC 989129 BC 989128 BC 989127 BC 989126 BC 989125 BC 989124 BC 989123 BC 989122 BC 989121 BC
989120 BC 989119 BC 989118 BC 989117 BC 989116 BC 989115 BC 989114 BC 989113 BC 989112 BC 989111 BC
989110 BC 989109 BC 989108 BC 989107 BC 989106 BC 989105 BC 989104 BC 989103 BC 989102 BC 989101 BC

989100 BC 989099 BC 989098 BC 989097 BC 989096 BC 989095 BC 989094 BC 989093 BC 989092 BC 989091 BC
989090 BC 989089 BC 989088 BC 989087 BC 989086 BC 989085 BC 989084 BC 989083 BC 989082 BC 989081 BC
989080 BC 989079 BC 989078 BC 989077 BC 989076 BC 989075 BC 989074 BC 989073 BC 989072 BC 989071 BC
989070 BC 989069 BC 989068 BC 989067 BC 989066 BC 989065 BC 989064 BC 989063 BC 989062 BC 989061 BC
989060 BC 989059 BC 989058 BC 989057 BC 989056 BC 989055 BC 989054 BC 989053 BC 989052 BC 989051 BC
989050 BC 989049 BC 989048 BC 989047 BC 989046 BC 989045 BC 989044 BC 989043 BC 989042 BC 989041 BC
989040 BC 989039 BC 989038 BC 989037 BC 989036 BC 989035 BC 989034 BC 989033 BC 989032 BC 989031 BC
989030 BC 989029 BC 989028 BC 989027 BC 989026 BC 989025 BC 989024 BC 989023 BC 989022 BC 989021 BC
989020 BC 989019 BC 989018 BC 989017 BC 989016 BC 989015 BC 989014 BC 989013 BC 989012 BC 989011 BC
989010 BC 989009 BC 989008 BC 989007 BC 989006 BC 989005 BC 989004 BC 989003 BC 989002 BC 989001 BC

989000 BC 988999 BC 988998 BC 988997 BC 988996 BC 988995 BC 988994 BC 988993 BC 988992 BC 988991 BC
988990 BC 988989 BC 988988 BC 988987 BC 988986 BC 988985 BC 988984 BC 988983 BC 988982 BC 988981 BC
988980 BC 988979 BC 988978 BC 988977 BC 988976 BC 988975 BC 988974 BC 988973 BC 988972 BC 988971 BC
988970 BC 988969 BC 988968 BC 988967 BC 988966 BC 988965 BC 988964 BC 988963 BC 988962 BC 988961 BC
988960 BC 988959 BC 988958 BC 988957 BC 988956 BC 988955 BC 988954 BC 988953 BC 988952 BC 988951 BC
988950 BC 988949 BC 988948 BC 988947 BC 988946 BC 988945 BC 988944 BC 988943 BC 988942 BC 988941 BC
988940 BC 988939 BC 988938 BC 988937 BC 988936 BC 988935 BC 988934 BC 988933 BC 988932 BC 988931 BC
988930 BC 988929 BC 988928 BC 988927 BC 988926 BC 988925 BC 988924 BC 988923 BC 988922 BC 988921 BC
988920 BC 988919 BC 988918 BC 988917 BC 988916 BC 988915 BC 988914 BC 988913 BC 988912 BC 988911 BC
988910 BC 988909 BC 988908 BC 988907 BC 988906 BC 988905 BC 988904 BC 988903 BC 988902 BC 988901 BC

988900 BC 988899 BC 988898 BC 988897 BC 988896 BC 988895 BC 988894 BC 988893 BC 988892 BC 988891 BC
988890 BC 988889 BC 988888 BC 988887 BC 988886 BC 988885 BC 988884 BC 988883 BC 988882 BC 988881 BC
988880 BC 988879 BC 988878 BC 988877 BC 988876 BC 988875 BC 988874 BC 988873 BC 988872 BC 988871 BC
988870 BC 988869 BC 988868 BC 988867 BC 988866 BC 988865 BC 988864 BC 988863 BC 988862 BC 988861 BC
988860 BC 988859 BC 988858 BC 988857 BC 988856 BC 988855 BC 988854 BC 988853 BC 988852 BC 988851 BC
988850 BC 988849 BC 988848 BC 988847 BC 988846 BC 988845 BC 988844 BC 988843 BC 988842 BC 988841 BC
988840 BC 988839 BC 988838 BC 988837 BC 988836 BC 988835 BC 988834 BC 988833 BC 988832 BC 988831 BC
988830 BC 988829 BC 988828 BC 988827 BC 988826 BC 988825 BC 988824 BC 988823 BC 988822 BC 988821 BC
988820 BC 988819 BC 988818 BC 988817 BC 988816 BC 988815 BC 988814 BC 988813 BC 988812 BC 988811 BC
988810 BC 988809 BC 988808 BC 988807 BC 988806 BC 988805 BC 988804 BC 988803 BC 988802 BC 988801 BC

988800 BC 988799 BC 988798 BC 988797 BC 988796 BC 988795 BC 988794 BC 988793 BC 988792 BC 988791 BC
988790 BC 988789 BC 988788 BC 988787 BC 988786 BC 988785 BC 988784 BC 988783 BC 988782 BC 988781 BC
988780 BC 988779 BC 988778 BC 988777 BC 988776 BC 988775 BC 988774 BC 988773 BC 988772 BC 988771 BC
988770 BC 988769 BC 988768 BC 988767 BC 988766 BC 988765 BC 988764 BC 988763 BC 988762 BC 988761 BC
988760 BC 988759 BC 988758 BC 988757 BC 988756 BC 988755 BC 988754 BC 988753 BC 988752 BC 988751 BC
988750 BC 988749 BC 988748 BC 988747 BC 988746 BC 988745 BC 988744 BC 988743 BC 988742 BC 988741 BC
988740 BC 988739 BC 988738 BC 988737 BC 988736 BC 988735 BC 988734 BC 988733 BC 988732 BC 988731 BC
988730 BC 988729 BC 988728 BC 988727 BC 988726 BC 988725 BC 988724 BC 988723 BC 988722 BC 988721 BC
988720 BC 988719 BC 988718 BC 988717 BC 988716 BC 988715 BC 988714 BC 988713 BC 988712 BC 988711 BC
988710 BC 988709 BC 988708 BC 988707 BC 988706 BC 988705 BC 988704 BC 988703 BC 988702 BC 988701 BC

988700 BC 988699 BC 988698 BC 988697 BC 988696 BC 988695 BC 988694 BC 988693 BC 988692 BC 988691 BC
988690 BC 988689 BC 988688 BC 988687 BC 988686 BC 988685 BC 988684 BC 988683 BC 988682 BC 988681 BC
988680 BC 988679 BC 988678 BC 988677 BC 988676 BC 988675 BC 988674 BC 988673 BC 988672 BC 988671 BC
988670 BC 988669 BC 988668 BC 988667 BC 988666 BC 988665 BC 988664 BC 988663 BC 988662 BC 988661 BC
988660 BC 988659 BC 988658 BC 988657 BC 988656 BC 988655 BC 988654 BC 988653 BC 988652 BC 988651 BC
988650 BC 988649 BC 988648 BC 988647 BC 988646 BC 988645 BC 988644 BC 988643 BC 988642 BC 988641 BC
988640 BC 988639 BC 988638 BC 988637 BC 988636 BC 988635 BC 988634 BC 988633 BC 988632 BC 988631 BC
988630 BC 988629 BC 988628 BC 988627 BC 988626 BC 988625 BC 988624 BC 988623 BC 988622 BC 988621 BC
988620 BC 988619 BC 988618 BC 988617 BC 988616 BC 988615 BC 988614 BC 988613 BC 988612 BC 988611 BC
988610 BC 988609 BC 988608 BC 988607 BC 988606 BC 988605 BC 988604 BC 988603 BC 988602 BC 988601 BC

988600 BC 988599 BC 988598 BC 988597 BC 988596 BC 988595 BC 988594 BC 988593 BC 988592 BC 988591 BC
988590 BC 988589 BC 988588 BC 988587 BC 988586 BC 988585 BC 988584 BC 988583 BC 988582 BC 988581 BC
988580 BC 988579 BC 988578 BC 988577 BC 988576 BC 988575 BC 988574 BC 988573 BC 988572 BC 988571 BC
988570 BC 988569 BC 988568 BC 988567 BC 988566 BC 988565 BC 988564 BC 988563 BC 988562 BC 988561 BC
988560 BC 988559 BC 988558 BC 988557 BC 988556 BC 988555 BC 988554 BC 988553 BC 988552 BC 988551 BC
988550 BC 988549 BC 988548 BC 988547 BC 988546 BC 988545 BC 988544 BC 988543 BC 988542 BC 988541 BC
988540 BC 988539 BC 988538 BC 988537 BC 988536 BC 988535 BC 988534 BC 988533 BC 988532 BC 988531 BC
988530 BC 988529 BC 988528 BC 988527 BC 988526 BC 988525 BC 988524 BC 988523 BC 988522 BC 988521 BC
988520 BC 988519 BC 988518 BC 988517 BC 988516 BC 988515 BC 988514 BC 988513 BC 988512 BC 988511 BC
988510 BC 988509 BC 988508 BC 988507 BC 988506 BC 988505 BC 988504 BC 988503 BC 988502 BC 988501 BC

988500 BC 988499 BC 988498 BC 988497 BC 988496 BC 988495 BC 988494 BC 988493 BC 988492 BC 988491 BC
988490 BC 988489 BC 988488 BC 988487 BC 988486 BC 988485 BC 988484 BC 988483 BC 988482 BC 988481 BC
988480 BC 988479 BC 988478 BC 988477 BC 988476 BC 988475 BC 988474 BC 988473 BC 988472 BC 988471 BC
988470 BC 988469 BC 988468 BC 988467 BC 988466 BC 988465 BC 988464 BC 988463 BC 988462 BC 988461 BC
988460 BC 988459 BC 988458 BC 988457 BC 988456 BC 988455 BC 988454 BC 988453 BC 988452 BC 988451 BC
988450 BC 988449 BC 988448 BC 988447 BC 988446 BC 988445 BC 988444 BC 988443 BC 988442 BC 988441 BC
988440 BC 988439 BC 988438 BC 988437 BC 988436 BC 988435 BC 988434 BC 988433 BC 988432 BC 988431 BC
988430 BC 988429 BC 988428 BC 988427 BC 988426 BC 988425 BC 988424 BC 988423 BC 988422 BC 988421 BC
988420 BC 988419 BC 988418 BC 988417 BC 988416 BC 988415 BC 988414 BC 988413 BC 988412 BC 988411 BC
988410 BC 988409 BC 988408 BC 988407 BC 988406 BC 988405 BC 988404 BC 988403 BC 988402 BC 988401 BC

988400 BC 988399 BC 988398 BC 988397 BC 988396 BC 988395 BC 988394 BC 988393 BC 988392 BC 988391 BC
988390 BC 988389 BC 988388 BC 988387 BC 988386 BC 988385 BC 988384 BC 988383 BC 988382 BC 988381 BC
988380 BC 988379 BC 988378 BC 988377 BC 988376 BC 988375 BC 988374 BC 988373 BC 988372 BC 988371 BC
988370 BC 988369 BC 988368 BC 988367 BC 988366 BC 988365 BC 988364 BC 988363 BC 988362 BC 988361 BC
988360 BC 988359 BC 988358 BC 988357 BC 988356 BC 988355 BC 988354 BC 988353 BC 988352 BC 988351 BC
988350 BC 988349 BC 988348 BC 988347 BC 988346 BC 988345 BC 988344 BC 988343 BC 988342 BC 988341 BC
988340 BC 988339 BC 988338 BC 988337 BC 988336 BC 988335 BC 988334 BC 988333 BC 988332 BC 988331 BC
988330 BC 988329 BC 988328 BC 988327 BC 988326 BC 988325 BC 988324 BC 988323 BC 988322 BC 988321 BC
988320 BC 988319 BC 988318 BC 988317 BC 988316 BC 988315 BC 988314 BC 988313 BC 988312 BC 988311 BC
988310 BC 988309 BC 988308 BC 988307 BC 988306 BC 988305 BC 988304 BC 988303 BC 988302 BC 988301 BC

988300 BC 988299 BC 988298 BC 988297 BC 988296 BC 988295 BC 988294 BC 988293 BC 988292 BC 988291 BC
988290 BC 988289 BC 988288 BC 988287 BC 988286 BC 988285 BC 988284 BC 988283 BC 988282 BC 988281 BC
988280 BC 988279 BC 988278 BC 988277 BC 988276 BC 988275 BC 988274 BC 988273 BC 988272 BC 988271 BC
988270 BC 988269 BC 988268 BC 988267 BC 988266 BC 988265 BC 988264 BC 988263 BC 988262 BC 988261 BC
988260 BC 988259 BC 988258 BC 988257 BC 988256 BC 988255 BC 988254 BC 988253 BC 988252 BC 988251 BC
988250 BC 988249 BC 988248 BC 988247 BC 988246 BC 988245 BC 988244 BC 988243 BC 988242 BC 988241 BC
988240 BC 988239 BC 988238 BC 988237 BC 988236 BC 988235 BC 988234 BC 988233 BC 988232 BC 988231 BC
988230 BC 988229 BC 988228 BC 988227 BC 988226 BC 988225 BC 988224 BC 988223 BC 988222 BC 988221 BC
988220 BC 988219 BC 988218 BC 988217 BC 988216 BC 988215 BC 988214 BC 988213 BC 988212 BC 988211 BC
988210 BC 988209 BC 988208 BC 988207 BC 988206 BC 988205 BC 988204 BC 988203 BC 988202 BC 988201 BC

988200 BC 988199 BC 988198 BC 988197 BC 988196 BC 988195 BC 988194 BC 988193 BC 988192 BC 988191 BC
988190 BC 988189 BC 988188 BC 988187 BC 988186 BC 988185 BC 988184 BC 988183 BC 988182 BC 988181 BC
988180 BC 988179 BC 988178 BC 988177 BC 988176 BC 988175 BC 988174 BC 988173 BC 988172 BC 988171 BC
988170 BC 988169 BC 988168 BC 988167 BC 988166 BC 988165 BC 988164 BC 988163 BC 988162 BC 988161 BC
988160 BC 988159 BC 988158 BC 988157 BC 988156 BC 988155 BC 988154 BC 988153 BC 988152 BC 988151 BC
988150 BC 988149 BC 988148 BC 988147 BC 988146 BC 988145 BC 988144 BC 988143 BC 988142 BC 988141 BC
988140 BC 988139 BC 988138 BC 988137 BC 988136 BC 988135 BC 988134 BC 988133 BC 988132 BC 988131 BC
988130 BC 988129 BC 988128 BC 988127 BC 988126 BC 988125 BC 988124 BC 988123 BC 988122 BC 988121 BC
988120 BC 988119 BC 988118 BC 988117 BC 988116 BC 988115 BC 988114 BC 988113 BC 988112 BC 988111 BC
988110 BC 988109 BC 988108 BC 988107 BC 988106 BC 988105 BC 988104 BC 988103 BC 988102 BC 988101 BC

988100 BC 988099 BC 988098 BC 988097 BC 988096 BC 988095 BC 988094 BC 988093 BC 988092 BC 988091 BC
988090 BC 988089 BC 988088 BC 988087 BC 988086 BC 988085 BC 988084 BC 988083 BC 988082 BC 988081 BC
988080 BC 988079 BC 988078 BC 988077 BC 988076 BC 988075 BC 988074 BC 988073 BC 988072 BC 988071 BC
988070 BC 988069 BC 988068 BC 988067 BC 988066 BC 988065 BC 988064 BC 988063 BC 988062 BC 988061 BC
988060 BC 988059 BC 988058 BC 988057 BC 988056 BC 988055 BC 988054 BC 988053 BC 988052 BC 988051 BC
988050 BC 988049 BC 988048 BC 988047 BC 988046 BC 988045 BC 988044 BC 988043 BC 988042 BC 988041 BC
988040 BC 988039 BC 988038 BC 988037 BC 988036 BC 988035 BC 988034 BC 988033 BC 988032 BC 988031 BC
988030 BC 988029 BC 988028 BC 988027 BC 988026 BC 988025 BC 988024 BC 988023 BC 988022 BC 988021 BC
988020 BC 988019 BC 988018 BC 988017 BC 988016 BC 988015 BC 988014 BC 988013 BC 988012 BC 988011 BC
988010 BC 988009 BC 988008 BC 988007 BC 988006 BC 988005 BC 988004 BC 988003 BC 988002 BC 988001 BC

988000 BC 987999 BC 987998 BC 987997 BC 987996 BC 987995 BC 987994 BC 987993 BC 987992 BC 987991 BC
987990 BC 987989 BC 987988 BC 987987 BC 987986 BC 987985 BC 987984 BC 987983 BC 987982 BC 987981 BC
987980 BC 987979 BC 987978 BC 987977 BC 987976 BC 987975 BC 987974 BC 987973 BC 987972 BC 987971 BC
987970 BC 987969 BC 987968 BC 987967 BC 987966 BC 987965 BC 987964 BC 987963 BC 987962 BC 987961 BC
987960 BC 987959 BC 987958 BC 987957 BC 987956 BC 987955 BC 987954 BC 987953 BC 987952 BC 987951 BC
987950 BC 987949 BC 987948 BC 987947 BC 987946 BC 987945 BC 987944 BC 987943 BC 987942 BC 987941 BC
987940 BC 987939 BC 987938 BC 987937 BC 987936 BC 987935 BC 987934 BC 987933 BC 987932 BC 987931 BC
987930 BC 987929 BC 987928 BC 987927 BC 987926 BC 987925 BC 987924 BC 987923 BC 987922 BC 987921 BC
987920 BC 987919 BC 987918 BC 987917 BC 987916 BC 987915 BC 987914 BC 987913 BC 987912 BC 987911 BC
987910 BC 987909 BC 987908 BC 987907 BC 987906 BC 987905 BC 987904 BC 987903 BC 987902 BC 987901 BC

987900 BC 987899 BC 987898 BC 987897 BC 987896 BC 987895 BC 987894 BC 987893 BC 987892 BC 987891 BC
987890 BC 987889 BC 987888 BC 987887 BC 987886 BC 987885 BC 987884 BC 987883 BC 987882 BC 987881 BC
987880 BC 987879 BC 987878 BC 987877 BC 987876 BC 987875 BC 987874 BC 987873 BC 987872 BC 987871 BC
987870 BC 987869 BC 987868 BC 987867 BC 987866 BC 987865 BC 987864 BC 987863 BC 987862 BC 987861 BC
987860 BC 987859 BC 987858 BC 987857 BC 987856 BC 987855 BC 987854 BC 987853 BC 987852 BC 987851 BC
987850 BC 987849 BC 987848 BC 987847 BC 987846 BC 987845 BC 987844 BC 987843 BC 987842 BC 987841 BC
987840 BC 987839 BC 987838 BC 987837 BC 987836 BC 987835 BC 987834 BC 987833 BC 987832 BC 987831 BC
987830 BC 987829 BC 987828 BC 987827 BC 987826 BC 987825 BC 987824 BC 987823 BC 987822 BC 987821 BC
987820 BC 987819 BC 987818 BC 987817 BC 987816 BC 987815 BC 987814 BC 987813 BC 987812 BC 987811 BC
987810 BC 987809 BC 987808 BC 987807 BC 987806 BC 987805 BC 987804 BC 987803 BC 987802 BC 987801 BC

987800 BC 987799 BC 987798 BC 987797 BC 987796 BC 987795 BC 987794 BC 987793 BC 987792 BC 987791 BC
987790 BC 987789 BC 987788 BC 987787 BC 987786 BC 987785 BC 987784 BC 987783 BC 987782 BC 987781 BC
987780 BC 987779 BC 987778 BC 987777 BC 987776 BC 987775 BC 987774 BC 987773 BC 987772 BC 987771 BC
987770 BC 987769 BC 987768 BC 987767 BC 987766 BC 987765 BC 987764 BC 987763 BC 987762 BC 987761 BC
987760 BC 987759 BC 987758 BC 987757 BC 987756 BC 987755 BC 987754 BC 987753 BC 987752 BC 987751 BC
987750 BC 987749 BC 987748 BC 987747 BC 987746 BC 987745 BC 987744 BC 987743 BC 987742 BC 987741 BC
987740 BC 987739 BC 987738 BC 987737 BC 987736 BC 987735 BC 987734 BC 987733 BC 987732 BC 987731 BC
987730 BC 987729 BC 987728 BC 987727 BC 987726 BC 987725 BC 987724 BC 987723 BC 987722 BC 987721 BC
987720 BC 987719 BC 987718 BC 987717 BC 987716 BC 987715 BC 987714 BC 987713 BC 987712 BC 987711 BC
987710 BC 987709 BC 987708 BC 987707 BC 987706 BC 987705 BC 987704 BC 987703 BC 987702 BC 987701 BC

987700 BC 987699 BC 987698 BC 987697 BC 987696 BC 987695 BC 987694 BC 987693 BC 987692 BC 987691 BC
987690 BC 987689 BC 987688 BC 987687 BC 987686 BC 987685 BC 987684 BC 987683 BC 987682 BC 987681 BC
987680 BC 987679 BC 987678 BC 987677 BC 987676 BC 987675 BC 987674 BC 987673 BC 987672 BC 987671 BC
987670 BC 987669 BC 987668 BC 987667 BC 987666 BC 987665 BC 987664 BC 987663 BC 987662 BC 987661 BC
987660 BC 987659 BC 987658 BC 987657 BC 987656 BC 987655 BC 987654 BC 987653 BC 987652 BC 987651 BC
987650 BC 987649 BC 987648 BC 987647 BC 987646 BC 987645 BC 987644 BC 987643 BC 987642 BC 987641 BC
987640 BC 987639 BC 987638 BC 987637 BC 987636 BC 987635 BC 987634 BC 987633 BC 987632 BC 987631 BC
987630 BC 987629 BC 987628 BC 987627 BC 987626 BC 987625 BC 987624 BC 987623 BC 987622 BC 987621 BC
987620 BC 987619 BC 987618 BC 987617 BC 987616 BC 987615 BC 987614 BC 987613 BC 987612 BC 987611 BC
987610 BC 987609 BC 987608 BC 987607 BC 987606 BC 987605 BC 987604 BC 987603 BC 987602 BC 987601 BC

987000 BC 987599 BC 987598 BC 987597 BC 987596 BC 987595 BC 987594 BC 987593 BC 987592 BC 987591 BC
987590 BC 987589 BC 987588 BC 987587 BC 987586 BC 987585 BC 987584 BC 987583 BC 987582 BC 987581 BC
987580 BC 987579 BC 987578 BC 987577 BC 987576 BC 987575 BC 987574 BC 987573 BC 987572 BC 987571 BC
987570 BC 987569 BC 987568 BC 987567 BC 987566 BC 987565 BC 987564 BC 987563 BC 987562 BC 987561 BC
987560 BC 987559 BC 987558 BC 987557 BC 987556 BC 987555 BC 987554 BC 987553 BC 987552 BC 987551 BC
987550 BC 987549 BC 987548 BC 987547 BC 987546 BC 987545 BC 987544 BC 987543 BC 987542 BC 987541 BC
987540 BC 987539 BC 987538 BC 987537 BC 987536 BC 987535 BC 987534 BC 987533 BC 987532 BC 987531 BC
987530 BC 987529 BC 987528 BC 987527 BC 987526 BC 987525 BC 987524 BC 987523 BC 987522 BC 987521 BC
987520 BC 987519 BC 987518 BC 987517 BC 987516 BC 987515 BC 987514 BC 987513 BC 987512 BC 987511 BC
987510 BC 987509 BC 987508 BC 987507 BC 987506 BC 987505 BC 987504 BC 987503 BC 987502 BC 987501 BC

987500 BC 987499 BC 987498 BC 987497 BC 987496 BC 987495 BC 987494 BC 987493 BC 987492 BC 987491 BC
987490 BC 987489 BC 987488 BC 987487 BC 987486 BC 987485 BC 987484 BC 987483 BC 987482 BC 987481 BC
987480 BC 987479 BC 987478 BC 987477 BC 987476 BC 987475 BC 987474 BC 987473 BC 987472 BC 987471 BC
987470 BC 987469 BC 987468 BC 987467 BC 987466 BC 987465 BC 987464 BC 987463 BC 987462 BC 987461 BC
987460 BC 987459 BC 987458 BC 987457 BC 987456 BC 987455 BC 987454 BC 987453 BC 987452 BC 987451 BC
987450 BC 987449 BC 987448 BC 987447 BC 987446 BC 987445 BC 987444 BC 987443 BC 987442 BC 987441 BC
987440 BC 987439 BC 987438 BC 987437 BC 987436 BC 987435 BC 987434 BC 987433 BC 987432 BC 987431 BC
987430 BC 987429 BC 987428 BC 987427 BC 987426 BC 987425 BC 987424 BC 987423 BC 987422 BC 987421 BC
987420 BC 987419 BC 987418 BC 987417 BC 987416 BC 987415 BC 987414 BC 987413 BC 987412 BC 987411 BC
987410 BC 987409 BC 987408 BC 987407 BC 987406 BC 987405 BC 987404 BC 987403 BC 987402 BC 987401 BC

987400 BC 987399 BC 987398 BC 987397 BC 987396 BC 987395 BC 987394 BC 987393 BC 987392 BC 987391 BC
987390 BC 987389 BC 987388 BC 987387 BC 987386 BC 987385 BC 987384 BC 987383 BC 987382 BC 987381 BC
987380 BC 987379 BC 987378 BC 987377 BC 987376 BC 987375 BC 987374 BC 987373 BC 987372 BC 987371 BC
987370 BC 987369 BC 987368 BC 987367 BC 987366 BC 987365 BC 987364 BC 987363 BC 987362 BC 987361 BC
987360 BC 987359 BC 987358 BC 987357 BC 987356 BC 987355 BC 987354 BC 987353 BC 987352 BC 987351 BC
987350 BC 987349 BC 987348 BC 987347 BC 987346 BC 987345 BC 987344 BC 987343 BC 987342 BC 987341 BC
987340 BC 987339 BC 987338 BC 987337 BC 987336 BC 987335 BC 987334 BC 987333 BC 987332 BC 987331 BC
987330 BC 987329 BC 987328 BC 987327 BC 987326 BC 987325 BC 987324 BC 987323 BC 987322 BC 987321 BC
987320 BC 987319 BC 987318 BC 987317 BC 987316 BC 987315 BC 987314 BC 987313 BC 987312 BC 987311 BC
987310 BC 987309 BC 987308 BC 987307 BC 987306 BC 987305 BC 987304 BC 987303 BC 987302 BC 987301 BC

987300 BC 987299 BC 987298 BC 987297 BC 987296 BC 987295 BC 987294 BC 987293 BC 987292 BC 987291 BC
987290 BC 987289 BC 987288 BC 987287 BC 987286 BC 987285 BC 987284 BC 987283 BC 987282 BC 987281 BC
987280 BC 987279 BC 987278 BC 987277 BC 987276 BC 987275 BC 987274 BC 987273 BC 987272 BC 987271 BC
987270 BC 987269 BC 987268 BC 987267 BC 987266 BC 987265 BC 987264 BC 987263 BC 987262 BC 987261 BC
987260 BC 987259 BC 987258 BC 987257 BC 987256 BC 987255 BC 987254 BC 987253 BC 987252 BC 987251 BC
987250 BC 987249 BC 987248 BC 987247 BC 987246 BC 987245 BC 987244 BC 987243 BC 987242 BC 987241 BC
987240 BC 987239 BC 987238 BC 987237 BC 987236 BC 987235 BC 987234 BC 987233 BC 987232 BC 987231 BC
987230 BC 987229 BC 987228 BC 987227 BC 987226 BC 987225 BC 987224 BC 987223 BC 987222 BC 987221 BC
987220 BC 987219 BC 987218 BC 987217 BC 987216 BC 987215 BC 987214 BC 987213 BC 987212 BC 987211 BC
987210 BC 987209 BC 987208 BC 987207 BC 987206 BC 987205 BC 987204 BC 987203 BC 987202 BC 987201 BC

987200 BC 987199 BC 987198 BC 987197 BC 987196 BC 987195 BC 987194 BC 987193 BC 987192 BC 987191 BC
987190 BC 987189 BC 987188 BC 987187 BC 987186 BC 987185 BC 987184 BC 987183 BC 987182 BC 987181 BC
987180 BC 987179 BC 987178 BC 987177 BC 987176 BC 987175 BC 987174 BC 987173 BC 987172 BC 987171 BC
987170 BC 987169 BC 987168 BC 987167 BC 987166 BC 987165 BC 987164 BC 987163 BC 987162 BC 987161 BC
987160 BC 987159 BC 987158 BC 987157 BC 987156 BC 987155 BC 987154 BC 987153 BC 987152 BC 987151 BC
987150 BC 987149 BC 987148 BC 987147 BC 987146 BC 987145 BC 987144 BC 987143 BC 987142 BC 987141 BC
987140 BC 987139 BC 987138 BC 987137 BC 987136 BC 987135 BC 987134 BC 987133 BC 987132 BC 987131 BC
987130 BC 987129 BC 987128 BC 987127 BC 987126 BC 987125 BC 987124 BC 987123 BC 987122 BC 987121 BC
987120 BC 987119 BC 987118 BC 987117 BC 987116 BC 987115 BC 987114 BC 987113 BC 987112 BC 987111 BC
987110 BC 987109 BC 987108 BC 987107 BC 987106 BC 987105 BC 987104 BC 987103 BC 987102 BC 987101 BC

987100 BC 987099 BC 987098 BC 987097 BC 987096 BC 987095 BC 987094 BC 987093 BC 987092 BC 987091 BC
987090 BC 987089 BC 987088 BC 987087 BC 987086 BC 987085 BC 987084 BC 987083 BC 987082 BC 987081 BC
987080 BC 987079 BC 987078 BC 987077 BC 987076 BC 987075 BC 987074 BC 987073 BC 987072 BC 987071 BC
987070 BC 987069 BC 987068 BC 987067 BC 987066 BC 987065 BC 987064 BC 987063 BC 987062 BC 987061 BC
987060 BC 987059 BC 987058 BC 987057 BC 987056 BC 987055 BC 987054 BC 987053 BC 987052 BC 987051 BC
987050 BC 987049 BC 987048 BC 987047 BC 987046 BC 987045 BC 987044 BC 987043 BC 987042 BC 987041 BC
987040 BC 987039 BC 987038 BC 987037 BC 987036 BC 987035 BC 987034 BC 987033 BC 987032 BC 987031 BC
987030 BC 987029 BC 987028 BC 987027 BC 987026 BC 987025 BC 987024 BC 987023 BC 987022 BC 987021 BC
987020 BC 987019 BC 987018 BC 987017 BC 987016 BC 987015 BC 987014 BC 987013 BC 987012 BC 987011 BC
987010 BC 987009 BC 987008 BC 987007 BC 987006 BC 987005 BC 987004 BC 987003 BC 987002 BC 987001 BC

— 23 —

986 99*...

987000 BC 986999 BC 986998 BC 986997 BC 986996 BC 986995 BC 986994 BC 986993 BC 986992 BC 986991 BC
986990 BC 986989 BC 986988 BC 986987 BC 986986 BC 986985 BC 986984 BC 986983 BC 986982 BC 986981 BC
986980 BC 986979 BC 986978 BC 986977 BC 986976 BC 986975 BC 986974 BC 986973 BC 986972 BC 986971 BC
986970 BC 986969 BC 986968 BC 986967 BC 986966 BC 986965 BC 986964 BC 986963 BC 986962 BC 986961 BC
986960 BC 986959 BC 986958 BC 986957 BC 986956 BC 986955 BC 986954 BC 986953 BC 986952 BC 986951 BC
986950 BC 986949 BC 986948 BC 986947 BC 986946 BC 986945 BC 986944 BC 986943 BC 986942 BC 986941 BC
986940 BC 986939 BC 986938 BC 986937 BC 986936 BC 986935 BC 986934 BC 986933 BC 986932 BC 986931 BC
986930 BC 986929 BC 986928 BC 986927 BC 986926 BC 986925 BC 986924 BC 986923 BC 986922 BC 986921 BC
986920 BC 986919 BC 986918 BC 986917 BC 986916 BC 986915 BC 986914 BC 986913 BC 986912 BC 986911 BC
986910 BC 986909 BC 986908 BC 986907 BC 986906 BC 986905 BC 986904 BC 986903 BC 986902 BC 986901 BC

986900 BC 986899 BC 986898 BC 986897 BC 986896 BC 986895 BC 986894 BC 986893 BC 986892 BC 986891 BC
986890 BC 986889 BC 986888 BC 986887 BC 986886 BC 986885 BC 986884 BC 986883 BC 986882 BC 986881 BC
986880 BC 986879 BC 986878 BC 986877 BC 986876 BC 986875 BC 986874 BC 986873 BC 986872 BC 986871 BC
986870 BC 986869 BC 986868 BC 986867 BC 986866 BC 986865 BC 986864 BC 986863 BC 986862 BC 986861 BC
986860 BC 986859 BC 986858 BC 986857 BC 986856 BC 986855 BC 986854 BC 986853 BC 986852 BC 986851 BC
986850 BC 986849 BC 986848 BC 986847 BC 986846 BC 986845 BC 986844 BC 986843 BC 986842 BC 986841 BC
986840 BC 986839 BC 986838 BC 986837 BC 986836 BC 986835 BC 986834 BC 986833 BC 986832 BC 986831 BC
986830 BC 986829 BC 986828 BC 986827 BC 986826 BC 986825 BC 986824 BC 986823 BC 986822 BC 986821 BC
986820 BC 986819 BC 986818 BC 986817 BC 986816 BC 986815 BC 986814 BC 986813 BC 986812 BC 986811 BC
986810 BC 986809 BC 986808 BC 986807 BC 986806 BC 986805 BC 986804 BC 986803 BC 986802 BC 986801 BC

986800 BC 986799 BC 986798 BC 986797 BC 986796 BC 986795 BC 986794 BC 986793 BC 986792 BC 986791 BC
986790 BC 986789 BC 986788 BC 986787 BC 986786 BC 986785 BC 986784 BC 986783 BC 986782 BC 986781 BC
986780 BC 986779 BC 986778 BC 986777 BC 986776 BC 986775 BC 986774 BC 986773 BC 986772 BC 986771 BC
986770 BC 986769 BC 986768 BC 986767 BC 986766 BC 986765 BC 986764 BC 986763 BC 986762 BC 986761 BC
986760 BC 986759 BC 986758 BC 986757 BC 986756 BC 986755 BC 986754 BC 986753 BC 986752 BC 986751 BC
986750 BC 986749 BC 986748 BC 986747 BC 986746 BC 986745 BC 986744 BC 986743 BC 986742 BC 986741 BC
986740 BC 986739 BC 986738 BC 986737 BC 986736 BC 986735 BC 986734 BC 986733 BC 986732 BC 986731 BC
986730 BC 986729 BC 986728 BC 986727 BC 986726 BC 986725 BC 986724 BC 986723 BC 986722 BC 986721 BC
986720 BC 986719 BC 986718 BC 986717 BC 986716 BC 986715 BC 986714 BC 986713 BC 986712 BC 986711 BC
986710 BC 986709 BC 986708 BC 986707 BC 986706 BC 986705 BC 986704 BC 986703 BC 986702 BC 986701 BC

986700 BC 986699 BC 986698 BC 986697 BC 986696 BC 986695 BC 986694 BC 986693 BC 986692 BC 986691 BC
986690 BC 986689 BC 986688 BC 986687 BC 986686 BC 986685 BC 986684 BC 986683 BC 986682 BC 986681 BC
986680 BC 986679 BC 986678 BC 986677 BC 986676 BC 986675 BC 986674 BC 986673 BC 986672 BC 986671 BC
986670 BC 986669 BC 986668 BC 986667 BC 986666 BC 986665 BC 986664 BC 986663 BC 986662 BC 986661 BC
986660 BC 986659 BC 986658 BC 986657 BC 986656 BC 986655 BC 986654 BC 986653 BC 986652 BC 986651 BC
986650 BC 986649 BC 986648 BC 986647 BC 986646 BC 986645 BC 986644 BC 986643 BC 986642 BC 986641 BC
986640 BC 986639 BC 986638 BC 986637 BC 986636 BC 986635 BC 986634 BC 986633 BC 986632 BC 986631 BC
986630 BC 986629 BC 986628 BC 986627 BC 986626 BC 986625 BC 986624 BC 986623 BC 986622 BC 986621 BC
986620 BC 986619 BC 986618 BC 986617 BC 986616 BC 986615 BC 986614 BC 986613 BC 986612 BC 986611 BC
986610 BC 986609 BC 986608 BC 986607 BC 986606 BC 986605 BC 986604 BC 986603 BC 986602 BC 986601 BC

986600 BC 986599 BC 986598 BC 986597 BC 986596 BC 986595 BC 986594 BC 986593 BC 986592 BC 986591 BC
986590 BC 986589 BC 986588 BC 986587 BC 986586 BC 986585 BC 986584 BC 986583 BC 986582 BC 986581 BC
986580 BC 986579 BC 986578 BC 986577 BC 986576 BC 986575 BC 986574 BC 986573 BC 986572 BC 986571 BC
986570 BC 986569 BC 986568 BC 986567 BC 986566 BC 986565 BC 986564 BC 986563 BC 986562 BC 986561 BC
986560 BC 986559 BC 986558 BC 986557 BC 986556 BC 986555 BC 986554 BC 986553 BC 986552 BC 986551 BC
986550 BC 986549 BC 986548 BC 986547 BC 986546 BC 986545 BC 986544 BC 986543 BC 986542 BC 986541 BC
986540 BC 986539 BC 986538 BC 986537 BC 986536 BC 986535 BC 986534 BC 986533 BC 986532 BC 986531 BC
986530 BC 986529 BC 986528 BC 986527 BC 986526 BC 986525 BC 986524 BC 986523 BC 986522 BC 986521 BC
986520 BC 986519 BC 986518 BC 986517 BC 986516 BC 986515 BC 986514 BC 986513 BC 986512 BC 986511 BC
986510 BC 986509 BC 986508 BC 986507 BC 986506 BC 986505 BC 986504 BC 986503 BC 986502 BC 986501 BC

986500 BC 986499 BC 986498 BC 986497 BC 986496 BC 986495 BC 986494 BC 986493 BC 986492 BC 986491 BC
986490 BC 986489 BC 986488 BC 986487 BC 986486 BC 986485 BC 986484 BC 986483 BC 986482 BC 986481 BC
986480 BC 986479 BC 986478 BC 986477 BC 986476 BC 986475 BC 986474 BC 986473 BC 986472 BC 986471 BC
986470 BC 986469 BC 986468 BC 986467 BC 986466 BC 986465 BC 986464 BC 986463 BC 986462 BC 986461 BC
986460 BC 986459 BC 986458 BC 986457 BC 986456 BC 986455 BC 986454 BC 986453 BC 986452 BC 986451 BC
986450 BC 986449 BC 986448 BC 986447 BC 986446 BC 986445 BC 986444 BC 986443 BC 986442 BC 986441 BC
986440 BC 986439 BC 986438 BC 986437 BC 986436 BC 986435 BC 986434 BC 986433 BC 986432 BC 986431 BC
986430 BC 986429 BC 986428 BC 986427 BC 986426 BC 986425 BC 986424 BC 986423 BC 986422 BC 986421 BC
986420 BC 986419 BC 986418 BC 986417 BC 986416 BC 986415 BC 986414 BC 986413 BC 986412 BC 986411 BC
986410 BC 986409 BC 986408 BC 986407 BC 986406 BC 986405 BC 986404 BC 986403 BC 986402 BC 986401 BC

986400 BC 986399 BC 986398 BC 986397 BC 986396 BC 986395 BC 986394 BC 986393 BC 986392 BC 986391 BC
986390 BC 986389 BC 986388 BC 986387 BC 986386 BC 986385 BC 986384 BC 986383 BC 986382 BC 986381 BC
986380 BC 986379 BC 986378 BC 986377 BC 986376 BC 986375 BC 986374 BC 986373 BC 986372 BC 986371 BC
986370 BC 986369 BC 986368 BC 986367 BC 986366 BC 986365 BC 986364 BC 986363 BC 986362 BC 986361 BC
986360 BC 986359 BC 986358 BC 986357 BC 986356 BC 986355 BC 986354 BC 986353 BC 986352 BC 986351 BC
986350 BC 986349 BC 986348 BC 986347 BC 986346 BC 986345 BC 986344 BC 986343 BC 986342 BC 986341 BC
986340 BC 986339 BC 986338 BC 986337 BC 986336 BC 986335 BC 986334 BC 986333 BC 986332 BC 986331 BC
986330 BC 986329 BC 986328 BC 986327 BC 986326 BC 986325 BC 986324 BC 986323 BC 986322 BC 986321 BC
986320 BC 986319 BC 986318 BC 986317 BC 986316 BC 986315 BC 986314 BC 986313 BC 986312 BC 986311 BC
986310 BC 986309 BC 986308 BC 986307 BC 986306 BC 986305 BC 986304 BC 986303 BC 986302 BC 986301 BC

986300 BC 986299 BC 986298 BC 986297 BC 986296 BC 986295 BC 986294 BC 986293 BC 986292 BC 986291 BC
986290 BC 986289 BC 986288 BC 986287 BC 986286 BC 986285 BC 986284 BC 986283 BC 986282 BC 986281 BC
986280 BC 986279 BC 986278 BC 986277 BC 986276 BC 986275 BC 986274 BC 986273 BC 986272 BC 986271 BC
986270 BC 986269 BC 986268 BC 986267 BC 986266 BC 986265 BC 986264 BC 986263 BC 986262 BC 986261 BC
986260 BC 986259 BC 986258 BC 986257 BC 986256 BC 986255 BC 986254 BC 986253 BC 986252 BC 986251 BC
986250 BC 986249 BC 986248 BC 986247 BC 986246 BC 986245 BC 986244 BC 986243 BC 986242 BC 986241 BC
986240 BC 986239 BC 986238 BC 986237 BC 986236 BC 986235 BC 986234 BC 986233 BC 986232 BC 986231 BC
986230 BC 986229 BC 986228 BC 986227 BC 986226 BC 986225 BC 986224 BC 986223 BC 986222 BC 986221 BC
986220 BC 986219 BC 986218 BC 986217 BC 986216 BC 986215 BC 986214 BC 986213 BC 986212 BC 986211 BC
986210 BC 986209 BC 986208 BC 986207 BC 986206 BC 986205 BC 986204 BC 986203 BC 986202 BC 986201 BC

986200 BC 986199 BC 986198 BC 986197 BC 986196 BC 986195 BC 986194 BC 986193 BC 986192 BC 986191 BC
986190 BC 986189 BC 986188 BC 986187 BC 986186 BC 986185 BC 986184 BC 986183 BC 986182 BC 986181 BC
986180 BC 986179 BC 986178 BC 986177 BC 986176 BC 986175 BC 986174 BC 986173 BC 986172 BC 986171 BC
986170 BC 986169 BC 986168 BC 986167 BC 986166 BC 986165 BC 986164 BC 986163 BC 986162 BC 986161 BC
986160 BC 986159 BC 986158 BC 986157 BC 986156 BC 986155 BC 986154 BC 986153 BC 986152 BC 986151 BC
986150 BC 986149 BC 986148 BC 986147 BC 986146 BC 986145 BC 986144 BC 986143 BC 986142 BC 986141 BC
986140 BC 986139 BC 986138 BC 986137 BC 986136 BC 986135 BC 986134 BC 986133 BC 986132 BC 986131 BC
986130 BC 986129 BC 986128 BC 986127 BC 986126 BC 986125 BC 986124 BC 986123 BC 986122 BC 986121 BC
986120 BC 986119 BC 986118 BC 986117 BC 986116 BC 986115 BC 986114 BC 986113 BC 986112 BC 986111 BC
986110 BC 986109 BC 986108 BC 986107 BC 986106 BC 986105 BC 986104 BC 986103 BC 986102 BC 986101 BC

986100 BC 986099 BC 986098 BC 986097 BC 986096 BC 986095 BC 986094 BC 986093 BC 986092 BC 986091 BC
986090 BC 986089 BC 986088 BC 986087 BC 986086 BC 986085 BC 986084 BC 986083 BC 986082 BC 986081 BC
986080 BC 986079 BC 986078 BC 986077 BC 986076 BC 986075 BC 986074 BC 986073 BC 986072 BC 986071 BC
986070 BC 986069 BC 986068 BC 986067 BC 986066 BC 986065 BC 986064 BC 986063 BC 986062 BC 986061 BC
986060 BC 986059 BC 986058 BC 986057 BC 986056 BC 986055 BC 986054 BC 986053 BC 986052 BC 986051 BC
986050 BC 986049 BC 986048 BC 986047 BC 986046 BC 986045 BC 986044 BC 986043 BC 986042 BC 986041 BC
986040 BC 986039 BC 986038 BC 986037 BC 986036 BC 986035 BC 986034 BC 986033 BC 986032 BC 986031 BC
986030 BC 986029 BC 986028 BC 986027 BC 986026 BC 986025 BC 986024 BC 986023 BC 986022 BC 986021 BC
986020 BC 986019 BC 986018 BC 986017 BC 986016 BC 986015 BC 986014 BC 986013 BC 986012 BC 986011 BC
986010 BC 986009 BC 986008 BC 986007 BC 986006 BC 986005 BC 986004 BC 986003 BC 986002 BC 986001 BC

985000 BC 985999 BC 985998 BC 985997 BC 985996 BC 985995 BC 985994 BC 985993 BC 985992 BC 985991 BC
985990 BC 985989 BC 985988 BC 985987 BC 985986 BC 985985 BC 985984 BC 985983 BC 985982 BC 985981 BC
985980 BC 985979 BC 985978 BC 985977 BC 985976 BC 985975 BC 985974 BC 985973 BC 985972 BC 985971 BC
985970 BC 985969 BC 985968 BC 985967 BC 985966 BC 985965 BC 985964 BC 985963 BC 985962 BC 985961 BC
985960 BC 985959 BC 985958 BC 985957 BC 985956 BC 985955 BC 985954 BC 985953 BC 985952 BC 985951 BC
985950 BC 985949 BC 985948 BC 985947 BC 985946 BC 985945 BC 985944 BC 985943 BC 985942 BC 985941 BC
985940 BC 985939 BC 985938 BC 985937 BC 985936 BC 985935 BC 985934 BC 985933 BC 985932 BC 985931 BC
985930 BC 985929 BC 985928 BC 985927 BC 985926 BC 985925 BC 985924 BC 985923 BC 985922 BC 985921 BC
985920 BC 985919 BC 985918 BC 985917 BC 985916 BC 985915 BC 985914 BC 985913 BC 985912 BC 985911 BC
985910 BC 985909 BC 985908 BC 985907 BC 985906 BC 985905 BC 985904 BC 985903 BC 985902 BC 985901 BC

985900 BC 985899 BC 985898 BC 985897 BC 985896 BC 985895 BC 985894 BC 985893 BC 985892 BC 985891 BC
985890 BC 985889 BC 985888 BC 985887 BC 985886 BC 985885 BC 985884 BC 985883 BC 985882 BC 985881 BC
985880 BC 985879 BC 985878 BC 985877 BC 985876 BC 985875 BC 985874 BC 985873 BC 985872 BC 985871 BC
985870 BC 985869 BC 985868 BC 985867 BC 985866 BC 985865 BC 985864 BC 985863 BC 985862 BC 985861 BC
985860 BC 985859 BC 985858 BC 985857 BC 985856 BC 985855 BC 985854 BC 985853 BC 985852 BC 985851 BC
985850 BC 985849 BC 985848 BC 985847 BC 985846 BC 985845 BC 985844 BC 985843 BC 985842 BC 985841 BC
985840 BC 985839 BC 985838 BC 985837 BC 985836 BC 985835 BC 985834 BC 985833 BC 985832 BC 985831 BC
985830 BC 985829 BC 985828 BC 985827 BC 985826 BC 985825 BC 985824 BC 985823 BC 985822 BC 985821 BC
985820 BC 985819 BC 985818 BC 985817 BC 985816 BC 985815 BC 985814 BC 985813 BC 985812 BC 985811 BC
985810 BC 985809 BC 985808 BC 985807 BC 985806 BC 985805 BC 985804 BC 985803 BC 985802 BC 985801 BC

985800 BC 985799 BC 985798 BC 985797 BC 985796 BC 985795 BC 985794 BC 985793 BC 985792 BC 985791 BC
985790 BC 985789 BC 985788 BC 985787 BC 985786 BC 985785 BC 985784 BC 985783 BC 985782 BC 985781 BC
985780 BC 985779 BC 985778 BC 985777 BC 985776 BC 985775 BC 985774 BC 985773 BC 985772 BC 985771 BC
985770 BC 985769 BC 985768 BC 985767 BC 985766 BC 985765 BC 985764 BC 985763 BC 985762 BC 985761 BC
985760 BC 985759 BC 985758 BC 985757 BC 985756 BC 985755 BC 985754 BC 985753 BC 985752 BC 985751 BC
985750 BC 985749 BC 985748 BC 985747 BC 985746 BC 985745 BC 985744 BC 985743 BC 985742 BC 985741 BC
985740 BC 985739 BC 985738 BC 985737 BC 985736 BC 985735 BC 985734 BC 985733 BC 985732 BC 985731 BC
985730 BC 985729 BC 985728 BC 985727 BC 985726 BC 985725 BC 985724 BC 985723 BC 985722 BC 985721 BC
985720 BC 985719 BC 985718 BC 985717 BC 985716 BC 985715 BC 985714 BC 985713 BC 985712 BC 985711 BC
985710 BC 985709 BC 985708 BC 985707 BC 985706 BC 985705 BC 985704 BC 985703 BC 985702 BC 985701 BC

985700 BC 985699 BC 985698 BC 985697 BC 985696 BC 985695 BC 985694 BC 985693 BC 985692 BC 985691 BC
985690 BC 985689 BC 985688 BC 985687 BC 985686 BC 985685 BC 985684 BC 985683 BC 985682 BC 985681 BC
985680 BC 985679 BC 985678 BC 985677 BC 985676 BC 985675 BC 985674 BC 985673 BC 985672 BC 985671 BC
985670 BC 985669 BC 985668 BC 985667 BC 985666 BC 985665 BC 985664 BC 985663 BC 985662 BC 985661 BC
985660 BC 985659 BC 985658 BC 985657 BC 985656 BC 985655 BC 985654 BC 985653 BC 985652 BC 985651 BC
985650 BC 985649 BC 985648 BC 985647 BC 985646 BC 985645 BC 985644 BC 985643 BC 985642 BC 985641 BC
985640 BC 985639 BC 985638 BC 985637 BC 985636 BC 985635 BC 985634 BC 985633 BC 985632 BC 985631 BC
985630 BC 985629 BC 985628 BC 985627 BC 985626 BC 985625 BC 985624 BC 985623 BC 985622 BC 985621 BC
985620 BC 985619 BC 985618 BC 985617 BC 985616 BC 985615 BC 985614 BC 985613 BC 985612 BC 985611 BC
985610 BC 985609 BC 985608 BC 985607 BC 985606 BC 985605 BC 985604 BC 985603 BC 985602 BC 985601 BC

985600 BC 985599 BC 985598 BC 985597 BC 985596 BC 985595 BC 985594 BC 985593 BC 985592 BC 985591 BC
985590 BC 985589 BC 985588 BC 985587 BC 985586 BC 985585 BC 985584 BC 985583 BC 985582 BC 985581 BC
985580 BC 985579 BC 985578 BC 985577 BC 985576 BC 985575 BC 985574 BC 985573 BC 985572 BC 985571 BC
985570 BC 985569 BC 985568 BC 985567 BC 985566 BC 985565 BC 985564 BC 985563 BC 985562 BC 985561 BC
985560 BC 985559 BC 985558 BC 985557 BC 985556 BC 985555 BC 985554 BC 985553 BC 985552 BC 985551 BC
985550 BC 985549 BC 985548 BC 985547 BC 985546 BC 985545 BC 985544 BC 985543 BC 985542 BC 985541 BC
985540 BC 985539 BC 985538 BC 985537 BC 985536 BC 985535 BC 985534 BC 985533 BC 985532 BC 985531 BC
985530 BC 985529 BC 985528 BC 985527 BC 985526 BC 985525 BC 985524 BC 985523 BC 985522 BC 985521 BC
985520 BC 985519 BC 985518 BC 985517 BC 985516 BC 985515 BC 985514 BC 985513 BC 985512 BC 985511 BC
985510 BC 985509 BC 985508 BC 985507 BC 985506 BC 985505 BC 985504 BC 985503 BC 985502 BC 985501 BC

985500 BC 985499 BC 985498 BC 985497 BC 985496 BC 985495 BC 985494 BC 985493 BC 985492 BC 985491 BC
985490 BC 985489 BC 985488 BC 985487 BC 985486 BC 985485 BC 985484 BC 985483 BC 985482 BC 985481 BC
985480 BC 985479 BC 985478 BC 985477 BC 985476 BC 985475 BC 985474 BC 985473 BC 985472 BC 985471 BC
985470 BC 985469 BC 985468 BC 985467 BC 985466 BC 985465 BC 985464 BC 985463 BC 985462 BC 985461 BC
985460 BC 985459 BC 985458 BC 985457 BC 985456 BC 985455 BC 985454 BC 985453 BC 985452 BC 985451 BC
985450 BC 985449 BC 985448 BC 985447 BC 985446 BC 985445 BC 985444 BC 985443 BC 985442 BC 985441 BC
985440 BC 985439 BC 985438 BC 985437 BC 985436 BC 985435 BC 985434 BC 985433 BC 985432 BC 985431 BC
985430 BC 985429 BC 985428 BC 985427 BC 985426 BC 985425 BC 985424 BC 985423 BC 985422 BC 985421 BC
985420 BC 985419 BC 985418 BC 985417 BC 985416 BC 985415 BC 985414 BC 985413 BC 985412 BC 985411 BC
985410 BC 985409 BC 985408 BC 985407 BC 985406 BC 985405 BC 985404 BC 985403 BC 985402 BC 985401 BC

985400 BC 985399 BC 985398 BC 985397 BC 985396 BC 985395 BC 985394 BC 985393 BC 985392 BC 985391 BC
985390 BC 985389 BC 985388 BC 985387 BC 985386 BC 985385 BC 985384 BC 985383 BC 985382 BC 985381 BC
985380 BC 985379 BC 985378 BC 985377 BC 985376 BC 985375 BC 985374 BC 985373 BC 985372 BC 985371 BC
985370 BC 985369 BC 985368 BC 985367 BC 985366 BC 985365 BC 985364 BC 985363 BC 985362 BC 985361 BC
985360 BC 985359 BC 985358 BC 985357 BC 985356 BC 985355 BC 985354 BC 985353 BC 985352 BC 985351 BC
985350 BC 985349 BC 985348 BC 985347 BC 985346 BC 985345 BC 985344 BC 985343 BC 985342 BC 985341 BC
985340 BC 985339 BC 985338 BC 985337 BC 985336 BC 985335 BC 985334 BC 985333 BC 985332 BC 985331 BC
985330 BC 985329 BC 985328 BC 985327 BC 985326 BC 985325 BC 985324 BC 985323 BC 985322 BC 985321 BC
985320 BC 985319 BC 985318 BC 985317 BC 985316 BC 985315 BC 985314 BC 985313 BC 985312 BC 985311 BC
985310 BC 985309 BC 985308 BC 985307 BC 985306 BC 985305 BC 985304 BC 985303 BC 985302 BC 985301 BC

985300 BC 985299 BC 985298 BC 985297 BC 985296 BC 985295 BC 985294 BC 985293 BC 985292 BC 985291 BC
985290 BC 985289 BC 985288 BC 985287 BC 985286 BC 985285 BC 985284 BC 985283 BC 985282 BC 985281 BC
985280 BC 985279 BC 985278 BC 985277 BC 985276 BC 985275 BC 985274 BC 985273 BC 985272 BC 985271 BC
985270 BC 985269 BC 985268 BC 985267 BC 985266 BC 985265 BC 985264 BC 985263 BC 985262 BC 985261 BC
985260 BC 985259 BC 985258 BC 985257 BC 985256 BC 985255 BC 985254 BC 985253 BC 985252 BC 985251 BC
985250 BC 985249 BC 985248 BC 985247 BC 985246 BC 985245 BC 985244 BC 985243 BC 985242 BC 985241 BC
985240 BC 985239 BC 985238 BC 985237 BC 985236 BC 985235 BC 985234 BC 985233 BC 985232 BC 985231 BC
985230 BC 985229 BC 985228 BC 985227 BC 985226 BC 985225 BC 985224 BC 985223 BC 985222 BC 985221 BC
985220 BC 985219 BC 985218 BC 985217 BC 985216 BC 985215 BC 985214 BC 985213 BC 985212 BC 985211 BC
985210 BC 985209 BC 985208 BC 985207 BC 985206 BC 985205 BC 985204 BC 985203 BC 985202 BC 985201 BC

985200 BC 985199 BC 985198 BC 985197 BC 985196 BC 985195 BC 985194 BC 985193 BC 985192 BC 985191 BC
985190 BC 985189 BC 985188 BC 985187 BC 985186 BC 985185 BC 985184 BC 985183 BC 985182 BC 985181 BC
985180 BC 985179 BC 985178 BC 985177 BC 985176 BC 985175 BC 985174 BC 985173 BC 985172 BC 985171 BC
985170 BC 985169 BC 985168 BC 985167 BC 985166 BC 985165 BC 985164 BC 985163 BC 985162 BC 985161 BC
985160 BC 985159 BC 985158 BC 985157 BC 985156 BC 985155 BC 985154 BC 985153 BC 985152 BC 985151 BC
985150 BC 985149 BC 985148 BC 985147 BC 985146 BC 985145 BC 985144 BC 985143 BC 985142 BC 985141 BC
985140 BC 985139 BC 985138 BC 985137 BC 985136 BC 985135 BC 985134 BC 985133 BC 985132 BC 985131 BC
985130 BC 985129 BC 985128 BC 985127 BC 985126 BC 985125 BC 985124 BC 985123 BC 985122 BC 985121 BC
985120 BC 985119 BC 985118 BC 985117 BC 985116 BC 985115 BC 985114 BC 985113 BC 985112 BC 985111 BC
985110 BC 985109 BC 985108 BC 985107 BC 985106 BC 985105 BC 985104 BC 985103 BC 985102 BC 985101 BC

985100 BC 985099 BC 985098 BC 985097 BC 985096 BC 985095 BC 985094 BC 985093 BC 985092 BC 985091 BC
985090 BC 985089 BC 985088 BC 985087 BC 985086 BC 985085 BC 985084 BC 985083 BC 985082 BC 985081 BC
985080 BC 985079 BC 985078 BC 985077 BC 985076 BC 985075 BC 985074 BC 985073 BC 985072 BC 985071 BC
985070 BC 985069 BC 985068 BC 985067 BC 985066 BC 985065 BC 985064 BC 985063 BC 985062 BC 985061 BC
985060 BC 985059 BC 985058 BC 985057 BC 985056 BC 985055 BC 985054 BC 985053 BC 985052 BC 985051 BC
985050 BC 985049 BC 985048 BC 985047 BC 985046 BC 985045 BC 985044 BC 985043 BC 985042 BC 985041 BC
985040 BC 985039 BC 985038 BC 985037 BC 985036 BC 985035 BC 985034 BC 985033 BC 985032 BC 985031 BC
985030 BC 985029 BC 985028 BC 985027 BC 985026 BC 985025 BC 985024 BC 985023 BC 985022 BC 985021 BC
985020 BC 985019 BC 985018 BC 985017 BC 985016 BC 985015 BC 985014 BC 985013 BC 985012 BC 985011 BC
985010 BC 985009 BC 985008 BC 985007 BC 985006 BC 985005 BC 985004 BC 985003 BC 985002 BC 985001 BC

— 27 —

985000 BC 984999 BC 984998 BC 984997 BC 984996 BC 984995 BC 984994 BC 984993 BC 984992 BC 984991 BC
984990 BC 984989 BC 984988 BC 984987 BC 984986 BC 984985 BC 984984 BC 984983 BC 984982 BC 984981 BC
984980 BC 984979 BC 984978 BC 984977 BC 984976 BC 984975 BC 984974 BC 984973 BC 984972 BC 984971 BC
984970 BC 984969 BC 984968 BC 984967 BC 984966 BC 984965 BC 984964 BC 984963 BC 984962 BC 984961 BC
984960 BC 984959 BC 984958 BC 984957 BC 984956 BC 984955 BC 984954 BC 984953 BC 984952 BC 984951 BC
984950 BC 984949 BC 984948 BC 984947 BC 984946 BC 984945 BC 984944 BC 984943 BC 984942 BC 984941 BC
984940 BC 984939 BC 984938 BC 984937 BC 984936 BC 984935 BC 984934 BC 984933 BC 984932 BC 984931 BC
984930 BC 984929 BC 984928 BC 984927 BC 984926 BC 984925 BC 984924 BC 984923 BC 984922 BC 984921 BC
984920 BC 984919 BC 984918 BC 984917 BC 984916 BC 984915 BC 984914 BC 984913 BC 984912 BC 984911 BC
984910 BC 984909 BC 984908 BC 984907 BC 984906 BC 984905 BC 984904 BC 984903 BC 984902 BC 984901 BC

984900 BC 984899 BC 984898 BC 984897 BC 984896 BC 984895 BC 984894 BC 984893 BC 984892 BC 984891 BC
984890 BC 984889 BC 984888 BC 984887 BC 984886 BC 984885 BC 984884 BC 984883 BC 984882 BC 984881 BC
984880 BC 984879 BC 984878 BC 984877 BC 984876 BC 984875 BC 984874 BC 984873 BC 984872 BC 984871 BC
984870 BC 984869 BC 984868 BC 984867 BC 984866 BC 984865 BC 984864 BC 984863 BC 984862 BC 984861 BC
984860 BC 984859 BC 984858 BC 984857 BC 984856 BC 984855 BC 984854 BC 984853 BC 984852 BC 984851 BC
984850 BC 984849 BC 984848 BC 984847 BC 984846 BC 984845 BC 984844 BC 984843 BC 984842 BC 984841 BC
984840 BC 984839 BC 984838 BC 984837 BC 984836 BC 984835 BC 984834 BC 984833 BC 984832 BC 984831 BC
984830 BC 984829 BC 984828 BC 984827 BC 984826 BC 984825 BC 984824 BC 984823 BC 984822 BC 984821 BC
984820 BC 984819 BC 984818 BC 984817 BC 984816 BC 984815 BC 984814 BC 984813 BC 984812 BC 984811 BC
984810 BC 984809 BC 984808 BC 984807 BC 984806 BC 984805 BC 984804 BC 984803 BC 984802 BC 984801 BC

984800 BC 984799 BC 984798 BC 984797 BC 984796 BC 984795 BC 984794 BC 984793 BC 984792 BC 984791 BC
984790 BC 984789 BC 984788 BC 984787 BC 984786 BC 984785 BC 984784 BC 984783 BC 984782 BC 984781 BC
984780 BC 984779 BC 984778 BC 984777 BC 984776 BC 984775 BC 984774 BC 984773 BC 984772 BC 984771 BC
984770 BC 984769 BC 984768 BC 984767 BC 984766 BC 984765 BC 984764 BC 984763 BC 984762 BC 984761 BC
984760 BC 984759 BC 984758 BC 984757 BC 984756 BC 984755 BC 984754 BC 984753 BC 984752 BC 984751 BC
984750 BC 984749 BC 984748 BC 984747 BC 984746 BC 984745 BC 984744 BC 984743 BC 984742 BC 984741 BC
984740 BC 984739 BC 984738 BC 984737 BC 984736 BC 984735 BC 984734 BC 984733 BC 984732 BC 984731 BC
984730 BC 984729 BC 984728 BC 984727 BC 984726 BC 984725 BC 984724 BC 984723 BC 984722 BC 984721 BC
984720 BC 984719 BC 984718 BC 984717 BC 984716 BC 984715 BC 984714 BC 984713 BC 984712 BC 984711 BC
984710 BC 984709 BC 984708 BC 984707 BC 984706 BC 984705 BC 984704 BC 984703 BC 984702 BC 984701 BC

984700 BC 984699 BC 984698 BC 984697 BC 984696 BC 984695 BC 984694 BC 984693 BC 984692 BC 984691 BC
984690 BC 984689 BC 984688 BC 984687 BC 984686 BC 984685 BC 984684 BC 984683 BC 984682 BC 984681 BC
984680 BC 984679 BC 984678 BC 984677 BC 984676 BC 984675 BC 984674 BC 984673 BC 984672 BC 984671 BC
984670 BC 984669 BC 984668 BC 984667 BC 984666 BC 984665 BC 984664 BC 984663 BC 984662 BC 984661 BC
984660 BC 984659 BC 984658 BC 984657 BC 984656 BC 984655 BC 984654 BC 984653 BC 984652 BC 984651 BC
984650 BC 984649 BC 984648 BC 984647 BC 984646 BC 984645 BC 984644 BC 984643 BC 984642 BC 984641 BC
984640 BC 984639 BC 984638 BC 984637 BC 984636 BC 984635 BC 984634 BC 984633 BC 984632 BC 984631 BC
984630 BC 984629 BC 984628 BC 984627 BC 984626 BC 984625 BC 984624 BC 984623 BC 984622 BC 984621 BC
984620 BC 984619 BC 984618 BC 984617 BC 984616 BC 984615 BC 984614 BC 984613 BC 984612 BC 984611 BC
984610 BC 984609 BC 984608 BC 984607 BC 984606 BC 984605 BC 984604 BC 984603 BC 984602 BC 984601 BC

984600 BC 984599 BC 984598 BC 984597 BC 984596 BC 984595 BC 984594 BC 984593 BC 984592 BC 984591 BC
984590 BC 984589 BC 984588 BC 984587 BC 984586 BC 984585 BC 984584 BC 984583 BC 984582 BC 984581 BC
984580 BC 984579 BC 984578 BC 984577 BC 984576 BC 984575 BC 984574 BC 984573 BC 984572 BC 984571 BC
984570 BC 984569 BC 984568 BC 984567 BC 984566 BC 984565 BC 984564 BC 984563 BC 984562 BC 984561 BC
984560 BC 984559 BC 984558 BC 984557 BC 984556 BC 984555 BC 984554 BC 984553 BC 984552 BC 984551 BC
984550 BC 984549 BC 984548 BC 984547 BC 984546 BC 984545 BC 984544 BC 984543 BC 984542 BC 984541 BC
984540 BC 984539 BC 984538 BC 984537 BC 984536 BC 984535 BC 984534 BC 984533 BC 984532 BC 984531 BC
984530 BC 984529 BC 984528 BC 984527 BC 984526 BC 984525 BC 984524 BC 984523 BC 984522 BC 984521 BC
984520 BC 984519 BC 984518 BC 984517 BC 984516 BC 984515 BC 984514 BC 984513 BC 984512 BC 984511 BC
984510 BC 984509 BC 984508 BC 984507 BC 984506 BC 984505 BC 984504 BC 984503 BC 984502 BC 984501 BC

— 28 —

984500 BC 984499 BC 984498 BC 984497 BC 984496 BC 984495 BC 984494 BC 984493 BC 984492 BC 984491 BC
984490 BC 984489 BC 984488 BC 984487 BC 984486 BC 984485 BC 984484 BC 984483 BC 984482 BC 984481 BC
984480 BC 984479 BC 984478 BC 984477 BC 984476 BC 984475 BC 984474 BC 984473 BC 984472 BC 984471 BC
984470 BC 984469 BC 984468 BC 984467 BC 984466 BC 984465 BC 984464 BC 984463 BC 984462 BC 984461 BC
984460 BC 984459 BC 984458 BC 984457 BC 984456 BC 984455 BC 984454 BC 984453 BC 984452 BC 984451 BC
984450 BC 984449 BC 984448 BC 984447 BC 984446 BC 984445 BC 984444 BC 984443 BC 984442 BC 984441 BC
984440 BC 984439 BC 984438 BC 984437 BC 984436 BC 984435 BC 984434 BC 984433 BC 984432 BC 984431 BC
984430 BC 984429 BC 984428 BC 984427 BC 984426 BC 984425 BC 984424 BC 984423 BC 984422 BC 984421 BC
984420 BC 984419 BC 984418 BC 984417 BC 984416 BC 984415 BC 984414 BC 984413 BC 984412 BC 984411 BC
984410 BC 984409 BC 984408 BC 984407 BC 984406 BC 984405 BC 984404 BC 984403 BC 984402 BC 984401 BC

984400 BC 984399 BC 984398 BC 984397 BC 984396 BC 984395 BC 984394 BC 984393 BC 984392 BC 984391 BC
984390 BC 984389 BC 984388 BC 984387 BC 984386 BC 984385 BC 984384 BC 984383 BC 984382 BC 984381 BC
984380 BC 984379 BC 984378 BC 984377 BC 984376 BC 984375 BC 984374 BC 984373 BC 984372 BC 984371 BC
984370 BC 984369 BC 984368 BC 984367 BC 984366 BC 984365 BC 984364 BC 984363 BC 984362 BC 984361 BC
984360 BC 984359 BC 984358 BC 984357 BC 984356 BC 984355 BC 984354 BC 984353 BC 984352 BC 984351 BC
984350 BC 984349 BC 984348 BC 984347 BC 984346 BC 984345 BC 984344 BC 984343 BC 984342 BC 984341 BC
984340 BC 984339 BC 984338 BC 984337 BC 984336 BC 984335 BC 984334 BC 984333 BC 984332 BC 984331 BC
984330 BC 984329 BC 984328 BC 984327 BC 984326 BC 984325 BC 984324 BC 984323 BC 984322 BC 984321 BC
984320 BC 984319 BC 984318 BC 984317 BC 984316 BC 984315 BC 984314 BC 984313 BC 984312 BC 984311 BC
984310 BC 984309 BC 984308 BC 984307 BC 984306 BC 984305 BC 984304 BC 984303 BC 984302 BC 984301 BC

984300 BC 984299 BC 984298 BC 984297 BC 984296 BC 984295 BC 984294 BC 984293 BC 984292 BC 984291 BC
984290 BC 984289 BC 984288 BC 984287 BC 984286 BC 984285 BC 984284 BC 984283 BC 984282 BC 984281 BC
984280 BC 984279 BC 984278 BC 984277 BC 984276 BC 984275 BC 984274 BC 984273 BC 984272 BC 984271 BC
984270 BC 984269 BC 984268 BC 984267 BC 984266 BC 984265 BC 984264 BC 984263 BC 984262 BC 984261 BC
984260 BC 984259 BC 984258 BC 984257 BC 984256 BC 984255 BC 984254 BC 984253 BC 984252 BC 984251 BC
984250 BC 984249 BC 984248 BC 984247 BC 984246 BC 984245 BC 984244 BC 984243 BC 984242 BC 984241 BC
984240 BC 984239 BC 984238 BC 984237 BC 984236 BC 984235 BC 984234 BC 984233 BC 984232 BC 984231 BC
984230 BC 984229 BC 984228 BC 984227 BC 984226 BC 984225 BC 984224 BC 984223 BC 984222 BC 984221 BC
984220 BC 984219 BC 984218 BC 984217 BC 984216 BC 984215 BC 984214 BC 984213 BC 984212 BC 984211 BC
984210 BC 984209 BC 984208 BC 984207 BC 984206 BC 984205 BC 984204 BC 984203 BC 984202 BC 984201 BC

984200 BC 984199 BC 984198 BC 984197 BC 984196 BC 984195 BC 984194 BC 984193 BC 984192 BC 984191 BC
984190 BC 984189 BC 984188 BC 984187 BC 984186 BC 984185 BC 984184 BC 984183 BC 984182 BC 984181 BC
984180 BC 984179 BC 984178 BC 984177 BC 984176 BC 984175 BC 984174 BC 984173 BC 984172 BC 984171 BC
984170 BC 984169 BC 984168 BC 984167 BC 984166 BC 984165 BC 984164 BC 984163 BC 984162 BC 984161 BC
984160 BC 984159 BC 984158 BC 984157 BC 984156 BC 984155 BC 984154 BC 984153 BC 984152 BC 984151 BC
984150 BC 984149 BC 984148 BC 984147 BC 984146 BC 984145 BC 984144 BC 984143 BC 984142 BC 984141 BC
984140 BC 984139 BC 984138 BC 984137 BC 984136 BC 984135 BC 984134 BC 984133 BC 984132 BC 984131 BC
984130 BC 984129 BC 984128 BC 984127 BC 984126 BC 984125 BC 984124 BC 984123 BC 984122 BC 984121 BC
984120 BC 984119 BC 984118 BC 984117 BC 984116 BC 984115 BC 984114 BC 984113 BC 984112 BC 984111 BC
984110 BC 984109 BC 984108 BC 984107 BC 984106 BC 984105 BC 984104 BC 984103 BC 984102 BC 984101 BC

984100 BC 984099 BC 984098 BC 984097 BC 984096 BC 984095 BC 984094 BC 984093 BC 984092 BC 984091 BC
984090 BC 984089 BC 984088 BC 984087 BC 984086 BC 984085 BC 984084 BC 984083 BC 984082 BC 984081 BC
984080 BC 984079 BC 984078 BC 984077 BC 984076 BC 984075 BC 984074 BC 984073 BC 984072 BC 984071 BC
984070 BC 984069 BC 984068 BC 984067 BC 984066 BC 984065 BC 984064 BC 984063 BC 984062 BC 984061 BC
984060 BC 984059 BC 984058 BC 984057 BC 984056 BC 984055 BC 984054 BC 984053 BC 984052 BC 984051 BC
984050 BC 984049 BC 984048 BC 984047 BC 984046 BC 984045 BC 984044 BC 984043 BC 984042 BC 984041 BC
984040 BC 984039 BC 984038 BC 984037 BC 984036 BC 984035 BC 984034 BC 984033 BC 984032 BC 984031 BC
984030 BC 984029 BC 984028 BC 984027 BC 984026 BC 984025 BC 984024 BC 984023 BC 984022 BC 984021 BC
984020 BC 984019 BC 984018 BC 984017 BC 984016 BC 984015 BC 984014 BC 984013 BC 984012 BC 984011 BC
984010 BC 984009 BC 984008 BC 984007 BC 984006 BC 984005 BC 984004 BC 984003 BC 984002 BC 984001 BC

— 29 —

984000 BC 983999 BC 983998 BC 983997 BC 983996 BC 983995 BC 983994 BC 983993 BC 983992 BC 983991 BC
983990 BC 983989 BC 983988 BC 983987 BC 983986 BC 983985 BC 983984 BC 983983 BC 983982 BC 983981 BC
983980 BC 983979 BC 983978 BC 983977 BC 983976 BC 983975 BC 983974 BC 983973 BC 983972 BC 983971 BC
983970 BC 983969 BC 983968 BC 983967 BC 983966 BC 983965 BC 983964 BC 983963 BC 983962 BC 983961 BC
983960 BC 983959 BC 983958 BC 983957 BC 983956 BC 983955 BC 983954 BC 983953 BC 983952 BC 983951 BC
983950 BC 983949 BC 983948 BC 983947 BC 983946 BC 983945 BC 983944 BC 983943 BC 983942 BC 983941 BC
983940 BC 983939 BC 983938 BC 983937 BC 983936 BC 983935 BC 983934 BC 983933 BC 983932 BC 983931 BC
983930 BC 983929 BC 983928 BC 983927 BC 983926 BC 983925 BC 983924 BC 983923 BC 983922 BC 983921 BC
983920 BC 983919 BC 983918 BC 983917 BC 983916 BC 983915 BC 983914 BC 983913 BC 983912 BC 983911 BC
983910 BC 983909 BC 983908 BC 983907 BC 983906 BC 983905 BC 983904 BC 983903 BC 983902 BC 983901 BC

983900 BC 983899 BC 983898 BC 983897 BC 983896 BC 983895 BC 983894 BC 983893 BC 983892 BC 983891 BC
983890 BC 983889 BC 983888 BC 983887 BC 983886 BC 983885 BC 983884 BC 983883 BC 983882 BC 983881 BC
983880 BC 983879 BC 983878 BC 983877 BC 983876 BC 983875 BC 983874 BC 983873 BC 983872 BC 983871 BC
983870 BC 983869 BC 983868 BC 983867 BC 983866 BC 983865 BC 983864 BC 983863 BC 983862 BC 983861 BC
983860 BC 983859 BC 983858 BC 983857 BC 983856 BC 983855 BC 983854 BC 983853 BC 983852 BC 983851 BC
983850 BC 983849 BC 983848 BC 983847 BC 983846 BC 983845 BC 983844 BC 983843 BC 983842 BC 983841 BC
983840 BC 983839 BC 983838 BC 983837 BC 983836 BC 983835 BC 983834 BC 983833 BC 983832 BC 983831 BC
983830 BC 983829 BC 983828 BC 983827 BC 983826 BC 983825 BC 983824 BC 983823 BC 983822 BC 983821 BC
983820 BC 983819 BC 983818 BC 983817 BC 983816 BC 983815 BC 983814 BC 983813 BC 983812 BC 983811 BC
983810 BC 983809 BC 983808 BC 983807 BC 983806 BC 983805 BC 983804 BC 983803 BC 983802 BC 983801 BC

983800 BC 983799 BC 983798 BC 983797 BC 983796 BC 983795 BC 983794 BC 983793 BC 983792 BC 983791 BC
983790 BC 983789 BC 983788 BC 983787 BC 983786 BC 983785 BC 983784 BC 983783 BC 983782 BC 983781 BC
983780 BC 983779 BC 983778 BC 983777 BC 983776 BC 983775 BC 983774 BC 983773 BC 983772 BC 983771 BC
983770 BC 983769 BC 983768 BC 983767 BC 983766 BC 983765 BC 983764 BC 983763 BC 983762 BC 983761 BC
983760 BC 983759 BC 983758 BC 983757 BC 983756 BC 983755 BC 983754 BC 983753 BC 983752 BC 983751 BC
983750 BC 983749 BC 983748 BC 983747 BC 983746 BC 983745 BC 983744 BC 983743 BC 983742 BC 983741 BC
983740 BC 983739 BC 983738 BC 983737 BC 983736 BC 983735 BC 983734 BC 983733 BC 983732 BC 983731 BC
983730 BC 983729 BC 983728 BC 983727 BC 983726 BC 983725 BC 983724 BC 983723 BC 983722 BC 983721 BC
983720 BC 983719 BC 983718 BC 983717 BC 983716 BC 983715 BC 983714 BC 983713 BC 983712 BC 983711 BC
983710 BC 983709 BC 983708 BC 983707 BC 983706 BC 983705 BC 983704 BC 983703 BC 983702 BC 983701 BC

983700 BC 983699 BC 983698 BC 983697 BC 983696 BC 983695 BC 983694 BC 983693 BC 983692 BC 983691 BC
983690 BC 983689 BC 983688 BC 983687 BC 983686 BC 983685 BC 983684 BC 983683 BC 983682 BC 983681 BC
983680 BC 983679 BC 983678 BC 983677 BC 983676 BC 983675 BC 983674 BC 983673 BC 983672 BC 983671 BC
983670 BC 983669 BC 983668 BC 983667 BC 983666 BC 983665 BC 983664 BC 983663 BC 983662 BC 983661 BC
983660 BC 983659 BC 983658 BC 983657 BC 983656 BC 983655 BC 983654 BC 983653 BC 983652 BC 983651 BC
983650 BC 983649 BC 983648 BC 983647 BC 983646 BC 983645 BC 983644 BC 983643 BC 983642 BC 983641 BC
983640 BC 983639 BC 983638 BC 983637 BC 983636 BC 983635 BC 983634 BC 983633 BC 983632 BC 983631 BC
983630 BC 983629 BC 983628 BC 983627 BC 983626 BC 983625 BC 983624 BC 983623 BC 983622 BC 983621 BC
983620 BC 983619 BC 983618 BC 983617 BC 983616 BC 983615 BC 983614 BC 983613 BC 983612 BC 983611 BC
983610 BC 983609 BC 983608 BC 983607 BC 983606 BC 983605 BC 983604 BC 983603 BC 983602 BC 983601 BC

983600 BC 983599 BC 983598 BC 983597 BC 983596 BC 983595 BC 983594 BC 983593 BC 983592 BC 983591 BC
983590 BC 983589 BC 983588 BC 983587 BC 983586 BC 983585 BC 983584 BC 983583 BC 983582 BC 983581 BC
983580 BC 983579 BC 983578 BC 983577 BC 983576 BC 983575 BC 983574 BC 983573 BC 983572 BC 983571 BC
983570 BC 983569 BC 983568 BC 983567 BC 983566 BC 983565 BC 983564 BC 983563 BC 983562 BC 983561 BC
983560 BC 983559 BC 983558 BC 983557 BC 983556 BC 983555 BC 983554 BC 983553 BC 983552 BC 983551 BC
983550 BC 983549 BC 983548 BC 983547 BC 983546 BC 983545 BC 983544 BC 983543 BC 983542 BC 983541 BC
983540 BC 983539 BC 983538 BC 983537 BC 983536 BC 983535 BC 983534 BC 983533 BC 983532 BC 983531 BC
983530 BC 983529 BC 983528 BC 983527 BC 983526 BC 983525 BC 983524 BC 983523 BC 983522 BC 983521 BC
983520 BC 983519 BC 983518 BC 983517 BC 983516 BC 983515 BC 983514 BC 983513 BC 983512 BC 983511 BC
983510 BC 983509 BC 983508 BC 983507 BC 983506 BC 983505 BC 983504 BC 983503 BC 983502 BC 983501 BC

— 30 —

983500 BC 983499 BC 983498 BC 983497 BC 983496 BC 983495 BC 983494 BC 983493 BC 983492 BC 983491 BC
983490 BC 983489 BC 983488 BC 983487 BC 983486 BC 983485 BC 983484 BC 983483 BC 983482 BC 983481 BC
983480 BC 983479 BC 983478 BC 983477 BC 983476 BC 983475 BC 983474 BC 983473 BC 983472 BC 983471 BC
983470 BC 983469 BC 983468 BC 983467 BC 983466 BC 983465 BC 983464 BC 983463 BC 983462 BC 983461 BC
983460 BC 983459 BC 983458 BC 983457 BC 983456 BC 983455 BC 983454 BC 983453 BC 983452 BC 983451 BC
983450 BC 983449 BC 983448 BC 983447 BC 983446 BC 983445 BC 983444 BC 983443 BC 983442 BC 983441 BC
983440 BC 983439 BC 983438 BC 983437 BC 983436 BC 983435 BC 983434 BC 983433 BC 983432 BC 983431 BC
983430 BC 983429 BC 983428 BC 983427 BC 983426 BC 983425 BC 983424 BC 983423 BC 983422 BC 983421 BC
983420 BC 983419 BC 983418 BC 983417 BC 983416 BC 983415 BC 983414 BC 983413 BC 983412 BC 983411 BC
983410 BC 983409 BC 983408 BC 983407 BC 983406 BC 983405 BC 983404 BC 983403 BC 983402 BC 983401 BC

983400 BC 983399 BC 983398 BC 983397 BC 983396 BC 983395 BC 983394 BC 983393 BC 983392 BC 983391 BC
983390 BC 983389 BC 983388 BC 983387 BC 983386 BC 983385 BC 983384 BC 983383 BC 983382 BC 983381 BC
983380 BC 983379 BC 983378 BC 983377 BC 983376 BC 983375 BC 983374 BC 983373 BC 983372 BC 983371 BC
983370 BC 983369 BC 983368 BC 983367 BC 983366 BC 983365 BC 983364 BC 983363 BC 983362 BC 983361 BC
983360 BC 983359 BC 983358 BC 983357 BC 983356 BC 983355 BC 983354 BC 983353 BC 983352 BC 983351 BC
983350 BC 983349 BC 983348 BC 983347 BC 983346 BC 983345 BC 983344 BC 983343 BC 983342 BC 983341 BC
983340 BC 983339 BC 983338 BC 983337 BC 983336 BC 983335 BC 983334 BC 983333 BC 983332 BC 983331 BC
983330 BC 983329 BC 983328 BC 983327 BC 983326 BC 983325 BC 983324 BC 983323 BC 983322 BC 983321 BC
983320 BC 983319 BC 983318 BC 983317 BC 983316 BC 983315 BC 983314 BC 983313 BC 983312 BC 983311 BC
983310 BC 983309 BC 983308 BC 983307 BC 983306 BC 983305 BC 983304 BC 983303 BC 983302 BC 983301 BC

983300 BC 983299 BC 983298 BC 983297 BC 983296 BC 983295 BC 983294 BC 983293 BC 983292 BC 983291 BC
983290 BC 983289 BC 983288 BC 983287 BC 983286 BC 983285 BC 983284 BC 983283 BC 983282 BC 983281 BC
983280 BC 983279 BC 983278 BC 983277 BC 983276 BC 983275 BC 983274 BC 983273 BC 983272 BC 983271 BC
983270 BC 983269 BC 983268 BC 983267 BC 983266 BC 983265 BC 983264 BC 983263 BC 983262 BC 983261 BC
983260 BC 983259 BC 983258 BC 983257 BC 983256 BC 983255 BC 983254 BC 983253 BC 983252 BC 983251 BC
983250 BC 983249 BC 983248 BC 983247 BC 983246 BC 983245 BC 983244 BC 983243 BC 983242 BC 983241 BC
983240 BC 983239 BC 983238 BC 983237 BC 983236 BC 983235 BC 983234 BC 983233 BC 983232 BC 983231 BC
983230 BC 983229 BC 983228 BC 983227 BC 983226 BC 983225 BC 983224 BC 983223 BC 983222 BC 983221 BC
983220 BC 983219 BC 983218 BC 983217 BC 983216 BC 983215 BC 983214 BC 983213 BC 983212 BC 983211 BC
983210 BC 983209 BC 983208 BC 983207 BC 983206 BC 983205 BC 983204 BC 983203 BC 983202 BC 983201 BC

983200 BC 983199 BC 983198 BC 983197 BC 983196 BC 983195 BC 983194 BC 983193 BC 983192 BC 983191 BC
983190 BC 983189 BC 983188 BC 983187 BC 983186 BC 983185 BC 983184 BC 983183 BC 983182 BC 983181 BC
983180 BC 983179 BC 983178 BC 983177 BC 983176 BC 983175 BC 983174 BC 983173 BC 983172 BC 983171 BC
983170 BC 983169 BC 983168 BC 983167 BC 983166 BC 983165 BC 983164 BC 983163 BC 983162 BC 983161 BC
983160 BC 983159 BC 983158 BC 983157 BC 983156 BC 983155 BC 983154 BC 983153 BC 983152 BC 983151 BC
983150 BC 983149 BC 983148 BC 983147 BC 983146 BC 983145 BC 983144 BC 983143 BC 983142 BC 983141 BC
983140 BC 983139 BC 983138 BC 983137 BC 983136 BC 983135 BC 983134 BC 983133 BC 983132 BC 983131 BC
983130 BC 983129 BC 983128 BC 983127 BC 983126 BC 983125 BC 983124 BC 983123 BC 983122 BC 983121 BC
983120 BC 983119 BC 983118 BC 983117 BC 983116 BC 983115 BC 983114 BC 983113 BC 983112 BC 983111 BC
983110 BC 983109 BC 983108 BC 983107 BC 983106 BC 983105 BC 983104 BC 983103 BC 983102 BC 983101 BC

983100 BC 983099 BC 983098 BC 983097 BC 983096 BC 983095 BC 983094 BC 983093 BC 983092 BC 983091 BC
983090 BC 983089 BC 983088 BC 983087 BC 983086 BC 983085 BC 983084 BC 983083 BC 983082 BC 983081 BC
983080 BC 983079 BC 983078 BC 983077 BC 983076 BC 983075 BC 983074 BC 983073 BC 983072 BC 983071 BC
983070 BC 983069 BC 983068 BC 983067 BC 983066 BC 983065 BC 983064 BC 983063 BC 983062 BC 983061 BC
983060 BC 983059 BC 983058 BC 983057 BC 983056 BC 983055 BC 983054 BC 983053 BC 983052 BC 983051 BC
983050 BC 983049 BC 983048 BC 983047 BC 983046 BC 983045 BC 983044 BC 983043 BC 983042 BC 983041 BC
983040 BC 983039 BC 983038 BC 983037 BC 983036 BC 983035 BC 983034 BC 983033 BC 983032 BC 983031 BC
983030 BC 983029 BC 983028 BC 983027 BC 983026 BC 983025 BC 983024 BC 983023 BC 983022 BC 983021 BC
983020 BC 983019 BC 983018 BC 983017 BC 983016 BC 983015 BC 983014 BC 983013 BC 983012 BC 983011 BC
983010 BC 983009 BC 983008 BC 983007 BC 983006 BC 983005 BC 983004 BC 983003 BC 983002 BC 983001 BC

— 31 —

```
983000 BC  982999 BC  982998 BC  982997 BC  982996 BC  982995 BC  982994 BC  982993 BC  982992 BC  982991 BC
982990 BC  982989 BC  982988 BC  982987 BC  982986 BC  982985 BC  982984 BC  982983 BC  982982 BC  982981 BC
982980 BC  982979 BC  982978 BC  982977 BC  982976 BC  982975 BC  982974 BC  982973 BC  982972 BC  982971 BC
982970 BC  982969 BC  982968 BC  982967 BC  982966 BC  982965 BC  982964 BC  982963 BC  982962 BC  982961 BC
982960 BC  982959 BC  982958 BC  982957 BC  982956 BC  982955 BC  982954 BC  982953 BC  982952 BC  982951 BC
982950 BC  982949 BC  982948 BC  982947 BC  982946 BC  982945 BC  982944 BC  982943 BC  982942 BC  982941 BC
982940 BC  982939 BC  982938 BC  982937 BC  982936 BC  982935 BC  982934 BC  982933 BC  982932 BC  982931 BC
982930 BC  982929 BC  982928 BC  982927 BC  982926 BC  982925 BC  982924 BC  982923 BC  982922 BC  982921 BC
982920 BC  982919 BC  982918 BC  982917 BC  982916 BC  982915 BC  982914 BC  982913 BC  982912 BC  982911 BC
982910 BC  982909 BC  982908 BC  982907 BC  982906 BC  982905 BC  982904 BC  982903 BC  982902 BC  982901 BC

982900 BC  982899 BC  982898 BC  982897 BC  982896 BC  982895 BC  982894 BC  982893 BC  982892 BC  982891 BC
982890 BC  982889 BC  982888 BC  982887 BC  982886 BC  982885 BC  982884 BC  982883 BC  982882 BC  982881 BC
982880 BC  982879 BC  982878 BC  982877 BC  982876 BC  982875 BC  982874 BC  982873 BC  982872 BC  982871 BC
982870 BC  982869 BC  982868 BC  982867 BC  982866 BC  982865 BC  982864 BC  982863 BC  982862 BC  982861 BC
982860 BC  982859 BC  982858 BC  982857 BC  982856 BC  982855 BC  982854 BC  982853 BC  982852 BC  982851 BC
982850 BC  982849 BC  982848 BC  982847 BC  982846 BC  982845 BC  982844 BC  982843 BC  982842 BC  982841 BC
982840 BC  982839 BC  982838 BC  982837 BC  982836 BC  982835 BC  982834 BC  982833 BC  982832 BC  982831 BC
982830 BC  982829 BC  982828 BC  982827 BC  982826 BC  982825 BC  982824 BC  982823 BC  982822 BC  982821 BC
982820 BC  982819 BC  982818 BC  982817 BC  982816 BC  982815 BC  982814 BC  982813 BC  982812 BC  982811 BC
982810 BC  982809 BC  982808 BC  982807 BC  982806 BC  982805 BC  982804 BC  982803 BC  982802 BC  982801 BC

982800 BC  982799 BC  982798 BC  982797 BC  982796 BC  982795 BC  982794 BC  982793 BC  982792 BC  982791 BC
982790 BC  982789 BC  982788 BC  982787 BC  982786 BC  982785 BC  982784 BC  982783 BC  982782 BC  982781 BC
982780 BC  982779 BC  982778 BC  982777 BC  982776 BC  982775 BC  982774 BC  982773 BC  982772 BC  982771 BC
982770 BC  982769 BC  982768 BC  982767 BC  982766 BC  982765 BC  982764 BC  982763 BC  982762 BC  982761 BC
982760 BC  982759 BC  982758 BC  982757 BC  982756 BC  982755 BC  982754 BC  982753 BC  982752 BC  982751 BC
982750 BC  982749 BC  982748 BC  982747 BC  982746 BC  982745 BC  982744 BC  982743 BC  982742 BC  982741 BC
982740 BC  982739 BC  982738 BC  982737 BC  982736 BC  982735 BC  982734 BC  982733 BC  982732 BC  982731 BC
982730 BC  982729 BC  982728 BC  982727 BC  982726 BC  982725 BC  982724 BC  982723 BC  982722 BC  982721 BC
982720 BC  982719 BC  982718 BC  982717 BC  982716 BC  982715 BC  982714 BC  982713 BC  982712 BC  982711 BC
982710 BC  982709 BC  982708 BC  982707 BC  982706 BC  982705 BC  982704 BC  982703 BC  982702 BC  982701 BC

982700 BC  982699 BC  982698 BC  982697 BC  982696 BC  982695 BC  982694 BC  982693 BC  982692 BC  982691 BC
982690 BC  982689 BC  982688 BC  982687 BC  982686 BC  982685 BC  982684 BC  982683 BC  982682 BC  982681 BC
982680 BC  982679 BC  982678 BC  982677 BC  982676 BC  982675 BC  982674 BC  982673 BC  982672 BC  982671 BC
982670 BC  982669 BC  982668 BC  982667 BC  982666 BC  982665 BC  982664 BC  982663 BC  982662 BC  982661 BC
982660 BC  982659 BC  982658 BC  982657 BC  982656 BC  982655 BC  982654 BC  982653 BC  982652 BC  982651 BC
982650 BC  982649 BC  982648 BC  982647 BC  982646 BC  982645 BC  982644 BC  982643 BC  982642 BC  982641 BC
982640 BC  982639 BC  982638 BC  982637 BC  982636 BC  982635 BC  982634 BC  982633 BC  982632 BC  982631 BC
982630 BC  982629 BC  982628 BC  982627 BC  982626 BC  982625 BC  982624 BC  982623 BC  982622 BC  982621 BC
982620 BC  982619 BC  982618 BC  982617 BC  982616 BC  982615 BC  982614 BC  982613 BC  982612 BC  982611 BC
982610 BC  982609 BC  982608 BC  982607 BC  982606 BC  982605 BC  982604 BC  982603 BC  982602 BC  982601 BC

982600 BC  982599 BC  982598 BC  982597 BC  982596 BC  982595 BC  982594 BC  982593 BC  982592 BC  982591 BC
982590 BC  982589 BC  982588 BC  982587 BC  982586 BC  982585 BC  982584 BC  982583 BC  982582 BC  982581 BC
982580 BC  982579 BC  982578 BC  982577 BC  982576 BC  982575 BC  982574 BC  982573 BC  982572 BC  982571 BC
982570 BC  982569 BC  982568 BC  982567 BC  982566 BC  982565 BC  982564 BC  982563 BC  982562 BC  982561 BC
982560 BC  982559 BC  982558 BC  982557 BC  982556 BC  982555 BC  982554 BC  982553 BC  982552 BC  982551 BC
982550 BC  982549 BC  982548 BC  982547 BC  982546 BC  982545 BC  982544 BC  982543 BC  982542 BC  982541 BC
982540 BC  982539 BC  982538 BC  982537 BC  982536 BC  982535 BC  982534 BC  982533 BC  982532 BC  982531 BC
982530 BC  982529 BC  982528 BC  982527 BC  982526 BC  982525 BC  982524 BC  982523 BC  982522 BC  982521 BC
982520 BC  982519 BC  982518 BC  982517 BC  982516 BC  982515 BC  982514 BC  982513 BC  982512 BC  982511 BC
982510 BC  982509 BC  982508 BC  982507 BC  982506 BC  982505 BC  982504 BC  982503 BC  982502 BC  982501 BC
```

— 32 —

ONE MILLION YEARS

I

ON KAWARA

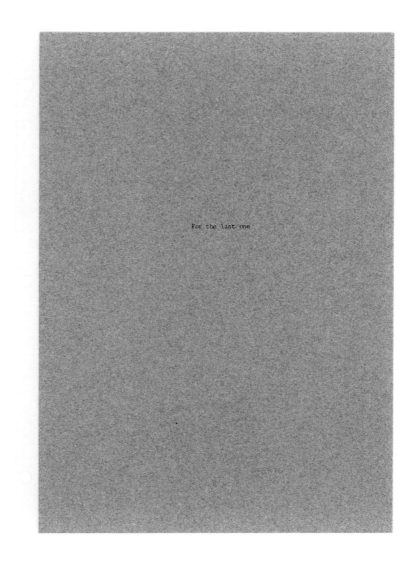

For the last one

1981 AD	1982 AD	1983 AD	1984 AD	1985 AD	1986 AD	1987 AD	1988 AD	1989 AD	1990 AD
1991 AD	1992 AD	1993 AD	1994 AD	1995 AD	1996 AD	1997 AD	1998 AD	1999 AD	2000 AD

— 1 —

2001 AD	2002 AD	2003 AD	2004 AD	2005 AD	2006 AD	2007 AD	2008 AD	2009 AD	2010 AD
2011 AD	2012 AD	2013 AD	2014 AD	2015 AD	2016 AD	2017 AD	2018 AD	2019 AD	2020 AD
2021 AD	2022 AD	2023 AD	2024 AD	2025 AD	2026 AD	2027 AD	2028 AD	2029 AD	2030 AD
2031 AD	2032 AD	2033 AD	2034 AD	2035 AD	2036 AD	2037 AD	2038 AD	2039 AD	2040 AD
2041 AD	2042 AD	2043 AD	2044 AD	2045 AD	2046 AD	2047 AD	2048 AD	2049 AD	2050 AD
2051 AD	2052 AD	2053 AD	2054 AD	2055 AD	2056 AD	2057 AD	2058 AD	2059 AD	2060 AD
2061 AD	2062 AD	2063 AD	2064 AD	2065 AD	2066 AD	2067 AD	2068 AD	2069 AD	2070 AD
2071 AD	2072 AD	2073 AD	2074 AD	2075 AD	2076 AD	2077 AD	2078 AD	2079 AD	2080 AD
2081 AD	2082 AD	2083 AD	2084 AD	2085 AD	2086 AD	2087 AD	2088 AD	2089 AD	2090 AD
2091 AD	2092 AD	2093 AD	2094 AD	2095 AD	2096 AD	2097 AD	2098 AD	2099 AD	2100 AD
2101 AD	2102 AD	2103 AD	2104 AD	2105 AD	2106 AD	2107 AD	2108 AD	2109 AD	2110 AD
2111 AD	2112 AD	2113 AD	2114 AD	2115 AD	2116 AD	2117 AD	2118 AD	2119 AD	2120 AD
2121 AD	2122 AD	2123 AD	2124 AD	2125 AD	2126 AD	2127 AD	2128 AD	2129 AD	2130 AD
2131 AD	2132 AD	2133 AD	2134 AD	2135 AD	2136 AD	2137 AD	2138 AD	2139 AD	2140 AD
2141 AD	2142 AD	2143 AD	2144 AD	2145 AD	2146 AD	2147 AD	2148 AD	2149 AD	2150 AD
2151 AD	2152 AD	2153 AD	2154 AD	2155 AD	2156 AD	2157 AD	2158 AD	2159 AD	2160 AD
2161 AD	2162 AD	2163 AD	2164 AD	2165 AD	2166 AD	2167 AD	2168 AD	2169 AD	2170 AD
2171 AD	2172 AD	2173 AD	2174 AD	2175 AD	2176 AD	2177 AD	2178 AD	2179 AD	2180 AD
2181 AD	2182 AD	2183 AD	2184 AD	2185 AD	2186 AD	2187 AD	2188 AD	2189 AD	2190 AD
2191 AD	2192 AD	2193 AD	2194 AD	2195 AD	2196 AD	2197 AD	2198 AD	2199 AD	2200 AD
2201 AD	2202 AD	2203 AD	2204 AD	2205 AD	2206 AD	2207 AD	2208 AD	2209 AD	2210 AD
2211 AD	2212 AD	2213 AD	2214 AD	2215 AD	2216 AD	2217 AD	2218 AD	2219 AD	2220 AD
2221 AD	2222 AD	2223 AD	2224 AD	2225 AD	2226 AD	2227 AD	2228 AD	2229 AD	2230 AD
2231 AD	2232 AD	2233 AD	2234 AD	2235 AD	2236 AD	2237 AD	2238 AD	2239 AD	2240 AD
2241 AD	2242 AD	2243 AD	2244 AD	2245 AD	2246 AD	2247 AD	2248 AD	2249 AD	2250 AD
2251 AD	2252 AD	2253 AD	2254 AD	2255 AD	2256 AD	2257 AD	2258 AD	2259 AD	2260 AD
2261 AD	2262 AD	2263 AD	2264 AD	2265 AD	2266 AD	2267 AD	2268 AD	2269 AD	2270 AD
2271 AD	2272 AD	2273 AD	2274 AD	2275 AD	2276 AD	2277 AD	2278 AD	2279 AD	2280 AD
2281 AD	2282 AD	2283 AD	2284 AD	2285 AD	2286 AD	2287 AD	2288 AD	2289 AD	2290 AD
2291 AD	2292 AD	2293 AD	2294 AD	2295 AD	2296 AD	2297 AD	2298 AD	2299 AD	2300 AD
2301 AD	2302 AD	2303 AD	2304 AD	2305 AD	2306 AD	2307 AD	2308 AD	2309 AD	2310 AD
2311 AD	2312 AD	2313 AD	2314 AD	2315 AD	2316 AD	2317 AD	2318 AD	2319 AD	2320 AD
2321 AD	2322 AD	2323 AD	2324 AD	2325 AD	2326 AD	2327 AD	2328 AD	2329 AD	2330 AD
2331 AD	2332 AD	2333 AD	2334 AD	2335 AD	2336 AD	2337 AD	2338 AD	2339 AD	2340 AD
2341 AD	2342 AD	2343 AD	2344 AD	2345 AD	2346 AD	2347 AD	2348 AD	2349 AD	2350 AD
2351 AD	2352 AD	2353 AD	2354 AD	2355 AD	2356 AD	2357 AD	2358 AD	2359 AD	2360 AD
2361 AD	2362 AD	2363 AD	2364 AD	2365 AD	2366 AD	2367 AD	2368 AD	2369 AD	2370 AD
2371 AD	2372 AD	2373 AD	2374 AD	2375 AD	2376 AD	2377 AD	2378 AD	2379 AD	2380 AD
2381 AD	2382 AD	2383 AD	2384 AD	2385 AD	2386 AD	2387 AD	2388 AD	2389 AD	2390 AD
2391 AD	2392 AD	2393 AD	2394 AD	2395 AD	2396 AD	2397 AD	2398 AD	2399 AD	2400 AD
2401 AD	2402 AD	2403 AD	2404 AD	2405 AD	2406 AD	2407 AD	2408 AD	2409 AD	2410 AD
2411 AD	2412 AD	2413 AD	2414 AD	2415 AD	2416 AD	2417 AD	2418 AD	2419 AD	2420 AD
2421 AD	2422 AD	2423 AD	2424 AD	2425 AD	2426 AD	2427 AD	2428 AD	2429 AD	2430 AD
2431 AD	2432 AD	2433 AD	2434 AD	2435 AD	2436 AD	2437 AD	2438 AD	2439 AD	2440 AD
2441 AD	2442 AD	2443 AD	2444 AD	2445 AD	2446 AD	2447 AD	2448 AD	2449 AD	2450 AD
2451 AD	2452 AD	2453 AD	2454 AD	2455 AD	2456 AD	2457 AD	2458 AD	2459 AD	2460 AD
2461 AD	2462 AD	2463 AD	2464 AD	2465 AD	2466 AD	2467 AD	2468 AD	2469 AD	2470 AD
2471 AD	2472 AD	2473 AD	2474 AD	2475 AD	2476 AD	2477 AD	2478 AD	2479 AD	2480 AD
2481 AD	2482 AD	2483 AD	2484 AD	2485 AD	2486 AD	2487 AD	2488 AD	2489 AD	2490 AD
2491 AD	2492 AD	2493 AD	2494 AD	2495 AD	2496 AD	2497 AD	2498 AD	2499 AD	2500 AD

2501 AD	2502 AD	2503 AD	2504 AD	2505 AD	2506 AD	2507 AD	2508 AD	2509 AD	2510 AD
2511 AD	2512 AD	2513 AD	2514 AD	2515 AD	2516 AD	2517 AD	2518 AD	2519 AD	2520 AD
2521 AD	2522 AD	2523 AD	2524 AD	2525 AD	2526 AD	2527 AD	2528 AD	2529 AD	2530 AD
2531 AD	2532 AD	2533 AD	2534 AD	2535 AD	2536 AD	2537 AD	2538 AD	2539 AD	2540 AD
2541 AD	2542 AD	2543 AD	2544 AD	2545 AD	2546 AD	2547 AD	2548 AD	2549 AD	2550 AD
2551 AD	2552 AD	2553 AD	2554 AD	2555 AD	2556 AD	2557 AD	2558 AD	2559 AD	2560 AD
2561 AD	2562 AD	2563 AD	2564 AD	2565 AD	2566 AD	2567 AD	2568 AD	2569 AD	2570 AD
2571 AD	2572 AD	2573 AD	2574 AD	2575 AD	2576 AD	2577 AD	2578 AD	2579 AD	2580 AD
2581 AD	2582 AD	2583 AD	2584 AD	2585 AD	2586 AD	2587 AD	2588 AD	2589 AD	2590 AD
2591 AD	2592 AD	2593 AD	2594 AD	2595 AD	2596 AD	2597 AD	2598 AD	2599 AD	2600 AD

2601 AD	2602 AD	2603 AD	2604 AD	2605 AD	2606 AD	2607 AD	2608 AD	2609 AD	2610 AD
2611 AD	2612 AD	2613 AD	2614 AD	2615 AD	2616 AD	2617 AD	2618 AD	2619 AD	2620 AD
2621 AD	2622 AD	2623 AD	2624 AD	2625 AD	2626 AD	2627 AD	2628 AD	2629 AD	2630 AD
2631 AD	2632 AD	2633 AD	2634 AD	2635 AD	2636 AD	2637 AD	2638 AD	2639 AD	2640 AD
2641 AD	2642 AD	2643 AD	2644 AD	2645 AD	2646 AD	2647 AD	2648 AD	2649 AD	2650 AD
2651 AD	2652 AD	2653 AD	2654 AD	2655 AD	2656 AD	2657 AD	2658 AD	2659 AD	2660 AD
2661 AD	2662 AD	2663 AD	2664 AD	2665 AD	2666 AD	2667 AD	2668 AD	2669 AD	2670 AD
2671 AD	2672 AD	2673 AD	2674 AD	2675 AD	2676 AD	2677 AD	2678 AD	2679 AD	2680 AD
2681 AD	2682 AD	2683 AD	2684 AD	2685 AD	2686 AD	2687 AD	2688 AD	2689 AD	2690 AD
2691 AD	2692 AD	2693 AD	2694 AD	2695 AD	2696 AD	2697 AD	2698 AD	2699 AD	2700 AD

2701 AD	2702 AD	2703 AD	2704 AD	2705 AD	2706 AD	2707 AD	2708 AD	2709 AD	2710 AD
2711 AD	2712 AD	2713 AD	2714 AD	2715 AD	2716 AD	2717 AD	2718 AD	2719 AD	2720 AD
2721 AD	2722 AD	2723 AD	2724 AD	2725 AD	2726 AD	2727 AD	2728 AD	2729 AD	2730 AD
2731 AD	2732 AD	2733 AD	2734 AD	2735 AD	2736 AD	2737 AD	2738 AD	2739 AD	2740 AD
2741 AD	2742 AD	2743 AD	2744 AD	2745 AD	2746 AD	2747 AD	2748 AD	2749 AD	2750 AD
2751 AD	2752 AD	2753 AD	2754 AD	2755 AD	2756 AD	2757 AD	2758 AD	2759 AD	2760 AD
2761 AD	2762 AD	2763 AD	2764 AD	2765 AD	2766 AD	2767 AD	2768 AD	2769 AD	2770 AD
2771 AD	2772 AD	2773 AD	2774 AD	2775 AD	2776 AD	2777 AD	2778 AD	2779 AD	2780 AD
2781 AD	2782 AD	2783 AD	2784 AD	2785 AD	2786 AD	2787 AD	2788 AD	2789 AD	2790 AD
2791 AD	2792 AD	2793 AD	2794 AD	2795 AD	2796 AD	2797 AD	2798 AD	2799 AD	2800 AD

2801 AD	2802 AD	2803 AD	2804 AD	2805 AD	2806 AD	2807 AD	2808 AD	2809 AD	2810 AD
2811 AD	2812 AD	2813 AD	2814 AD	2815 AD	2816 AD	2817 AD	2818 AD	2819 AD	2820 AD
2821 AD	2822 AD	2823 AD	2824 AD	2825 AD	2826 AD	2827 AD	2828 AD	2829 AD	2830 AD
2831 AD	2832 AD	2833 AD	2834 AD	2835 AD	2836 AD	2837 AD	2838 AD	2839 AD	2840 AD
2841 AD	2842 AD	2843 AD	2844 AD	2845 AD	2846 AD	2847 AD	2848 AD	2849 AD	2850 AD
2851 AD	2852 AD	2853 AD	2854 AD	2855 AD	2856 AD	2857 AD	2858 AD	2859 AD	2860 AD
2861 AD	2862 AD	2863 AD	2864 AD	2865 AD	2866 AD	2867 AD	2868 AD	2869 AD	2870 AD
2871 AD	2872 AD	2873 AD	2874 AD	2875 AD	2876 AD	2877 AD	2878 AD	2879 AD	2880 AD
2881 AD	2882 AD	2883 AD	2884 AD	2885 AD	2886 AD	2887 AD	2888 AD	2889 AD	2890 AD
2891 AD	2892 AD	2893 AD	2894 AD	2895 AD	2896 AD	2897 AD	2898 AD	2899 AD	2900 AD

2901 AD	2902 AD	2903 AD	2904 AD	2905 AD	2906 AD	2907 AD	2908 AD	2909 AD	2910 AD
2911 AD	2912 AD	2913 AD	2914 AD	2915 AD	2916 AD	2917 AD	2918 AD	2919 AD	2920 AD
2921 AD	2922 AD	2923 AD	2924 AD	2925 AD	2926 AD	2927 AD	2928 AD	2929 AD	2930 AD
2931 AD	2932 AD	2933 AD	2934 AD	2935 AD	2936 AD	2937 AD	2938 AD	2939 AD	2940 AD
2941 AD	2942 AD	2943 AD	2944 AD	2945 AD	2946 AD	2947 AD	2948 AD	2949 AD	2950 AD
2951 AD	2952 AD	2953 AD	2954 AD	2955 AD	2956 AD	2957 AD	2958 AD	2959 AD	2960 AD
2961 AD	2962 AD	2963 AD	2964 AD	2965 AD	2966 AD	2967 AD	2968 AD	2969 AD	2970 AD
2971 AD	2972 AD	2973 AD	2974 AD	2975 AD	2976 AD	2977 AD	2978 AD	2979 AD	2980 AD
2981 AD	2982 AD	2983 AD	2984 AD	2985 AD	2986 AD	2987 AD	2988 AD	2989 AD	2990 AD
2991 AD	2992 AD	2993 AD	2994 AD	2995 AD	2996 AD	2997 AD	2998 AD	2999 AD	3000 AD

— 3 —

3001 AD	3002 AD	3003 AD	3004 AD	3005 AD	3006 AD	3007 AD	3008 AD	3009 AD	3010 AD
3011 AD	3012 AD	3013 AD	3014 AD	3015 AD	3016 AD	3017 AD	3018 AD	3019 AD	3020 AD
3021 AD	3022 AD	3023 AD	3024 AD	3025 AD	3026 AD	3027 AD	3028 AD	3029 AD	3030 AD
3031 AD	3032 AD	3033 AD	3034 AD	3035 AD	3036 AD	3037 AD	3038 AD	3039 AD	3040 AD
3041 AD	3042 AD	3043 AD	3044 AD	3045 AD	3046 AD	3047 AD	3048 AD	3049 AD	3050 AD
3051 AD	3052 AD	3053 AD	3054 AD	3055 AD	3056 AD	3057 AD	3058 AD	3059 AD	3060 AD
3061 AD	3062 AD	3063 AD	3064 AD	3065 AD	3066 AD	3067 AD	3068 AD	3069 AD	3070 AD
3071 AD	3072 AD	3073 AD	3074 AD	3075 AD	3076 AD	3077 AD	3078 AD	3079 AD	3080 AD
3081 AD	3082 AD	3083 AD	3084 AD	3085 AD	3086 AD	3087 AD	3088 AD	3089 AD	3090 AD
3091 AD	3092 AD	3093 AD	3094 AD	3095 AD	3096 AD	3097 AD	3098 AD	3099 AD	3100 AD
3101 AD	3102 AD	3103 AD	3104 AD	3105 AD	3106 AD	3107 AD	3108 AD	3109 AD	3110 AD
3111 AD	3112 AD	3113 AD	3114 AD	3115 AD	3116 AD	3117 AD	3118 AD	3119 AD	3120 AD
3121 AD	3122 AD	3123 AD	3124 AD	3125 AD	3126 AD	3127 AD	3128 AD	3129 AD	3130 AD
3131 AD	3132 AD	3133 AD	3134 AD	3135 AD	3136 AD	3137 AD	3138 AD	3139 AD	3140 AD
3141 AD	3142 AD	3143 AD	3144 AD	3145 AD	3146 AD	3147 AD	3148 AD	3149 AD	3150 AD
3151 AD	3152 AD	3153 AD	3154 AD	3155 AD	3156 AD	3157 AD	3158 AD	3159 AD	3160 AD
3161 AD	3162 AD	3163 AD	3164 AD	3165 AD	3166 AD	3167 AD	3168 AD	3169 AD	3170 AD
3171 AD	3172 AD	3173 AD	3174 AD	3175 AD	3176 AD	3177 AD	3178 AD	3179 AD	3180 AD
3181 AD	3182 AD	3183 AD	3184 AD	3185 AD	3186 AD	3187 AD	3188 AD	3189 AD	3190 AD
3191 AD	3192 AD	3193 AD	3194 AD	3195 AD	3196 AD	3197 AD	3198 AD	3199 AD	3200 AD
3201 AD	3202 AD	3203 AD	3204 AD	3205 AD	3206 AD	3207 AD	3208 AD	3209 AD	3210 AD
3211 AD	3212 AD	3213 AD	3214 AD	3215 AD	3216 AD	3217 AD	3218 AD	3219 AD	3220 AD
3221 AD	3222 AD	3223 AD	3224 AD	3225 AD	3226 AD	3227 AD	3228 AD	3229 AD	3230 AD
3231 AD	3232 AD	3233 AD	3234 AD	3235 AD	3236 AD	3237 AD	3238 AD	3239 AD	3240 AD
3241 AD	3242 AD	3243 AD	3244 AD	3245 AD	3246 AD	3247 AD	3248 AD	3249 AD	3250 AD
3251 AD	3252 AD	3253 AD	3254 AD	3255 AD	3256 AD	3257 AD	3258 AD	3259 AD	3260 AD
3261 AD	3262 AD	3263 AD	3264 AD	3265 AD	3266 AD	3267 AD	3268 AD	3269 AD	3270 AD
3271 AD	3272 AD	3273 AD	3274 AD	3275 AD	3276 AD	3277 AD	3278 AD	3279 AD	3280 AD
3281 AD	3282 AD	3283 AD	3284 AD	3285 AD	3286 AD	3287 AD	3288 AD	3289 AD	3290 AD
3291 AD	3292 AD	3293 AD	3294 AD	3295 AD	3296 AD	3297 AD	3298 AD	3299 AD	3300 AD
3301 AD	3302 AD	3303 AD	3304 AD	3305 AD	3306 AD	3307 AD	3308 AD	3309 AD	3310 AD
3311 AD	3312 AD	3313 AD	3314 AD	3315 AD	3316 AD	3317 AD	3318 AD	3319 AD	3320 AD
3321 AD	3322 AD	3323 AD	3324 AD	3325 AD	3326 AD	3327 AD	3328 AD	3329 AD	3330 AD
3331 AD	3332 AD	3333 AD	3334 AD	3335 AD	3336 AD	3337 AD	3338 AD	3339 AD	3340 AD
3341 AD	3342 AD	3343 AD	3344 AD	3345 AD	3346 AD	3347 AD	3348 AD	3349 AD	3350 AD
3351 AD	3352 AD	3353 AD	3354 AD	3355 AD	3356 AD	3357 AD	3358 AD	3359 AD	3360 AD
3361 AD	3362 AD	3363 AD	3364 AD	3365 AD	3366 AD	3367 AD	3368 AD	3369 AD	3370 AD
3371 AD	3372 AD	3373 AD	3374 AD	3375 AD	3376 AD	3377 AD	3378 AD	3379 AD	3380 AD
3381 AD	3382 AD	3383 AD	3384 AD	3385 AD	3386 AD	3387 AD	3388 AD	3389 AD	3390 AD
3391 AD	3392 AD	3393 AD	3394 AD	3395 AD	3396 AD	3397 AD	3398 AD	3399 AD	3400 AD
3401 AD	3402 AD	3403 AD	3404 AD	3405 AD	3406 AD	3407 AD	3408 AD	3409 AD	3410 AD
3411 AD	3412 AD	3413 AD	3414 AD	3415 AD	3416 AD	3417 AD	3418 AD	3419 AD	3420 AD
3421 AD	3422 AD	3423 AD	3424 AD	3425 AD	3426 AD	3427 AD	3428 AD	3429 AD	3430 AD
3431 AD	3432 AD	3433 AD	3434 AD	3435 AD	3436 AD	3437 AD	3438 AD	3439 AD	3440 AD
3441 AD	3442 AD	3443 AD	3444 AD	3445 AD	3446 AD	3447 AD	3448 AD	3449 AD	3450 AD
3451 AD	3452 AD	3453 AD	3454 AD	3455 AD	3456 AD	3457 AD	3458 AD	3459 AD	3460 AD
3461 AD	3462 AD	3463 AD	3464 AD	3465 AD	3466 AD	3467 AD	3468 AD	3469 AD	3470 AD
3471 AD	3472 AD	3473 AD	3474 AD	3475 AD	3476 AD	3477 AD	3478 AD	3479 AD	3480 AD
3481 AD	3482 AD	3483 AD	3484 AD	3485 AD	3486 AD	3487 AD	3488 AD	3489 AD	3490 AD
3491 AD	3492 AD	3493 AD	3494 AD	3495 AD	3496 AD	3497 AD	3498 AD	3499 AD	3500 AD

3501 AD	3502 AD	3503 AD	3504 AD	3505 AD	3506 AD	3507 AD	3508 AD	3509 AD	3510 AD
3511 AD	3512 AD	3513 AD	3514 AD	3515 AD	3516 AD	3517 AD	3518 AD	3519 AD	3520 AD
3521 AD	3522 AD	3523 AD	3524 AD	3525 AD	3526 AD	3527 AD	3528 AD	3529 AD	3530 AD
3531 AD	3532 AD	3533 AD	3534 AD	3535 AD	3536 AD	3537 AD	3538 AD	3539 AD	3540 AD
3541 AD	3542 AD	3543 AD	3544 AD	3545 AD	3546 AD	3547 AD	3548 AD	3549 AD	3550 AD
3551 AD	3552 AD	3553 AD	3554 AD	3555 AD	3556 AD	3557 AD	3558 AD	3559 AD	3560 AD
3561 AD	3562 AD	3563 AD	3564 AD	3565 AD	3566 AD	3567 AD	3568 AD	3569 AD	3570 AD
3571 AD	3572 AD	3573 AD	3574 AD	3575 AD	3576 AD	3577 AD	3578 AD	3579 AD	3580 AD
3581 AD	3582 AD	3583 AD	3584 AD	3585 AD	3586 AD	3587 AD	3588 AD	3589 AD	3590 AD
3591 AD	3592 AD	3593 AD	3594 AD	3595 AD	3596 AD	3597 AD	3598 AD	3599 AD	3600 AD
3601 AD	3602 AD	3603 AD	3604 AD	3605 AD	3606 AD	3607 AD	3608 AD	3609 AD	3610 AD
3611 AD	3612 AD	3613 AD	3614 AD	3615 AD	3616 AD	3617 AD	3618 AD	3619 AD	3620 AD
3621 AD	3622 AD	3623 AD	3624 AD	3625 AD	3626 AD	3627 AD	3628 AD	3629 AD	3630 AD
3631 AD	3632 AD	3633 AD	3634 AD	3635 AD	3636 AD	3637 AD	3638 AD	3639 AD	3640 AD
3641 AD	3642 AD	3643 AD	3644 AD	3645 AD	3646 AD	3647 AD	3648 AD	3649 AD	3650 AD
3651 AD	3652 AD	3653 AD	3654 AD	3655 AD	3656 AD	3657 AD	3658 AD	3659 AD	3660 AD
3661 AD	3662 AD	3663 AD	3664 AD	3665 AD	3666 AD	3667 AD	3668 AD	3669 AD	3670 AD
3671 AD	3672 AD	3673 AD	3674 AD	3675 AD	3676 AD	3677 AD	3678 AD	3679 AD	3680 AD
3681 AD	3682 AD	3683 AD	3684 AD	3685 AD	3686 AD	3687 AD	3688 AD	3689 AD	3690 AD
3691 AD	3692 AD	3693 AD	3694 AD	3695 AD	3696 AD	3697 AD	3698 AD	3699 AD	3700 AD
3701 AD	3702 AD	3703 AD	3704 AD	3705 AD	3706 AD	3707 AD	3708 AD	3709 AD	3710 AD
3711 AD	3712 AD	3713 AD	3714 AD	3715 AD	3716 AD	3717 AD	3718 AD	3719 AD	3720 AD
3721 AD	3722 AD	3723 AD	3724 AD	3725 AD	3726 AD	3727 AD	3728 AD	3729 AD	3730 AD
3731 AD	3732 AD	3733 AD	3734 AD	3735 AD	3736 AD	3737 AD	3738 AD	3739 AD	3740 AD
3741 AD	3742 AD	3743 AD	3744 AD	3745 AD	3746 AD	3747 AD	3748 AD	3749 AD	3750 AD
3751 AD	3752 AD	3753 AD	3754 AD	3755 AD	3756 AD	3757 AD	3758 AD	3759 AD	3760 AD
3761 AD	3762 AD	3763 AD	3764 AD	3765 AD	3766 AD	3767 AD	3768 AD	3769 AD	3770 AD
3771 AD	3772 AD	3773 AD	3774 AD	3775 AD	3776 AD	3777 AD	3778 AD	3779 AD	3780 AD
3781 AD	3782 AD	3783 AD	3784 AD	3785 AD	3786 AD	3787 AD	3788 AD	3789 AD	3790 AD
3791 AD	3792 AD	3793 AD	3794 AD	3795 AD	3796 AD	3797 AD	3798 AD	3799 AD	3800 AD
3801 AD	3802 AD	3803 AD	3804 AD	3805 AD	3806 AD	3807 AD	3808 AD	3809 AD	3810 AD
3811 AD	3812 AD	3813 AD	3814 AD	3815 AD	3816 AD	3817 AD	3818 AD	3819 AD	3820 AD
3821 AD	3822 AD	3823 AD	3824 AD	3825 AD	3826 AD	3827 AD	3828 AD	3829 AD	3830 AD
3831 AD	3832 AD	3833 AD	3834 AD	3835 AD	3836 AD	3837 AD	3838 AD	3839 AD	3840 AD
3841 AD	3842 AD	3843 AD	3844 AD	3845 AD	3846 AD	3847 AD	3848 AD	3849 AD	3850 AD
3851 AD	3852 AD	3853 AD	3854 AD	3855 AD	3856 AD	3857 AD	3858 AD	3859 AD	3860 AD
3861 AD	3862 AD	3863 AD	3864 AD	3865 AD	3866 AD	3867 AD	3868 AD	3869 AD	3870 AD
3871 AD	3872 AD	3873 AD	3874 AD	3875 AD	3876 AD	3877 AD	3878 AD	3879 AD	3880 AD
3881 AD	3882 AD	3883 AD	3884 AD	3885 AD	3886 AD	3887 AD	3888 AD	3889 AD	3890 AD
3891 AD	3892 AD	3893 AD	3894 AD	3895 AD	3896 AD	3897 AD	3898 AD	3899 AD	3900 AD
3901 AD	3902 AD	3903 AD	3904 AD	3905 AD	3906 AD	3907 AD	3908 AD	3909 AD	3910 AD
3911 AD	3912 AD	3913 AD	3914 AD	3915 AD	3916 AD	3917 AD	3918 AD	3919 AD	3920 AD
3921 AD	3922 AD	3923 AD	3924 AD	3925 AD	3926 AD	3927 AD	3928 AD	3929 AD	3930 AD
3931 AD	3932 AD	3933 AD	3934 AD	3935 AD	3936 AD	3937 AD	3938 AD	3939 AD	3940 AD
3941 AD	3942 AD	3943 AD	3944 AD	3945 AD	3946 AD	3947 AD	3948 AD	3949 AD	3950 AD
3951 AD	3952 AD	3953 AD	3954 AD	3955 AD	3956 AD	3957 AD	3958 AD	3959 AD	3960 AD
3961 AD	3962 AD	3963 AD	3964 AD	3965 AD	3966 AD	3967 AD	3968 AD	3969 AD	3970 AD
3971 AD	3972 AD	3973 AD	3974 AD	3975 AD	3976 AD	3977 AD	3978 AD	3979 AD	3980 AD
3981 AD	3982 AD	3983 AD	3984 AD	3985 AD	3986 AD	3987 AD	3988 AD	3989 AD	3990 AD
3991 AD	3992 AD	3993 AD	3994 AD	3995 AD	3996 AD	3997 AD	3998 AD	3999 AD	4000 AD

4001 AD	4002 AD	4003 AD	4004 AD	4005 AD	4006 AD	4007 AD	4008 AD	4009 AD	4010 AD
4011 AD	4012 AD	4013 AD	4014 AD	4015 AD	4016 AD	4017 AD	4018 AD	4019 AD	4020 AD
4021 AD	4022 AD	4023 AD	4024 AD	4025 AD	4026 AD	4027 AD	4028 AD	4029 AD	4030 AD
4031 AD	4032 AD	4033 AD	4034 AD	4035 AD	4036 AD	4037 AD	4038 AD	4039 AD	4040 AD
4041 AD	4042 AD	4043 AD	4044 AD	4045 AD	4046 AD	4047 AD	4048 AD	4049 AD	4050 AD
4051 AD	4052 AD	4053 AD	4054 AD	4055 AD	4056 AD	4057 AD	4058 AD	4059 AD	4060 AD
4061 AD	4062 AD	4063 AD	4064 AD	4065 AD	4066 AD	4067 AD	4068 AD	4069 AD	4070 AD
4071 AD	4072 AD	4073 AD	4074 AD	4075 AD	4076 AD	4077 AD	4078 AD	4079 AD	4080 AD
4081 AD	4082 AD	4083 AD	4084 AD	4085 AD	4086 AD	4087 AD	4088 AD	4089 AD	4090 AD
4091 AD	4092 AD	4093 AD	4094 AD	4095 AD	4096 AD	4097 AD	4098 AD	4099 AD	4100 AD
4101 AD	4102 AD	4103 AD	4104 AD	4105 AD	4106 AD	4107 AD	4108 AD	4109 AD	4110 AD
4111 AD	4112 AD	4113 AD	4114 AD	4115 AD	4116 AD	4117 AD	4118 AD	4119 AD	4120 AD
4121 AD	4122 AD	4123 AD	4124 AD	4125 AD	4126 AD	4127 AD	4128 AD	4129 AD	4130 AD
4131 AD	4132 AD	4133 AD	4134 AD	4135 AD	4136 AD	4137 AD	4138 AD	4139 AD	4140 AD
4141 AD	4142 AD	4143 AD	4144 AD	4145 AD	4146 AD	4147 AD	4148 AD	4149 AD	4150 AD
4151 AD	4152 AD	4153 AD	4154 AD	4155 AD	4156 AD	4157 AD	4158 AD	4159 AD	4160 AD
4161 AD	4162 AD	4163 AD	4164 AD	4165 AD	4166 AD	4167 AD	4168 AD	4169 AD	4170 AD
4171 AD	4172 AD	4173 AD	4174 AD	4175 AD	4176 AD	4177 AD	4178 AD	4179 AD	4180 AD
4181 AD	4182 AD	4183 AD	4184 AD	4185 AD	4186 AD	4187 AD	4188 AD	4189 AD	4190 AD
4191 AD	4192 AD	4193 AD	4194 AD	4195 AD	4196 AD	4197 AD	4198 AD	4199 AD	4200 AD
4201 AD	4202 AD	4203 AD	4204 AD	4205 AD	4206 AD	4207 AD	4208 AD	4209 AD	4210 AD
4211 AD	4212 AD	4213 AD	4214 AD	4215 AD	4216 AD	4217 AD	4218 AD	4219 AD	4220 AD
4221 AD	4222 AD	4223 AD	4224 AD	4225 AD	4226 AD	4227 AD	4228 AD	4229 AD	4230 AD
4231 AD	4232 AD	4233 AD	4234 AD	4235 AD	4236 AD	4237 AD	4238 AD	4239 AD	4240 AD
4241 AD	4242 AD	4243 AD	4244 AD	4245 AD	4246 AD	4247 AD	4248 AD	4249 AD	4250 AD
4251 AD	4252 AD	4253 AD	4254 AD	4255 AD	4256 AD	4257 AD	4258 AD	4259 AD	4260 AD
4261 AD	4262 AD	4263 AD	4264 AD	4265 AD	4266 AD	4267 AD	4268 AD	4269 AD	4270 AD
4271 AD	4272 AD	4273 AD	4274 AD	4275 AD	4276 AD	4277 AD	4278 AD	4279 AD	4280 AD
4281 AD	4282 AD	4283 AD	4284 AD	4285 AD	4286 AD	4287 AD	4288 AD	4289 AD	4290 AD
4291 AD	4292 AD	4293 AD	4294 AD	4295 AD	4296 AD	4297 AD	4298 AD	4299 AD	4300 AD
4301 AD	4302 AD	4303 AD	4304 AD	4305 AD	4306 AD	4307 AD	4308 AD	4309 AD	4310 AD
4311 AD	4312 AD	4313 AD	4314 AD	4315 AD	4316 AD	4317 AD	4318 AD	4319 AD	4320 AD
4321 AD	4322 AD	4323 AD	4324 AD	4325 AD	4326 AD	4327 AD	4328 AD	4329 AD	4330 AD
4331 AD	4332 AD	4333 AD	4334 AD	4335 AD	4336 AD	4337 AD	4338 AD	4339 AD	4340 AD
4341 AD	4342 AD	4343 AD	4344 AD	4345 AD	4346 AD	4347 AD	4348 AD	4349 AD	4350 AD
4351 AD	4352 AD	4353 AD	4354 AD	4355 AD	4356 AD	4357 AD	4358 AD	4359 AD	4360 AD
4361 AD	4362 AD	4363 AD	4364 AD	4365 AD	4366 AD	4367 AD	4368 AD	4369 AD	4370 AD
4371 AD	4372 AD	4373 AD	4374 AD	4375 AD	4376 AD	4377 AD	4378 AD	4379 AD	4380 AD
4381 AD	4382 AD	4383 AD	4384 AD	4385 AD	4386 AD	4387 AD	4388 AD	4389 AD	4390 AD
4391 AD	4392 AD	4393 AD	4394 AD	4395 AD	4396 AD	4397 AD	4398 AD	4399 AD	4400 AD
4401 AD	4402 AD	4403 AD	4404 AD	4405 AD	4406 AD	4407 AD	4408 AD	4409 AD	4410 AD
4411 AD	4412 AD	4413 AD	4414 AD	4415 AD	4416 AD	4417 AD	4418 AD	4419 AD	4420 AD
4421 AD	4422 AD	4423 AD	4424 AD	4425 AD	4426 AD	4427 AD	4428 AD	4429 AD	4430 AD
4431 AD	4432 AD	4433 AD	4434 AD	4435 AD	4436 AD	4437 AD	4438 AD	4439 AD	4440 AD
4441 AD	4442 AD	4443 AD	4444 AD	4445 AD	4446 AD	4447 AD	4448 AD	4449 AD	4450 AD
4451 AD	4452 AD	4453 AD	4454 AD	4455 AD	4456 AD	4457 AD	4458 AD	4459 AD	4460 AD
4461 AD	4462 AD	4463 AD	4464 AD	4465 AD	4466 AD	4467 AD	4468 AD	4469 AD	4470 AD
4471 AD	4472 AD	4473 AD	4474 AD	4475 AD	4476 AD	4477 AD	4478 AD	4479 AD	4480 AD
4481 AD	4482 AD	4483 AD	4484 AD	4485 AD	4486 AD	4487 AD	4488 AD	4489 AD	4490 AD
4491 AD	4492 AD	4493 AD	4494 AD	4495 AD	4496 AD	4497 AD	4498 AD	4499 AD	4500 AD

4501 AD	4502 AD	4503 AD	4504 AD	4505 AD	4506 AD	4507 AD	4508 AD	4509 AD	4510 AD
4511 AD	4512 AD	4513 AD	4514 AD	4515 AD	4516 AD	4517 AD	4518 AD	4519 AD	4520 AD
4521 AD	4522 AD	4523 AD	4524 AD	4525 AD	4526 AD	4527 AD	4528 AD	4529 AD	4530 AD
4531 AD	4532 AD	4533 AD	4534 AD	4535 AD	4536 AD	4537 AD	4538 AD	4539 AD	4540 AD
4541 AD	4542 AD	4543 AD	4544 AD	4545 AD	4546 AD	4547 AD	4548 AD	4549 AD	4550 AD
4551 AD	4552 AD	4553 AD	4554 AD	4555 AD	4556 AD	4557 AD	4558 AD	4559 AD	4560 AD
4561 AD	4562 AD	4563 AD	4564 AD	4565 AD	4566 AD	4567 AD	4568 AD	4569 AD	4570 AD
4571 AD	4572 AD	4573 AD	4574 AD	4575 AD	4576 AD	4577 AD	4578 AD	4579 AD	4580 AD
4581 AD	4582 AD	4583 AD	4584 AD	4585 AD	4586 AD	4587 AD	4588 AD	4589 AD	4590 AD
4591 AD	4592 AD	4593 AD	4594 AD	4595 AD	4596 AD	4597 AD	4598 AD	4599 AD	4600 AD
4601 AD	4602 AD	4603 AD	4604 AD	4605 AD	4606 AD	4607 AD	4608 AD	4609 AD	4610 AD
4611 AD	4612 AD	4613 AD	4614 AD	4615 AD	4616 AD	4617 AD	4618 AD	4619 AD	4620 AD
4621 AD	4622 AD	4623 AD	4624 AD	4625 AD	4626 AD	4627 AD	4628 AD	4629 AD	4630 AD
4631 AD	4632 AD	4633 AD	4634 AD	4635 AD	4636 AD	4637 AD	4638 AD	4639 AD	4640 AD
4641 AD	4642 AD	4643 AD	4644 AD	4645 AD	4646 AD	4647 AD	4648 AD	4649 AD	4650 AD
4651 AD	4652 AD	4653 AD	4654 AD	4655 AD	4656 AD	4657 AD	4658 AD	4659 AD	4660 AD
4661 AD	4662 AD	4663 AD	4664 AD	4665 AD	4666 AD	4667 AD	4668 AD	4669 AD	4670 AD
4671 AD	4672 AD	4673 AD	4674 AD	4675 AD	4676 AD	4677 AD	4678 AD	4679 AD	4680 AD
4681 AD	4682 AD	4683 AD	4684 AD	4685 AD	4686 AD	4687 AD	4688 AD	4689 AD	4690 AD
4691 AD	4692 AD	4693 AD	4694 AD	4695 AD	4696 AD	4697 AD	4698 AD	4699 AD	4700 AD
4701 AD	4702 AD	4703 AD	4704 AD	4705 AD	4706 AD	4707 AD	4708 AD	4709 AD	4710 AD
4711 AD	4712 AD	4713 AD	4714 AD	4715 AD	4716 AD	4717 AD	4718 AD	4719 AD	4720 AD
4721 AD	4722 AD	4723 AD	4724 AD	4725 AD	4726 AD	4727 AD	4728 AD	4729 AD	4730 AD
4731 AD	4732 AD	4733 AD	4734 AD	4735 AD	4736 AD	4737 AD	4738 AD	4739 AD	4740 AD
4741 AD	4742 AD	4743 AD	4744 AD	4745 AD	4746 AD	4747 AD	4748 AD	4749 AD	4750 AD
4751 AD	4752 AD	4753 AD	4754 AD	4755 AD	4756 AD	4757 AD	4758 AD	4759 AD	4760 AD
4761 AD	4762 AD	4763 AD	4764 AD	4765 AD	4766 AD	4767 AD	4768 AD	4769 AD	4770 AD
4771 AD	4772 AD	4773 AD	4774 AD	4775 AD	4776 AD	4777 AD	4778 AD	4779 AD	4780 AD
4781 AD	4782 AD	4783 AD	4784 AD	4785 AD	4786 AD	4787 AD	4788 AD	4789 AD	4790 AD
4791 AD	4792 AD	4793 AD	4794 AD	4795 AD	4796 AD	4797 AD	4798 AD	4799 AD	4800 AD
4801 AD	4802 AD	4803 AD	4804 AD	4805 AD	4806 AD	4807 AD	4808 AD	4809 AD	4810 AD
4811 AD	4812 AD	4813 AD	4814 AD	4815 AD	4816 AD	4817 AD	4818 AD	4819 AD	4820 AD
4821 AD	4822 AD	4823 AD	4824 AD	4825 AD	4826 AD	4827 AD	4828 AD	4829 AD	4830 AD
4831 AD	4832 AD	4833 AD	4834 AD	4835 AD	4836 AD	4837 AD	4838 AD	4839 AD	4840 AD
4841 AD	4842 AD	4843 AD	4844 AD	4845 AD	4846 AD	4847 AD	4848 AD	4849 AD	4850 AD
4851 AD	4852 AD	4853 AD	4854 AD	4855 AD	4856 AD	4857 AD	4858 AD	4859 AD	4860 AD
4861 AD	4862 AD	4863 AD	4864 AD	4865 AD	4866 AD	4867 AD	4868 AD	4869 AD	4870 AD
4871 AD	4872 AD	4873 AD	4874 AD	4875 AD	4876 AD	4877 AD	4878 AD	4879 AD	4880 AD
4881 AD	4882 AD	4883 AD	4884 AD	4885 AD	4886 AD	4887 AD	4888 AD	4889 AD	4890 AD
4891 AD	4892 AD	4893 AD	4894 AD	4895 AD	4896 AD	4897 AD	4898 AD	4899 AD	4900 AD
4901 AD	4902 AD	4903 AD	4904 AD	4905 AD	4906 AD	4907 AD	4908 AD	4909 AD	4910 AD
4911 AD	4912 AD	4913 AD	4914 AD	4915 AD	4916 AD	4917 AD	4918 AD	4919 AD	4920 AD
4921 AD	4922 AD	4923 AD	4924 AD	4925 AD	4926 AD	4927 AD	4928 AD	4929 AD	4930 AD
4931 AD	4932 AD	4933 AD	4934 AD	4935 AD	4936 AD	4937 AD	4938 AD	4939 AD	4940 AD
4941 AD	4942 AD	4943 AD	4944 AD	4945 AD	4946 AD	4947 AD	4948 AD	4949 AD	4950 AD
4951 AD	4952 AD	4953 AD	4954 AD	4955 AD	4956 AD	4957 AD	4958 AD	4959 AD	4960 AD
4961 AD	4962 AD	4963 AD	4964 AD	4965 AD	4966 AD	4967 AD	4968 AD	4969 AD	4970 AD
4971 AD	4972 AD	4973 AD	4974 AD	4975 AD	4976 AD	4977 AD	4978 AD	4979 AD	4980 AD
4981 AD	4982 AD	4983 AD	4984 AD	4985 AD	4986 AD	4987 AD	4988 AD	4989 AD	4990 AD
4991 AD	4992 AD	4993 AD	4994 AD	4995 AD	4996 AD	4997 AD	4998 AD	4999 AD	5000 AD

— 7 —

5001 AD	5002 AD	5003 AD	5004 AD	5005 AD	5006 AD	5007 AD	5008 AD	5009 AD	5010 AD
5011 AD	5012 AD	5013 AD	5014 AD	5015 AD	5016 AD	5017 AD	5018 AD	5019 AD	5020 AD
5021 AD	5022 AD	5023 AD	5024 AD	5025 AD	5026 AD	5027 AD	5028 AD	5029 AD	5030 AD
5031 AD	5032 AD	5033 AD	5034 AD	5035 AD	5036 AD	5037 AD	5038 AD	5039 AD	5040 AD
5041 AD	5042 AD	5043 AD	5044 AD	5045 AD	5046 AD	5047 AD	5048 AD	5049 AD	5050 AD
5051 AD	5052 AD	5053 AD	5054 AD	5055 AD	5056 AD	5057 AD	5058 AD	5059 AD	5060 AD
5061 AD	5062 AD	5063 AD	5064 AD	5065 AD	5066 AD	5067 AD	5068 AD	5069 AD	5070 AD
5071 AD	5072 AD	5073 AD	5074 AD	5075 AD	5076 AD	5077 AD	5078 AD	5079 AD	5080 AD
5081 AD	5082 AD	5083 AD	5084 AD	5085 AD	5086 AD	5087 AD	5088 AD	5089 AD	5090 AD
5091 AD	5092 AD	5093 AD	5094 AD	5095 AD	5096 AD	5097 AD	5098 AD	5099 AD	5100 AD
5101 AD	5102 AD	5103 AD	5104 AD	5105 AD	5106 AD	5107 AD	5108 AD	5109 AD	5110 AD
5111 AD	5112 AD	5113 AD	5114 AD	5115 AD	5116 AD	5117 AD	5118 AD	5119 AD	5120 AD
5121 AD	5122 AD	5123 AD	5124 AD	5125 AD	5126 AD	5127 AD	5128 AD	5129 AD	5130 AD
5131 AD	5132 AD	5133 AD	5134 AD	5135 AD	5136 AD	5137 AD	5138 AD	5139 AD	5140 AD
5141 AD	5142 AD	5143 AD	5144 AD	5145 AD	5146 AD	5147 AD	5148 AD	5149 AD	5150 AD
5151 AD	5152 AD	5153 AD	5154 AD	5155 AD	5156 AD	5157 AD	5158 AD	5159 AD	5160 AD
5161 AD	5162 AD	5163 AD	5164 AD	5165 AD	5166 AD	5167 AD	5168 AD	5169 AD	5170 AD
5171 AD	5172 AD	5173 AD	5174 AD	5175 AD	5176 AD	5177 AD	5178 AD	5179 AD	5180 AD
5181 AD	5182 AD	5183 AD	5184 AD	5185 AD	5186 AD	5187 AD	5188 AD	5189 AD	5190 AD
5191 AD	5192 AD	5193 AD	5194 AD	5195 AD	5196 AD	5197 AD	5198 AD	5199 AD	5200 AD
5201 AD	5202 AD	5203 AD	5204 AD	5205 AD	5206 AD	5207 AD	5208 AD	5209 AD	5210 AD
5211 AD	5212 AD	5213 AD	5214 AD	5215 AD	5216 AD	5217 AD	5218 AD	5219 AD	5220 AD
5221 AD	5222 AD	5223 AD	5224 AD	5225 AD	5226 AD	5227 AD	5228 AD	5229 AD	5230 AD
5231 AD	5232 AD	5233 AD	5234 AD	5235 AD	5236 AD	5237 AD	5238 AD	5239 AD	5240 AD
5241 AD	5342 AD	5243 AD	5244 AD	5245 AD	5246 AD	5247 AD	5248 AD	5249 AD	5250 AD
5251 AD	5252 AD	5253 AD	5254 AD	5255 AD	5256 AD	5257 AD	5258 AD	5259 AD	5260 AD
5261 AD	5262 AD	5263 AD	5264 AD	5265 AD	5266 AD	5267 AD	5268 AD	5269 AD	5270 AD
5271 AD	5272 AD	5273 AD	5274 AD	5275 AD	5276 AD	5277 AD	5278 AD	5279 AD	5280 AD
5281 AD	5282 AD	5283 AD	5284 AD	5285 AD	5286 AD	5287 AD	5288 AD	5289 AD	5290 AD
5291 AD	5292 AD	5293 AD	5294 AD	5295 AD	5296 AD	5297 AD	5298 AD	5299 AD	5300 AD
5301 AD	5302 AD	5303 AD	5304 AD	5305 AD	5306 AD	5307 AD	5308 AD	5309 AD	5310 AD
5311 AD	5312 AD	5313 AD	5314 AD	5315 AD	5316 AD	5317 AD	5318 AD	5319 AD	5320 AD
5321 AD	5322 AD	5323 AD	5324 AD	5325 AD	5326 AD	5327 AD	5328 AD	5329 AD	5330 AD
5331 AD	5332 AD	5333 AD	5334 AD	5335 AD	5336 AD	5337 AD	5338 AD	5339 AD	5340 AD
5341 AD	5342 AD	5343 AD	5344 AD	5345 AD	5346 AD	5347 AD	5348 AD	5349 AD	5350 AD
5351 AD	5352 AD	5353 AD	5354 AD	5355 AD	5356 AD	5357 AD	5358 AD	5359 AD	5360 AD
5361 AD	5362 AD	5363 AD	5364 AD	5365 AD	5366 AD	5367 AD	5368 AD	5369 AD	5370 AD
5371 AD	5372 AD	5373 AD	5374 AD	5375 AD	5376 AD	5377 AD	5378 AD	5379 AD	5380 AD
5381 AD	5382 AD	5383 AD	5384 AD	5385 AD	5386 AD	5387 AD	5388 AD	5389 AD	5390 AD
5391 AD	5392 AD	5393 AD	5394 AD	5395 AD	5396 AD	5397 AD	5398 AD	5399 AD	5400 AD
5401 AD	5402 AD	5403 AD	5404 AD	5405 AD	5406 AD	5407 AD	5408 AD	5409 AD	5410 AD
5411 AD	5412 AD	5413 AD	5414 AD	5415 AD	5416 AD	5417 AD	5418 AD	5419 AD	5420 AD
5421 AD	5422 AD	5423 AD	5424 AD	5425 AD	5426 AD	5427 AD	5428 AD	5429 AD	5430 AD
5431 AD	5432 AD	5433 AD	5434 AD	5435 AD	5436 AD	5437 AD	5438 AD	5439 AD	5440 AD
5441 AD	5442 AD	5443 AD	5444 AD	5445 AD	5446 AD	5447 AD	5448 AD	5449 AD	5450 AD
5451 AD	5452 AD	5453 AD	5454 AD	5455 AD	5456 AD	5457 AD	5458 AD	5459 AD	5460 AD
5461 AD	5462 AD	5463 AD	5464 AD	5465 AD	5466 AD	5467 AD	5468 AD	5469 AD	5470 AD
5471 AD	5472 AD	5473 AD	5474 AD	5475 AD	5476 AD	5477 AD	5478 AD	5479 AD	5480 AD
5481 AD	5482 AD	5483 AD	5484 AD	5485 AD	5486 AD	5487 AD	5488 AD	5489 AD	5490 AD
5491 AD	5492 AD	5493 AD	5494 AD	5495 AD	5496 AD	5497 AD	5498 AD	5499 AD	5500 AD

5501 AD	5502 AD	5503 AD	5504 AD	5505 AD	5506 AD	5507 AD	5508 AD	5509 AD	5510 AD
5511 AD	5512 AD	5513 AD	5514 AD	5515 AD	5516 AD	5517 AD	5518 AD	5519 AD	5520 AD
5521 AD	5522 AD	5523 AD	5524 AD	5525 AD	5526 AD	5527 AD	5528 AD	5529 AD	5530 AD
5531 AD	5532 AD	5533 AD	5534 AD	5535 AD	5536 AD	5537 AD	5538 AD	5539 AD	5540 AD
5541 AD	5542 AD	5543 AD	5544 AD	5545 AD	5546 AD	5547 AD	5548 AD	5549 AD	5550 AD
5551 AD	5552 AD	5553 AD	5554 AD	5555 AD	5556 AD	5557 AD	5558 AD	5559 AD	5560 AD
5561 AD	5562 AD	5563 AD	5564 AD	5565 AD	5566 AD	5567 AD	5568 AD	5569 AD	5570 AD
5571 AD	5572 AD	5573 AD	5574 AD	5575 AD	5576 AD	5577 AD	5578 AD	5579 AD	5580 AD
5581 AD	5582 AD	5583 AD	5584 AD	5585 AD	5586 AD	5587 AD	5588 AD	5589 AD	5590 AD
5591 AD	5592 AD	5593 AD	5594 AD	5595 AD	5596 AD	5597 AD	5598 AD	5599 AD	5600 AD
5601 AD	5602 AD	5603 AD	5604 AD	5605 AD	5606 AD	5607 AD	5608 AD	5609 AD	5610 AD
5611 AD	5612 AD	5613 AD	5614 AD	5615 AD	5616 AD	5617 AD	5618 AD	5619 AD	5620 AD
5621 AD	5622 AD	5623 AD	5624 AD	5625 AD	5626 AD	5627 AD	5628 AD	5629 AD	5630 AD
5631 AD	5632 AD	5633 AD	5634 AD	5635 AD	5636 AD	5637 AD	5638 AD	5639 AD	5640 AD
5641 AD	5642 AD	5643 AD	5644 AD	5645 AD	5646 AD	5647 AD	5648 AD	5649 AD	5650 AD
5651 AD	5652 AD	5653 AD	5654 AD	5655 AD	5656 AD	5657 AD	5658 AD	5659 AD	5660 AD
5661 AD	5662 AD	5663 AD	5664 AD	5665 AD	5666 AD	5667 AD	5668 AD	5669 AD	5670 AD
5671 AD	5672 AD	5673 AD	5674 AD	5675 AD	5676 AD	5677 AD	5678 AD	5679 AD	5680 AD
5681 AD	5682 AD	5683 AD	5684 AD	5685 AD	5686 AD	5687 AD	5688 AD	5689 AD	5690 AD
5691 AD	5692 AD	5693 AD	5694 AD	5695 AD	5696 AD	5697 AD	5698 AD	5699 AD	5700 AD
5701 AD	5702 AD	5703 AD	5704 AD	5705 AD	5706 AD	5707 AD	5708 AD	5709 AD	5710 AD
5711 AD	5712 AD	5713 AD	5714 AD	5715 AD	5716 AD	5717 AD	5718 AD	5719 AD	5720 AD
5721 AD	5722 AD	5723 AD	5724 AD	5725 AD	5726 AD	5727 AD	5728 AD	5729 AD	5730 AD
5731 AD	5732 AD	5733 AD	5734 AD	5735 AD	5736 AD	5737 AD	5738 AD	5739 AD	5740 AD
5741 AD	5742 AD	5743 AD	5744 AD	5745 AD	5746 AD	5747 AD	5748 AD	5749 AD	5750 AD
5751 AD	5752 AD	5753 AD	5754 AD	5755 AD	5756 AD	5757 AD	5758 AD	5759 AD	5760 AD
5761 AD	5762 AD	5763 AD	5764 AD	5765 AD	5766 AD	5767 AD	5768 AD	5769 AD	5770 AD
5771 AD	5772 AD	5773 AD	5774 AD	5775 AD	5776 AD	5777 AD	5778 AD	5779 AD	5780 AD
5781 AD	5782 AD	5783 AD	5784 AD	5785 AD	5786 AD	5787 AD	5788 AD	5789 AD	5790 AD
5791 AD	5792 AD	5793 AD	5794 AD	5795 AD	5796 AD	5797 AD	5798 AD	5799 AD	5800 AD
5801 AD	5802 AD	5803 AD	5804 AD	5805 AD	5806 AD	5807 AD	5808 AD	5809 AD	5810 AD
5811 AD	5812 AD	5813 AD	5814 AD	5815 AD	5816 AD	5817 AD	5818 AD	5819 AD	5820 AD
5821 AD	5822 AD	5823 AD	5824 AD	5825 AD	5826 AD	5827 AD	5828 AD	5829 AD	5830 AD
5831 AD	5832 AD	5833 AD	5834 AD	5835 AD	5836 AD	5837 AD	5838 AD	5839 AD	5840 AD
5841 AD	5842 AD	5843 AD	5844 AD	5845 AD	5846 AD	5847 AD	5848 AD	5849 AD	5850 AD
5851 AD	5852 AD	5853 AD	5854 AD	5855 AD	5856 AD	5857 AD	5858 AD	5859 AD	5860 AD
5861 AD	5862 AD	5863 AD	5864 AD	5865 AD	5866 AD	5867 AD	5868 AD	5869 AD	5870 AD
5871 AD	5872 AD	5873 AD	5874 AD	5875 AD	5876 AD	5877 AD	5878 AD	5879 AD	5880 AD
5881 AD	5882 AD	5883 AD	5884 AD	5885 AD	5886 AD	5887 AD	5888 AD	5889 AD	5890 AD
5891 AD	5892 AD	5893 AD	5894 AD	5895 AD	5896 AD	5897 AD	5898 AD	5899 AD	5900 AD
5901 AD	5902 AD	5903 AD	5904 AD	5905 AD	5906 AD	5907 AD	5908 AD	5909 AD	5910 AD
5911 AD	5912 AD	5913 AD	5914 AD	5915 AD	5916 AD	5917 AD	5918 AD	5919 AD	5920 AD
5921 AD	5922 AD	5923 AD	5924 AD	5925 AD	5926 AD	5927 AD	5928 AD	5929 AD	5930 AD
5931 AD	5932 AD	5933 AD	5934 AD	5935 AD	5936 AD	5937 AD	5938 AD	5939 AD	5940 AD
5941 AD	5942 AD	5943 AD	5944 AD	5945 AD	5946 AD	5947 AD	5948 AD	5949 AD	5950 AD
5951 AD	5952 AD	5953 AD	5954 AD	5955 AD	5956 AD	5957 AD	5958 AD	5959 AD	5960 AD
5961 AD	5962 AD	5963 AD	5964 AD	5965 AD	5966 AD	5967 AD	5968 AD	5969 AD	5970 AD
5971 AD	5972 AD	5973 AD	5974 AD	5975 AD	5976 AD	5977 AD	5978 AD	5979 AD	5980 AD
5981 AD	5982 AD	5983 AD	5984 AD	5985 AD	5986 AD	5987 AD	5988 AD	5989 AD	5990 AD
5991 AD	5992 AD	5993 AD	5994 AD	5995 AD	5996 AD	5997 AD	5998 AD	5999 AD	6000 AD

6001 AD	6002 AD	6003 AD	6004 AD	6005 AD	6006 AD	6007 AD	6008 AD	6009 AD	6010 AD
6011 AD	6012 AD	6013 AD	6014 AD	6015 AD	6016 AD	6017 AD	6018 AD	6019 AD	6020 AD
6021 AD	6022 AD	6023 AD	6024 AD	6025 AD	6026 AD	6027 AD	6028 AD	6029 AD	6030 AD
6031 AD	6032 AD	6033 AD	6034 AD	6035 AD	6036 AD	6037 AD	6038 AD	6039 AD	6040 AD
6041 AD	6042 AD	6043 AD	6044 AD	6045 AD	6046 AD	6047 AD	6048 AD	6049 AD	6050 AD
6051 AD	6052 AD	6053 AD	6054 AD	6055 AD	6056 AD	6057 AD	6058 AD	6059 AD	6060 AD
6061 AD	6062 AD	6063 AD	6064 AD	6065 AD	6066 AD	6067 AD	6068 AD	6069 AD	6070 AD
6071 AD	6072 AD	6073 AD	6074 AD	6075 AD	6076 AD	6077 AD	6078 AD	6079 AD	6080 AD
6081 AD	6082 AD	6083 AD	6084 AD	6085 AD	6086 AD	6087 AD	6088 AD	6089 AD	6090 AD
6091 AD	6092 AD	6093 AD	6094 AD	6095 AD	6096 AD	6097 AD	6098 AD	6099 AD	6100 AD
6101 AD	6102 AD	6103 AD	6104 AD	6105 AD	6106 AD	6107 AD	6108 AD	6109 AD	6110 AD
6111 AD	6112 AD	6113 AD	6114 AD	6115 AD	6116 AD	6117 AD	6118 AD	6119 AD	6120 AD
6121 AD	6122 AD	6123 AD	6124 AD	6125 AD	6126 AD	6127 AD	6128 AD	6129 AD	6130 AD
6131 AD	6132 AD	6133 AD	6134 AD	6135 AD	6136 AD	6137 AD	6138 AD	6139 AD	6140 AD
6141 AD	6142 AD	6143 AD	6144 AD	6145 AD	6146 AD	6147 AD	6148 AD	6149 AD	6150 AD
6151 AD	6152 AD	6153 AD	6154 AD	6155 AD	6156 AD	6157 AD	6158 AD	6159 AD	6160 AD
6161 AD	6162 AD	6163 AD	6164 AD	6165 AD	6166 AD	6167 AD	6168 AD	6169 AD	6170 AD
6171 AD	6172 AD	6173 AD	6174 AD	6175 AD	6176 AD	6177 AD	6178 AD	6179 AD	6180 AD
6181 AD	6182 AD	6183 AD	6184 AD	6185 AD	6186 AD	6187 AD	6188 AD	6189 AD	6190 AD
6191 AD	6192 AD	6193 AD	6194 AD	6195 AD	6196 AD	6197 AD	6198 AD	6199 AD	6200 AD
6201 AD	6202 AD	6203 AD	6204 AD	6205 AD	6206 AD	6207 AD	6208 AD	6209 AD	6210 AD
6211 AD	6212 AD	6213 AD	6214 AD	6215 AD	6216 AD	6217 AD	6218 AD	6219 AD	6220 AD
6221 AD	6222 AD	6223 AD	6224 AD	6225 AD	6226 AD	6227 AD	6228 AD	6229 AD	6230 AD
6231 AD	6232 AD	6233 AD	6234 AD	6235 AD	6236 AD	6237 AD	6238 AD	6239 AD	6240 AD
6241 AD	6242 AD	6243 AD	6244 AD	6245 AD	6246 AD	6247 AD	6248 AD	6249 AD	6250 AD
6251 AD	6252 AD	6253 AD	6254 AD	6255 AD	6256 AD	6257 AD	6258 AD	6259 AD	6260 AD
6261 AD	6262 AD	6263 AD	6264 AD	6265 AD	6266 AD	6267 AD	6268 AD	6269 AD	6270 AD
6271 AD	6272 AD	6273 AD	6274 AD	6275 AD	6276 AD	6277 AD	6278 AD	6279 AD	6280 AD
6281 AD	6282 AD	6283 AD	6284 AD	6285 AD	6286 AD	6287 AD	6288 AD	6289 AD	6290 AD
6291 AD	6292 AD	6293 AD	6294 AD	6295 AD	6296 AD	6297 AD	6298 AD	6299 AD	6300 AD
6301 AD	6302 AD	6303 AD	6304 AD	6305 AD	6306 AD	6307 AD	6308 AD	6309 AD	6310 AD
6311 AD	6312 AD	6313 AD	6314 AD	6315 AD	6316 AD	6317 AD	6318 AD	6319 AD	6320 AD
6321 AD	6322 AD	6323 AD	6324 AD	6325 AD	6326 AD	6327 AD	6328 AD	6329 AD	6330 AD
6331 AD	6332 AD	6333 AD	6334 AD	6335 AD	6336 AD	6337 AD	6338 AD	6339 AD	6340 AD
6341 AD	6342 AD	6343 AD	6344 AD	6345 AD	6346 AD	6347 AD	6348 AD	6349 AD	6350 AD
6351 AD	6352 AD	6353 AD	6354 AD	6355 AD	6356 AD	6357 AD	6358 AD	6359 AD	6360 AD
6361 AD	6362 AD	6363 AD	6364 AD	6365 AD	6366 AD	6367 AD	6368 AD	6369 AD	6370 AD
6371 AD	6372 AD	6373 AD	6374 AD	6375 AD	6376 AD	6377 AD	6378 AD	6379 AD	6380 AD
6381 AD	6382 AD	6383 AD	6384 AD	6385 AD	6386 AD	6387 AD	6388 AD	6389 AD	6390 AD
6391 AD	6392 AD	6393 AD	6394 AD	6395 AD	6396 AD	6397 AD	6398 AD	6399 AD	6400 AD
6401 AD	6402 AD	6403 AD	6404 AD	6405 AD	6406 AD	6407 AD	6408 AD	6409 AD	6410 AD
6411 AD	6412 AD	6413 AD	6414 AD	6415 AD	6416 AD	6417 AD	6418 AD	6419 AD	6420 AD
6421 AD	6422 AD	6423 AD	6424 AD	6425 AD	6426 AD	6427 AD	6428 AD	6429 AD	6430 AD
6431 AD	6432 AD	6433 AD	6434 AD	6435 AD	6436 AD	6437 AD	6438 AD	6439 AD	6440 AD
6441 AD	6442 AD	6443 AD	6444 AD	6445 AD	6446 AD	6447 AD	6448 AD	6449 AD	6450 AD
6451 AD	6452 AD	6453 AD	6454 AD	6455 AD	6456 AD	6457 AD	6458 AD	6459 AD	6460 AD
6461 AD	6462 AD	6463 AD	6464 AD	6465 AD	6466 AD	6467 AD	6468 AD	6469 AD	6470 AD
6471 AD	6472 AD	6473 AD	6474 AD	6475 AD	6476 AD	6477 AD	6478 AD	6479 AD	6480 AD
6481 AD	6482 AD	6483 AD	6484 AD	6485 AD	6486 AD	6487 AD	6488 AD	6489 AD	6490 AD
6491 AD	6492 AD	6493 AD	6494 AD	6495 AD	6496 AD	6497 AD	6498 AD	6499 AD	6500 AD

6501 AD	6502 AD	6503 AD	6504 AD	6505 AD	6506 AD	6507 AD	6508 AD	6509 AD	6510 AD
6511 AD	6512 AD	6513 AD	6514 AD	6515 AD	6516 AD	6517 AD	6518 AD	6519 AD	6520 AD
6521 AD	6522 AD	6523 AD	6524 AD	6525 AD	6526 AD	6527 AD	6528 AD	6529 AD	6530 AD
6531 AD	6532 AD	6533 AD	6534 AD	6535 AD	6536 AD	6537 AD	6538 AD	6539 AD	6540 AD
6541 AD	6542 AD	6543 AD	6544 AD	6545 AD	6546 AD	6547 AD	6548 AD	6549 AD	6550 AD
6551 AD	6552 AD	6553 AD	6554 AD	6555 AD	6556 AD	6557 AD	6558 AD	6559 AD	6560 AD
6561 AD	6562 AD	6563 AD	6564 AD	6565 AD	6566 AD	6567 AD	6568 AD	6569 AD	6570 AD
6571 AD	6572 AD	6573 AD	6574 AD	6575 AD	6576 AD	6577 AD	6578 AD	6579 AD	6580 AD
6581 AD	6582 AD	6583 AD	6584 AD	6585 AD	6586 AD	6587 AD	6588 AD	6589 AD	6590 AD
6591 AD	6592 AD	6593 AD	6594 AD	6595 AD	6596 AD	6597 AD	6598 AD	6599 AD	6600 AD
6601 AD	6602 AD	6603 AD	6604 AD	6605 AD	6606 AD	6607 AD	6608 AD	6609 AD	6610 AD
6611 AD	6612 AD	6613 AD	6614 AD	6615 AD	6616 AD	6617 AD	6618 AD	6619 AD	6620 AD
6621 AD	6622 AD	6623 AD	6624 AD	6625 AD	6626 AD	6627 AD	6628 AD	6629 AD	6630 AD
6631 AD	6632 AD	6633 AD	6634 AD	6635 AD	6636 AD	6637 AD	6638 AD	6639 AD	6640 AD
6641 AD	6642 AD	6643 AD	6644 AD	6645 AD	6646 AD	6647 AD	6648 AD	6649 AD	6650 AD
6651 AD	6652 AD	6653 AD	6654 AD	6655 AD	6656 AD	6657 AD	6658 AD	6659 AD	6660 AD
6661 AD	6662 AD	6663 AD	6664 AD	6665 AD	6666 AD	6667 AD	6668 AD	6669 AD	6670 AD
6671 AD	6672 AD	6673 AD	6674 AD	6675 AD	6676 AD	6677 AD	6678 AD	6679 AD	6680 AD
6681 AD	6682 AD	6683 AD	6684 AD	6685 AD	6686 AD	6687 AD	6688 AD	6689 AD	6690 AD
6691 AD	6692 AD	6693 AD	6694 AD	6695 AD	6696 AD	6697 AD	6698 AD	6699 AD	6700 AD
6701 AD	6702 AD	6703 AD	6704 AD	6705 AD	6706 AD	6707 AD	6708 AD	6709 AD	6710 AD
6711 AD	6712 AD	6713 AD	6714 AD	6715 AD	6716 AD	6717 AD	6718 AD	6719 AD	6720 AD
6721 AD	6722 AD	6723 AD	6724 AD	6725 AD	6726 AD	6727 AD	6728 AD	6729 AD	6730 AD
6731 AD	6732 AD	6733 AD	6734 AD	6735 AD	6736 AD	6737 AD	6738 AD	6739 AD	6740 AD
6741 AD	6742 AD	6743 AD	6744 AD	6745 AD	6746 AD	6747 AD	6748 AD	6749 AD	6750 AD
6751 AD	6752 AD	6753 AD	6754 AD	6755 AD	6756 AD	6757 AD	6758 AD	6759 AD	6760 AD
6761 AD	6762 AD	6763 AD	6764 AD	6165 AD	6766 AD	6767 AD	6768 AD	6769 AD	6770 AD
6771 AD	6772 AD	6773 AD	6774 AD	6775 AD	6776 AD	6777 AD	6778 AD	6779 AD	6780 AD
6781 AD	6782 AD	6783 AD	6784 AD	6785 AD	6786 AD	6787 AD	6788 AD	6789 AD	6790 AD
6791 AD	6792 AD	6793 AD	6794 AD	6795 AD	6796 AD	6797 AD	6798 AD	6799 AD	6800 AD
6801 AD	6802 AD	6803 AD	6804 AD	6805 AD	6806 AD	6807 AD	6808 AD	6809 AD	6810 AD
6811 AD	6812 AD	6813 AD	6814 AD	6815 AD	6816 AD	6817 AD	6818 AD	6819 AD	6820 AD
6821 AD	6822 AD	6823 AD	6824 AD	6825 AD	6826 AD	6827 AD	6828 AD	6829 AD	6830 AD
6831 AD	6832 AD	6833 AD	6834 AD	6835 AD	6836 AD	6837 AD	6838 AD	6839 AD	6840 AD
6841 AD	6842 AD	6843 AD	6844 AD	6845 AD	6846 AD	6847 AD	6848 AD	6849 AD	6850 AD
6851 AD	6852 AD	6853 AD	6854 AD	6855 AD	6856 AD	6857 AD	6858 AD	6859 AD	6860 AD
6861 AD	6862 AD	6863 AD	6864 AD	6865 AD	6866 AD	6867 AD	6868 AD	6869 AD	6870 AD
6871 AD	6872 AD	6873 AD	6874 AD	6875 AD	6876 AD	6877 AD	6878 AD	6879 AD	6880 AD
6881 AD	6882 AD	6883 AD	6884 AD	6885 AD	6886 AD	6887 AD	6888 AD	6889 AD	6890 AD
6891 AD	6892 AD	6893 AD	6894 AD	6895 AD	6896 AD	6897 AD	6898 AD	6899 AD	6900 AD
6901 AD	6902 AD	6903 AD	6904 AD	6905 AD	6906 AD	6907 AD	6908 AD	6909 AD	6910 AD
6911 AD	6912 AD	6913 AD	6914 AD	6915 AD	6916 AD	6917 AD	6918 AD	6919 AD	6920 AD
6921 AD	6922 AD	6923 AD	6924 AD	6925 AD	6926 AD	6927 AD	6928 AD	6929 AD	6930 AD
6931 AD	6932 AD	6933 AD	6934 AD	6935 AD	6936 AD	6937 AD	6938 AD	6939 AD	6940 AD
6941 AD	6942 AD	6943 AD	6944 AD	6945 AD	6946 AD	6947 AD	6948 AD	6949 AD	6950 AD
6951 AD	6952 AD	6953 AD	6954 AD	6955 AD	6956 AD	6957 AD	6958 AD	6959 AD	6960 AD
6961 AD	6962 AD	6963 AD	6964 AD	6965 AD	6966 AD	6967 AD	6968 AD	6969 AD	6970 AD
6971 AD	6972 AD	6973 AD	6974 AD	6975 AD	6976 AD	6977 AD	6978 AD	6979 AD	6980 AD
6981 AD	6982 AD	6983 AD	6984 AD	6985 AD	6986 AD	6987 AD	6988 AD	6989 AD	6990 AD
6991 AD	6992 AD	6993 AD	6994 AD	6995 AD	6996 AD	6997 AD	6998 AD	6999 AD	7000 AD

7001 AD	7002 AD	7003 AD	7004 AD	7005 AD	7006 AD	7007 AD	7008 AD	7009 AD	7010 AD
7011 AD	7012 AD	7013 AD	7014 AD	7015 AD	7016 AD	7017 AD	7018 AD	7019 AD	7020 AD
7021 AD	7022 AD	7023 AD	7024 AD	7025 AD	7026 AD	7027 AD	7028 AD	7029 AD	7030 AD
7031 AD	7032 AD	7033 AD	7034 AD	7035 AD	7036 AD	7037 AD	7038 AD	7039 AD	7040 AD
7041 AD	7042 AD	7043 AD	7044 AD	7045 AD	7046 AD	7047 AD	7048 AD	7049 AD	7050 AD
7051 AD	7052 AD	7053 AD	7054 AD	7055 AD	7056 AD	7057 AD	7058 AD	7059 AD	7060 AD
7061 AD	7062 AD	7063 AD	7064 AD	7065 AD	7066 AD	7067 AD	7068 AD	7069 AD	7070 AD
7071 AD	7072 AD	7073 AD	7074 AD	7075 AD	7076 AD	7077 AD	7078 AD	7079 AD	7080 AD
7081 AD	7082 AD	7083 AD	7084 AD	7085 AD	7086 AD	7087 AD	7088 AD	7089 AD	7090 AD
7091 AD	7092 AD	7093 AD	7094 AD	7095 AD	7096 AD	7097 AD	7098 AD	7099 AD	7100 AD
7101 AD	7102 AD	7103 AD	7104 AD	7105 AD	7106 AD	7107 AD	7108 AD	7109 AD	7110 AD
7111 AD	7112 AD	7113 AD	7114 AD	7115 AD	7116 AD	7117 AD	7118 AD	7119 AD	7120 AD
7121 AD	7122 AD	7123 AD	7124 AD	7125 AD	7126 AD	7127 AD	7128 AD	7129 AD	7130 AD
7131 AD	7132 AD	7133 AD	7134 AD	7135 AD	7136 AD	7137 AD	7138 AD	7139 AD	7140 AD
7141 AD	7142 AD	7143 AD	7144 AD	7145 AD	7146 AD	7147 AD	7148 AD	7149 AD	7150 AD
7151 AD	7152 AD	7153 AD	7154 AD	7155 AD	7156 AD	7157 AD	7158 AD	7159 AD	7160 AD
7161 AD	7162 AD	7163 AD	7164 AD	7165 AD	7166 AD	7167 AD	7168 AD	7169 AD	7170 AD
7171 AD	7172 AD	7173 AD	7174 AD	7175 AD	7176 AD	7177 AD	7178 AD	7179 AD	7180 AD
7181 AD	7182 AD	7183 AD	7184 AD	7185 AD	7186 AD	7187 AD	7188 AD	7189 AD	7190 AD
7191 AD	7192 AD	7193 AD	7194 AD	7195 AD	7196 AD	7197 AD	7198 AD	7199 AD	7200 AD
7201 AD	7202 AD	7203 AD	7204 AD	7205 AD	7206 AD	7207 AD	7208 AD	7209 AD	7210 AD
7211 AD	7212 AD	7213 AD	7214 AD	7215 AD	7216 AD	7217 AD	7218 AD	7219 AD	7220 AD
7221 AD	7222 AD	7223 AD	7224 AD	7225 AD	7226 AD	7227 AD	7228 AD	7229 AD	7230 AD
7231 AD	7232 AD	7233 AD	7234 AD	7235 AD	7236 AD	7237 AD	7238 AD	7239 AD	7240 AD
7241 AD	7242 AD	7243 AD	7244 AD	7245 AD	7246 AD	7247 AD	7248 AD	7249 AD	7250 AD
7251 AD	7252 AD	7253 AD	7254 AD	7255 AD	7256 AD	7257 AD	7258 AD	7259 AD	7260 AD
7261 AD	7262 AD	7263 AD	7264 AD	7265 AD	7266 AD	7267 AD	7268 AD	7269 AD	7270 AD
7271 AD	7272 AD	7273 AD	7274 AD	7275 AD	7276 AD	7277 AD	7278 AD	7279 AD	7280 AD
7281 AD	7282 AD	7283 AD	7284 AD	7285 AD	7286 AD	7287 AD	7288 AD	7289 AD	7290 AD
7291 AD	7292 AD	7293 AD	7294 AD	7295 AD	7296 AD	7297 AD	7298 AD	7299 AD	7300 AD
7301 AD	7302 AD	7303 AD	7304 AD	7305 AD	7306 AD	7307 AD	7308 AD	7309 AD	7310 AD
7311 AD	7312 AD	7313 AD	7314 AD	7315 AD	7316 AD	7317 AD	7318 AD	7319 AD	7320 AD
7321 AD	7322 AD	7323 AD	7324 AD	7325 AD	7326 AD	7327 AD	7328 AD	7329 AD	7330 AD
7331 AD	7332 AD	7333 AD	7334 AD	7335 AD	7336 AD	7337 AD	7338 AD	7339 AD	7340 AD
7341 AD	7342 AD	7343 AD	7344 AD	7345 AD	7346 AD	7347 AD	7348 AD	7349 AD	7350 AD
7351 AD	7352 AD	7353 AD	7354 AD	7355 AD	7356 AD	7357 AD	7358 AD	7359 AD	7360 AD
7361 AD	7362 AD	7363 AD	7364 AD	7365 AD	7366 AD	7367 AD	7368 AD	7369 AD	7370 AD
7371 AD	7372 AD	7373 AD	7374 AD	7375 AD	7376 AD	7377 AD	7378 AD	7379 AD	7380 AD
7381 AD	7382 AD	7383 AD	7384 AD	7385 AD	7386 AD	7387 AD	7388 AD	7389 AD	7390 AD
7391 AD	7392 AD	7393 AD	7394 AD	7395 AD	7396 AD	7397 AD	7398 AD	7399 AD	7400 AD
7401 AD	7402 AD	7403 AD	7404 AD	7405 AD	7406 AD	7407 AD	7408 AD	7409 AD	7410 AD
7411 AD	7412 AD	7413 AD	7414 AD	7415 AD	7416 AD	7417 AD	7418 AD	7419 AD	7420 AD
7421 AD	7422 AD	7423 AD	7424 AD	7425 AD	7426 AD	7427 AD	7428 AD	7429 AD	7430 AD
7431 AD	7432 AD	7433 AD	7434 AD	7435 AD	7436 AD	7437 AD	7438 AD	7439 AD	7440 AD
7441 AD	7442 AD	7443 AD	7444 AD	7445 AD	7446 AD	7447 AD	7448 AD	7449 AD	7450 AD
7451 AD	7452 AD	7453 AD	7454 AD	7455 AD	7456 AD	7457 AD	7458 AD	7459 AD	7460 AD
7461 AD	7462 AD	7463 AD	7464 AD	7465 AD	7466 AD	7467 AD	7468 AD	7469 AD	7470 AD
7471 AD	7472 AD	7473 AD	7474 AD	7475 AD	7476 AD	7477 AD	7478 AD	7479 AD	7480 AD
7481 AD	7482 AD	7483 AD	7484 AD	7485 AD	7486 AD	7487 AD	7488 AD	7489 AD	7490 AD
7491 AD	7492 AD	7493 AD	7494 AD	7495 AD	7496 AD	7497 AD	7498 AD	7499 AD	7500 AD

— 12 —

7501 AD	7502 AD	7503 AD	7504 AD	7505 AD	7506 AD	7507 AD	7508 AD	7509 AD	7510 AD
7511 AD	7512 AD	7513 AD	7514 AD	7515 AD	7516 AD	7517 AD	7518 AD	7519 AD	7520 AD
7521 AD	7522 AD	7523 AD	7524 AD	7525 AD	7526 AD	7527 AD	7528 AD	7529 AD	7530 AD
7531 AD	7532 AD	7533 AD	7534 AD	7535 AD	7536 AD	7537 AD	7538 AD	7539 AD	7540 AD
7541 AD	7542 AD	7543 AD	7544 AD	7545 AD	7546 AD	7547 AD	7548 AD	7549 AD	7550 AD
7551 AD	7552 AD	7553 AD	7554 AD	7555 AD	7556 AD	7557 AD	7558 AD	7559 AD	7560 AD
7561 AD	7562 AD	7563 AD	7564 AD	7565 AD	7566 AD	7567 AD	7568 AD	7569 AD	7570 AD
7571 AD	7572 AD	7573 AD	7574 AD	7575 AD	7576 AD	7577 AD	7578 AD	7579 AD	7580 AD
7581 AD	7582 AD	7583 AD	7584 AD	7585 AD	7586 AD	7587 AD	7588 AD	7589 AD	7590 AD
7591 AD	7592 AD	7593 AD	7594 AD	7595 AD	7596 AD	7597 AD	7598 AD	7599 AD	7600 AD
7601 AD	7602 AD	7603 AD	7604 AD	7605 AD	7606 AD	7607 AD	7608 AD	7609 AD	7610 AD
7611 AD	7612 AD	7613 AD	7614 AD	7615 AD	7616 AD	7617 AD	7618 AD	7619 AD	7620 AD
7621 AD	7622 AD	7623 AD	7624 AD	7625 AD	7626 AD	7627 AD	7628 AD	7629 AD	7630 AD
7631 AD	7632 AD	7633 AD	7634 AD	7635 AD	7636 AD	7637 AD	7638 AD	7639 AD	7640 AD
7641 AD	7642 AD	7643 AD	7644 AD	7645 AD	7646 AD	7647 AD	7648 AD	7649 AD	7650 AD
7651 AD	7652 AD	7653 AD	7654 AD	7655 AD	7656 AD	7657 AD	7658 AD	7659 AD	7660 AD
7661 AD	7662 AD	7663 AD	7664 AD	7665 AD	7666 AD	7667 AD	7668 AD	7669 AD	7670 AD
7671 AD	7672 AD	7673 AD	7674 AD	7675 AD	7676 AD	7677 AD	7678 AD	7679 AD	7680 AD
7681 AD	7682 AD	7683 AD	7684 AD	7685 AD	7686 AD	7687 AD	7688 AD	7689 AD	7690 AD
7691 AD	7692 AD	7693 AD	7694 AD	7695 AD	7696 AD	7697 AD	7698 AD	7699 AD	7700 AD
7701 AD	7702 AD	7703 AD	7704 AD	7705 AD	7706 AD	7707 AD	7708 AD	7709 AD	7710 AD
7711 AD	7712 AD	7713 AD	7714 AD	7715 AD	7716 AD	7717 AD	7718 AD	7719 AD	7720 AD
7721 AD	7722 AD	7723 AD	7724 AD	7725 AD	7726 AD	7727 AD	7728 AD	7729 AD	7730 AD
7731 AD	7732 AD	7733 AD	7734 AD	7735 AD	7736 AD	7737 AD	7738 AD	7739 AD	7740 AD
7741 AD	7742 AD	7743 AD	7744 AD	7745 AD	7746 AD	7747 AD	7748 AD	7749 AD	7750 AD
7751 AD	7752 AD	7753 AD	7754 AD	7755 AD	7756 AD	7757 AD	7758 AD	7759 AD	7760 AD
7761 AD	7762 AD	7763 AD	7764 AD	7765 AD	7766 AD	7767 AD	7768 AD	7769 AD	7770 AD
7771 AD	7772 AD	7773 AD	7774 AD	7775 AD	7776 AD	7777 AD	7778 AD	7779 AD	7780 AD
7781 AD	7782 AD	7783 AD	7784 AD	7785 AD	7786 AD	7787 AD	7788 AD	7789 AD	7790 AD
7791 AD	7792 AD	7793 AD	7794 AD	7795 AD	7796 AD	7797 AD	7798 AD	7799 AD	7800 AD
7801 AD	7802 AD	7803 AD	7804 AD	7805 AD	7806 AD	7807 AD	7808 AD	7809 AD	7810 AD
7811 AD	7812 AD	7813 AD	7814 AD	7815 AD	7816 AD	7817 AD	7818 AD	7819 AD	7820 AD
7821 AD	7822 AD	7823 AD	7824 AD	7825 AD	7826 AD	7827 AD	7828 AD	7829 AD	7830 AD
7831 AD	7832 AD	7833 AD	7834 AD	7835 AD	7836 AD	7837 AD	7838 AD	7839 AD	7840 AD
7841 AD	7842 AD	7843 AD	7844 AD	7845 AD	7846 AD	7847 AD	7848 AD	7849 AD	7850 AD
7851 AD	7852 AD	7853 AD	7854 AD	7855 AD	7856 AD	7857 AD	7858 AD	7859 AD	7860 AD
7861 AD	7862 AD	7863 AD	7864 AD	7865 AD	7866 AD	7867 AD	7868 AD	7869 AD	7870 AD
7871 AD	7872 AD	7873 AD	7874 AD	7875 AD	7876 AD	7877 AD	7878 AD	7879 AD	7880 AD
7881 AD	7882 AD	7883 AD	7884 AD	7885 AD	7886 AD	7887 AD	7888 AD	7889 AD	7890 AD
7891 AD	7892 AD	7893 AD	7894 AD	7895 AD	7896 AD	7897 AD	7898 AD	7899 AD	7900 AD
7901 AD	7902 AD	7903 AD	7904 AD	7905 AD	7906 AD	7907 AD	7908 AD	7909 AD	7910 AD
7911 AD	7912 AD	7913 AD	7914 AD	7915 AD	7916 AD	7917 AD	7918 AD	7919 AD	7920 AD
7921 AD	7922 AD	7923 AD	7924 AD	7925 AD	7926 AD	7927 AD	7928 AD	7929 AD	7930 AD
7931 AD	7932 AD	7933 AD	7934 AD	7935 AD	7936 AD	7937 AD	7938 AD	7939 AD	7940 AD
7941 AD	7942 AD	7943 AD	7944 AD	7945 AD	7946 AD	7947 AD	7948 AD	7949 AD	7950 AD
7951 AD	7952 AD	7953 AD	7954 AD	7955 AD	7956 AD	7957 AD	7958 AD	7959 AD	7960 AD
7961 AD	7962 AD	7963 AD	7964 AD	7965 AD	7966 AD	7967 AD	7968 AD	7969 AD	7970 AD
7971 AD	7972 AD	7973 AD	7974 AD	7975 AD	7976 AD	7977 AD	7978 AD	7979 AD	7980 AD
7981 AD	7982 AD	7983 AD	7984 AD	7985 AD	7986 AD	7987 AD	7988 AD	7989 AD	7990 AD
7991 AD	7992 AD	7993 AD	7994 AD	7995 AD	7996 AD	7997 AD	7998 AD	7999 AD	8000 AD

— 13 —

8001 AD	8002 AD	8003 AD	8004 AD	8005 AD	8006 AD	8007 AD	8008 AD	8009 AD	8010 AD
8011 AD	8012 AD	8013 AD	8014 AD	8015 AD	8016 AD	8017 AD	8018 AD	8019 AD	8020 AD
8021 AD	8022 AD	8023 AD	8024 AD	8025 AD	8026 AD	8027 AD	8028 AD	8029 AD	8030 AD
8031 AD	8032 AD	8033 AD	8034 AD	8035 AD	8036 AD	8037 AD	8038 AD	8039 AD	8040 AD
8041 AD	8042 AD	8043 AD	8044 AD	8045 AD	8046 AD	8047 AD	8048 AD	8049 AD	8050 AD
8051 AD	8052 AD	8053 AD	8054 AD	8055 AD	8056 AD	8057 AD	8058 AD	8059 AD	8060 AD
8061 AD	8062 AD	8063 AD	8064 AD	8065 AD	8066 AD	8067 AD	8068 AD	8069 AD	8070 AD
8071 AD	8072 AD	8073 AD	8074 AD	8075 AD	8076 AD	8077 AD	8078 AD	8079 AD	8080 AD
8081 AD	8082 AD	8083 AD	8084 AD	8085 AD	8086 AD	8087 AD	8088 AD	8089 AD	8090 AD
8091 AD	8092 AD	8093 AD	8094 AD	8095 AD	8096 AD	8097 AD	8098 AD	8099 AD	8100 AD
8101 AD	8102 AD	8103 AD	8104 AD	8105 AD	8106 AD	8107 AD	8108 AD	8109 AD	8110 AD
8111 AD	8112 AD	8113 AD	8114 AD	8115 AD	8116 AD	8117 AD	8118 AD	8119 AD	8120 AD
8121 AD	8122 AD	8123 AD	8124 AD	8125 AD	8126 AD	8127 AD	8128 AD	8129 AD	8130 AD
8131 AD	8132 AD	8133 AD	8134 AD	8135 AD	8136 AD	8137 AD	8138 AD	8139 AD	8140 AD
8141 AD	8142 AD	8143 AD	8144 AD	8145 AD	8146 AD	8147 AD	8148 AD	8149 AD	8150 AD
8151 AD	8152 AD	8153 AD	8154 AD	8155 AD	8156 AD	8157 AD	8158 AD	8159 AD	8160 AD
8161 AD	8162 AD	8163 AD	8164 AD	8165 AD	8166 AD	8167 AD	8168 AD	8169 AD	8170 AD
8171 AD	8172 AD	8173 AD	8174 AD	8175 AD	8176 AD	8177 AD	8178 AD	8179 AD	8180 AD
8181 AD	8182 AD	8183 AD	8184 AD	8185 AD	8186 AD	8187 AD	8188 AD	8189 AD	8190 AD
8191 AD	8192 AD	8193 AD	8194 AD	8195 AD	8196 AD	8197 AD	8198 AD	8199 AD	8200 AD
8201 AD	8202 AD	8203 AD	8204 AD	8205 AD	8206 AD	8207 AD	8208 AD	8209 AD	8210 AD
8211 AD	8212 AD	8213 AD	8214 AD	8215 AD	8216 AD	8217 AD	8218 AD	8219 AD	8220 AD
8221 AD	8222 AD	8223 AD	8224 AD	8225 AD	8226 AD	8227 AD	8228 AD	8229 AD	8230 AD
8231 AD	8232 AD	8233 AD	8234 AD	8235 AD	8236 AD	8237 AD	8238 AD	8239 AD	8240 AD
8241 AD	8242 AD	8243 AD	8244 AD	8245 AD	8246 AD	8247 AD	8248 AD	8249 AD	8250 AD
8251 AD	8252 AD	8253 AD	8254 AD	8255 AD	8256 AD	8257 AD	8258 AD	8259 AD	8260 AD
8261 AD	8262 AD	8263 AD	8264 AD	8265 AD	8266 AD	8267 AD	8268 AD	8269 AD	8270 AD
8271 AD	8272 AD	8273 AD	8274 AD	8275 AD	8276 AD	8277 AD	8278 AD	8279 AD	8280 AD
8281 AD	8282 AD	8283 AD	8284 AD	8285 AD	8286 AD	8287 AD	8288 AD	8289 AD	8290 AD
8291 AD	8292 AD	8293 AD	8294 AD	8295 AD	8296 AD	8297 AD	8298 AD	8299 AD	8300 AD
8301 AD	8302 AD	8303 AD	8304 AD	8305 AD	8306 AD	8307 AD	8308 AD	8309 AD	8310 AD
8311 AD	8312 AD	8313 AD	8314 AD	8315 AD	8316 AD	8317 AD	8318 AD	8319 AD	8320 AD
8321 AD	8322 AD	8323 AD	8324 AD	8325 AD	8326 AD	8327 AD	8328 AD	8329 AD	8330 AD
8331 AD	8332 AD	8333 AD	8334 AD	8335 AD	8336 AD	8337 AD	8338 AD	8339 AD	8340 AD
8341 AD	8342 AD	8343 AD	8344 AD	8345 AD	8346 AD	8347 AD	8348 AD	8349 AD	8350 AD
8351 AD	8352 AD	8353 AD	8354 AD	8355 AD	8356 AD	8357 AD	8358 AD	8359 AD	8360 AD
8361 AD	8362 AD	8363 AD	8364 AD	8365 AD	8366 AD	8367 AD	8368 AD	8369 AD	8370 AD
8371 AD	8372 AD	8373 AD	8374 AD	8375 AD	8376 AD	8377 AD	8378 AD	8379 AD	8380 AD
8381 AD	8382 AD	8383 AD	8384 AD	8385 AD	8386 AD	8387 AD	8388 AD	8389 AD	8390 AD
8391 AD	8392 AD	8393 AD	8394 AD	8395 AD	8396 AD	8397 AD	8398 AD	8399 AD	8400 AD
8401 AD	8402 AD	8403 AD	8404 AD	8405 AD	8406 AD	8407 AD	8408 AD	8409 AD	8410 AD
8411 AD	8412 AD	8413 AD	8414 AD	8415 AD	8416 AD	8417 AD	8418 AD	8419 AD	8420 AD
8421 AD	8422 AD	8423 AD	8424 AD	8425 AD	8426 AD	8427 AD	8428 AD	8429 AD	8430 AD
8431 AD	8432 AD	8433 AD	8434 AD	8435 AD	8436 AD	8437 AD	8438 AD	8439 AD	8440 AD
8441 AD	8442 AD	8443 AD	8444 AD	8445 AD	8446 AD	8447 AD	8448 AD	8449 AD	8450 AD
8451 AD	8452 AD	8453 AD	8454 AD	8455 AD	8456 AD	8457 AD	8458 AD	8459 AD	8460 AD
8461 AD	8462 AD	8463 AD	8464 AD	8465 AD	8466 AD	8467 AD	8468 AD	8469 AD	8470 AD
8471 AD	8472 AD	8473 AD	8474 AD	8475 AD	8476 AD	8477 AD	8478 AD	8479 AD	8480 AD
8481 AD	8482 AD	8483 AD	8484 AD	8485 AD	8486 AD	8487 AD	8488 AD	8489 AD	8490 AD
8491 AD	8492 AD	8493 AD	8494 AD	8495 AD	8496 AD	8497 AD	8498 AD	8499 AD	8500 AD

8501 AD	8502 AD	8503 AD	8504 AD	8505 AD	8506 AD	8507 AD	8508 AD	8509 AD	8510 AD
8511 AD	8512 AD	8513 AD	8514 AD	8515 AD	8516 AD	8517 AD	8518 AD	8519 AD	8520 AD
8521 AD	8522 AD	8523 AD	8524 AD	8525 AD	8526 AD	8527 AD	8528 AD	8529 AD	8530 AD
8531 AD	8532 AD	8533 AD	8534 AD	8535 AD	8536 AD	8537 AD	8538 AD	8539 AD	8540 AD
8541 AD	8542 AD	8543 AD	8544 AD	8545 AD	8546 AD	8547 AD	8548 AD	8549 AD	8550 AD
8551 AD	8552 AD	8553 AD	8554 AD	8555 AD	8556 AD	8557 AD	8558 AD	8559 AD	8560 AD
8561 AD	8562 AD	8563 AD	8564 AD	8565 AD	8566 AD	8567 AD	8568 AD	8569 AD	8570 AD
8571 AD	8572 AD	8573 AD	8574 AD	8575 AD	8576 AD	8577 AD	8578 AD	8579 AD	8580 AD
8581 AD	8582 AD	8583 AD	8584 AD	8585 AD	8586 AD	8587 AD	8588 AD	8589 AD	8590 AD
8591 AD	8592 AD	8593 AD	8594 AD	8595 AD	8596 AD	8597 AD	8598 AD	8599 AD	8600 AD
8601 AD	8602 AD	8603 AD	8604 AD	8605 AD	8606 AD	8607 AD	8608 AD	8609 AD	8610 AD
8611 AD	8612 AD	8613 AD	8614 AD	8615 AD	8616 AD	8617 AD	8618 AD	8619 AD	8620 AD
8621 AD	8622 AD	8623 AD	8624 AD	8625 AD	8626 AD	8627 AD	8628 AD	8629 AD	8630 AD
8631 AD	8632 AD	8633 AD	8634 AD	8635 AD	8636 AD	8637 AD	8638 AD	8639 AD	8640 AD
8641 AD	8642 AD	8643 AD	8644 AD	8645 AD	8646 AD	8647 AD	8648 AD	8649 AD	8650 AD
8651 AD	8652 AD	8653 AD	8654 AD	8655 AD	8656 AD	8657 AD	8658 AD	8659 AD	8660 AD
8661 AD	8662 AD	8663 AD	8664 AD	8665 AD	8666 AD	8667 AD	8668 AD	8669 AD	8670 AD
8671 AD	8672 AD	8673 AD	8674 AD	8675 AD	8676 AD	8677 AD	8678 AD	8679 AD	8680 AD
8681 AD	8682 AD	8683 AD	8684 AD	8685 AD	8686 AD	8687 AD	8688 AD	8689 AD	8690 AD
8691 AD	8692 AD	8693 AD	8694 AD	8695 AD	8696 AD	8697 AD	8698 AD	8699 AD	8700 AD
8701 AD	8702 AD	8703 AD	8704 AD	8705 AD	8706 AD	8707 AD	8708 AD	8709 AD	8710 AD
8711 AD	8712 AD	8713 AD	8714 AD	8715 AD	8716 AD	8717 AD	8718 AD	8719 AD	8720 AD
8721 AD	8722 AD	8723 AD	8724 AD	8725 AD	8726 AD	8727 AD	8728 AD	8729 AD	8730 AD
8731 AD	8732 AD	8733 AD	8734 AD	8735 AD	8736 AD	8737 AD	8738 AD	8739 AD	8740 AD
8741 AD	8742 AD	8743 AD	8744 AD	8745 AD	8746 AD	8747 AD	8748 AD	8749 AD	8750 AD
8751 AD	8752 AD	8753 AD	8754 AD	8755 AD	8756 AD	8757 AD	8758 AD	8759 AD	8760 AD
8761 AD	8762 AD	8763 AD	8764 AD	8765 AD	8766 AD	8767 AD	8768 AD	8769 AD	8770 AD
8771 AD	8772 AD	8773 AD	8774 AD	8775 AD	8776 AD	8777 AD	8778 AD	8779 AD	8780 AD
8781 AD	8782 AD	8783 AD	8784 AD	8785 AD	8786 AD	8787 AD	8788 AD	8789 AD	8790 AD
8791 AD	8792 AD	8793 AD	8794 AD	8795 AD	8796 AD	8797 AD	8798 AD	8799 AD	8800 AD
8801 AD	8802 AD	8803 AD	8804 AD	8805 AD	8806 AD	8807 AD	8808 AD	8809 AD	8810 AD
8811 AD	8812 AD	8813 AD	8814 AD	8815 AD	8816 AD	8817 AD	8818 AD	8819 AD	8820 AD
8821 AD	8822 AD	8823 AD	8824 AD	8825 AD	8826 AD	8827 AD	8828 AD	8829 AD	8830 AD
8831 AD	8832 AD	8833 AD	8834 AD	8835 AD	8836 AD	8837 AD	8838 AD	8839 AD	8840 AD
8841 AD	8842 AD	8843 AD	8844 AD	8845 AD	8846 AD	8847 AD	8848 AD	8849 AD	8850 AD
8851 AD	8852 AD	8853 AD	8854 AD	8855 AD	8856 AD	8857 AD	8858 AD	8859 AD	8860 AD
8861 AD	8862 AD	8863 AD	8864 AD	8865 AD	8866 AD	8867 AD	8868 AD	8869 AD	8870 AD
8871 AD	8872 AD	8873 AD	8874 AD	8875 AD	8876 AD	8877 AD	8878 AD	8879 AD	8880 AD
8881 AD	8882 AD	8883 AD	8884 AD	8885 AD	8886 AD	8887 AD	8888 AD	8889 AD	8890 AD
8891 AD	8892 AD	8893 AD	8894 AD	8895 AD	8896 AD	8897 AD	8898 AD	8899 AD	8900 AD
8901 AD	8902 AD	8903 AD	8904 AD	8905 AD	8906 AD	8907 AD	8908 AD	8909 AD	8910 AD
8911 AD	8912 AD	8913 AD	8914 AD	8915 AD	8916 AD	8917 AD	8918 AD	8919 AD	8920 AD
8921 AD	8922 AD	8923 AD	8924 AD	8925 AD	8926 AD	8927 AD	8928 AD	8929 AD	8930 AD
8931 AD	8932 AD	8933 AD	8934 AD	8935 AD	8936 AD	8937 AD	8938 AD	8939 AD	8940 AD
8941 AD	8942 AD	8943 AD	8944 AD	8945 AD	8946 AD	8947 AD	8948 AD	8949 AD	8950 AD
8951 AD	8952 AD	8953 AD	8954 AD	8955 AD	8956 AD	8957 AD	8958 AD	8959 AD	8960 AD
8961 AD	8962 AD	8963 AD	8964 AD	8965 AD	8966 AD	8967 AD	8968 AD	8969 AD	8970 AD
8971 AD	8972 AD	8973 AD	8974 AD	8975 AD	8976 AD	8977 AD	8978 AD	8979 AD	8980 AD
8981 AD	8982 AD	8983 AD	8984 AD	8985 AD	8986 AD	8987 AD	8988 AD	8989 AD	8990 AD
8991 AD	8992 AD	8993 AD	8994 AD	8995 AD	8996 AD	8997 AD	8998 AD	8999 AD	9000 AD

9001 AD	9002 AD	9003 AD	9004 AD	9005 AD	9006 AD	9007 AD	9008 AD	9009 AD	9010 AD
9011 AD	9012 AD	9013 AD	9014 AD	9015 AD	9016 AD	9017 AD	9018 AD	9019 AD	9020 AD
9021 AD	9022 AD	9023 AD	9024 AD	9025 AD	9026 AD	9027 AD	9028 AD	9029 AD	9030 AD
9031 AD	9032 AD	9033 AD	9034 AD	9035 AD	9036 AD	9037 AD	9038 AD	9039 AD	9040 AD
9041 AD	9042 AD	9043 AD	9044 AD	9045 AD	9046 AD	9047 AD	9048 AD	9049 AD	9050 AD
9051 AD	9052 AD	9053 AD	9054 AD	9055 AD	9056 AD	9057 AD	9058 AD	9059 AD	9060 AD
9061 AD	9062 AD	9063 AD	9064 AD	9065 AD	9066 AD	9067 AD	9068 AD	9069 AD	9070 AD
9071 AD	9072 AD	9073 AD	9074 AD	9075 AD	9076 AD	9077 AD	9078 AD	9079 AD	9080 AD
9081 AD	9082 AD	9083 AD	9084 AD	9085 AD	9086 AD	9087 AD	9088 AD	9089 AD	9090 AD
9091 AD	9092 AD	9093 AD	9094 AD	9095 AD	9096 AD	9097 AD	9098 AD	9099 AD	9100 AD
9101 AD	9102 AD	9103 AD	9104 AD	9105 AD	9106 AD	9107 AD	9108 AD	9109 AD	9110 AD
9111 AD	9112 AD	9113 AD	9114 AD	9115 AD	9116 AD	9117 AD	9118 AD	9119 AD	9120 AD
9121 AD	9122 AD	9123 AD	9124 AD	9125 AD	9126 AD	9127 AD	9128 AD	9129 AD	9130 AD
9131 AD	9132 AD	9133 AD	9134 AD	9135 AD	9136 AD	9137 AD	9138 AD	9139 AD	9140 AD
9141 AD	9142 AD	9143 AD	9144 AD	9145 AD	9146 AD	9147 AD	9148 AD	9149 AD	9150 AD
9151 AD	9152 AD	9153 AD	9154 AD	9155 AD	9156 AD	9157 AD	9158 AD	9159 AD	9160 AD
9161 AD	9162 AD	9163 AD	9164 AD	9165 AD	9166 AD	9167 AD	9168 AD	9169 AD	9170 AD
9171 AD	9172 AD	9173 AD	9174 AD	9175 AD	9176 AD	9177 AD	9178 AD	9179 AD	9180 AD
9181 AD	9182 AD	9183 AD	9184 AD	9185 AD	9186 AD	9187 AD	9188 AD	9189 AD	9190 AD
9191 AD	9192 AD	9193 AD	9194 AD	9195 AD	9196 AD	9197 AD	9198 AD	9199 AD	9200 AD
9201 AD	9202 AD	9203 AD	9204 AD	9205 AD	9206 AD	9207 AD	9208 AD	9209 AD	9210 AD
9211 AD	9212 AD	9213 AD	9214 AD	9215 AD	9216 AD	9217 AD	9218 AD	9219 AD	9220 AD
9221 AD	9222 AD	9223 AD	9224 AD	9225 AD	9226 AD	9227 AD	9228 AD	9229 AD	9230 AD
9231 AD	9232 AD	9233 AD	9234 AD	9235 AD	9236 AD	9237 AD	9238 AD	9239 AD	9240 AD
9241 AD	9242 AD	9243 AD	9244 AD	9245 AD	9246 AD	9247 AD	9248 AD	9249 AD	9250 AD
9251 AD	9252 AD	9253 AD	9254 AD	9255 AD	9256 AD	9257 AD	9258 AD	9259 AD	9260 AD
9261 AD	9262 AD	9263 AD	9264 AD	9265 AD	9266 AD	9267 AD	9268 AD	9269 AD	9270 AD
9271 AD	9272 AD	9273 AD	9274 AD	9275 AD	9276 AD	9277 AD	9278 AD	9279 AD	9280 AD
9281 AD	9282 AD	9283 AD	9284 AD	9285 AD	9286 AD	9287 AD	9288 AD	9289 AD	9290 AD
9291 AD	9292 AD	9293 AD	9294 AD	9295 AD	9296 AD	9297 AD	9298 AD	9299 AD	9300 AD
9301 AD	9302 AD	9303 AD	9304 AD	9305 AD	9306 AD	9307 AD	9308 AD	9309 AD	9310 AD
9311 AD	9312 AD	9313 AD	9314 AD	9315 AD	9316 AD	9317 AD	9318 AD	9319 AD	9320 AD
9321 AD	9322 AD	9323 AD	9324 AD	9325 AD	9326 AD	9327 AD	9328 AD	9329 AD	9330 AD
9331 AD	9332 AD	9333 AD	9334 AD	9335 AD	9336 AD	9337 AD	9338 AD	9339 AD	9340 AD
9341 AD	9342 AD	9343 AD	9344 AD	9345 AD	9346 AD	9347 AD	9348 AD	9349 AD	9350 AD
9351 AD	9352 AD	9353 AD	9354 AD	9355 AD	9356 AD	9357 AD	9358 AD	9359 AD	9360 AD
9361 AD	9362 AD	9363 AD	9364 AD	9365 AD	9366 AD	9367 AD	9368 AD	9369 AD	9370 AD
9371 AD	9372 AD	9373 AD	9374 AD	9375 AD	9376 AD	9377 AD	9378 AD	9379 AD	9380 AD
9381 AD	9382 AD	9383 AD	9384 AD	9385 AD	9386 AD	9387 AD	9388 AD	9389 AD	9390 AD
9391 AD	9392 AD	9393 AD	9394 AD	9395 AD	9396 AD	9397 AD	9398 AD	9399 AD	9400 AD
9401 AD	9402 AD	9403 AD	9404 AD	9405 AD	9406 AD	9407 AD	9408 AD	9409 AD	9410 AD
9411 AD	9412 AD	9413 AD	9414 AD	9415 AD	9416 AD	9417 AD	9418 AD	9419 AD	9420 AD
9421 AD	9422 AD	9423 AD	9424 AD	9425 AD	9426 AD	9427 AD	9428 AD	9429 AD	9430 AD
9431 AD	9432 AD	9433 AD	9434 AD	9435 AD	9436 AD	9437 AD	9438 AD	9439 AD	9440 AD
9441 AD	9442 AD	9443 AD	9444 AD	9445 AD	9446 AD	9447 AD	9448 AD	9449 AD	9450 AD
9451 AD	9452 AD	9453 AD	9454 AD	9455 AD	9456 AD	9457 AD	9458 AD	9459 AD	9460 AD
9461 AD	9462 AD	9463 AD	9464 AD	9465 AD	9466 AD	9467 AD	9468 AD	9469 AD	9470 AD
9471 AD	9472 AD	9473 AD	9474 AD	9475 AD	9476 AD	9477 AD	9478 AD	9479 AD	9480 AD
9481 AD	9482 AD	9483 AD	9484 AD	9485 AD	9486 AD	9487 AD	9488 AD	9489 AD	9490 AD
9491 AD	9492 AD	9493 AD	9494 AD	9495 AD	9496 AD	9497 AD	9498 AD	9499 AD	9500 AD

9501 AD	9502 AD	9503 AD	9504 AD	9505 AD	9506 AD	9507 AD	9508 AD	9509 AD	9510 AD
9511 AD	9512 AD	9513 AD	9514 AD	9515 AD	9516 AD	9517 AD	9518 AD	9519 AD	9520 AD
9521 AD	9522 AD	9523 AD	9524 AD	9525 AD	9526 AD	9527 AD	9528 AD	9529 AD	9530 AD
9531 AD	9532 AD	9533 AD	9534 AD	9535 AD	9536 AD	9537 AD	9538 AD	9539 AD	9540 AD
9541 AD	9542 AD	9543 AD	9544 AD	9545 AD	9546 AD	9547 AD	9548 AD	9549 AD	9550 AD
9551 AD	9552 AD	9553 AD	9554 AD	9555 AD	9556 AD	9557 AD	9558 AD	9559 AD	9560 AD
9561 AD	9562 AD	9563 AD	9564 AD	9565 AD	9566 AD	9567 AD	9568 AD	9569 AD	9570 AD
9571 AD	9572 AD	9573 AD	9574 AD	9575 AD	9576 AD	9577 AD	9578 AD	9579 AD	9580 AD
9581 AD	9582 AD	9583 AD	9584 AD	9585 AD	9586 AD	9587 AD	9588 AD	9589 AD	9590 AD
9591 AD	9592 AD	9593 AD	9594 AD	9595 AD	9596 AD	9597 AD	9598 AD	9599 AD	9600 AD
9601 AD	9602 AD	9603 AD	9604 AD	9605 AD	9606 AD	9607 AD	9608 AD	9609 AD	9610 AD
9611 AD	9612 AD	9613 AD	9614 AD	9615 AD	9616 AD	9617 AD	9618 AD	9619 AD	9620 AD
9621 AD	9622 AD	9623 AD	9624 AD	9625 AD	9626 AD	9627 AD	9628 AD	9629 AD	9630 AD
9631 AD	9632 AD	9633 AD	9634 AD	9635 AD	9636 AD	9637 AD	9638 AD	9639 AD	9640 AD
9641 AD	9642 AD	9643 AD	9644 AD	9645 AD	9646 AD	9647 AD	9648 AD	9649 AD	9650 AD
9651 AD	9652 AD	9653 AD	9654 AD	9655 AD	9656 AD	9657 AD	9658 AD	9659 AD	9660 AD
9661 AD	9662 AD	9663 AD	9664 AD	9665 AD	9666 AD	9667 AD	9668 AD	9669 AD	9670 AD
9671 AD	9672 AD	9673 AD	9674 AD	9675 AD	9676 AD	9677 AD	9678 AD	9679 AD	9680 AD
9681 AD	9682 AD	9683 AD	9684 AD	9685 AD	9686 AD	9687 AD	9688 AD	9689 AD	9690 AD
9691 AD	9692 AD	9693 AD	9694 AD	9695 AD	9696 AD	9697 AD	9698 AD	9699 AD	9700 AD
9701 AD	9702 AD	9703 AD	9704 AD	9705 AD	9706 AD	9707 AD	9708 AD	9709 AD	9710 AD
9711 AD	9712 AD	9713 AD	9714 AD	9715 AD	9716 AD	9717 AD	9718 AD	9719 AD	9720 AD
9721 AD	9722 AD	9723 AD	9724 AD	9725 AD	9726 AD	9727 AD	9728 AD	9729 AD	9730 AD
9731 AD	9732 AD	9733 AD	9734 AD	9735 AD	9736 AD	9737 AD	9738 AD	9739 AD	9740 AD
9741 AD	9742 AD	9743 AD	9744 AD	9745 AD	9746 AD	9747 AD	9748 AD	9749 AD	9750 AD
9751 AD	9752 AD	9753 AD	9754 AD	9755 AD	9756 AD	9757 AD	9758 AD	9759 AD	9760 AD
9761 AD	9762 AD	9763 AD	9764 AD	9765 AD	9766 AD	9767 AD	9768 AD	9769 AD	9770 AD
9771 AD	9772 AD	9773 AD	9774 AD	9775 AD	9776 AD	9777 AD	9778 AD	9779 AD	9780 AD
9781 AD	9782 AD	9783 AD	9784 AD	9785 AD	9786 AD	9787 AD	9788 AD	9789 AD	9790 AD
9791 AD	9792 AD	9793 AD	9794 AD	9795 AD	9796 AD	9797 AD	9798 AD	9799 AD	9800 AD
9801 AD	9802 AD	9803 AD	9804 AD	9805 AD	9806 AD	9807 AD	9808 AD	9809 AD	9810 AD
9811 AD	9812 AD	9813 AD	9814 AD	9815 AD	9816 AD	9817 AD	9818 AD	9819 AD	9820 AD
9821 AD	9822 AD	9823 AD	9824 AD	9825 AD	9826 AD	9827 AD	9828 AD	9829 AD	9830 AD
9831 AD	9832 AD	9833 AD	9834 AD	9835 AD	9836 AD	9837 AD	9838 AD	9839 AD	9840 AD
9841 AD	9842 AD	9843 AD	9844 AD	9845 AD	9846 AD	9847 AD	9848 AD	9849 AD	9850 AD
9851 AD	9852 AD	9853 AD	9854 AD	9855 AD	9856 AD	9857 AD	9858 AD	9859 AD	9860 AD
9861 AD	9862 AD	9863 AD	9864 AD	9865 AD	9866 AD	9867 AD	9868 AD	9869 AD	9870 AD
9871 AD	9872 AD	9873 AD	9874 AD	9875 AD	9876 AD	9877 AD	9878 AD	9879 AD	9880 AD
9881 AD	9882 AD	9883 AD	9884 AD	9885 AD	9886 AD	9887 AD	9888 AD	9889 AD	9890 AD
9891 AD	9892 AD	9893 AD	9894 AD	9895 AD	9896 AD	9897 AD	9898 AD	9899 AD	9900 AD
9901 AD	9902 AD	9903 AD	9904 AD	9905 AD	9906 AD	9907 AD	9908 AD	9909 AD	9910 AD
9911 AD	9912 AD	9913 AD	9914 AD	9915 AD	9916 AD	9917 AD	9918 AD	9919 AD	9920 AD
9921 AD	9922 AD	9923 AD	9924 AD	9925 AD	9926 AD	9927 AD	9928 AD	9929 AD	9930 AD
9931 AD	9932 AD	9933 AD	9934 AD	9935 AD	9936 AD	9937 AD	9938 AD	9939 AD	9940 AD
9941 AD	9942 AD	9943 AD	9944 AD	9945 AD	9946 AD	9947 AD	9948 AD	9949 AD	9950 AD
9951 AD	9952 AD	9953 AD	9954 AD	9955 AD	9956 AD	9957 AD	9958 AD	9959 AD	9960 AD
9961 AD	9962 AD	9963 AD	9964 AD	9965 AD	9966 AD	9967 AD	9968 AD	9969 AD	9970 AD
9971 AD	9972 AD	9973 AD	9974 AD	9975 AD	9976 AD	9977 AD	9978 AD	9979 AD	9980 AD
9981 AD	9982 AD	9983 AD	9984 AD	9985 AD	9986 AD	9987 AD	9988 AD	9989 AD	9990 AD
9991 AD	9992 AD	9993 AD	9994 AD	9995 AD	9996 AD	9997 AD	9998 AD	9999 AD	10000 AD

10001 AD	10002 AD	10003 AD	10004 AD	10005 AD	10006 AD	10007 AD	10008 AD	10009 AD	10010 AD
10011 AD	10012 AD	10013 AD	10014 AD	10015 AD	10016 AD	10017 AD	10018 AD	10019 AD	10020 AD
10021 AD	10022 AD	10023 AD	10024 AD	10025 AD	10026 AD	10027 AD	10028 AD	10029 AD	10030 AD
10031 AD	10032 AD	10033 AD	10034 AD	10035 AD	10036 AD	10037 AD	10038 AD	10039 AD	10040 AD
10041 AD	10042 AD	10043 AD	10044 AD	10045 AD	10046 AD	10047 AD	10048 AD	10049 AD	10050 AD
10051 AD	10052 AD	10053 AD	10054 AD	10055 AD	10056 AD	10057 AD	10058 AD	10059 AD	10060 AD
10061 AD	10062 AD	10063 AD	10064 AD	10065 AD	10066 AD	10067 AD	10068 AD	10069 AD	10070 AD
10071 AD	10072 AD	10073 AD	10074 AD	10075 AD	10076 AD	10077 AD	10078 AD	10079 AD	10080 AD
10081 AD	10082 AD	10083 AD	10084 AD	10085 AD	10086 AD	10087 AD	10088 AD	10089 AD	10090 AD
10091 AD	10092 AD	10093 AD	10094 AD	10095 AD	10096 AD	10097 AD	10098 AD	10099 AD	10100 AD
10101 AD	10102 AD	10103 AD	10104 AD	10105 AD	10106 AD	10107 AD	10108 AD	10109 AD	10110 AD
10111 AD	10112 AD	10113 AD	10114 AD	10115 AD	10116 AD	10117 AD	10118 AD	10119 AD	10120 AD
10121 AD	10122 AD	10123 AD	10124 AD	10125 AD	10126 AD	10127 AD	10128 AD	10129 AD	10130 AD
10131 AD	10132 AD	10133 AD	10134 AD	10135 AD	10136 AD	10137 AD	10138 AD	10139 AD	10140 AD
10141 AD	10142 AD	10143 AD	10144 AD	10145 AD	10146 AD	10147 AD	10148 AD	10149 AD	10150 AD
10151 AD	10152 AD	10153 AD	10154 AD	10155 AD	10156 AD	10157 AD	10158 AD	10159 AD	10160 AD
10161 AD	10162 AD	10163 AD	10164 AD	10165 AD	10166 AD	10167 AD	10168 AD	10169 AD	10170 AD
10171 AD	10172 AD	10173 AD	10174 AD	10175 AD	10176 AD	10177 AD	10178 AD	10179 AD	10180 AD
10181 AD	10182 AD	10183 AD	10184 AD	10185 AD	10186 AD	10187 AD	10188 AD	10189 AD	10190 AD
10191 AD	10192 AD	10193 AD	10194 AD	10195 AD	10196 AD	10197 AD	10198 AD	10199 AD	10200 AD
10201 AD	10202 AD	10203 AD	10204 AD	10205 AD	10206 AD	10207 AD	10208 AD	10209 AD	10210 AD
10211 AD	10212 AD	10213 AD	10214 AD	10215 AD	10216 AD	10217 AD	10218 AD	10219 AD	10220 AD
10221 AD	10222 AD	10223 AD	10224 AD	10225 AD	10226 AD	10227 AD	10228 AD	10229 AD	10230 AD
10231 AD	10232 AD	10233 AD	10234 AD	10235 AD	10236 AD	10237 AD	10238 AD	10239 AD	10240 AD
10241 AD	10242 AD	10243 AD	10244 AD	10245 AD	10246 AD	10247 AD	10248 AD	10249 AD	10250 AD
10251 AD	10252 AD	10253 AD	10254 AD	10255 AD	10256 AD	10257 AD	10258 AD	10259 AD	10260 AD
10261 AD	10262 AD	10263 AD	10264 AD	10265 AD	10266 AD	10267 AD	10268 AD	10269 AD	10270 AD
10271 AD	10272 AD	10273 AD	10274 AD	10275 AD	10276 AD	10277 AD	10278 AD	10279 AD	10280 AD
10281 AD	10282 AD	10283 AD	10284 AD	10285 AD	10286 AD	10287 AD	10288 AD	10289 AD	10290 AD
10291 AD	10292 AD	10293 AD	10294 AD	10295 AD	10296 AD	10297 AD	10298 AD	10299 AD	10300 AD
10301 AD	10302 AD	10303 AD	10304 AD	10305 AD	10306 AD	10307 AD	10308 AD	10309 AD	10310 AD
10311 AD	10312 AD	10313 AD	10314 AD	10315 AD	10316 AD	10317 AD	10318 AD	10319 AD	10320 AD
10321 AD	10322 AD	10323 AD	10324 AD	10325 AD	10326 AD	10327 AD	10328 AD	10329 AD	10330 AD
10331 AD	10332 AD	10333 AD	10334 AD	10335 AD	10336 AD	10337 AD	10338 AD	10339 AD	10340 AD
10341 AD	10342 AD	10343 AD	10344 AD	10345 AD	10346 AD	10347 AD	10348 AD	10349 AD	10350 AD
10351 AD	10352 AD	10353 AD	10354 AD	10355 AD	10356 AD	10357 AD	10358 AD	10359 AD	10360 AD
10361 AD	10362 AD	10363 AD	10364 AD	10365 AD	10366 AD	10367 AD	10368 AD	10369 AD	10370 AD
10371 AD	10372 AD	10373 AD	10374 AD	10375 AD	10376 AD	10377 AD	10378 AD	10379 AD	10380 AD
10381 AD	10382 AD	10383 AD	10384 AD	10385 AD	10386 AD	10387 AD	10388 AD	10389 AD	10390 AD
10391 AD	10392 AD	10393 AD	10394 AD	10395 AD	10396 AD	10397 AD	10398 AD	10399 AD	10400 AD
10401 AD	10402 AD	10403 AD	10404 AD	10405 AD	10406 AD	10407 AD	10408 AD	10409 AD	10410 AD
10411 AD	10412 AD	10413 AD	10414 AD	10415 AD	10416 AD	10417 AD	10418 AD	10419 AD	10420 AD
10421 AD	10422 AD	10423 AD	10424 AD	10425 AD	10426 AD	10427 AD	10428 AD	10429 AD	10430 AD
10431 AD	10432 AD	10433 AD	10434 AD	10435 AD	10436 AD	10437 AD	10438 AD	10439 AD	10440 AD
10441 AD	10442 AD	10443 AD	10444 AD	10445 AD	10446 AD	10447 AD	10448 AD	10449 AD	10450 AD
10451 AD	10452 AD	10453 AD	10454 AD	10455 AD	10456 AD	10457 AD	10458 AD	10459 AD	10460 AD
10461 AD	10462 AD	10463 AD	10464 AD	10465 AD	10466 AD	10467 AD	10468 AD	10469 AD	10470 AD
10471 AD	10472 AD	10473 AD	10474 AD	10475 AD	10476 AD	10477 AD	10478 AD	10479 AD	10480 AD
10481 AD	10482 AD	10483 AD	10484 AD	10485 AD	10486 AD	10487 AD	10488 AD	10489 AD	10490 AD
10491 AD	10492 AD	10493 AD	10494 AD	10495 AD	10496 AD	10497 AD	10498 AD	10499 AD	10500 AD

10501 AD	10502 AD	10503 AD	10504 AD	10505 AD	10506 AD	10507 AD	10508 AD	10509 AD	10510 AD
10511 AD	10512 AD	10513 AD	10514 AD	10515 AD	10516 AD	10517 AD	10518 AD	10519 AD	10520 AD
10521 AD	10522 AD	10523 AD	10524 AD	10525 AD	10526 AD	10527 AD	10528 AD	10529 AD	10530 AD
10531 AD	10532 AD	10533 AD	10534 AD	10535 AD	10536 AD	10537 AD	10538 AD	10539 AD	10540 AD
10541 AD	10542 AD	10543 AD	10544 AD	10545 AD	10546 AD	10547 AD	10548 AD	10549 AD	10550 AD
10551 AD	10552 AD	10553 AD	10554 AD	10555 AD	10556 AD	10557 AD	10558 AD	10559 AD	10560 AD
10561 AD	10562 AD	10563 AD	10564 AD	10565 AD	10566 AD	10567 AD	10568 AD	10569 AD	10570 AD
10571 AD	10572 AD	10573 AD	10574 AD	10575 AD	10576 AD	10577 AD	10578 AD	10579 AD	10580 AD
10581 AD	10582 AD	10583 AD	10584 AD	10585 AD	10586 AD	10587 AD	10588 AD	10589 AD	10590 AD
10591 AD	10592 AD	10593 AD	10594 AD	10595 AD	10596 AD	10597 AD	10598 AD	10599 AD	10600 AD
10601 AD	10602 AD	10603 AD	10604 AD	10605 AD	10606 AD	10607 AD	10608 AD	10609 AD	10610 AD
10611 AD	10612 AD	10613 AD	10614 AD	10615 AD	10616 AD	10617 AD	10618 AD	10619 AD	10620 AD
10621 AD	10622 AD	10623 AD	10624 AD	10625 AD	10626 AD	10627 AD	10628 AD	10629 AD	10630 AD
10631 AD	10632 AD	10633 AD	10634 AD	10635 AD	10636 AD	10637 AD	10638 AD	10639 AD	10640 AD
10641 AD	10642 AD	10643 AD	10644 AD	10645 AD	10646 AD	10647 AD	10648 AD	10649 AD	10650 AD
10651 AD	10652 AD	10653 AD	10654 AD	10655 AD	10656 AD	10657 AD	10658 AD	10659 AD	10660 AD
10661 AD	10662 AD	10663 AD	10664 AD	10665 AD	10666 AD	10667 AD	10668 AD	10669 AD	10670 AD
10671 AD	10672 AD	10673 AD	10674 AD	10675 AD	10676 AD	10677 AD	10678 AD	10679 AD	10680 AD
10681 AD	10682 AD	10683 AD	10684 AD	10685 AD	10686 AD	10687 AD	10688 AD	10689 AD	10690 AD
10691 AD	10692 AD	10693 AD	10694 AD	10695 AD	10696 AD	10697 AD	10698 AD	10699 AD	10700 AD
10701 AD	10702 AD	10703 AD	10704 AD	10705 AD	10706 AD	10707 AD	10708 AD	10709 AD	10710 AD
10711 AD	10712 AD	10713 AD	10714 AD	10715 AD	10716 AD	10717 AD	10718 AD	10719 AD	10720 AD
10721 AD	10722 AD	10723 AD	10724 AD	10725 AD	10726 AD	10727 AD	10728 AD	10729 AD	10730 AD
10731 AD	10732 AD	10733 AD	10734 AD	10735 AD	10736 AD	10737 AD	10738 AD	10739 AD	10740 AD
10741 AD	10742 AD	10743 AD	10744 AD	10745 AD	10746 AD	10747 AD	10748 AD	10749 AD	10750 AD
10751 AD	10752 AD	10753 AD	10754 AD	10755 AD	10756 AD	10757 AD	10758 AD	10759 AD	10760 AD
10761 AD	10762 AD	10763 AD	10764 AD	10765 AD	10766 AD	10767 AD	10768 AD	10769 AD	10770 AD
10771 AD	10772 AD	10773 AD	10774 AD	10775 AD	10776 AD	10777 AD	10778 AD	10779 AD	10780 AD
10781 AD	10782 AD	10783 AD	10784 AD	10785 AD	10786 AD	10787 AD	10788 AD	10789 AD	10790 AD
10791 AD	10792 AD	10793 AD	10794 AD	10795 AD	10796 AD	10797 AD	10798 AD	10799 AD	10800 AD
10801 AD	10802 AD	10803 AD	10804 AD	10805 AD	10806 AD	10807 AD	10808 AD	10809 AD	10810 AD
10811 AD	10812 AD	10813 AD	10814 AD	10815 AD	10816 AD	10817 AD	10818 AD	10819 AD	10820 AD
10821 AD	10822 AD	10823 AD	10824 AD	10825 AD	10826 AD	10827 AD	10828 AD	10829 AD	10830 AD
10831 AD	10832 AD	10833 AD	10834 AD	10835 AD	10836 AD	10837 AD	10838 AD	10839 AD	10840 AD
10841 AD	10842 AD	10843 AD	10844 AD	10845 AD	10846 AD	10847 AD	10848 AD	10849 AD	10850 AD
10851 AD	10852 AD	10853 AD	10854 AD	10855 AD	10856 AD	10857 AD	10858 AD	10859 AD	10860 AD
10861 AD	10862 AD	10863 AD	10864 AD	10865 AD	10866 AD	10867 AD	10868 AD	10869 AD	10870 AD
10871 AD	10872 AD	10873 AD	10874 AD	10875 AD	10876 AD	10877 AD	10878 AD	10879 AD	10880 AD
10881 AD	10882 AD	10883 AD	10884 AD	10885 AD	10886 AD	10887 AD	10888 AD	10889 AD	10890 AD
10891 AD	10892 AD	10893 AD	10894 AD	10895 AD	10896 AD	10897 AD	10898 AD	10899 AD	10900 AD
10901 AD	10902 AD	10903 AD	10904 AD	10905 AD	10906 AD	10907 AD	10908 AD	10909 AD	10910 AD
10911 AD	10912 AD	10913 AD	10914 AD	10915 AD	10916 AD	10917 AD	10918 AD	10919 AD	10920 AD
10921 AD	10922 AD	10923 AD	10924 AD	10925 AD	10926 AD	10927 AD	10928 AD	10929 AD	10930 AD
10931 AD	10932 AD	10933 AD	10934 AD	10935 AD	10936 AD	10937 AD	10938 AD	10939 AD	10940 AD
10941 AD	10942 AD	10943 AD	10944 AD	10945 AD	10946 AD	10947 AD	10948 AD	10949 AD	10950 AD
10951 AD	10952 AD	10953 AD	10954 AD	10955 AD	10956 AD	10957 AD	10958 AD	10959 AD	10960 AD
10961 AD	10962 AD	10963 AD	10964 AD	10965 AD	10966 AD	10967 AD	10968 AD	10969 AD	10970 AD
10971 AD	10972 AD	10973 AD	10974 AD	10975 AD	10976 AD	10977 AD	10978 AD	10979 AD	10980 AD
10981 AD	10982 AD	10983 AD	10984 AD	10985 AD	10986 AD	10987 AD	10988 AD	10989 AD	10990 AD
10991 AD	10992 AD	10993 AD	10994 AD	10995 AD	10996 AD	10997 AD	10998 AD	10999 AD	11000 AD

11001 AD	11002 AD	11003 AD	11004 AD	11005 AD	11006 AD	11007 AD	11008 AD	11009 AD	11010 AD
11011 AD	11012 AD	11013 AD	11014 AD	11015 AD	11016 AD	11017 AD	11018 AD	11019 AD	11020 AD
11021 AD	11022 AD	11023 AD	11024 AD	11025 AD	11026 AD	11027 AD	11028 AD	11029 AD	11030 AD
11031 AD	11032 AD	11033 AD	11034 AD	11035 AD	11036 AD	11037 AD	11038 AD	11039 AD	11040 AD
11041 AD	11042 AD	11043 AD	11044 AD	11045 AD	11046 AD	11047 AD	11048 AD	11049 AD	11050 AD
11051 AD	11052 AD	11053 AD	11054 AD	11055 AD	11056 AD	11057 AD	11058 AD	11059 AD	11060 AD
11061 AD	11062 AD	11063 AD	11064 AD	11065 AD	11066 AD	11067 AD	11068 AD	11069 AD	11070 AD
11071 AD	11072 AD	11073 AD	11074 AD	11075 AD	11076 AD	11077 AD	11078 AD	11079 AD	11080 AD
11081 AD	11082 AD	11083 AD	11084 AD	11085 AD	11086 AD	11087 AD	11088 AD	11089 AD	11090 AD
11091 AD	11092 AD	11093 AD	11094 AD	11095 AD	11096 AD	11097 AD	11098 AD	11099 AD	11100 AD
11101 AD	11102 AD	11103 AD	11104 AD	11105 AD	11106 AD	11107 AD	11108 AD	11109 AD	11110 AD
11111 AD	11112 AD	11113 AD	11114 AD	11115 AD	11116 AD	11117 AD	11118 AD	11119 AD	11120 AD
11121 AD	11122 AD	11123 AD	11124 AD	11125 AD	11126 AD	11127 AD	11128 AD	11129 AD	11130 AD
11131 AD	11132 AD	11133 AD	11134 AD	11135 AD	11136 AD	11137 AD	11138 AD	11139 AD	11140 AD
11141 AD	11142 AD	11143 AD	11144 AD	11145 AD	11146 AD	11147 AD	11148 AD	11149 AD	11150 AD
11151 AD	11152 AD	11153 AD	11154 AD	11155 AD	11156 AD	11157 AD	11158 AD	11159 AD	11160 AD
11161 AD	11162 AD	11163 AD	11164 AD	11165 AD	11166 AD	11167 AD	11168 AD	11169 AD	11170 AD
11171 AD	11172 AD	11173 AD	11174 AD	11175 AD	11176 AD	11177 AD	11178 AD	11179 AD	11180 AD
11181 AD	11182 AD	11183 AD	11184 AD	11185 AD	11186 AD	11187 AD	11188 AD	11189 AD	11190 AD
11191 AD	11192 AD	11193 AD	11194 AD	11195 AD	11196 AD	11197 AD	11198 AD	11199 AD	11200 AD
11201 AD	11202 AD	11203 AD	11204 AD	11205 AD	11206 AD	11207 AD	11208 AD	11209 AD	11210 AD
11211 AD	11212 AD	11213 AD	11214 AD	11215 AD	11216 AD	11217 AD	11218 AD	11219 AD	11220 AD
11221 AD	11222 AD	11223 AD	11224 AD	11225 AD	11226 AD	11227 AD	11228 AD	11229 AD	11230 AD
11231 AD	11232 AD	11233 AD	11234 AD	11235 AD	11236 AD	11237 AD	11238 AD	11239 AD	11240 AD
11241 AD	11242 AD	11243 AD	11244 AD	11245 AD	11246 AD	11247 AD	11248 AD	11249 AD	11250 AD
11251 AD	11252 AD	11253 AD	11254 AD	11255 AD	11256 AD	11257 AD	11258 AD	11259 AD	11260 AD
11261 AD	11262 AD	11263 AD	11264 AD	11265 AD	11266 AD	11267 AD	11268 AD	11269 AD	11270 AD
11271 AD	11272 AD	11273 AD	11274 AD	11275 AD	11276 AD	11277 AD	11278 AD	11279 AD	11280 AD
11281 AD	11282 AD	11283 AD	11284 AD	11285 AD	11286 AD	11287 AD	11288 AD	11289 AD	11290 AD
11291 AD	11292 AD	11293 AD	11294 AD	11295 AD	11296 AD	11297 AD	11298 AD	11299 AD	11300 AD
11301 AD	11302 AD	11303 AD	11304 AD	11305 AD	11306 AD	11307 AD	11308 AD	11309 AD	11310 AD
11311 AD	11312 AD	11313 AD	11314 AD	11315 AD	11316 AD	11317 AD	11318 AD	11319 AD	11320 AD
11321 AD	11322 AD	11323 AD	11324 AD	11325 AD	11326 AD	11327 AD	11328 AD	11329 AD	11330 AD
11331 AD	11332 AD	11333 AD	11334 AD	11335 AD	11336 AD	11337 AD	11338 AD	11339 AD	11340 AD
11341 AD	11342 AD	11343 AD	11344 AD	11345 AD	11346 AD	11347 AD	11348 AD	11349 AD	11350 AD
11351 AD	11352 AD	11353 AD	11354 AD	11355 AD	11356 AD	11357 AD	11358 AD	11359 AD	11360 AD
11361 AD	11362 AD	11363 AD	11364 AD	11365 AD	11366 AD	11367 AD	11368 AD	11369 AD	11370 AD
11371 AD	11372 AD	11373 AD	11374 AD	11375 AD	11376 AD	11377 AD	11378 AD	11379 AD	11380 AD
11381 AD	11382 AD	11383 AD	11384 AD	11385 AD	11386 AD	11387 AD	11388 AD	11389 AD	11390 AD
11391 AD	11392 AD	11393 AD	11394 AD	11395 AD	11396 AD	11397 AD	11398 AD	11399 AD	11400 AD
11401 AD	11402 AD	11403 AD	11404 AD	11405 AD	11406 AD	11407 AD	11408 AD	11409 AD	11410 AD
11411 AD	11412 AD	11413 AD	11414 AD	11415 AD	11416 AD	11417 AD	11418 AD	11419 AD	11420 AD
11421 AD	11422 AD	11423 AD	11424 AD	11425 AD	11426 AD	11427 AD	11428 AD	11429 AD	11430 AD
11431 AD	11432 AD	11433 AD	11434 AD	11435 AD	11436 AD	11437 AD	11438 AD	11439 AD	11440 AD
11441 AD	11442 AD	11443 AD	11444 AD	11445 AD	11446 AD	11447 AD	11448 AD	11449 AD	11450 AD
11451 AD	11452 AD	11453 AD	11454 AD	11455 AD	11456 AD	11457 AD	11458 AD	11459 AD	11460 AD
11461 AD	11462 AD	11463 AD	11464 AD	11465 AD	11466 AD	11467 AD	11468 AD	11469 AD	11470 AD
11471 AD	11472 AD	11473 AD	11474 AD	11475 AD	11476 AD	11477 AD	11478 AD	11479 AD	11480 AD
11481 AD	11482 AD	11483 AD	11484 AD	11485 AD	11486 AD	11487 AD	11488 AD	11489 AD	11490 AD
11491 AD	11492 AD	11493 AD	11494 AD	11495 AD	11496 AD	11497 AD	11498 AD	11499 AD	11500 AD

11501 AD	11502 AD	11503 AD	11504 AD	11505 AD	11506 AD	11507 AD	11508 AD	11509 AD	11510 AD
11511 AD	11512 AD	11513 AD	11514 AD	11515 AD	11516 AD	11517 AD	11518 AD	11519 AD	11520 AD
11521 AD	11522 AD	11523 AD	11524 AD	11525 AD	11526 AD	11527 AD	11528 AD	11529 AD	11530 AD
11531 AD	11532 AD	11533 AD	11534 AD	11535 AD	11536 AD	11537 AD	11538 AD	11539 AD	11540 AD
11541 AD	11542 AD	11543 AD	11544 AD	11545 AD	11546 AD	11547 AD	11548 AD	11549 AD	11550 AD
11551 AD	11552 AD	11553 AD	11554 AD	11555 AD	11556 AD	11557 AD	11558 AD	11559 AD	11560 AD
11561 AD	11562 AD	11563 AD	11564 AD	11565 AD	11566 AD	11567 AD	11568 AD	11569 AD	11570 AD
11571 AD	11572 AD	11573 AD	11574 AD	11575 AD	11576 AD	11577 AD	11578 AD	11579 AD	11580 AD
11581 AD	11582 AD	11583 AD	11584 AD	11585 AD	11586 AD	11587 AD	11588 AD	11589 AD	11590 AD
11591 AD	11592 AD	11593 AD	11594 AD	11595 AD	11596 AD	11597 AD	11598 AD	11599 AD	11600 AD
11601 AD	11602 AD	11603 AD	11604 AD	11605 AD	11606 AD	11607 AD	11608 AD	11609 AD	11610 AD
11611 AD	11612 AD	11613 AD	11614 AD	11615 AD	11616 AD	11617 AD	11618 AD	11619 AD	11620 AD
11621 AD	11622 AD	11623 AD	11624 AD	11625 AD	11626 AD	11627 AD	11628 AD	11629 AD	11630 AD
11631 AD	11632 AD	11633 AD	11634 AD	11635 AD	11636 AD	11637 AD	11638 AD	11639 AD	11640 AD
11641 AD	11642 AD	11643 AD	11644 AD	11645 AD	11646 AD	11647 AD	11648 AD	11649 AD	11650 AD
11651 AD	11652 AD	11653 AD	11654 AD	11655 AD	11656 AD	11657 AD	11658 AD	11659 AD	11660 AD
11661 AD	11662 AD	11663 AD	11664 AD	11665 AD	11666 AD	11667 AD	11668 AD	11669 AD	11670 AD
11671 AD	11672 AD	11673 AD	11674 AD	11675 AD	11676 AD	11677 AD	11678 AD	11679 AD	11680 AD
11681 AD	11682 AD	11683 AD	11684 AD	11685 AD	11686 AD	11687 AD	11688 AD	11689 AD	11690 AD
11691 AD	11692 AD	11693 AD	11694 AD	11695 AD	11696 AD	11697 AD	11698 AD	11699 AD	11700 AD
11701 AD	11702 AD	11703 AD	11704 AD	11705 AD	11706 AD	11707 AD	11708 AD	11709 AD	11710 AD
11711 AD	11712 AD	11713 AD	11714 AD	11715 AD	11716 AD	11717 AD	11718 AD	11719 AD	11720 AD
11721 AD	11722 AD	11723 AD	11724 AD	11725 AD	11726 AD	11727 AD	11728 AD	11729 AD	11730 AD
11731 AD	11732 AD	11733 AD	11734 AD	11735 AD	11736 AD	11737 AD	11738 AD	11739 AD	11740 AD
11741 AD	11742 AD	11743 AD	11744 AD	11745 AD	11746 AD	11747 AD	11748 AD	11749 AD	11750 AD
11751 AD	11752 AD	11753 AD	11754 AD	11755 AD	11756 AD	11757 AD	11758 AD	11759 AD	11760 AD
11761 AD	11762 AD	11763 AD	11764 AD	11765 AD	11766 AD	11767 AD	11768 AD	11769 AD	11770 AD
11771 AD	11772 AD	11773 AD	11774 AD	11775 AD	11776 AD	11777 AD	11778 AD	11779 AD	11780 AD
11781 AD	11782 AD	11783 AD	11784 AD	11785 AD	11786 AD	11787 AD	11788 AD	11789 AD	11790 AD
11791 AD	11792 AD	11793 AD	11794 AD	11795 AD	11796 AD	11797 AD	11798 AD	11799 AD	11800 AD
11801 AD	11802 AD	11803 AD	11804 AD	11805 AD	11806 AD	11807 AD	11808 AD	11809 AD	11810 AD
11811 AD	11812 AD	11813 AD	11814 AD	11815 AD	11816 AD	11817 AD	11818 AD	11819 AD	11820 AD
11821 AD	11822 AD	11823 AD	11824 AD	11825 AD	11826 AD	11827 AD	11828 AD	11829 AD	11830 AD
11831 AD	11832 AD	11833 AD	11834 AD	11835 AD	11836 AD	11837 AD	11838 AD	11839 AD	11840 AD
11841 AD	11842 AD	11843 AD	11844 AD	11845 AD	11846 AD	11847 AD	11848 AD	11849 AD	11850 AD
11851 AD	11852 AD	11853 AD	11854 AD	11855 AD	11856 AD	11857 AD	11858 AD	11859 AD	11860 AD
11861 AD	11862 AD	11863 AD	11864 AD	11865 AD	11866 AD	11867 AD	11868 AD	11869 AD	11870 AD
11871 AD	11872 AD	11873 AD	11874 AD	11875 AD	11876 AD	11877 AD	11878 AD	11879 AD	11880 AD
11881 AD	11882 AD	11883 AD	11884 AD	11885 AD	11886 AD	11887 AD	11888 AD	11889 AD	11890 AD
11891 AD	11892 AD	11893 AD	11894 AD	11895 AD	11896 AD	11897 AD	11898 AD	11899 AD	11900 AD
11901 AD	11902 AD	11903 AD	11904 AD	11905 AD	11906 AD	11907 AD	11908 AD	11909 AD	11910 AD
11911 AD	11912 AD	11913 AD	11914 AD	11915 AD	11916 AD	11917 AD	11918 AD	11919 AD	11920 AD
11921 AD	11922 AD	11923 AD	11924 AD	11925 AD	11926 AD	11927 AD	11928 AD	11929 AD	11930 AD
11931 AD	11932 AD	11933 AD	11934 AD	11935 AD	11936 AD	11937 AD	11938 AD	11939 AD	11940 AD
11941 AD	11942 AD	11943 AD	11944 AD	11945 AD	11946 AD	11947 AD	11948 AD	11949 AD	11950 AD
11951 AD	11952 AD	11953 AD	11954 AD	11955 AD	11956 AD	11957 AD	11958 AD	11959 AD	11960 AD
11961 AD	11962 AD	11963 AD	11964 AD	11965 AD	11966 AD	11967 AD	11968 AD	11969 AD	11970 AD
11971 AD	11972 AD	11973 AD	11974 AD	11975 AD	11976 AD	11977 AD	11978 AD	11979 AD	11980 AD
11981 AD	11982 AD	11983 AD	11984 AD	11985 AD	11986 AD	11987 AD	11988 AD	11989 AD	11990 AD
11991 AD	11992 AD	11993 AD	11994 AD	11995 AD	11996 AD	11997 AD	11998 AD	11999 AD	12000 AD

12001 AD	12002 AD	12003 AD	12004 AD	12005 AD	12006 AD	12007 AD	12008 AD	12009 AD	12010 AD
12011 AD	12012 AD	12013 AD	12014 AD	12015 AD	12016 AD	12017 AD	12018 AD	12019 AD	12020 AD
12021 AD	12022 AD	12023 AD	12024 AD	12025 AD	12026 AD	12027 AD	12028 AD	12029 AD	12030 AD
12031 AD	12032 AD	12033 AD	12034 AD	12035 AD	12036 AD	12037 AD	12038 AD	12039 AD	12040 AD
12041 AD	12042 AD	12043 AD	12044 AD	12045 AD	12046 AD	12047 AD	12048 AD	12049 AD	12050 AD
12051 AD	12052 AD	12053 AD	12054 AD	12055 AD	12056 AD	12057 AD	12058 AD	12059 AD	12060 AD
12061 AD	12062 AD	12063 AD	12064 AD	12065 AD	12066 AD	12067 AD	12068 AD	12069 AD	12070 AD
12071 AD	12072 AD	12073 AD	12074 AD	12075 AD	12076 AD	12077 AD	12078 AD	12079 AD	12080 AD
12081 AD	12082 AD	12083 AD	12084 AD	12085 AD	12086 AD	12087 AD	12088 AD	12089 AD	12090 AD
12091 AD	12092 AD	12093 AD	12094 AD	12095 AD	12096 AD	12097 AD	12098 AD	12099 AD	12100 AD
12101 AD	12102 AD	12103 AD	12104 AD	12105 AD	12106 AD	12107 AD	12108 AD	12109 AD	12110 AD
12111 AD	12112 AD	12113 AD	12114 AD	12115 AD	12116 AD	12117 AD	12118 AD	12119 AD	12120 AD
12121 AD	12122 AD	12123 AD	12124 AD	12125 AD	12126 AD	12127 AD	12128 AD	12129 AD	12130 AD
12131 AD	12132 AD	12133 AD	12134 AD	12135 AD	12136 AD	12137 AD	12138 AD	12139 AD	12140 AD
12141 AD	12142 AD	12143 AD	12144 AD	12145 AD	12146 AD	12147 AD	12148 AD	12149 AD	12150 AD
12151 AD	12152 AD	12153 AD	12154 AD	12155 AD	12156 AD	12157 AD	12158 AD	12159 AD	12160 AD
12161 AD	12162 AD	12163 AD	12164 AD	12165 AD	12166 AD	12167 AD	12168 AD	12169 AD	12170 AD
12171 AD	12172 AD	12173 AD	12174 AD	12175 AD	12176 AD	12177 AD	12178 AD	12179 AD	12180 AD
12181 AD	12182 AD	12183 AD	12184 AD	12185 AD	12186 AD	12187 AD	12188 AD	12189 AD	12190 AD
12191 AD	12192 AD	12193 AD	12194 AD	12195 AD	12196 AD	12197 AD	12198 AD	12199 AD	12200 AD
12201 AD	12202 AD	12203 AD	12204 AD	12205 AD	12206 AD	12207 AD	12208 AD	12209 AD	12210 AD
12211 AD	12212 AD	12213 AD	12214 AD	12215 AD	12216 AD	12217 AD	12218 AD	12219 AD	12220 AD
12221 AD	12222 AD	12223 AD	12224 AD	12225 AD	12226 AD	12227 AD	12228 AD	12229 AD	12230 AD
12231 AD	12232 AD	12233 AD	12234 AD	12235 AD	12236 AD	12237 AD	12238 AD	12239 AD	12240 AD
12241 AD	12242 AD	12243 AD	12244 AD	12245 AD	12246 AD	12247 AD	12248 AD	12249 AD	12250 AD
12251 AD	12252 AD	12253 AD	12254 AD	12255 AD	12256 AD	12257 AD	12258 AD	12259 AD	12260 AD
12261 AD	12262 AD	12263 AD	12264 AD	12265 AD	12266 AD	12267 AD	12268 AD	12269 AD	12270 AD
12271 AD	12272 AD	12273 AD	12274 AD	12275 AD	12276 AD	12277 AD	12278 AD	12279 AD	12280 AD
12281 AD	12282 AD	12283 AD	12284 AD	12285 AD	12286 AD	12287 AD	12288 AD	12289 AD	12290 AD
12291 AD	12292 AD	12293 AD	12294 AD	12295 AD	12296 AD	12297 AD	12298 AD	12299 AD	12300 AD
12301 AD	12302 AD	12303 AD	12304 AD	12305 AD	12306 AD	12307 AD	12308 AD	12309 AD	12310 AD
12311 AD	12312 AD	12313 AD	12314 AD	12315 AD	12316 AD	12317 AD	12318 AD	12319 AD	12320 AD
12321 AD	12322 AD	12323 AD	12324 AD	12325 AD	12326 AD	12327 AD	12328 AD	12329 AD	12330 AD
12331 AD	12332 AD	12333 AD	12334 AD	12335 AD	12336 AD	12337 AD	12338 AD	12339 AD	12340 AD
12341 AD	12342 AD	12343 AD	12344 AD	12345 AD	12346 AD	12347 AD	12348 AD	12349 AD	12350 AD
12351 AD	12352 AD	12353 AD	12354 AD	12355 AD	12356 AD	12357 AD	12358 AD	12359 AD	12360 AD
12361 AD	12362 AD	12363 AD	12364 AD	12365 AD	12366 AD	12367 AD	12368 AD	12369 AD	12370 AD
12371 AD	12372 AD	12373 AD	12374 AD	12375 AD	12376 AD	12377 AD	12378 AD	12379 AD	12380 AD
12381 AD	12382 AD	12383 AD	12384 AD	12385 AD	12386 AD	12387 AD	12388 AD	12389 AD	12390 AD
12391 AD	12392 AD	12393 AD	12394 AD	12395 AD	12396 AD	12397 AD	12398 AD	12399 AD	12400 AD
12401 AD	12402 AD	12403 AD	12404 AD	12405 AD	12406 AD	12407 AD	12408 AD	12409 AD	12410 AD
12411 AD	12412 AD	12413 AD	12414 AD	12415 AD	12416 AD	12417 AD	12418 AD	12419 AD	12420 AD
12421 AD	12422 AD	12423 AD	12424 AD	12425 AD	12426 AD	12427 AD	12428 AD	12429 AD	12430 AD
12431 AD	12432 AD	12433 AD	12434 AD	12435 AD	12436 AD	12437 AD	12438 AD	12439 AD	12440 AD
12441 AD	12442 AD	12443 AD	12444 AD	12445 AD	12446 AD	12447 AD	12448 AD	12449 AD	12450 AD
12451 AD	12452 AD	12453 AD	12454 AD	12455 AD	12456 AD	12457 AD	12458 AD	12459 AD	12460 AD
12461 AD	12462 AD	12463 AD	12464 AD	12465 AD	12466 AD	12467 AD	12468 AD	12469 AD	12470 AD
12471 AD	12472 AD	12473 AD	12474 AD	12475 AD	12476 AD	12477 AD	12478 AD	12479 AD	12480 AD
12481 AD	12482 AD	12483 AD	12484 AD	12485 AD	12486 AD	12487 AD	12488 AD	12489 AD	12490 AD
12491 AD	12492 AD	12493 AD	12494 AD	12495 AD	12496 AD	12497 AD	12498 AD	12499 AD	12500 AD

12501 AD	12502 AD	12503 AD	12504 AD	12505 AD	12506 AD	12507 AD	12508 AD	12509 AD	12510 AD
12511 AD	12512 AD	12513 AD	12514 AD	12515 AD	12516 AD	12517 AD	12518 AD	12519 AD	12520 AD
12521 AD	12522 AD	12523 AD	12524 AD	12525 AD	12526 AD	12527 AD	12528 AD	12529 AD	12530 AD
12531 AD	12532 AD	12533 AD	12534 AD	12535 AD	12536 AD	12537 AD	12538 AD	12539 AD	12540 AD
12541 AD	12542 AD	12543 AD	12544 AD	12545 AD	12546 AD	12547 AD	12548 AD	12549 AD	12550 AD
12551 AD	12552 AD	12553 AD	12554 AD	12555 AD	12556 AD	12557 AD	12558 AD	12559 AD	12560 AD
12561 AD	12562 AD	12563 AD	12564 AD	12565 AD	12566 AD	12567 AD	12568 AD	12569 AD	12570 AD
12571 AD	12572 AD	12573 AD	12574 AD	12575 AD	12576 AD	12577 AD	12578 AD	12579 AD	12580 AD
12581 AD	12582 AD	12583 AD	12584 AD	12585 AD	12586 AD	12587 AD	12588 AD	12589 AD	12590 AD
12591 AD	12592 AD	12593 AD	12594 AD	12595 AD	12596 AD	12597 AD	12598 AD	12599 AD	12600 AD
12601 AD	12602 AD	12603 AD	12604 AD	12605 AD	12606 AD	12607 AD	12608 AD	12609 AD	12610 AD
12611 AD	12612 AD	12613 AD	12614 AD	12615 AD	12616 AD	12617 AD	12618 AD	12619 AD	12620 AD
12621 AD	12622 AD	12623 AD	12624 AD	12625 AD	12626 AD	12627 AD	12628 AD	12629 AD	12630 AD
12631 AD	12632 AD	12633 AD	12634 AD	12635 AD	12636 AD	12637 AD	12638 AD	12639 AD	12640 AD
12641 AD	12642 AD	12643 AD	12644 AD	12645 AD	12646 AD	12647 AD	12648 AD	12649 AD	12650 AD
12651 AD	12652 AD	12653 AD	12654 AD	12655 AD	12656 AD	12657 AD	12658 AD	12659 AD	12660 AD
12661 AD	12662 AD	12663 AD	12664 AD	12665 AD	12666 AD	12667 AD	12668 AD	12669 AD	12670 AD
12671 AD	12672 AD	12673 AD	12674 AD	12675 AD	12676 AD	12677 AD	12678 AD	12679 AD	12680 AD
12681 AD	12682 AD	12683 AD	12684 AD	12685 AD	12686 AD	12687 AD	12688 AD	12689 AD	12690 AD
12691 AD	12692 AD	12693 AD	12694 AD	12695 AD	12696 AD	12697 AD	12698 AD	12699 AD	12700 AD
12701 AD	12702 AD	12703 AD	12704 AD	12705 AD	12706 AD	12707 AD	12708 AD	12709 AD	12710 AD
12711 AD	12712 AD	12713 AD	12714 AD	12715 AD	12716 AD	12717 AD	12718 AD	12719 AD	12720 AD
12721 AD	12722 AD	12723 AD	12724 AD	12725 AD	12726 AD	12727 AD	12728 AD	12729 AD	12730 AD
12731 AD	12732 AD	12733 AD	12734 AD	12735 AD	12736 AD	12737 AD	12738 AD	12739 AD	12740 AD
12741 AD	12742 AD	12743 AD	12744 AD	12745 AD	12746 AD	12747 AD	12748 AD	12749 AD	12750 AD
12751 AD	12752 AD	12753 AD	12754 AD	12755 AD	12756 AD	12757 AD	12758 AD	12759 AD	12760 AD
12761 AD	12762 AD	12763 AD	12764 AD	12765 AD	12766 AD	12767 AD	12768 AD	12769 AD	12770 AD
12771 AD	12772 AD	12773 AD	12774 AD	12775 AD	12776 AD	12777 AD	12778 AD	12779 AD	12780 AD
12781 AD	12782 AD	12783 AD	12784 AD	12785 AD	12786 AD	12787 AD	12788 AD	12789 AD	12790 AD
12791 AD	12792 AD	12793 AD	12794 AD	12795 AD	12796 AD	12797 AD	12798 AD	12799 AD	12800 AD
12801 AD	12802 AD	12803 AD	12804 AD	12805 AD	12806 AD	12807 AD	12808 AD	12809 AD	12810 AD
12811 AD	12812 AD	12813 AD	12814 AD	12815 AD	12816 AD	12817 AD	12818 AD	12819 AD	12820 AD
12821 AD	12822 AD	12823 AD	12824 AD	12825 AD	12826 AD	12827 AD	12828 AD	12829 AD	12830 AD
12831 AD	12832 AD	12833 AD	12834 AD	12835 AD	12836 AD	12837 AD	12838 AD	12839 AD	12840 AD
12841 AD	12842 AD	12843 AD	12844 AD	12845 AD	12846 AD	12847 AD	12848 AD	12849 AD	12850 AD
12851 AD	12852 AD	12853 AD	12854 AD	12855 AD	12856 AD	12857 AD	12858 AD	12859 AD	12860 AD
12861 AD	12862 AD	12863 AD	12864 AD	12865 AD	12866 AD	12867 AD	12868 AD	12869 AD	12870 AD
12871 AD	12872 AD	12873 AD	12874 AD	12875 AD	12876 AD	12877 AD	12878 AD	12879 AD	12880 AD
12881 AD	12882 AD	12883 AD	12884 AD	12885 AD	12886 AD	12887 AD	12888 AD	12889 AD	12890 AD
12891 AD	12892 AD	12893 AD	12894 AD	12895 AD	12896 AD	12897 AD	12898 AD	12899 AD	12900 AD
12901 AD	12902 AD	12903 AD	12904 AD	12905 AD	12906 AD	12907 AD	12908 AD	12909 AD	12910 AD
12911 AD	12912 AD	12913 AD	12914 AD	12915 AD	12916 AD	12917 AD	12918 AD	12919 AD	12920 AD
12921 AD	12922 AD	12923 AD	12924 AD	12925 AD	12926 AD	12927 AD	12928 AD	12929 AD	12930 AD
12931 AD	12932 AD	12933 AD	12934 AD	12935 AD	12936 AD	12937 AD	12938 AD	12939 AD	12940 AD
12941 AD	12942 AD	12943 AD	12944 AD	12945 AD	12946 AD	12947 AD	12948 AD	12949 AD	12950 AD
12951 AD	12952 AD	12953 AD	12954 AD	12955 AD	12956 AD	12957 AD	12958 AD	12959 AD	12960 AD
12961 AD	12962 AD	12963 AD	12964 AD	12965 AD	12966 AD	12967 AD	12968 AD	12969 AD	12970 AD
12971 AD	12972 AD	12973 AD	12974 AD	12975 AD	12976 AD	12977 AD	12978 AD	12979 AD	12980 AD
12981 AD	12982 AD	12983 AD	12984 AD	12985 AD	12986 AD	12987 AD	12988 AD	12989 AD	12990 AD
12991 AD	12992 AD	12993 AD	12994 AD	12995 AD	12996 AD	12997 AD	12998 AD	12999 AD	13000 AD

13001 AD	13002 AD	13003 AD	13004 AD	13005 AD	13006 AD	13007 AD	13008 AD	13009 AD	13010 AD
13011 AD	13012 AD	13013 AD	13014 AD	13015 AD	13016 AD	13017 AD	13018 AD	13019 AD	13020 AD
13021 AD	13022 AD	13023 AD	13024 AD	13025 AD	13026 AD	13027 AD	13028 AD	13029 AD	13030 AD
13031 AD	13032 AD	13033 AD	13034 AD	13035 AD	13036 AD	13037 AD	13038 AD	13039 AD	13040 AD
13041 AD	13042 AD	13043 AD	13044 AD	13045 AD	13046 AD	13047 AD	13048 AD	13049 AD	13050 AD
13051 AD	13052 AD	13053 AD	13054 AD	13055 AD	13056 AD	13057 AD	13058 AD	13059 AD	13060 AD
13061 AD	13062 AD	13063 AD	13064 AD	13065 AD	13066 AD	13067 AD	13068 AD	13069 AD	13070 AD
13071 AD	13072 AD	13073 AD	13074 AD	13075 AD	13076 AD	13077 AD	13078 AD	13079 AD	13080 AD
13081 AD	13082 AD	13083 AD	13084 AD	13085 AD	13086 AD	13087 AD	13088 AD	13089 AD	13090 AD
13091 AD	13092 AD	13093 AD	13094 AD	13095 AD	13096 AD	13097 AD	13098 AD	13099 AD	13100 AD
13101 AD	13102 AD	13103 AD	13104 AD	13105 AD	13106 AD	13107 AD	13108 AD	13109 AD	13110 AD
13111 AD	13112 AD	13113 AD	13114 AD	13115 AD	13116 AD	13117 AD	13118 AD	13119 AD	13120 AD
13121 AD	13122 AD	13123 AD	13124 AD	13125 AD	13126 AD	13127 AD	13128 AD	13129 AD	13130 AD
13131 AD	13132 AD	13133 AD	13134 AD	13135 AD	13136 AD	13137 AD	13138 AD	13139 AD	13140 AD
13141 AD	13142 AD	13143 AD	13144 AD	13145 AD	13146 AD	13147 AD	13148 AD	13149 AD	13150 AD
13151 AD	13152 AD	13153 AD	13154 AD	13155 AD	13156 AD	13157 AD	13158 AD	13159 AD	13160 AD
13161 AD	13162 AD	13163 AD	13164 AD	13165 AD	13166 AD	13167 AD	13168 AD	13169 AD	13170 AD
13171 AD	13172 AD	13173 AD	13174 AD	13175 AD	13176 AD	13177 AD	13178 AD	13179 AD	13180 AD
13181 AD	13182 AD	13183 AD	13184 AD	13185 AD	13186 AD	13187 AD	13188 AD	13189 AD	13190 AD
13191 AD	13192 AD	13193 AD	13194 AD	13195 AD	13196 AD	13197 AD	13198 AD	13199 AD	13200 AD
13201 AD	13202 AD	13203 AD	13204 AD	13205 AD	13206 AD	13207 AD	13208 AD	13209 AD	13210 AD
13211 AD	13212 AD	13213 AD	13214 AD	13215 AD	13216 AD	13217 AD	13218 AD	13219 AD	13220 AD
13221 AD	13222 AD	13223 AD	13224 AD	13225 AD	13226 AD	13227 AD	13228 AD	13229 AD	13230 AD
13231 AD	13232 AD	13233 AD	13234 AD	13235 AD	13236 AD	13237 AD	13238 AD	13239 AD	13240 AD
13241 AD	13242 AD	13243 AD	13244 AD	13245 AD	13246 AD	13247 AD	13248 AD	13249 AD	13250 AD
13251 AD	13252 AD	13253 AD	13254 AD	13255 AD	13256 AD	13257 AD	13258 AD	13259 AD	13260 AD
13261 AD	13262 AD	13263 AD	13264 AD	13265 AD	13266 AD	13267 AD	13268 AD	13269 AD	13270 AD
13271 AD	13272 AD	13273 AD	13274 AD	13275 AD	13276 AD	13277 AD	13278 AD	13279 AD	13280 AD
13281 AD	13282 AD	13283 AD	13284 AD	13285 AD	13286 AD	13287 AD	13288 AD	13289 AD	13290 AD
13291 AD	13292 AD	13293 AD	13294 AD	13295 AD	13296 AD	13297 AD	13298 AD	13299 AD	13300 AD
13301 AD	13302 AD	13303 AD	13304 AD	13305 AD	13306 AD	13307 AD	13308 AD	13309 AD	13310 AD
13311 AD	13312 AD	13313 AD	13314 AD	13315 AD	13316 AD	13317 AD	13318 AD	13319 AD	13320 AD
13321 AD	13322 AD	13323 AD	13324 AD	13325 AD	13326 AD	13327 AD	13328 AD	13329 AD	13330 AD
13331 AD	13332 AD	13333 AD	13334 AD	13335 AD	13336 AD	13337 AD	13338 AD	13339 AD	13340 AD
13341 AD	13342 AD	13343 AD	13344 AD	13345 AD	13346 AD	13347 AD	13348 AD	13349 AD	13350 AD
13351 AD	13352 AD	13353 AD	13354 AD	13355 AD	13356 AD	13357 AD	13358 AD	13359 AD	13360 AD
13361 AD	13362 AD	13363 AD	13364 AD	13365 AD	13366 AD	13367 AD	13368 AD	13369 AD	13370 AD
13371 AD	13372 AD	13373 AD	13374 AD	13375 AD	13376 AD	13377 AD	13378 AD	13379 AD	13380 AD
13381 AD	13382 AD	13383 AD	13384 AD	13385 AD	13386 AD	13387 AD	13388 AD	13389 AD	13390 AD
13391 AD	13392 AD	13393 AD	13394 AD	13395 AD	13396 AD	13397 AD	13398 AD	13399 AD	13400 AD
13401 AD	13402 AD	13403 AD	13404 AD	13405 AD	13406 AD	13407 AD	13408 AD	13409 AD	13410 AD
13411 AD	13412 AD	13413 AD	13414 AD	13415 AD	13416 AD	13417 AD	13418 AD	13419 AD	13420 AD
13421 AD	13422 AD	13423 AD	13424 AD	13425 AD	13426 AD	13427 AD	13428 AD	13429 AD	13430 AD
13431 AD	13432 AD	13433 AD	13434 AD	13435 AD	13436 AD	13437 AD	13438 AD	13439 AD	13440 AD
13441 AD	13442 AD	13443 AD	13444 AD	13445 AD	13446 AD	13447 AD	13448 AD	13449 AD	13450 AD
13451 AD	13452 AD	13453 AD	13454 AD	13455 AD	13456 AD	13457 AD	13458 AD	13459 AD	13460 AD
13461 AD	13462 AD	13463 AD	13464 AD	13465 AD	13466 AD	13467 AD	13468 AD	13469 AD	13470 AD
13471 AD	13472 AD	13473 AD	13474 AD	13475 AD	13476 AD	13477 AD	13478 AD	13479 AD	13480 AD
13481 AD	13482 AD	13483 AD	13484 AD	13485 AD	13486 AD	13487 AD	13488 AD	13489 AD	13490 AD
13491 AD	13492 AD	13493 AD	13494 AD	13495 AD	13496 AD	13497 AD	13498 AD	13499 AD	13500 AD

13501 AD	13502 AD	13503 AD	13504 AD	13505 AD	13506 AD	13507 AD	13508 AD	13509 AD	13510 AD
13511 AD	13512 AD	13513 AD	13514 AD	13515 AD	13516 AD	13517 AD	13518 AD	13519 AD	13520 AD
13521 AD	13522 AD	13523 AD	13524 AD	13525 AD	13526 AD	13527 AD	13528 AD	13529 AD	13530 AD
13531 AD	13532 AD	13533 AD	13534 AD	13535 AD	13536 AD	13537 AD	13538 AD	13539 AD	13540 AD
13541 AD	13542 AD	13543 AD	13544 AD	13545 AD	13546 AD	13547 AD	13548 AD	13549 AD	13550 AD
13551 AD	13552 AD	13553 AD	13554 AD	13555 AD	13556 AD	13557 AD	13558 AD	13559 AD	13560 AD
13561 AD	13562 AD	13563 AD	13564 AD	13565 AD	13566 AD	13567 AD	13568 AD	13569 AD	13570 AD
13571 AD	13572 AD	13573 AD	13574 AD	13575 AD	13576 AD	13577 AD	13578 AD	13579 AD	13580 AD
13581 AD	13582 AD	13583 AD	13584 AD	13585 AD	13586 AD	13587 AD	13588 AD	13589 AD	13590 AD
13591 AD	13592 AD	13593 AD	13594 AD	13595 AD	13596 AD	13597 AD	13598 AD	13599 AD	13600 AD
13601 AD	13602 AD	13603 AD	13604 AD	13605 AD	13606 AD	13607 AD	13608 AD	13609 AD	13610 AD
13611 AD	13612 AD	13613 AD	13614 AD	13615 AD	13616 AD	13617 AD	13618 AD	13619 AD	13620 AD
13621 AD	13622 AD	13623 AD	13624 AD	13625 AD	13626 AD	13627 AD	13628 AD	13629 AD	13630 AD
13631 AD	13632 AD	13633 AD	13634 AD	13635 AD	13636 AD	13637 AD	13638 AD	13639 AD	13640 AD
13641 AD	13642 AD	13643 AD	13644 AD	13645 AD	13646 AD	13647 AD	13648 AD	13649 AD	13650 AD
13651 AD	13652 AD	13653 AD	13654 AD	13655 AD	13656 AD	13657 AD	13658 AD	13659 AD	13660 AD
13661 AD	13662 AD	13663 AD	13664 AD	13665 AD	13666 AD	13667 AD	13668 AD	13669 AD	13670 AD
13671 AD	13672 AD	13673 AD	13674 AD	13675 AD	13676 AD	13677 AD	13678 AD	13679 AD	13680 AD
13681 AD	13682 AD	13683 AD	13684 AD	13685 AD	13686 AD	13687 AD	13688 AD	13689 AD	13690 AD
13691 AD	13692 AD	13693 AD	13694 AD	13695 AD	13696 AD	13697 AD	13698 AD	13699 AD	13700 AD
13701 AD	13702 AD	13703 AD	13704 AD	13705 AD	13706 AD	13707 AD	13708 AD	13709 AD	13710 AD
13711 AD	13712 AD	13713 AD	13714 AD	13715 AD	13716 AD	13717 AD	13718 AD	13719 AD	13720 AD
13721 AD	13722 AD	13723 AD	13724 AD	13725 AD	13726 AD	13727 AD	13728 AD	13729 AD	13730 AD
13731 AD	13732 AD	13733 AD	13734 AD	13735 AD	13736 AD	13737 AD	13738 AD	13739 AD	13740 AD
13741 AD	13742 AD	13743 AD	13744 AD	13745 AD	13746 AD	13747 AD	13748 AD	13749 AD	13750 AD
13751 AD	13752 AD	13753 AD	13754 AD	13755 AD	13756 AD	13757 AD	13758 AD	13759 AD	13760 AD
13761 AD	13762 AD	13763 AD	13764 AD	13765 AD	13766 AD	13767 AD	13768 AD	13769 AD	13770 AD
13771 AD	13772 AD	13773 AD	13774 AD	13775 AD	13776 AD	13777 AD	13778 AD	13779 AD	13780 AD
13781 AD	13782 AD	13783 AD	13784 AD	13785 AD	13786 AD	13787 AD	13788 AD	13789 AD	13790 AD
13791 AD	13792 AD	13793 AD	13794 AD	13795 AD	13796 AD	13797 AD	13798 AD	13799 AD	13800 AD
13801 AD	13802 AD	13803 AD	13804 AD	13805 AD	13806 AD	13807 AD	13808 AD	13809 AD	13810 AD
13811 AD	13812 AD	13813 AD	13814 AD	13815 AD	13816 AD	13817 AD	13818 AD	13819 AD	13820 AD
13821 AD	13822 AD	13823 AD	13824 AD	13825 AD	13826 AD	13827 AD	13828 AD	13829 AD	13830 AD
13831 AD	13832 AD	13833 AD	13834 AD	13835 AD	13836 AD	13837 AD	13838 AD	13839 AD	13840 AD
13841 AD	13842 AD	13843 AD	13844 AD	13845 AD	13846 AD	13847 AD	13848 AD	13849 AD	13850 AD
13851 AD	13852 AD	13853 AD	13854 AD	13855 AD	13856 AD	13857 AD	13858 AD	13859 AD	13860 AD
13861 AD	13862 AD	13863 AD	13864 AD	13865 AD	13866 AD	13867 AD	13868 AD	13869 AD	13870 AD
13871 AD	13872 AD	13873 AD	13874 AD	13875 AD	13876 AD	13877 AD	13878 AD	13879 AD	13880 AD
13881 AD	13882 AD	13883 AD	13884 AD	13885 AD	13886 AD	13887 AD	13888 AD	13889 AD	13890 AD
13891 AD	13892 AD	13893 AD	13894 AD	13895 AD	13896 AD	13897 AD	13898 AD	13899 AD	13900 AD
13901 AD	13902 AD	13903 AD	13904 AD	13905 AD	13906 AD	13907 AD	13908 AD	13909 AD	13910 AD
13911 AD	13912 AD	13913 AD	13914 AD	13915 AD	13916 AD	13917 AD	13918 AD	13919 AD	13920 AD
13921 AD	13922 AD	13923 AD	13924 AD	13925 AD	13926 AD	13927 AD	13928 AD	13929 AD	13930 AD
13931 AD	13932 AD	13933 AD	13934 AD	13935 AD	13936 AD	13937 AD	13938 AD	13939 AD	13940 AD
13941 AD	13942 AD	13943 AD	13944 AD	13945 AD	13946 AD	13947 AD	13948 AD	13949 AD	13950 AD
13951 AD	13952 AD	13953 AD	13954 AD	13955 AD	13956 AD	13957 AD	13958 AD	13959 AD	13960 AD
13961 AD	13962 AD	13963 AD	13964 AD	13965 AD	13966 AD	13967 AD	13968 AD	13969 AD	13970 AD
13971 AD	13972 AD	13973 AD	13974 AD	13975 AD	13976 AD	13977 AD	13978 AD	13979 AD	13980 AD
13981 AD	13982 AD	13983 AD	13984 AD	13985 AD	13986 AD	13987 AD	13988 AD	13989 AD	13990 AD
13991 AD	13992 AD	13993 AD	13994 AD	13995 AD	13996 AD	13997 AD	13998 AD	13999 AD	14000 AD

```
14001 AD  14002 AD  14003 AD  14004 AD  14005 AD  14006 AD  14007 AD  14008 AD  14009 AD  14010 AD
14011 AD  14012 AD  14013 AD  14014 AD  14015 AD  14016 AD  14017 AD  14018 AD  14019 AD  14020 AD
14021 AD  14022 AD  14023 AD  14024 AD  14025 AD  14026 AD  14027 AD  14028 AD  14029 AD  14030 AD
14031 AD  14032 AD  14033 AD  14034 AD  14035 AD  14036 AD  14037 AD  14038 AD  14039 AD  14040 AD
14041 AD  14042 AD  14043 AD  14044 AD  14045 AD  14046 AD  14047 AD  14048 AD  14049 AD  14050 AD
14051 AD  14052 AD  14053 AD  14054 AD  14055 AD  14056 AD  14057 AD  14058 AD  14059 AD  14060 AD
14061 AD  14062 AD  14063 AD  14064 AD  14065 AD  14066 AD  14067 AD  14068 AD  14069 AD  14070 AD
14071 AD  14072 AD  14073 AD  14074 AD  14075 AD  14076 AD  14077 AD  14078 AD  14079 AD  14080 AD
14081 AD  14082 AD  14083 AD  14084 AD  14085 AD  14086 AD  14087 AD  14088 AD  14089 AD  14090 AD
14091 AD  14092 AD  14093 AD  14094 AD  14095 AD  14096 AD  14097 AD  14098 AD  14099 AD  14100 AD

14101 AD  14102 AD  14103 AD  14104 AD  14105 AD  14106 AD  14107 AD  14108 AD  14109 AD  14110 AD
14111 AD  14112 AD  14113 AD  14114 AD  14115 AD  14116 AD  14117 AD  14118 AD  14119 AD  14120 AD
14121 AD  14122 AD  14123 AD  14124 AD  14125 AD  14126 AD  14127 AD  14128 AD  14129 AD  14130 AD
14131 AD  14132 AD  14133 AD  14134 AD  14135 AD  14136 AD  14137 AD  14138 AD  14139 AD  14140 AD
14141 AD  14142 AD  14143 AD  14144 AD  14145 AD  14146 AD  14147 AD  14148 AD  14149 AD  14150 AD
14151 AD  14152 AD  14153 AD  14154 AD  14155 AD  14156 AD  14157 AD  14158 AD  14159 AD  14160 AD
14161 AD  14162 AD  14163 AD  14164 AD  14165 AD  14166 AD  14167 AD  14168 AD  14169 AD  14170 AD
14171 AD  14172 AD  14173 AD  14174 AD  14175 AD  14176 AD  14177 AD  14178 AD  14179 AD  14180 AD
14181 AD  14182 AD  14183 AD  14184 AD  14185 AD  14186 AD  14187 AD  14188 AD  14189 AD  14190 AD
14191 AD  14192 AD  14193 AD  14194 AD  14195 AD  14196 AD  14197 AD  14198 AD  14199 AD  14200 AD

14201 AD  14202 AD  14203 AD  14204 AD  14205 AD  14206 AD  14207 AD  14208 AD  14209 AD  14210 AD
14211 AD  14212 AD  14213 AD  14214 AD  14215 AD  14216 AD  14217 AD  14218 AD  14219 AD  14220 AD
14221 AD  14222 AD  14223 AD  14224 AD  14225 AD  14226 AD  14227 AD  14228 AD  14229 AD  14230 AD
14231 AD  14232 AD  14233 AD  14234 AD  14235 AD  14236 AD  14237 AD  14238 AD  14239 AD  14240 AD
14241 AD  14242 AD  14243 AD  14244 AD  14245 AD  14246 AD  14247 AD  14248 AD  14249 AD  14250 AD
14251 AD  14252 AD  14253 AD  14254 AD  14255 AD  14256 AD  14257 AD  14258 AD  14259 AD  14260 AD
14261 AD  14262 AD  14263 AD  14264 AD  14265 AD  14266 AD  14267 AD  14268 AD  14269 AD  14270 AD
14271 AD  14272 AD  14273 AD  14274 AD  14275 AD  14276 AD  14277 AD  14278 AD  14279 AD  14280 AD
14281 AD  14282 AD  14283 AD  14284 AD  14285 AD  14286 AD  14287 AD  14288 AD  14289 AD  14290 AD
14291 AD  14292 AD  14293 AD  14294 AD  14295 AD  14296 AD  14297 AD  14298 AD  14299 AD  14300 AD

14301 AD  14302 AD  14303 AD  14304 AD  14305 AD  14306 AD  14307 AD  14308 AD  14309 AD  14310 AD
14311 AD  14312 AD  14313 AD  14314 AD  14315 AD  14316 AD  14317 AD  14318 AD  14319 AD  14320 AD
14321 AD  14322 AD  14323 AD  14324 AD  14325 AD  14326 AD  14327 AD  14328 AD  14329 AD  14330 AD
14331 AD  14332 AD  14333 AD  14334 AD  14335 AD  14336 AD  14337 AD  14338 AD  14339 AD  14340 AD
14341 AD  14342 AD  14343 AD  14344 AD  14345 AD  14346 AD  14347 AD  14348 AD  14349 AD  14350 AD
14351 AD  14352 AD  14353 AD  14354 AD  14355 AD  14356 AD  14357 AD  14358 AD  14359 AD  14360 AD
14361 AD  14362 AD  14363 AD  14364 AD  14365 AD  14366 AD  14367 AD  14368 AD  14369 AD  14370 AD
14371 AD  14372 AD  14373 AD  14374 AD  14375 AD  14376 AD  14377 AD  14378 AD  14379 AD  14380 AD
14381 AD  14382 AD  14383 AD  14384 AD  14385 AD  14386 AD  14387 AD  14388 AD  14389 AD  14390 AD
14391 AD  14392 AD  14393 AD  14394 AD  14395 AD  14396 AD  14397 AD  14398 AD  14399 AD  14400 AD

14401 AD  14402 AD  14403 AD  14404 AD  14405 AD  14406 AD  14407 AD  14408 AD  14409 AD  14410 AD
14411 AD  14412 AD  14413 AD  14414 AD  14415 AD  14416 AD  14417 AD  14418 AD  14419 AD  14420 AD
14421 AD  14422 AD  14423 AD  14424 AD  14425 AD  14426 AD  14427 AD  14428 AD  14429 AD  14430 AD
14431 AD  14432 AD  14433 AD  14434 AD  14435 AD  14436 AD  14437 AD  14438 AD  14439 AD  14440 AD
14441 AD  14442 AD  14443 AD  14444 AD  14445 AD  14446 AD  14447 AD  14448 AD  14449 AD  14450 AD
14451 AD  14452 AD  14453 AD  14454 AD  14455 AD  14456 AD  14457 AD  14458 AD  14459 AD  14460 AD
14461 AD  14462 AD  14463 AD  14464 AD  14465 AD  14466 AD  14467 AD  14468 AD  14469 AD  14470 AD
14471 AD  14472 AD  14473 AD  14474 AD  14475 AD  14476 AD  14477 AD  14478 AD  14479 AD  14480 AD
14481 AD  14482 AD  14483 AD  14484 AD  14485 AD  14486 AD  14487 AD  14488 AD  14489 AD  14490 AD
14491 AD  14492 AD  14493 AD  14494 AD  14495 AD  14496 AD  14497 AD  14498 AD  14499 AD  14500 AD
```

```
14501 AD  14502 AD  14503 AD  14504 AD  14505 AD  14506 AD  14507 AD  14508 AD  14509 AD  14510 AD
14511 AD  14512 AD  14513 AD  14514 AD  14515 AD  14516 AD  14517 AD  14518 AD  14519 AD  14520 AD
14521 AD  14522 AD  14523 AD  14524 AD  14525 AD  14526 AD  14527 AD  14528 AD  14529 AD  14530 AD
14531 AD  14532 AD  14533 AD  14534 AD  14535 AD  14536 AD  14537 AD  14538 AD  14539 AD  14540 AD
14541 AD  14542 AD  14543 AD  14544 AD  14545 AD  14546 AD  14547 AD  14548 AD  14549 AD  14550 AD
14551 AD  14552 AD  14553 AD  14554 AD  14555 AD  14556 AD  14557 AD  14558 AD  14559 AD  14560 AD
14561 AD  14562 AD  14563 AD  14564 AD  14565 AD  14566 AD  14567 AD  14568 AD  14569 AD  14570 AD
14571 AD  14572 AD  14573 AD  14574 AD  14575 AD  14576 AD  14577 AD  14578 AD  14579 AD  14580 AD
14581 AD  14582 AD  14583 AD  14584 AD  14585 AD  14586 AD  14587 AD  14588 AD  14589 AD  14590 AD
14591 AD  14592 AD  14593 AD  14594 AD  14595 AD  14596 AD  14597 AD  14598 AD  14599 AD  14600 AD

14601 AD  14602 AD  14603 AD  14604 AD  14605 AD  14606 AD  14607 AD  14608 AD  14609 AD  14610 AD
14611 AD  14612 AD  14613 AD  14614 AD  14615 AD  14616 AD  14617 AD  14618 AD  14619 AD  14620 AD
14621 AD  14622 AD  14623 AD  14624 AD  14625 AD  14626 AD  14627 AD  14628 AD  14629 AD  14630 AD
14631 AD  14632 AD  14633 AD  14634 AD  14635 AD  14636 AD  14637 AD  14638 AD  14639 AD  14640 AD
14641 AD  14642 AD  14643 AD  14644 AD  14645 AD  14646 AD  14647 AD  14648 AD  14649 AD  14650 AD
14651 AD  14652 AD  14653 AD  14654 AD  14655 AD  14656 AD  14657 AD  14658 AD  14659 AD  14660 AD
14661 AD  14662 AD  14663 AD  14664 AD  14665 AD  14666 AD  14667 AD  14668 AD  14669 AD  14670 AD
14671 AD  14672 AD  14673 AD  14674 AD  14675 AD  14676 AD  14677 AD  14678 AD  14679 AD  14680 AD
14681 AD  14682 AD  14683 AD  14684 AD  14685 AD  14686 AD  14687 AD  14688 AD  14689 AD  14690 AD
14691 AD  14692 AD  14693 AD  14694 AD  14695 AD  14696 AD  14697 AD  14698 AD  14699 AD  14700 AD

14701 AD  14702 AD  14703 AD  14704 AD  14705 AD  14706 AD  14707 AD  14708 AD  14709 AD  14710 AD
14711 AD  14712 AD  14713 AD  14714 AD  14715 AD  14716 AD  14717 AD  14718 AD  14719 AD  14720 AD
14721 AD  14722 AD  14723 AD  14724 AD  14725 AD  14726 AD  14727 AD  14728 AD  14729 AD  14730 AD
14731 AD  14732 AD  14733 AD  14734 AD  14735 AD  14736 AD  14737 AD  14738 AD  14739 AD  14740 AD
14741 AD  14742 AD  14743 AD  14744 AD  14745 AD  14746 AD  14747 AD  14748 AD  14749 AD  14750 AD
14751 AD  14752 AD  14753 AD  14754 AD  14755 AD  14756 AD  14757 AD  14758 AD  14759 AD  14760 AD
14761 AD  14762 AD  14763 AD  14764 AD  14765 AD  14766 AD  14767 AD  14768 AD  14769 AD  14770 AD
14771 AD  14772 AD  14773 AD  14774 AD  14775 AD  14776 AD  14777 AD  14778 AD  14779 AD  14780 AD
14781 AD  14782 AD  14783 AD  14784 AD  14785 AD  14786 AD  14787 AD  14788 AD  14789 AD  14790 AD
14791 AD  14792 AD  14793 AD  14794 AD  14795 AD  14796 AD  14797 AD  14798 AD  14799 AD  14800 AD

14801 AD  14802 AD  14803 AD  14804 AD  14805 AD  14806 AD  14807 AD  14808 AD  14809 AD  14810 AD
14811 AD  14812 AD  14813 AD  14814 AD  14815 AD  14816 AD  14817 AD  14818 AD  14819 AD  14820 AD
14821 AD  14822 AD  14823 AD  14824 AD  14825 AD  14826 AD  14827 AD  14828 AD  14829 AD  14830 AD
14831 AD  14832 AD  14833 AD  14834 AD  14835 AD  14836 AD  14837 AD  14838 AD  14839 AD  14840 AD
14841 AD  14842 AD  14843 AD  14844 AD  14845 AD  14846 AD  14847 AD  14848 AD  14849 AD  14850 AD
14851 AD  14852 AD  14853 AD  14854 AD  14855 AD  14856 AD  14857 AD  14858 AD  14859 AD  14860 AD
14861 AD  14862 AD  14863 AD  14864 AD  14865 AD  14866 AD  14867 AD  14868 AD  14869 AD  14870 AD
14871 AD  14872 AD  14873 AD  14874 AD  14875 AD  14876 AD  14877 AD  14878 AD  14879 AD  14880 AD
14881 AD  14882 AD  14883 AD  14884 AD  14885 AD  14886 AD  14887 AD  14888 AD  14889 AD  14890 AD
14891 AD  14892 AD  14893 AD  14894 AD  14895 AD  14896 AD  14897 AD  14898 AD  14899 AD  14900 AD

14901 AD  14902 AD  14903 AD  14904 AD  14905 AD  14906 AD  14907 AD  14908 AD  14909 AD  14910 AD
14911 AD  14912 AD  14913 AD  14914 AD  14915 AD  14916 AD  14917 AD  14918 AD  14919 AD  14920 AD
14921 AD  14922 AD  14923 AD  14924 AD  14925 AD  14926 AD  14927 AD  14928 AD  14929 AD  14930 AD
14931 AD  14932 AD  14933 AD  14934 AD  14935 AD  14936 AD  14937 AD  14938 AD  14939 AD  14940 AD
14941 AD  14942 AD  14943 AD  14944 AD  14945 AD  14946 AD  14947 AD  14948 AD  14949 AD  14950 AD
14951 AD  14952 AD  14953 AD  14954 AD  14955 AD  14956 AD  14957 AD  14958 AD  14959 AD  14960 AD
14961 AD  14962 AD  14963 AD  14964 AD  14965 AD  14966 AD  14967 AD  14968 AD  14969 AD  14970 AD
14971 AD  14972 AD  14973 AD  14974 AD  14975 AD  14976 AD  14977 AD  14978 AD  14979 AD  14980 AD
14981 AD  14982 AD  14983 AD  14984 AD  14985 AD  14986 AD  14987 AD  14988 AD  14989 AD  14990 AD
14991 AD  14992 AD  14993 AD  14994 AD  14995 AD  14996 AD  14997 AD  14998 AD  14999 AD  15000 AD
```

15001 AD	15002 AD	15003 AD	15004 AD	15005 AD	15006 AD	15007 AD	15008 AD	15009 AD	15010 AD
15011 AD	15012 AD	15013 AD	15014 AD	15015 AD	15016 AD	15017 AD	15018 AD	15019 AD	15020 AD
15021 AD	15022 AD	15023 AD	15024 AD	15025 AD	15026 AD	15027 AD	15028 AD	15029 AD	15030 AD
15031 AD	15032 AD	15033 AD	15034 AD	15035 AD	15036 AD	15037 AD	15038 AD	15039 AD	15040 AD
15041 AD	15042 AD	15043 AD	15044 AD	15045 AD	15046 AD	15047 AD	15048 AD	15049 AD	15050 AD
15051 AD	15052 AD	15053 AD	15054 AD	15055 AD	15056 AD	15057 AD	15058 AD	15059 AD	15060 AD
15061 AD	15062 AD	15063 AD	15064 AD	15065 AD	15066 AD	15067 AD	15068 AD	15069 AD	15070 AD
15071 AD	15072 AD	15073 AD	15074 AD	15075 AD	15076 AD	15077 AD	15078 AD	15079 AD	15080 AD
15081 AD	15082 AD	15083 AD	15084 AD	15085 AD	15086 AD	15087 AD	15088 AD	15089 AD	15090 AD
15091 AD	15092 AD	15093 AD	15094 AD	15095 AD	15096 AD	15097 AD	15098 AD	15099 AD	15100 AD
15101 AD	15102 AD	15103 AD	15104 AD	15105 AD	15106 AD	15107 AD	15108 AD	15109 AD	15110 AD
15111 AD	15112 AD	15113 AD	15114 AD	15115 AD	15116 AD	15117 AD	15118 AD	15119 AD	15120 AD
15121 AD	15122 AD	15123 AD	15124 AD	15125 AD	15126 AD	15127 AD	15128 AD	15129 AD	15130 AD
15131 AD	15132 AD	15133 AD	15134 AD	15135 AD	15136 AD	15137 AD	15138 AD	15139 AD	15140 AD
15141 AD	15142 AD	15143 AD	15144 AD	15145 AD	15146 AD	15147 AD	15148 AD	15149 AD	15150 AD
15151 AD	15152 AD	15153 AD	15154 AD	15155 AD	15156 AD	15157 AD	15158 AD	15159 AD	15160 AD
15161 AD	15162 AD	15163 AD	15164 AD	15165 AD	15166 AD	15167 AD	15168 AD	15169 AD	15170 AD
15171 AD	15172 AD	15173 AD	15174 AD	15175 AD	15176 AD	15177 AD	15178 AD	15179 AD	15180 AD
15181 AD	15182 AD	15183 AD	15184 AD	15185 AD	15186 AD	15187 AD	15188 AD	15189 AD	15190 AD
15191 AD	15192 AD	15193 AD	15194 AD	15195 AD	15196 AD	15197 AD	15198 AD	15199 AD	15200 AD
15201 AD	15202 AD	15203 AD	15204 AD	15205 AD	15206 AD	15207 AD	15208 AD	15209 AD	15210 AD
15211 AD	15212 AD	15213 AD	15214 AD	15215 AD	15216 AD	15217 AD	15218 AD	15219 AD	15220 AD
15221 AD	15222 AD	15223 AD	15224 AD	15225 AD	15226 AD	15227 AD	15228 AD	15229 AD	15230 AD
15231 AD	15232 AD	15233 AD	15234 AD	15235 AD	15236 AD	15237 AD	15238 AD	15239 AD	15240 AD
15241 AD	15342 AD	15243 AD	15244 AD	15245 AD	15246 AD	15247 AD	15248 AD	15249 AD	15250 AD
15251 AD	15252 AD	15253 AD	15254 AD	15255 AD	15256 AD	15257 AD	15258 AD	15259 AD	15260 AD
15261 AD	15262 AD	15263 AD	15264 AD	15265 AD	15266 AD	15267 AD	15268 AD	15269 AD	15270 AD
15271 AD	15272 AD	15273 AD	15274 AD	15275 AD	15276 AD	15277 AD	15278 AD	15279 AD	15280 AD
15281 AD	15282 AD	15283 AD	15284 AD	15285 AD	15286 AD	15287 AD	15288 AD	15289 AD	15290 AD
15291 AD	15292 AD	15293 AD	15294 AD	15295 AD	15296 AD	15297 AD	15298 AD	15299 AD	15300 AD
15301 AD	15302 AD	15303 AD	15304 AD	15305 AD	15306 AD	15307 AD	15308 AD	15309 AD	15310 AD
15311 AD	15312 AD	15313 AD	15314 AD	15315 AD	15316 AD	15317 AD	15318 AD	15319 AD	15320 AD
15321 AD	15322 AD	15323 AD	15324 AD	15325 AD	15326 AD	15327 AD	15328 AD	15329 AD	15330 AD
15331 AD	15332 AD	15333 AD	15334 AD	15335 AD	15336 AD	15337 AD	15338 AD	15339 AD	15340 AD
15341 AD	15342 AD	15343 AD	15344 AD	15345 AD	15346 AD	15347 AD	15348 AD	15349 AD	15350 AD
15351 AD	15352 AD	15353 AD	15354 AD	15355 AD	15356 AD	15357 AD	15358 AD	15359 AD	15360 AD
15361 AD	15362 AD	15363 AD	15364 AD	15365 AD	15366 AD	15367 AD	15368 AD	15369 AD	15370 AD
15371 AD	15372 AD	15373 AD	15374 AD	15375 AD	15376 AD	15377 AD	15378 AD	15379 AD	15380 AD
15381 AD	15382 AD	15383 AD	15384 AD	15385 AD	15386 AD	15387 AD	15388 AD	15389 AD	15390 AD
15391 AD	15392 AD	15393 AD	15394 AD	15395 AD	15396 AD	15397 AD	15398 AD	15399 AD	15400 AD
15401 AD	15402 AD	15403 AD	15404 AD	15405 AD	15406 AD	15407 AD	15408 AD	15409 AD	15410 AD
15411 AD	15412 AD	15413 AD	15414 AD	15415 AD	15416 AD	15417 AD	15418 AD	15419 AD	15420 AD
15421 AD	15422 AD	15423 AD	15424 AD	15425 AD	15426 AD	15427 AD	15428 AD	15429 AD	15430 AD
15431 AD	15432 AD	15433 AD	15434 AD	15435 AD	15436 AD	15437 AD	15438 AD	15439 AD	15440 AD
15441 AD	15442 AD	15443 AD	15444 AD	15445 AD	15446 AD	15447 AD	15448 AD	15449 AD	15450 AD
15451 AD	15452 AD	15453 AD	15454 AD	15455 AD	15456 AD	15457 AD	15458 AD	15459 AD	15460 AD
15461 AD	15462 AD	15463 AD	15464 AD	15465 AD	15466 AD	15467 AD	15468 AD	15469 AD	15470 AD
15471 AD	15472 AD	15473 AD	15474 AD	15475 AD	15476 AD	15477 AD	15478 AD	15479 AD	15480 AD
15481 AD	15482 AD	15483 AD	15484 AD	15485 AD	15486 AD	15487 AD	15488 AD	15489 AD	15490 AD
15491 AD	15492 AD	15493 AD	15494 AD	15495 AD	15496 AD	15497 AD	15498 AD	15499 AD	15500 AD

— 28 —

15501 AD	15502 AD	15503 AD	15504 AD	15505 AD	15506 AD	15507 AD	15508 AD	15509 AD	15510 AD
15511 AD	15512 AD	15513 AD	15514 AD	15515 AD	15516 AD	15517 AD	15518 AD	15519 AD	15520 AD
15521 AD	15522 AD	15523 AD	15524 AD	15525 AD	15526 AD	15527 AD	15528 AD	15529 AD	15530 AD
15531 AD	15532 AD	15533 AD	15534 AD	15535 AD	15536 AD	15537 AD	15538 AD	15539 AD	15540 AD
15541 AD	15542 AD	15543 AD	15544 AD	15545 AD	15546 AD	15547 AD	15548 AD	15549 AD	15550 AD
15551 AD	15552 AD	15553 AD	15554 AD	15555 AD	15556 AD	15557 AD	15558 AD	15559 AD	15560 AD
15561 AD	15562 AD	15563 AD	15564 AD	15565 AD	15566 AD	15567 AD	15568 AD	15569 AD	15570 AD
15571 AD	15572 AD	15573 AD	15574 AD	15575 AD	15576 AD	15577 AD	15578 AD	15579 AD	15580 AD
15581 AD	15582 AD	15583 AD	15584 AD	15585 AD	15586 AD	15587 AD	15588 AD	15589 AD	15590 AD
15591 AD	15592 AD	15593 AD	15594 AD	15595 AD	15596 AD	15597 AD	15598 AD	15599 AD	15600 AD
15601 AD	15602 AD	15603 AD	15604 AD	15605 AD	15606 AD	15607 AD	15608 AD	15609 AD	15610 AD
15611 AD	15612 AD	15613 AD	15614 AD	15615 AD	15616 AD	15617 AD	15618 AD	15619 AD	15620 AD
15621 AD	15622 AD	15623 AD	15624 AD	15625 AD	15626 AD	15627 AD	15628 AD	15629 AD	15630 AD
15631 AD	15632 AD	15633 AD	15634 AD	15635 AD	15636 AD	15637 AD	15638 AD	15639 AD	15640 AD
15641 AD	15642 AD	15643 AD	15644 AD	15645 AD	15646 AD	15647 AD	15648 AD	15649 AD	15650 AD
15651 AD	15652 AD	15653 AD	15654 AD	15655 AD	15656 AD	15657 AD	15658 AD	15659 AD	15660 AD
15661 AD	15662 AD	15663 AD	15664 AD	15665 AD	15666 AD	15667 AD	15668 AD	15669 AD	15670 AD
15671 AD	15672 AD	15673 AD	15674 AD	15675 AD	15676 AD	15677 AD	15678 AD	15679 AD	15680 AD
15681 AD	15682 AD	15683 AD	15684 AD	15685 AD	15686 AD	15687 AD	15688 AD	15689 AD	15690 AD
15691 AD	15692 AD	15693 AD	15694 AD	15695 AD	15696 AD	15697 AD	15698 AD	15699 AD	15700 AD
15701 AD	15702 AD	15703 AD	15704 AD	15705 AD	15706 AD	15707 AD	15708 AD	15709 AD	15710 AD
15711 AD	15712 AD	15713 AD	15714 AD	15715 AD	15716 AD	15717 AD	15718 AD	15719 AD	15720 AD
15721 AD	15722 AD	15723 AD	15724 AD	15725 AD	15726 AD	15727 AD	15728 AD	15729 AD	15730 AD
15731 AD	15732 AD	15733 AD	15734 AD	15735 AD	15736 AD	15737 AD	15738 AD	15739 AD	15740 AD
15741 AD	15742 AD	15743 AD	15744 AD	15745 AD	15746 AD	15747 AD	15748 AD	15749 AD	15750 AD
15751 AD	15752 AD	15753 AD	15754 AD	15755 AD	15756 AD	15757 AD	15758 AD	15759 AD	15760 AD
15761 AD	15762 AD	15763 AD	15764 AD	15765 AD	15766 AD	15767 AD	15768 AD	15769 AD	15770 AD
15771 AD	15772 AD	15773 AD	15774 AD	15775 AD	15776 AD	15777 AD	15778 AD	15779 AD	15780 AD
15781 AD	15782 AD	15783 AD	15784 AD	15785 AD	15786 AD	15787 AD	15788 AD	15789 AD	15790 AD
15791 AD	15792 AD	15793 AD	15794 AD	15795 AD	15796 AD	15797 AD	15798 AD	15799 AD	15800 AD
15801 AD	15802 AD	15803 AD	15804 AD	15805 AD	15806 AD	15807 AD	15808 AD	15809 AD	15810 AD
15811 AD	15812 AD	15813 AD	15814 AD	15815 AD	15816 AD	15817 AD	15818 AD	15819 AD	15820 AD
15821 AD	15822 AD	15823 AD	15824 AD	15825 AD	15826 AD	15827 AD	15828 AD	15829 AD	15830 AD
15831 AD	15832 AD	15833 AD	15834 AD	15835 AD	15836 AD	15837 AD	15838 AD	15839 AD	15840 AD
15841 AD	15842 AD	15843 AD	15844 AD	15845 AD	15846 AD	15847 AD	15848 AD	15849 AD	15850 AD
15851 AD	15852 AD	15853 AD	15854 AD	15855 AD	15856 AD	15857 AD	15858 AD	15859 AD	15860 AD
15861 AD	15862 AD	15863 AD	15864 AD	15865 AD	15866 AD	15867 AD	15868 AD	15869 AD	15870 AD
15871 AD	15872 AD	15873 AD	15874 AD	15875 AD	15876 AD	15877 AD	15878 AD	15879 AD	15880 AD
15881 AD	15882 AD	15883 AD	15884 AD	15885 AD	15886 AD	15887 AD	15888 AD	15889 AD	15890 AD
15891 AD	15892 AD	15893 AD	15894 AD	15895 AD	15896 AD	15897 AD	15898 AD	15899 AD	15900 AD
15901 AD	15902 AD	15903 AD	15904 AD	15905 AD	15906 AD	15907 AD	15908 AD	15909 AD	15910 AD
15911 AD	15912 AD	15913 AD	15914 AD	15915 AD	15916 AD	15917 AD	15918 AD	15919 AD	15920 AD
15921 AD	15922 AD	15923 AD	15924 AD	15925 AD	15926 AD	15927 AD	15928 AD	15929 AD	15930 AD
15931 AD	15932 AD	15933 AD	15934 AD	15935 AD	15936 AD	15937 AD	15938 AD	15939 AD	15940 AD
15941 AD	15942 AD	15943 AD	15944 AD	15945 AD	15946 AD	15947 AD	15948 AD	15949 AD	15950 AD
15951 AD	15952 AD	15953 AD	15954 AD	15955 AD	15956 AD	15957 AD	15958 AD	15959 AD	15960 AD
15961 AD	15962 AD	15963 AD	15964 AD	15965 AD	15966 AD	15967 AD	15968 AD	15969 AD	15970 AD
15971 AD	15972 AD	15973 AD	15974 AD	15975 AD	15976 AD	15977 AD	15978 AD	15979 AD	15980 AD
15981 AD	15982 AD	15983 AD	15984 AD	15985 AD	15986 AD	15987 AD	15988 AD	15989 AD	15990 AD
15991 AD	15992 AD	15993 AD	15994 AD	15995 AD	15996 AD	15997 AD	15998 AD	15999 AD	16000 AD

```
16001 AD  16002 AD  16003 AD  16004 AD  16005 AD  16006 AD  16007 AD  16008 AD  16009 AD  16010 AD
16011 AD  16012 AD  16013 AD  16014 AD  16015 AD  16016 AD  16017 AD  16018 AD  16019 AD  16020 AD
16021 AD  16022 AD  16023 AD  16024 AD  16025 AD  16026 AD  16027 AD  16028 AD  16029 AD  16030 AD
16031 AD  16032 AD  16033 AD  16034 AD  16035 AD  16036 AD  16037 AD  16038 AD  16039 AD  16040 AD
16041 AD  16042 AD  16043 AD  16044 AD  16045 AD  16046 AD  16047 AD  16048 AD  16049 AD  16050 AD
16051 AD  16052 AD  16053 AD  16054 AD  16055 AD  16056 AD  16057 AD  16058 AD  16059 AD  16060 AD
16061 AD  16062 AD  16063 AD  16064 AD  16065 AD  16066 AD  16067 AD  16068 AD  16069 AD  16070 AD
16071 AD  16072 AD  16073 AD  16074 AD  16075 AD  16076 AD  16077 AD  16078 AD  16079 AD  16080 AD
16081 AD  16082 AD  16083 AD  16084 AD  16085 AD  16086 AD  16087 AD  16088 AD  16089 AD  16090 AD
16091 AD  16092 AD  16093 AD  16094 AD  16095 AD  16096 AD  16097 AD  16098 AD  16099 AD  16100 AD

16101 AD  16102 AD  16103 AD  16104 AD  16105 AD  16106 AD  16107 AD  16108 AD  16109 AD  16110 AD
16111 AD  16112 AD  16113 AD  16114 AD  16115 AD  16116 AD  16117 AD  16118 AD  16119 AD  16120 AD
16121 AD  16122 AD  16123 AD  16124 AD  16125 AD  16126 AD  16127 AD  16128 AD  16129 AD  16130 AD
16131 AD  16132 AD  16133 AD  16134 AD  16135 AD  16136 AD  16137 AD  16138 AD  16139 AD  16140 AD
16141 AD  16142 AD  16143 AD  16144 AD  16145 AD  16146 AD  16147 AD  16148 AD  16149 AD  16150 AD
16151 AD  16152 AD  16153 AD  16154 AD  16155 AD  16156 AD  16157 AD  16158 AD  16159 AD  16160 AD
16161 AD  16162 AD  16163 AD  16164 AD  16165 AD  16166 AD  16167 AD  16168 AD  16169 AD  16170 AD
16171 AD  16172 AD  16173 AD  16174 AD  16175 AD  16176 AD  16177 AD  16178 AD  16179 AD  16180 AD
16181 AD  16182 AD  16183 AD  16184 AD  16185 AD  16186 AD  16187 AD  16188 AD  16189 AD  16190 AD
16191 AD  16192 AD  16193 AD  16194 AD  16195 AD  16196 AD  16197 AD  16198 AD  16199 AD  16200 AD

16201 AD  16202 AD  16203 AD  16204 AD  16205 AD  16206 AD  16207 AD  16208 AD  16209 AD  16210 AD
16211 AD  16212 AD  16213 AD  16214 AD  16215 AD  16216 AD  16217 AD  16218 AD  16219 AD  16220 AD
16221 AD  16222 AD  16223 AD  16224 AD  16225 AD  16226 AD  16227 AD  16228 AD  16229 AD  16230 AD
16231 AD  16232 AD  16233 AD  16234 AD  16235 AD  16236 AD  16237 AD  16238 AD  16239 AD  16240 AD
16241 AD  16242 AD  16243 AD  16244 AD  16245 AD  16246 AD  16247 AD  16248 AD  16249 AD  16250 AD
16251 AD  16252 AD  16253 AD  16254 AD  16255 AD  16256 AD  16257 AD  16258 AD  16259 AD  16260 AD
16261 AD  16262 AD  16263 AD  16264 AD  16265 AD  16266 AD  16267 AD  16268 AD  16269 AD  16270 AD
16271 AD  16272 AD  16273 AD  16274 AD  16275 AD  16276 AD  16277 AD  16278 AD  16279 AD  16280 AD
16281 AD  16282 AD  16283 AD  16284 AD  16285 AD  16286 AD  16287 AD  16288 AD  16289 AD  16290 AD
16291 AD  16292 AD  16293 AD  16294 AD  16295 AD  16296 AD  16297 AD  16298 AD  16299 AD  16300 AD

16301 AD  16302 AD  16303 AD  16304 AD  16305 AD  16306 AD  16307 AD  16308 AD  16309 AD  16310 AD
16311 AD  16312 AD  16313 AD  16314 AD  16315 AD  16316 AD  16317 AD  16318 AD  16319 AD  16320 AD
16321 AD  16322 AD  16323 AD  16324 AD  16325 AD  16326 AD  16327 AD  16328 AD  16329 AD  16330 AD
16331 AD  16332 AD  16333 AD  16334 AD  16335 AD  16336 AD  16337 AD  16338 AD  16339 AD  16340 AD
16341 AD  16342 AD  16343 AD  16344 AD  16345 AD  16346 AD  16347 AD  16348 AD  16349 AD  16350 AD
16351 AD  16352 AD  16353 AD  16354 AD  16355 AD  16356 AD  16357 AD  16358 AD  16359 AD  16360 AD
16361 AD  16362 AD  16363 AD  16364 AD  16365 AD  16366 AD  16367 AD  16368 AD  16369 AD  16370 AD
16371 AD  16372 AD  16373 AD  16374 AD  16375 AD  16376 AD  16377 AD  16378 AD  16379 AD  16380 AD
16381 AD  16382 AD  16383 AD  16384 AD  16385 AD  16386 AD  16387 AD  16388 AD  16389 AD  16390 AD
16391 AD  16392 AD  16393 AD  16394 AD  16395 AD  16396 AD  16397 AD  16398 AD  16399 AD  16400 AD

16401 AD  16402 AD  16403 AD  16404 AD  16405 AD  16406 AD  16407 AD  16408 AD  16409 AD  16410 AD
16411 AD  16412 AD  16413 AD  16414 AD  16415 AD  16416 AD  16417 AD  16418 AD  16419 AD  16420 AD
16421 AD  16422 AD  16423 AD  16424 AD  16425 AD  16426 AD  16427 AD  16428 AD  16429 AD  16430 AD
16431 AD  16432 AD  16433 AD  16434 AD  16435 AD  16436 AD  16437 AD  16438 AD  16439 AD  16440 AD
16441 AD  16442 AD  16443 AD  16444 AD  16445 AD  16446 AD  16447 AD  16448 AD  16449 AD  16450 AD
16451 AD  16452 AD  16453 AD  16454 AD  16455 AD  16456 AD  16457 AD  16458 AD  16459 AD  16460 AD
16461 AD  16462 AD  16463 AD  16464 AD  16465 AD  16466 AD  16467 AD  16468 AD  16469 AD  16470 AD
16471 AD  16472 AD  16473 AD  16474 AD  16475 AD  16476 AD  16477 AD  16478 AD  16479 AD  16480 AD
16481 AD  16482 AD  16483 AD  16484 AD  16485 AD  16486 AD  16487 AD  16488 AD  16489 AD  16490 AD
16491 AD  16492 AD  16493 AD  16494 AD  16495 AD  16496 AD  16497 AD  16498 AD  16499 AD  16500 AD
```

16501 AD	16502 AD	16503 AD	16504 AD	16505 AD	16506 AD	16507 AD	16508 AD	16509 AD	16510 AD
16511 AD	16512 AD	16513 AD	16514 AD	16515 AD	16516 AD	16517 AD	16518 AD	16519 AD	16520 AD
16521 AD	16522 AD	16523 AD	16524 AD	16525 AD	16526 AD	16527 AD	16528 AD	16529 AD	16530 AD
16531 AD	16532 AD	16533 AD	16534 AD	16535 AD	16536 AD	16537 AD	16538 AD	16539 AD	16540 AD
16541 AD	16542 AD	16543 AD	16544 AD	16545 AD	16546 AD	16547 AD	16548 AD	16549 AD	16550 AD
16551 AD	16552 AD	16553 AD	16554 AD	16555 AD	16556 AD	16557 AD	16558 AD	16559 AD	16560 AD
16561 AD	16562 AD	16563 AD	16564 AD	16565 AD	16566 AD	16567 AD	16568 AD	16569 AD	16570 AD
16571 AD	16572 AD	16573 AD	16574 AD	16575 AD	16576 AD	16577 AD	16578 AD	16579 AD	16580 AD
16581 AD	16582 AD	16583 AD	16584 AD	16585 AD	16586 AD	16587 AD	16588 AD	16589 AD	16590 AD
16591 AD	16592 AD	16593 AD	16594 AD	16595 AD	16596 AD	16597 AD	16598 AD	16599 AD	16600 AD
16601 AD	16602 AD	16603 AD	16604 AD	16605 AD	16606 AD	16607 AD	16608 AD	16609 AD	16610 AD
16611 AD	16612 AD	16613 AD	16614 AD	16615 AD	16616 AD	16617 AD	16618 AD	16619 AD	16620 AD
16621 AD	16622 AD	16623 AD	16624 AD	16625 AD	16626 AD	16627 AD	16628 AD	16629 AD	16630 AD
16631 AD	16632 AD	16633 AD	16634 AD	16635 AD	16636 AD	16637 AD	16638 AD	16639 AD	16640 AD
16641 AD	16642 AD	16643 AD	16644 AD	16645 AD	16646 AD	16647 AD	16648 AD	16649 AD	16650 AD
16651 AD	16652 AD	16653 AD	16654 AD	16655 AD	16656 AD	16657 AD	16658 AD	16659 AD	16660 AD
16661 AD	16662 AD	16663 AD	16664 AD	16665 AD	16666 AD	16667 AD	16668 AD	16669 AD	16670 AD
16671 AD	16672 AD	16673 AD	16674 AD	16675 AD	16676 AD	16677 AD	16678 AD	16679 AD	16680 AD
16681 AD	16682 AD	16683 AD	16684 AD	16685 AD	16686 AD	16687 AD	16688 AD	16689 AD	16690 AD
16691 AD	16692 AD	16693 AD	16694 AD	16695 AD	16696 AD	16697 AD	16698 AD	16699 AD	16700 AD
16701 AD	16702 AD	16703 AD	16704 AD	16705 AD	16706 AD	16707 AD	16708 AD	16709 AD	16710 AD
16711 AD	16712 AD	16713 AD	16714 AD	16715 AD	16716 AD	16717 AD	16718 AD	16719 AD	16720 AD
16721 AD	16722 AD	16723 AD	16724 AD	16725 AD	16726 AD	16727 AD	16728 AD	16729 AD	16730 AD
16731 AD	16732 AD	16733 AD	16734 AD	16735 AD	16736 AD	16737 AD	16738 AD	16739 AD	16740 AD
16741 AD	16742 AD	16743 AD	16744 AD	16745 AD	16746 AD	16747 AD	16748 AD	16749 AD	16750 AD
16751 AD	16752 AD	16753 AD	16754 AD	16755 AD	16756 AD	16757 AD	16758 AD	16759 AD	16760 AD
16761 AD	16762 AD	16763 AD	16764 AD	16765 AD	16766 AD	16767 AD	16768 AD	16769 AD	16770 AD
16771 AD	16772 AD	16773 AD	16774 AD	16775 AD	16776 AD	16777 AD	16778 AD	16779 AD	16780 AD
16781 AD	16782 AD	16783 AD	16784 AD	16785 AD	16786 AD	16787 AD	16788 AD	16789 AD	16790 AD
16791 AD	16792 AD	16793 AD	16794 AD	16795 AD	16796 AD	16797 AD	16798 AD	16799 AD	16800 AD
16801 AD	16802 AD	16803 AD	16804 AD	16805 AD	16806 AD	16807 AD	16808 AD	16809 AD	16810 AD
16811 AD	16812 AD	16813 AD	16814 AD	16815 AD	16816 AD	16817 AD	16818 AD	16819 AD	16820 AD
16821 AD	16822 AD	16823 AD	16824 AD	16825 AD	16826 AD	16827 AD	16828 AD	16829 AD	16830 AD
16831 AD	16832 AD	16833 AD	16834 AD	16835 AD	16836 AD	16837 AD	16838 AD	16839 AD	16840 AD
16841 AD	16842 AD	16843 AD	16844 AD	16845 AD	16846 AD	16847 AD	16848 AD	16849 AD	16850 AD
16851 AD	16852 AD	16853 AD	16854 AD	16855 AD	16856 AD	16857 AD	16858 AD	16859 AD	16860 AD
16861 AD	16862 AD	16863 AD	16864 AD	16865 AD	16866 AD	16867 AD	16868 AD	16869 AD	16870 AD
16871 AD	16872 AD	16873 AD	16874 AD	16875 AD	16876 AD	16877 AD	16878 AD	16879 AD	16880 AD
16881 AD	16882 AD	16883 AD	16884 AD	16885 AD	16886 AD	16887 AD	16888 AD	16889 AD	16890 AD
16891 AD	16892 AD	16893 AD	16894 AD	16895 AD	16896 AD	16897 AD	16898 AD	16899 AD	16900 AD
16901 AD	16902 AD	16903 AD	16904 AD	16905 AD	16906 AD	16907 AD	16908 AD	16909 AD	16910 AD
16911 AD	16912 AD	16913 AD	16914 AD	16915 AD	16916 AD	16917 AD	16918 AD	16919 AD	16920 AD
16921 AD	16922 AD	16923 AD	16924 AD	16925 AD	16926 AD	16927 AD	16928 AD	16929 AD	16930 AD
16931 AD	16932 AD	16933 AD	16934 AD	16935 AD	16936 AD	16937 AD	16938 AD	16939 AD	16940 AD
16941 AD	16942 AD	16943 AD	16944 AD	16945 AD	16946 AD	16947 AD	16948 AD	16949 AD	16950 AD
16951 AD	16952 AD	16953 AD	16954 AD	16955 AD	16956 AD	16957 AD	16958 AD	16959 AD	16960 AD
16961 AD	16962 AD	16963 AD	16964 AD	16965 AD	16966 AD	16967 AD	16968 AD	16969 AD	16970 AD
16971 AD	16972 AD	16973 AD	16974 AD	16975 AD	16976 AD	16977 AD	16978 AD	16979 AD	16980 AD
16981 AD	16982 AD	16983 AD	16984 AD	16985 AD	16986 AD	16987 AD	16988 AD	16989 AD	16990 AD
16991 AD	16992 AD	16993 AD	16994 AD	16995 AD	16996 AD	16997 AD	16998 AD	16999 AD	17000 AD

17001 AD 17002 AD 17003 AD 17004 AD 17005 AD 17006 AD 17007 AD 17008 AD 17009 AD 17010 AD
17011 AD 17012 AD 17013 AD 17014 AD 17015 AD 17016 AD 17017 AD 17018 AD 17019 AD 17020 AD
17021 AD 17022 AD 17023 AD 17024 AD 17025 AD 17026 AD 17027 AD 17028 AD 17029 AD 17030 AD
17031 AD 17032 AD 17033 AD 17034 AD 17035 AD 17036 AD 17037 AD 17038 AD 17039 AD 17040 AD
17041 AD 17042 AD 17043 AD 17044 AD 17045 AD 17046 AD 17047 AD 17048 AD 17049 AD 17050 AD
17051 AD 17052 AD 17053 AD 17054 AD 17055 AD 17056 AD 17057 AD 17058 AD 17059 AD 17060 AD
17061 AD 17062 AD 17063 AD 17064 AD 17065 AD 17066 AD 17067 AD 17068 AD 17069 AD 17070 AD
17071 AD 17072 AD 17073 AD 17074 AD 17075 AD 17076 AD 17077 AD 17078 AD 17079 AD 17080 AD
17081 AD 17082 AD 17083 AD 17084 AD 17085 AD 17086 AD 17087 AD 17088 AD 17089 AD 17090 AD
17091 AD 17092 AD 17093 AD 17094 AD 17095 AD 17096 AD 17097 AD 17098 AD 17099 AD 17100 AD

17101 AD 17102 AD 17103 AD 17104 AD 17105 AD 17106 AD 17107 AD 17108 AD 17109 AD 17110 AD
17111 AD 17112 AD 17113 AD 17114 AD 17115 AD 17116 AD 17117 AD 17118 AD 17119 AD 17120 AD
17121 AD 17122 AD 17123 AD 17124 AD 17125 AD 17126 AD 17127 AD 17128 AD 17129 AD 17130 AD
17131 AD 17132 AD 17133 AD 17134 AD 17135 AD 17136 AD 17137 AD 17138 AD 17139 AD 17140 AD
17141 AD 17142 AD 17143 AD 17144 AD 17145 AD 17146 AD 17147 AD 17148 AD 17149 AD 17150 AD
17151 AD 17152 AD 17153 AD 17154 AD 17155 AD 17156 AD 17157 AD 17158 AD 17159 AD 17160 AD
17161 AD 17162 AD 17163 AD 17164 AD 17165 AD 17166 AD 17167 AD 17168 AD 17169 AD 17170 AD
17171 AD 17172 AD 17173 AD 17174 AD 17175 AD 17176 AD 17177 AD 17178 AD 17179 AD 17180 AD
17181 AD 17182 AD 17183 AD 17184 AD 17185 AD 17186 AD 17187 AD 17188 AD 17189 AD 17190 AD
17191 AD 17192 AD 17193 AD 17194 AD 17195 AD 17196 AD 17197 AD 17198 AD 17199 AD 17200 AD

17201 AD 17202 AD 17203 AD 17204 AD 17205 AD 17206 AD 17207 AD 17208 AD 17209 AD 17210 AD
17211 AD 17212 AD 17213 AD 17214 AD 17215 AD 17216 AD 17217 AD 17218 AD 17219 AD 17220 AD
17221 AD 17222 AD 17223 AD 17224 AD 17225 AD 17226 AD 17227 AD 17228 AD 17229 AD 17230 AD
17231 AD 17232 AD 17233 AD 17234 AD 17235 AD 17236 AD 17237 AD 17238 AD 17239 AD 17240 AD
17241 AD 17242 AD 17243 AD 17244 AD 17245 AD 17246 AD 17247 AD 17248 AD 17249 AD 17250 AD
17251 AD 17252 AD 17253 AD 17254 AD 17255 AD 17256 AD 17257 AD 17258 AD 17259 AD 17260 AD
17261 AD 17262 AD 17263 AD 17264 AD 17265 AD 17266 AD 17267 AD 17268 AD 17269 AD 17270 AD
17271 AD 17272 AD 17273 AD 17274 AD 17275 AD 17276 AD 17277 AD 17278 AD 17279 AD 17280 AD
17281 AD 17282 AD 17283 AD 17284 AD 17285 AD 17286 AD 17287 AD 17288 AD 17289 AD 17290 AD
17291 AD 17292 AD 17293 AD 17294 AD 17295 AD 17296 AD 17297 AD 17298 AD 17299 AD 17300 AD

17301 AD 17302 AD 17303 AD 17304 AD 17305 AD 17306 AD 17307 AD 17308 AD 17309 AD 17310 AD
17311 AD 17312 AD 17313 AD 17314 AD 17315 AD 17316 AD 17317 AD 17318 AD 17319 AD 17320 AD
17321 AD 17322 AD 17323 AD 17324 AD 17325 AD 17326 AD 17327 AD 17328 AD 17329 AD 17330 AD
17331 AD 17332 AD 17333 AD 17334 AD 17335 AD 17336 AD 17337 AD 17338 AD 17339 AD 17340 AD
17341 AD 17342 AD 17343 AD 17344 AD 17345 AD 17346 AD 17347 AD 17348 AD 17349 AD 17350 AD
17351 AD 17352 AD 17353 AD 17354 AD 17355 AD 17356 AD 17357 AD 17358 AD 17359 AD 17360 AD
17361 AD 17362 AD 17363 AD 17364 AD 17365 AD 17366 AD 17367 AD 17368 AD 17369 AD 17370 AD
17371 AD 17372 AD 17373 AD 17374 AD 17375 AD 17376 AD 17377 AD 17378 AD 17379 AD 17380 AD
17381 AD 17382 AD 17383 AD 17384 AD 17385 AD 17386 AD 17387 AD 17388 AD 17389 AD 17390 AD
17391 AD 17392 AD 17393 AD 17394 AD 17395 AD 17396 AD 17397 AD 17398 AD 17399 AD 17400 AD

17401 AD 17402 AD 17403 AD 17404 AD 17405 AD 17406 AD 17407 AD 17408 AD 17409 AD 17410 AD
17411 AD 17412 AD 17413 AD 17414 AD 17415 AD 17416 AD 17417 AD 17418 AD 17419 AD 17420 AD
17421 AD 17422 AD 17423 AD 17424 AD 17425 AD 17426 AD 17427 AD 17428 AD 17429 AD 17430 AD
17431 AD 17432 AD 17433 AD 17434 AD 17435 AD 17436 AD 17437 AD 17438 AD 17439 AD 17440 AD
17441 AD 17442 AD 17443 AD 17444 AD 17445 AD 17446 AD 17447 AD 17448 AD 17449 AD 17450 AD
17451 AD 17452 AD 17453 AD 17454 AD 17455 AD 17456 AD 17457 AD 17458 AD 17459 AD 17460 AD
17461 AD 17462 AD 17463 AD 17464 AD 17465 AD 17466 AD 17467 AD 17468 AD 17469 AD 17470 AD
17471 AD 17472 AD 17473 AD 17474 AD 17475 AD 17476 AD 17477 AD 17478 AD 17479 AD 17480 AD
17481 AD 17482 AD 17483 AD 17484 AD 17485 AD 17486 AD 17487 AD 17488 AD 17489 AD 17490 AD
17491 AD 17492 AD 17493 AD 17494 AD 17495 AD 17496 AD 17497 AD 17498 AD 17499 AD 17500 AD

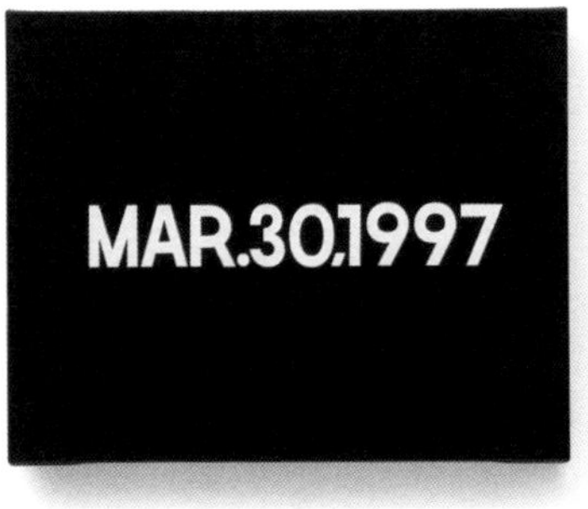
MAR.30.1997

Sundays, drawing, 1964

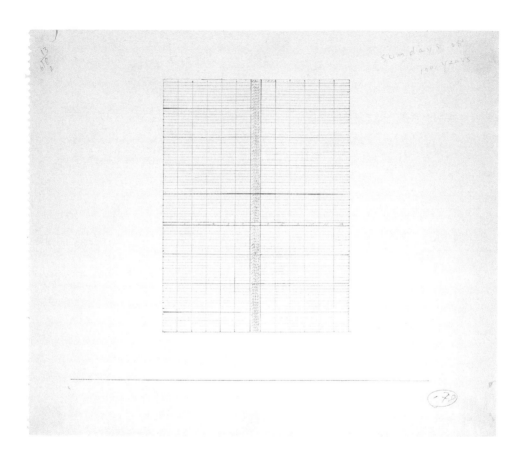

JAN. 16, 1966
JANUARY 30, 1966
FEB. 20, 1966
MAR. 13, 1966
MAR. 20, 1966
APR. 10, 1966
APR. 17, 1966
MAY 15, 1966
MAY 22, 1966
MAY 29, 1966
JUNE 5, 1966
JUNE 12, 1966
JULY 3, 1966
JULY 10, 1966
JULY 24, 1966
JULY 31, 1966
AUG. 7, 1966
SEPT. 4, 1966
SEPT. 18, 1966
SEPT. 25, 1966
OCT. 2, 1966
OCT. 9, 1966
OCT. 16, 1966
DEC. 4, 1966
DEC. 11, 1966
DEC. 25, 1966
JAN.8, 1967
JAN. 22, 1967
JAN. 29, 1967
FEB. 12, 1967
APR. 2, 1967
APR. 16, 1967
APR. 30, 1967
MAY 7, 1967
MAY 21, 1967

JUNE 4, 1967
JUNE 11, 1967
JUNE 18, 1967
JULY 16, 1967
AUG. 6, 1967
SEPT. 10, 1967
OCT. 1, 1967
OCT. 8, 1967
OCT. 15, 1967
OCT. 22, 1967
NOV. 12, 1967
NOV. 19, 1967
DEC. 17, 1967
DEC. 24, 1967
DEC. 31, 1967
14 ABR. 68
21 ABR. 68
28 ABR. 68
5 MAY. 68
12 MAY. 68
19 MAY. 68
26 MAY. 68
9 JUN. 68
30 JUN. 68
7 JUL. 68
14 JUL. 68
22 SEP. 68
29 SEP. 68
6 OCT. 68
20 OCT. 68
15 DIC. 68
29 DIC. 68
16 FEV. 1969
23 FEV. 1969
9 MAR. 69

MAY 11, 1969
MAY 18, 1969
JULY 20, 1969
AUG. 31, 1969
OCT. 26, 1969
JAN. 4, 1970
JAN. 11, 1970
JAN. 18, 1970
JAN. 25, 1970
FEB. 1, 1970
FEB. 8, 1970
FEB. 15, 1970
FEB. 22, 1970
MAR. 1, 1970
MAR. 8, 1970
MAR. 15, 1970
MAR. 22, 1970
MAR. 29, 1970
MAY 31, 1970
SEPT. 27, 1970
24 JAN. 1971
MAY 2, 1971
MAY 9, 1971
MAY 16, 1971
MAY 23, 1971
MAY 30, 1971
JULY 18, 1971
JULY 18, 1971
JULY 25, 1971
JULY 25, 1971
AUG. 1, 1971
AUG. 1, 1971
OCT. 17, 1971
OCT. 24, 1971
OCT. 31, 1971

NOV. 21, 1971
NOV. 28, 1971
FEB. 20, 1972
FEB. 27, 1972
APR. 2, 1972
APR. 16, 1972
JUNE 4, 1972
AUG. 27, 1972
31 DEC. 1972
7 JAN. 1973
14 JAN. 1973
11 FEV. 1973
18 FEB. 1973
4 MARS 1973
APR. 15, 1973
APR. 15, 1973
JUNE 17, 1973
JUNE 24, 1973
JULY 1, 1973
AUG. 26, 1973
OCT. 21, 1973
OCT. 28, 1973
NOV. 25, 1973
DEC. 30, 1973
MAR. 17, 1974
MAR. 24, 1974
MAR. 31, 1974
APR. 7, 1974
APR. 28, 1974
13 OKT. 1974
20 OCT. 1974
DEC. 1, 1974
DEC. 8, 1974
APR. 20, 1975
MAY 11, 1975

MAY 25, 1975
JUNE 1, 1975
JUNE 8, 1975
AUG. 17, 1975
SEPT. 14, 1975
SEPT. 21, 1975
NOV. 30, 1975
DEC. 28, 1975
JAN. 25, 1976
11. APR. 1976
1. AUG. 1976
21. NOV. 1976
28. NOV. 1976
JULY 17, 1977
OCT. 30, 1977
OCT. 29, 1978
DEC. 3, 1978
DEC. 24, 1978
DEC. 2, 1979
APR. 6, 1980
JULY 6, 1980
AUG. 10, 1980
NOV. 16, 1980
DEC. 21, 1980
DEC. 28, 1980
FEB. 22, 1981
NOV. 8, 1981
JAN. 17, 1982
JAN. 24, 1982
JAN. 31, 1982
FEB. 14, 1982
FEB. 28, 1982
18 JUL. 1982
17 JUL. 1983
NOV. 27, 1983

DEC. 18, 1983
JAN. 1, 1984
JAN. 22, 1984
APR. 22, 1984
15 JUL. 1984
12 AUG. 1984
OCT. 7, 1984
OCT. 14, 1984
JAN. 20, 1985
APR. 28, 1985
JUNE 2, 1985
JUNE 9, 1985
SEPT. 15, 1985
DEC. 8, 1985
JUNE 1, 1986
3 AUG. 1986
SEPT. 7, 1986
30. NOV. 1986
APR. 5, 1987
OCT. 4, 1987
MAY 15, 1988
DEC. 25, 1988
APR. 9, 1989
APR. 16, 1989
18 JUN. 1989
SEPT. 10, 1989
SEPT. 17, 1989
OCT. 29, 1989
DEC. 17, 1989
DEC. 24, 1989
MAR. 11, 1990
APR. 22, 1990
APR. 29, 1990
JUNE 17, 1990
AUG. 26, 1990

SEPT. 9, 1990	FEB. 6, 1994	APR. 19, 1998
SEPT. 16, 1990	FEB. 27, 1994	MAY 10, 1998
21 OTT. 1990	17 JUL. 1994	MAY 17, 1998
28 OTT. 1990	31 JUL. 1994	JULY 12, 1998
4 NOV. 1990	SEPT. 25, 1994	AUG. 2, 1998
11. NOV. 1990	OCT. 9, 1994	AUG. 23, 1998
DEC. 9, 1990	26 FEB. 1995	AUG. 23, 1998
JAN. 27, 1991	MAY 21, 1995	24 JAN. 1999
MAR. 24, 1991	MAY 28, 1995	MAR. 7, 1999
APR. 14, 1991	JUNE 4, 1995	MAR. 21, 1999
APR. 28, 1991	18 JUN. 1995	20. JUNI 1999
MAY 5, 1991	13. AUG. 1995	4 JUIL. 1999
MAY 19, 1991	27 AG. 1995	JULY 25, 1999
JUNE 9, 1991	3 SEPT. 1995	AUG. 1, 1999
JUNE 30, 1991	NOV. 5, 1995	AUG. 8, 1999
AUG. 25, 1991	FEB. 18, 1996	OCT. 10, 1999
NOV. 17, 1991	MAR. 17, 1996	9 JAN. 2000
DEC. 1, 1991	APR. 28, 1996	FEB. 27, 2000
29. DEZ. 1991	SEPT. 8, 1996	MAR. 5, 2000
FEB. 23, 1992	NOV. 3, 1996	MAR. 12, 2000
APR. 19, 1992	NOV. 17, 1996	APR. 16, 2000
SEPT. 6, 1992	NOV. 24, 1996	JULY 16, 2000
SEPT. 27, 1992	DEC. 1, 1996	12 NOV. 2000
OCT. 11, 1992	DEC. 8, 1996	21 JAN. 2001
6. DEZ. 1992	JAN. 5, 1997	FEB. 25, 2001
DEC. 27, 1992	MAR. 30, 1997	3. JUNI 2001
JAN. 10, 1993	APR. 13, 1997	JULY 1, 2001
FEB. 7, 1993	APR. 27, 1997	JULY 8, 2001
FEB. 14, 1993	JUNE 22, 1997	AUG. 19, 2001
APR. 18, 1993	NOV. 2, 1997	FEB. 3, 2002
MAY 16, 1993	NOV. 9, 1997	FEB. 24, 2002
30 MAI 1993	JAN. 18, 1998	MAR. 10, 2002
OCT. 17, 1993	MAR. 22, 1998	MAR. 31, 2002
NOV. 21, 1993	APR. 12, 1998	APR. 7, 2002

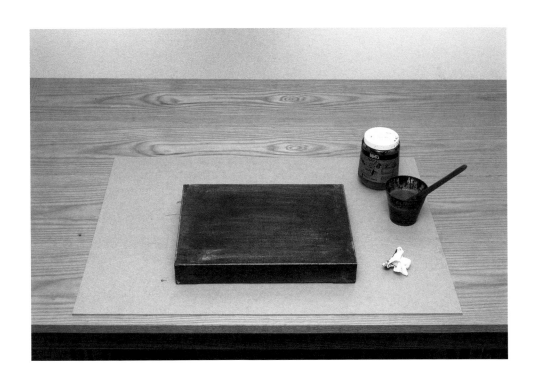

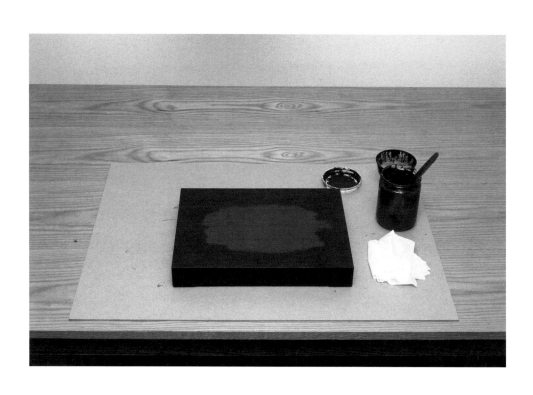

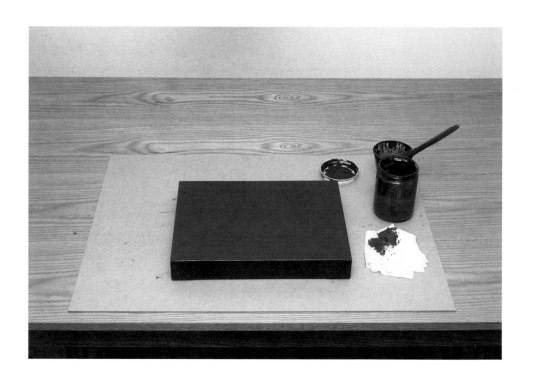

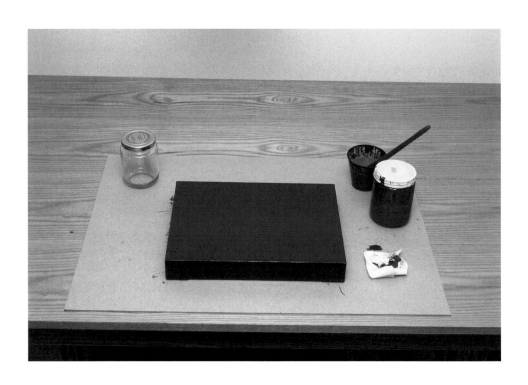

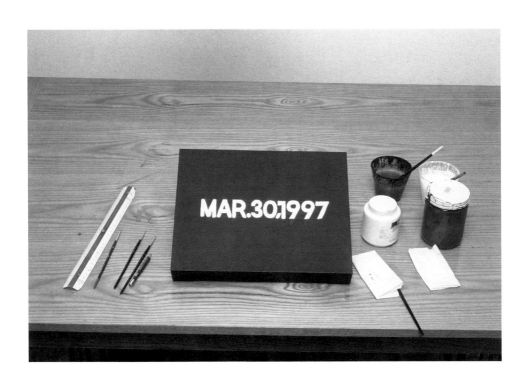

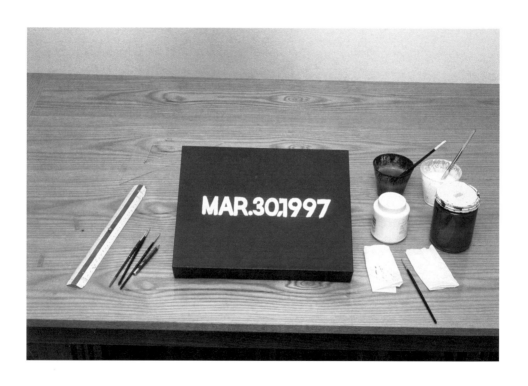

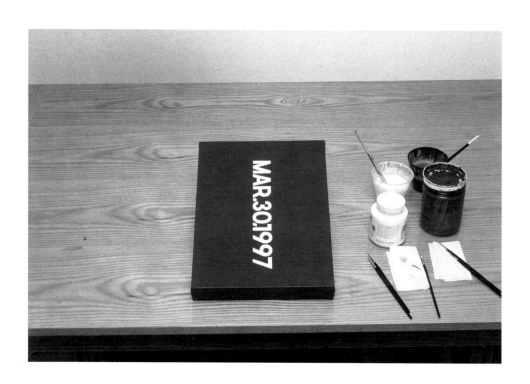

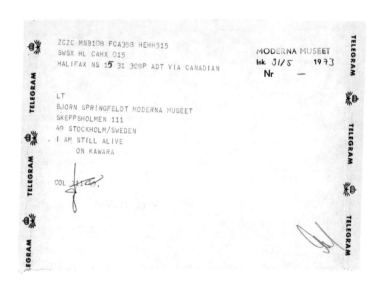

MODERNA MUSEET
Ink. 7/6   1973
Nr   —

NNNN
ZCZC MSD217 FCAO21 HXA592
SWSX HL CAHX 015
HALIFAX NS 15 7 205P ADT VIA CANADIAN

LT
MILLA TRAGARDH MODERNA MUSEET SKEPPSHOLMEN 111
49 STOCKHOLM

I AM STILL ALIVE
        ON KAWARA

COL 111 49.

42 7583

3000 BERN
-2 -6. 75
a
TELEGRAPH

```
zczc kjc570 nsw991 1-043369c157
dc newyork ny 015/015 06 630p ect

jbb8341 kt
johannes gachnang
kunsthalle bern helvetiaplatz 1
3005 bern



i am still alive
    on kawara col 1 3005

mnm  0123
```

h.a. 0856

zczc kja949 nsw768 1-030113a051
ys newyork ny 015/015 20 445p est

jbb9626 lt
johannes gachnang
kunsthalle bern helvetiaplatz 1 3005
(3000)bern

i am still alive
    on kawara col 1 3005

nnnn 20/02/76 2327

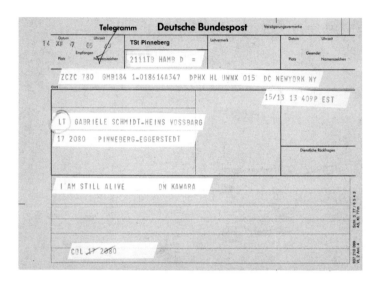

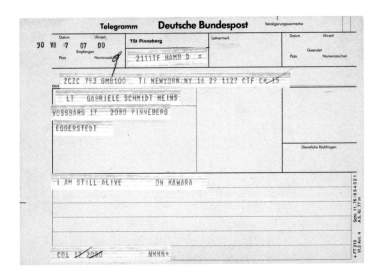

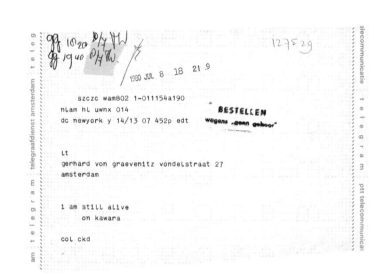

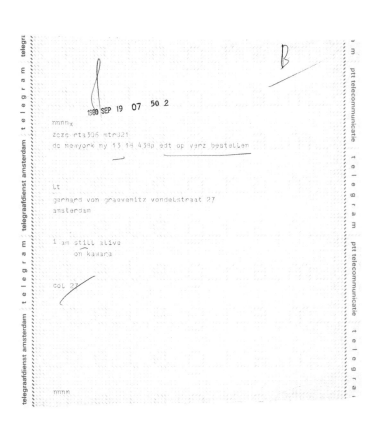

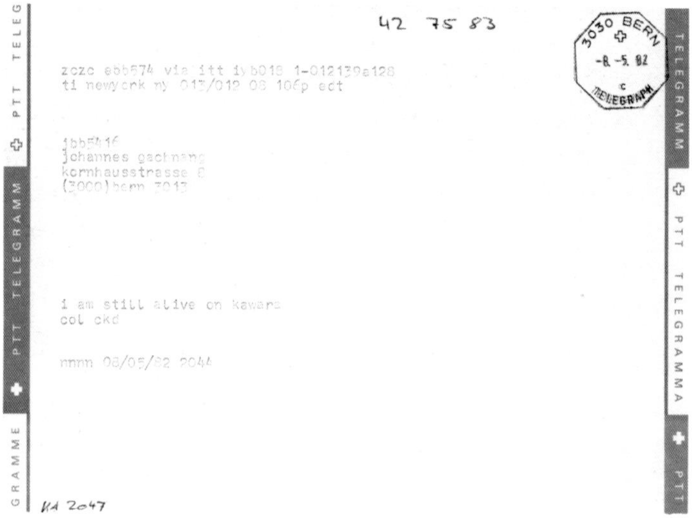

PTT TELEGRAMM PTT TELEGRAMME

42 75 83

3030 BERN
-8.-5.82
c
TELEGRAPH

zczc ebb574 via itt iyb018 1-012139a128
ti newyork ny 013/012 08 106p edt

ibb5416
johannes gachnang
kornhausstrasse 8
(3000)bern 3013

i am still alive on kawara
col ckd

nnnn 08/05/82 2044

KA 2047

PTT TELEGRAMMA PTT

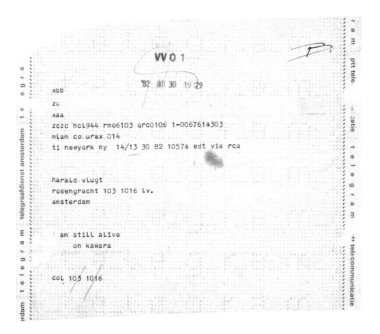

WW 0 1

'82 00 30 19:29

xbb
zc
xaa
zczc hcl944 rmo6103 qrc0106 1-006761a303
nlam co urax 014
t1 newyork ny 14/13 30 82 1057a edt via rca

harald vlugt
rosengracht 103 1016 lv.
amsterdam

i am still alive
     on kawara

col 103 1016

```
32221rb   ant b
29221to   bru b
zczc tob040
tokyo 13/11   7 1137


micheline szwajcer
venusstraat 17
(2000)antwerpen


i am still alive
    on kawara


col 17 2000
```

```
nnnn
32221rb   ant b
29221to   bru b
```

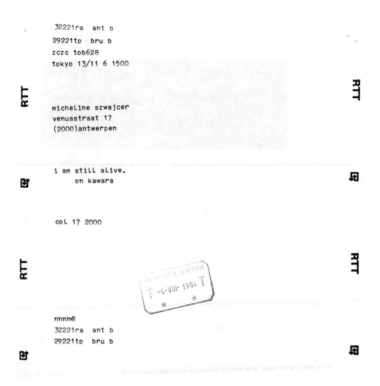

```
32221ra  ant b
29221tp  bru b
zczc tob628
tokyo 13/11 6 1500


micheline szwajcer
venusstraat 17
(2000)antwerpen


i am still alive.
        on kawara


col 17 2000


nnnn#
32221ra  ant b
29221tp  bru b
```

```
e
32221ra   ant b
29216a lisboa p
zczc pcb482 tap843 ioa091 1-006968b314
bean co udnx 012
dc newyork ny 12 09 1100


micheline szwajcer
venusstraat 17 2000
antwerpen


i am still alive on
       on kawara


col 17 2000




nnnne
32221ra   ant b
29216a lisboa p
```

ZCZC TDG791 053 2101 XBB370 UDF280 IOG191 1-014666A053
FRXX CO UDNX 019
DC NEWYORK NY 19 22 1439

XAVIER DOUROUX
CARE LE COIN DU MIROIR 55 RUE SAUMAISE
21000DIJONFRANCE

I AM STILL ALIVE
     ON KAWARA

COL 55 2 1000

NNNN

ZCZC RXV07U FER7629 WDT847 IODU73 1-UU5693A28U
ITRM CO UDNX 013
B.I BROOKLYN NY 13 U7 1UUU

ELEONORA VILLANTI
VIA CLEMENTINA 11
UU184ROMA

I AM STILL ALIVE
    ON KAWARA

COL 11 UU184

U7/1U 19.5U
NNNN

S

7C7C RX7455 BBR4526 ICT079 RMN5883 MIB0008 1-005788A314
ITRM CO URAX 012
BJ BROOKLYN NY 12 10 VIA RCA

ELEONORA VILLANTI
VIA CLEMENTINA 11
00184ROMA

AM STILL ALIVE
     ON KAWARA

COL 11 00184

10/11 19.06
NNNN

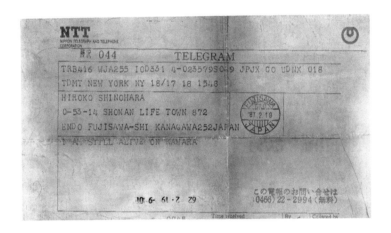

```
      ⊕
      29221z bru b
      1299 adx itt us
      zczc tlg900 via itt qic070 1-0033451030
      bebr co uiax 015
      ti newyork ny  15/14 30 138p est


      philippe-andre rihoux
      28a rue du lombard
      bruxelles 1000


      i am still alive.
       on kawara


      col  28a 1000
```

```
      nnnn
      ⊕=
      29221z bru b
      1299 adx itt us
      above sent via worldcom

      for 1988 horoscope and calendar telex usa 472222+ code 1988
```

```
⊕
29221z bru b
1299 adx itt us
zczc tlg838 via itt qib113 1-007716a079
bebr co uiax 014
ti newyork ny  14 19 1804p est


philippe andre rihoux
28a rue du Lombard
1000 bruxelles


i am stillalive
  on kawara


col  28a 1000
```

DEJA TELEPHONE
COPIE CONFIRMATIVE
————◆————
REEDS GETELEFONEERD
BEVESTIGEND AFSCHRIFT

```
nnnn
⊕=
29221z bru b
1299 adx itt us
above sent via worldcom

for easter greetings telex usa 472222+ enter code 836
```

RTT

RTT

```
⊕
29221z bru b
1299 adx itt us
zczc tlh307 via itt qia178 1-013494a139
bebr co uiax 015
ti newyork ny  15 18 88 326p edt


philippe andre rihoux
28a rue du lombard
1000 bruxelles


i am still alive
on kawara

col ckd
```

RTT

RTT

```
nnnn
⊕=
29221z bru b
1299 adx itt us
above sent via worldcom

euro 88 games special features call usa 472222+
enter code 3930
```

Het telegram wordt met de bode gezonden, daar de geadresseerde telefonisch niet kon worden bereikt.

Le destinataire n'ayant pu être atteint par téléphone.

Telegramme remis par messager.

```
'89-12-22 10:14 トウキョウチュウオウユウビンキョク

〒 214
TOSHIKI SASNUMA
1-5-5 NISHI IKUTA TAMA-KU
KAWASAKI-SHI KANAGAWA-KEN
JAPAN

                              (KP12220149/E )
```

P.1

① ② ③
④ ⑤ 月 日

```
〒163
KDD
国際電信センター
東京都新宿区
 西新宿2-3-2
 (国際電報在中)
```

```
ZCZC TLD831 WJA133 IOA195 1-0125601355
JPJX CO UDNX 016
TI NEWYORK NY 16/14 21 1900

TOSHIKI SASNUMA
1-5-5 NISHI IKUTA TAMA-KU
KAWASAKI-SHIKANAGAWA-KENJAPAN

I AM STILL ALIVE
     ON KAWARA

COL 1-5-5 TAMA-KU KAWASAKI-SHI KANAGAWA-KEN


NNNN
```

\

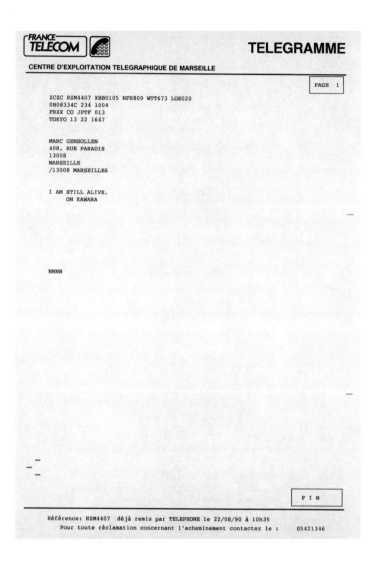

NNNN

==========

C.I.P.B - CENTRE TELEGRAPHIQUE INTERNATIONAL A VOTRE SERVICE 24H/24 -

    POUR DEPOSER VOS TELEGRAMMES A DESTINATION DE L'ETRANGER,

        DES DEPARTEMENTS ET TERRITOIRES D'OUTRE-MER.

-PAR TELEPHONE: 05.33.44.11 (NUMERO VERT)

-PAR TELEX: 250500 - RENSEIGNEMENTS AU 05.26.21.86

==========

XP0116 CEM197 COPIE 104 1927

UDF197 ICED79 1-002037S104

FRXX CO UDNX 019 FAX 142718747 TELECOPIE PAR PARIS-CIPB LE 13 A 2009

TDBN NEW YORK NY 19 13 1225

LUCIEN TERRAS

C/O GALERIE YVON LAMBERT

108 RUE VIEILLE DU TEMPLE

PARIS75003FRANCE

I AM STILL ALIVE.

    ON KAWARA

TELEGRAMME

CENTRE DE MESSAGERIE DE L'ECRIT DE BAR LE DUC

PAGE 1

```
ZCZC RZA4664 XBB0583 UDF850 ICC129 1-002309S195
08123C7F 195 2158
FRXX CO UDNX 013
TDBN NEW YORK NY  13 13 1450


ARNAUD LEFEBVRE
30 RUE MAZARINE
PARIS75006FRANCE
/75006 PARIS


I AM STILL ALIVE.
                ON KAWARA
```

```
NNNN
```

F I N

Référence: RZA4664   du 14/07/92 à 08h46
Pour toute réclamation concernant l'acheminement contactez le :   05040355

 **France Telecom**　　　　　　　　　**TELEGRAMME**

CENTRE DE MESSAGERIE DE L'ECRIT DE BAR LE DUC

PAGE 1

```
ZCZC RZA9340 XBA0395 UDF744 4246817 WUF-CA-9313602869489
030A1D72 136 2020
FRXX CO UDNX 013
TDEL UPPER SADDLE RIVE NJ 013 16 1307


DORA MALTZ
39 RUE PIGALLE
75009PARISFRANCE
/75009 PARIS


I AM STILL ALIVE.
   ON KAWARA




NNNN
```

F I N

Référence: RZA9340　　　　　　　　du 17/05/93 à 07h09
　Pour toute réclamation concernant l'acheminement contactez le :　　05040355

T E L E G R A M M. – ZTBSt Koblenz ☎ Telekom

'93 DEC 30 -9 :24

937 235 099 - 6 6.5

```
ZCZC GYY005 JGE771 VTT772 LOE001
DPXX CO JPTF 015
TOKYO 15/14 30 1719


HENNING WEIDEMANN
AM BOTANISCHEN GARTEN 45 5000
KOELN(60) 50735

I AM STILL ALIVE
       ON KAWARA




NNNN
```

1994

TELEGRAMM. –ZTBSt Bremen

Telekom

ZCZC CYY579 WCF233 9038961 WUF-EX-9435702416893
DPXX CO UDNX 011
TDEL NEW YORK NY 011/010 23 1602

DIETMAR ELGER
HAARSTR.14
30169HANNOVER

I AM STILL ALIVE
ON KAWARA

'94. DEO 24 -6 '55

NNNN

37235099-6 6.92

261

1994

TELEGRAMM.

```
ZCZC GYY208 WCFB78 0336249 WUF-EX-9436302448124
DPXX CO UDNX 014
TDEL NEW YORK NY 014/012 29 1411

JURGEN PARTENHEIMER
DRIESCHER STR 22
51588NUEMBRECHT(BIERENBACHTAL)

I AM STILL ALIVE.
  ON KAWARA



NNNN
```

1994

⊞ **Telegramm - Télégramme - Telegramma**
ZCZC JFX751 EBB319 0336189 WUF-EX-9436302448079
TDEL NEW YORK NY 012/011 29 1411

JFX751
NINO WEINSTOCK
BAUMLEINGASSE 11
(4051)BASEL

I AM STILL ALIVE.
  ON KAWARA

NNNN 29/12/94 2014

937 235 099-

'95 JAN -6 20.28

Telekom · T E L E G R A M M · -ZTBSt Koblenz   **Tetek**

```
ZCZC GYY596 WCF568 2817681 WUF-EX-9500602496340
DPXX CO UDNX 013
TDEL NEW YORK NY 013 06 1426

ERNST GEORG KUHLE
DURENER STR. 245
50931KOLN

I AM STILL ALIVE.
   ON  KAWARA


NNNN
```

I5 099 - 6   6.92

Telekom

'95 JAN 15 -5 :47

39

ZCZC EYY965 WCF140 5712041 WUF-EX-9501402552597

DPXX CO UDNX 012

TDEL NEW YORK NY 012 14 1639

IRM SOMMER

BUNSENWEG 12

STUTTGART 70191

I AM STILL ALIVE.

ON KAWARE

NNNN

TELEGRAMM - ZTBSt Mannheim

937235099-6 6.92

6.92

'95 APR 29 20:38

Telekom.

TELEGRAMM.

Telekom.

```
ZCZC KYY271 WCF454 2760068 WUF-EX-9511900120450
DPXX CO UDNX 014
TDEL NEW YORK NY 014/012 29 1338

JOSEPH W FROEHLICH
BRUNNENWIESEN 32
70619STUTTGART

I AM STILL ALIVE.
  ON KAWARA

NNNN
```

SÍMS 礠 SÍMSKEYTI SÍMSKEYTI 礠

SÍMSKEYTI

礠

```
ZCZC LRA234 NKY873 8241346 WUF-E X-9606801513876
19RX CO UDNX 015
IDEL NEW YORK NY 015/014 08 1731


PETUR ARASON
LAUGAVEGUR 37 P BOX 442
101REYKJAVIK


I AM STILL ALIVE.
   ON KAWARA
```

-8 MAR 96 22   52

YTI 礠 SÍMSKEYTI 礠 SÍMSKEYTI 礠

SÍMSKEYTI SÍMSKEYTI SÍMSKEYTI ÍMSKEYTI

SÍMSKEYTI SÍMSKEYTI SÍMSKEYTI SÍMSKEYT

29   10

ZCZC LRA648 NKY103 2909798 WUF-E X-9624202635647

ISRX CO UDNX 015

TDEL NEW YORK NY 015/014 29 1001

PETUR ARASON

LAUGAVEGUR 37

PO BOX 442

101REYKJAVIK

I AM STILL ALIVE.

    ON KAWARA

'97 12月 8日 7:14   100 トウキョウチュウオウ 2ゴウ 1407   FAX 03-3212-1407   P. 1

① □1 ② □1 ③ □1

④ □1 ⑤ □ 月 □ 日

〒135
YUSUKE MINAMI
MUSEUM OF CONTEMPORARY ART
TOKYO
4-1-1 MIYOSHI KOTO KU
TOKYO 135

(KP12080006/E)

〒163
KDD 国際電話センター
(国際電報担当)
東京都新宿区
西新宿2−3−2
(国際電報在中)

ZCZC TLD411 MJA752 5293937 WUF-EX-9734101121616
JPTK CO UDNX 020
TDEL NEW YORK NY 020/019 07 1549

YUSUKE MINAMI
MUSEUM OF CONTEMPORARY ART TOKYO
4-1-1 MIYOSHI KOTO KU
TOKYO 135

I AM STILL ALIVE
    ON KAWARA

NNNN

INTERNATIONAL TELEGRAM

KDD
国際電報をご利用いただきましてありがとうございます。
お届けしました国際電報についてのお問い合わせは、KDD
0120-115931(フリーダイヤルサービス)へお願いいたします。

FROM:100 トウキョウチュオウクヌゴウ 1375   100 81 3-3211-1375   1997/12/22 07:25 No.231 P01

〒 135
YUSUKE MINAMI
MUSEUM OF CONTEMPORARY ART
TOKYO
4-1-1 MIYOSHI KOTO-KU
TOKYO 135

　　　　　　　(KP12220004/E)

① 1　② 1　③ 1

④ 1　⑤ 月　日

〒163
KDD　国際電話センター
（国際電報担当）
東京都新宿区
　西新宿2－3－2
　　　（国際電報在中）

ZCZC ILE540 MJA257 2048747 WUF-EX-9735501185700
JPTK CO UDNX 019
TDEL NEW YORK NY 019/018 21 1604

YUSUKE MINAMI
MUSEUM OF CONTEMPORARY ART TOKYO
4-1-1 MIYOSHI KOTO-KU
TOKYO 135

I AM STILL ALIVE.
  ON KAWARA

NNNN

INTERNATIONAL TELEGRAM

KDD

国際電報をご利用いただきましてありがとうございます。
お届けしました国際電報についてのお問い合わせは、KDD
0120-115931（フリーダイヤルサービス）へお願いいたします。

1997

'97 12月 8日 7:14   100 トウキョウチュウオウ 2ゴウ 1407   FAX 03-3212-1407   P. 1

〒135
YUSUKE MINAMI
MUSEUM OF CONTEMPORARY ART
TOKYO
4-1-1 MIYOSHI KOTO KU
TOKYO 135

(KP12080006/E)

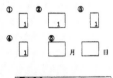

〒163
KDD 国際電話センター
（国際電報担当）
東京都新宿区
西新宿2-3-2
（国際電報在中）

ZCZC TLD411 MJA752 5293937 WUF-EX-9734101121616
JPTK CO UDNX 020
TDEL NEW YORK NY 020/019 07 1549

YUSUKE MINAMI
MUSEUM OF CONTEMPORARY ART TOKYO
4-1-1 MIYOSHI KOTO KU
TOKYO 135

I AM STILL ALIVE
    ON KAWARA

NNNN

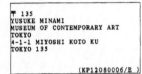

KDD ══ INTERNATIONAL TELEGRAM ══

国際電報をご利用いただきましてありがとうございます。
お届けしました国際電報についてのお問い合わせは、KDD
0120-115931（フリーダイヤルサービス）へお願いいたします。

1998

1998-01-18 06:11 FROM 100 トウキョウチュウオウ1ゴウ 1408 TO   135 フカガワ P.01

〒 135
YUSUKE MINAMI
CARE MUSEUM OF CONTEMPORARY
ART TOKYO
4-1-1 MIYOSHI KOTO-KU
TOKYO135

(KP01180022/E)

〒163
KDD 国際電話センター
（国際電報担当）
東京都新宿区
西新宿2－3－2
（国際電報在中）

ZCZC TLE595 MJA169 5225996 WUF-EX-9801701304564
JPTK CO UDNX 019
TDEL NEW YORK NY 019/018 17 1411

YUSUKE MINAMI
CARE MUSEUM OF CONTEMPORARY ART TOKYO
4-1-1 MIYOSHI KOTO-KU
TOKYO135

I AM STILL ALIVE.
  ON KAWARA

NNNN

═══════ INTERNATIONAL TELEGRAM ═══════

KDD 国際電報をご利用いただきましてありがとうございます。
お届けしました国際電報についてのお問い合わせは、ＫＤＤ
0120－115931(フリーダイヤルサービス)へお願いいたします。

トータル P.01

BELGACOM

TELEGRAAF
BRUSSEL
- 6 -06- 1998
TELEGRAPHE
BRUXELLES

```
ZCZC BRP3-049 B080261 EX10606185 U
BEBR CO UDNX 015
TDEL NEW YORK NY 015 06 1554
```

```
MICHEL ASSENMAKER
114 RUE DE LA MUTUALITE
BRUXELLES 1180
```

```
I AM STILL ALIVE
  ON KAWARA
```

TGM

TG8 094 434 09

‹10×100-0799#m#s0F01-J #1367 10○ 4 81-3-3211-1387 1998/10/00 02:00 No.015 P01

〒 471-0876
AOYAMA EIJI-SAMA
2-27 KANAYA-CHO
TOYOTA AICHI 471-0876

(KP10020001/E)

① ② ③
1 1 1

④ ⑤
月 日

〒163
KDD 国際電話センター
（国際電報担当）
東京都新宿区
西新宿2－3－2
（国際電報在中）

ZCZC TLE476 FRN738 AMI483 MIQ365 0153206263 693
JPJX CO FRXX 013
PARISPIGALLE 13 3 1545

AOYAMA EIJI-SAMA
2-27 KANAYA-CHO
TOYOTA AICHI 471-0876

I AM STILL ALIVE
ON KAWARA

NNNN

INTERNATIONAL TELEGRAM

KDD

FROM:100-8799トウキョウCPO[4] :1383   100 4 81-3-3211-1383   1999/06/14 18:53 No.285 P01

〒473-0914
MARIKO NAKANO
153-1 TANAA WAKABAYASHI HIGASHIMACHI
TOYOTA AICHI 473-0914

(0614TLJ580/ E)

① ② ③
| 1 | | 1 | | 1 |

④ ⑤
| 1 | | | 月 | | 日 |

〒１６３−８００３
ＫＤＤ
東京国際電報局
東京都新宿区
　西新宿２−３−２
（国際電報在中）

ZCZC TLJ580 FRN522 AMI188 MIQ021 0153206263 998
JPJX CO FRXX 016
PARISPIGALLE 16/14 14 1100

MARIKO NAKANO
153-1 TANAA WAKABAYASHI HIGASHIMACHI
TOYOTA AICHI 473-0914

I'AM STILL ALIVE
ON KAWARA

NNNN

===== INTERNATIONAL TELEGRAM =====

KDD　国際電報をご利用いただきましてありがとうございます。
お届けしました国際電報についてのお問い合わせは、ＫＤＤ
0120-115931 (フリーダイヤルサービス) へお願いいたします。

1999

FROM:100-8799ｹｮｳｷｮｳCPO[4] :1383 100 4 81-3-3211-1383 1999/06/30 17:51 No.416 P01

〒466-0011
KONDO, YUKI
1-15-1 TSURUHA-CHO, SHOWA-KU
NAGOYA, AICHI
JAPON

(0630TLJ966/ E)

① □ ② □ ③ □
  1   1   1
④ □ ⑤ □ 月 □ 日
  1

〒163-8003
KDD
東京国際電報局
東京都新宿区
西新宿2-3-2
(国際電報在中)

ZCZC TLJ966 RJN007 DRU423 TEH852
JPJX CO DPXX 016
FRANKFURT AM MAIN/FAX 16/14 30 0956

KONDO, YUKI
1-15-1 TSURUHA CHO, SHOWA-KU NAGOYA
(466-0011)AICHI/JAPON

I AM STILL ALIVE.
    ON KAWARA

2000-04-06 10:12 FROM 100-8799トウキョウCPO (1)/1408 TO   P.01

〒 473-0939
MARIKO SAKAI
52 NISHIKAWA TSUTSUMIHONMACHI
TOYOTA-SHI/AICHI

(0406TLJ036/ E)

①   ②   ③
  1   1   1

④   ⑤
  1   月   日

〒163-8003
KDD
東京国際電報局
東京都新宿区
　西新宿2-3-2
（国際電報在中）

ZCZC TLJ036 MJA141 2139703 WUF-EX-0009601684760
JPJX CO UDNX 014
TDEL NEW YORK NY 014/012 05 1150

MARIKO SAKAI
52 NISHIKAWA TSUTSUMIHONMACHI
TOYOTAAICHI473-0939

I AM STILL ALIVE.
  ON KAWARA

NNNN

INTERNATIONAL TELEGRAM

FROM:100-8799トウキョウCPO[4] :1383   100 4 81-3-3211-1383 2000/06/03 19:16 No.869 P01

〒 471-0851
YASUSHI ISHIGAI SAMA
3 18 JYUMOKU-CHO TOYOTA
AICHI 471-0851 JAPON

(0603TLI102/ E)

④   ⑤

月

〒163-8003
KDD
東京国際電報局
東京都新宿区
　西新宿2－3－2
（国際電報在中）

ZCZC TLI102 IJP063 ABR173 XIE189/302/EHO
JPTX CO CIAB 019
ABIDJANBCT 19/18 02/06 1605 AMPLIATION

YASUSHI ISHIGAI
3 18 JYUMOKU-CHO TOYOTA
AICHI 471-0851 JAPON

I AM STILL ALIVE
ON KAWARA
        ON KAWARA ONKAWARA

COL 3 18 471-0851

NNNN

KDD ════ INTERNATIONAL TELEGRAM ════

国際電報をご利用いただきましてありがとうございます。
お届けしました国際電報についてのお問い合わせは、KDD
0120-115931(フリーダイヤルサービス)へお願いいたします。

FROM:100-8799トウキョウCPO[2]   100-8799 1407   2000/10/17 08:57 No.499 P01

〒473-0932
TAKAYUKI TSHIKAWA SAMA
60-1 KURASHITA TSUTSUMI-CHO
TOYOTA-SHI AICHI-KEN

(1017TLI564/ E)

① ② ③
④ ⑤ 月 日

〒163-8003
KDDI
電信センター
東京都新宿区
　西新宿2-3-2
（国際電報在中）

ZCZC TLI564 WJA802 5260157 WUF-EX-0029002331423
JPJX CO UDNX 015
TDEL NEW YORK NY 015/014 16 1653

TAKAYUKI TSHIKAWA
60-1 KURASHITA TSUTSUMI-CHO
AICHI 473-0932
TOYOTA

I AM STILL ALIVE.
  ON KAWARA

NNNN

Consciousness, Dijon, 1990

René Denizot
On Kawara

At the Consortium, Dijon, a strange exhibition. Twenty-four canvases by On Kawara from the *Today* series of his *Date Paintings*, one per year from 1966 to 1989, encountered five sculptures by Alberto Giacometti: *Femme Haut Chignon* (1948), *La Cage* (1950), *Femme de Venise 7* and *8* (1956) and *Femme Debout* (1959-60). It was a seductive juxtaposition. One imagines the incisive, vertical statuary of the metal silhouettes and, from one painting to the next, the horizon of painting brought to light by the very dates of the canvases. A universal condition, that of time, indexes the wandering but rigorous figures of Giacometti's and Kawara's works. The image or the test of time? Conscience (consciousness) is the title of this exhibition. Without subject or object, it questions the present.

Of all the things about this exhibition, not the least strange was that it was neither a thematic showing nor a historicist display, but the untimely bringing to light of the very figures of time. Consciousness of the present is the condition for bringing them together in a real time and place. Outside the conventions of the image and the theatre of memory, the gravitation of the present restores to these given and dated pieces the difference of the work at work here and now. There is painting. There is sculpture. A double manifestation, double exhibition, irreducible to the period of a production that is symbolically marked in Giacometti and methodically dated with On Kawara. At the time of exhibition, the pieces presented are strictly timeless and singularly present. There is no aesthetic complicity, no dialectical exchange. There is the strangeness of the present raised to the manifestness of a condition, the appearance and disappearance of the work.

The question is resolutely modern. If, with nature lacking, one must be present, then the work has no other recourse than its artifices. What remains of the dated paintings and the given statues, if not the present of painting and the present of sculpture? The literal numerical inscription of both the date and the pictorial act, at the same time, on the same level, is not a residue of time, but a visual base of the present, a signal relief of the here and now, the salience of a gaze exposed to the countable manifestness of a definition that puts it beside itself. Face on, from the side, on the surface of the painting, the accomplishment of the gaze from painting to painting is freed from the images that ensured its representation. There is painting or there is nothing. Facing the date paintings, there is sculpture. Statuary, analogical matrix of the human figure, whose ageless bronze lets the emptied apparentness of a body to be worked appear within matter and form. Threshold, a simple, possible sign of bodies.

The cosmic, comic situation of an earthling walking is brought to light. Being there, here, now? An insistent, questioning occurrence, in the absence of nature. Letting the present be, the work's imperative. The work of the present? Artifice and measure or madness by the hour?

René Denizot, "On Kawara", *art press*, no. 150, 1990

Michel Gauthier
Parallel Lives (Addendum)

Plutarch's stroke of genius in his *Lives* of illustrious men, written in the early second century, was to pair Greeks with Romans – Theseus with Romulus, Alexander with Caesar and Demosthenes with Cicero, to mention only the most famous. An exhibition like *Conscience: On Kawara – Alberto Giacometti*, conceived by the first of the two, offers a visual, scenographic and non-literary example of two parallel lives. In those biographies, the historian sought to inspire belief in his great men, but what is the idea behind this parallel drawn, in the exhibition room, between Giacometti's frail women figures (*Femme au chignon*, *Femmes de Venise*, *Femme debout*, the woman in *La Cage*) and On Kawara's *date paintings* (one per year from 1966 to 1990)? If, in Plutarch, the parallel implies that Greeks and Romans partook of the same nature, believed in the same values – in a word, that they inhabited the same world, then what community is being implied by this juxtaposition of vertical sculptures and dated canvases?

As we know, since 1966 On Kawara has been making paintings in which letters and figures indicating the month, day and year are painted on a monochrome ground. It seems a fair bet that, for some future Plutarch recalling the great men of 20th-century art, On Kawara will be remembered – the other, considerable parts of his output notwithstanding – as the creator of these *date paintings*. If, amidst the avant-gardist euphoria of the 1960s with its militant contextualism, the great advantage of these paintings was that they drastically defined artistic activity by its temporal conditions, then today they stand, as they will even more certainly tomorrow, as pure emblems of that universal topos that is the flight of time. For these paintings will, effectively, show their age more and more as time goes by. Each one states the time of its making (in the same way as one states the accounts), and that time grows irremediably more distant. With these works, in a very different and much stricter sense than this expression usually has, painting is irrevocably *a thing of the past*. The multiplication of the *date paintings* (an artist's life) and the new atmosphere generally have changed our perspective: where once it indexed the time of its making, this painting now simply seems to index passing time.

Towards the middle of the 1940s, Giacometti began working in a vein of sculptural figuration whose thrust was essentially reductive: people become skeletons and their actions are limited to pure movement or mere immobility. Some of these figures highlight space by walking, by going *there*, by treading the ground with which sculpture, in the work of Carl Andre, would a few years later seek to merge. Others, on the contrary, choose to break off their movement and freeze on their base, out of the concern to assert their verticality, a will to celebrate that same *Here* which would soon be brought to a kind of apotheosis in the Barnett Newman series of that name. These figures by Giacometti trouble us, for they play on both presence (by walking or standing still, they make us aware of the space in which we too move) and absence (like any other classical representation, they point to an absent referent; that woman with the bun, standing up, in Venice, or the woman in the cage).

Perhaps, now, we can begin to glimpse a possible parallel. It is true, for a start, that this joint exhibition of these five sculptures and these twenty-four paintings takes advantage of an obvious affinity: a marked predilection for reduction (painting reduced to the date of its execution, a human body reduced to its line of force). It also plays on a few obvious polarities: sculptures on the ground, paintings on the wall, the former being vertical, the latter horizontal. But there is more than that. Giacometti's figures and On Kawara's *date paintings* exhibit two *a priori* forms of our sensibility, of our consciousness: space and time. In this sense, they are transcendental works. One manifests the fact that it exists in space, that it necessarily occupies a space, where it stands and remains for ever; the other declares that it exists in time, and that therefore it necessarily has a date: 20 November 1987, 29 February 1988 or 9 April 1989. A place, a date; stasis in space, stasis in time. They are, then, transcendental, in that they express those conditions which precede all human and, by the same token, aesthetic experience. But Giacometti's statues and On Kawara's chrono-paintings also share an absence: that of the woman figured by the bronze, who will never be there, and that of the long-gone day when the canvas was painted.

Space and time, then, are the terms of the parallel. At this point, it becomes possible for lives to cross paths, for destinies to echo one another. What if the past patterned on the walls was the past of these Beckettian figures? What if the dates stated here were when these same figures elected their permanent immobility? The more distant the dates, the more plausible this hypothesis appears, for these women seem to have been still like this for a very long time. Behind the fiction and its fantasies, what we see here is in reality the basic commerce of space and time: it takes time to occupy space, and space to inscribe time.

By putting the lives of Alexander and Caesar in parallel, Plutarch's aim was to allow us to decide which of the two, the Greek or the Roman, most fully embodied the figure of the great war leader. Clearly, the idea behind *Conscience* was never to show us which of the two propositions constituted the most effective allegory of Art, the Swiss sculptor's Women or the Japanese artist's *date paintings*. However, for us as members of the public, this juxtaposition may not be totally devoid of competition. Modern artists – and, Giacometti must be counted as one of them, not least because of these figures – set out to conquer space. The artists who came after modernism were more concerned not to forget time, and the *date paintings* were very probably one of the first symptoms of this reversal of priorities. By placing Giacometti's sculptures in a *cage* where a series of dates are being exhibited, is it not the case in some way that space is being measured up by time? To put it another way, it may be that an exhibition like this attests an awareness of time's future primacy over space. And if, with On Kawara, what is shown on the picture walls are small blocks of finished time, then soon clocks will be ticking off the hours, minutes and seconds there. It could be said that Giacometti's sculptures had a certain predisposition to be the perfect witnesses of this retemporalisation of the visual. And in fact, is that not what, in their mute and fascinated stasis, they are waiting for: lost time regained?

2002

PURE CONSCIOUSNESS, SYDNEY, 1998

Pure Consciousness

On Kawara's exhibition as part of the 11th Biennale of Sydney consisted of seven "date paintings" from his *Today* series, 1997. Entitled *Pure Consciousness,* it took place in a kindergarten, a classroom in Darlinghurst Public School, where local children attend for a year prior to their entry into primary school proper. With few other visitors to this room, and these being mainly teachers and parents, the work was thus installed ostensibly for a selected group of five and six year olds.

The kindergarten children at this school are encouraged to learn mainly through organised play, but also they have slightly more formal lessons in elementary maths, reading and writing, painting, drawing and modelling, science and general studies. Continually they are acquiring basic social skills and engaging at a seemingly exponential rate with the world beyond their families, encountering very many things for the first time.

The seven paintings, centred on the back wall of the classroom, were made on consecutive days, the first seven days of 1997. They were a combination of two sizes, 8"x 10"and 10"x 13" their stark white text super-imposed on a uniform dark grey-green ground. Around them the days came and went as they normally would, Kawara having insisted that his work not be used didactically – as teaching aids, for example – but instead simply to co-exist with the children's various activities. Nearby was a box of building blocks, a simple computer, charts indicating shapes and colours, and rhyming words, and shelves full of how-to-read books.

The poignancy of On Kawara's fundamental proposition is matched by the stringent formal quality of his work. The simple statement of the date, the date on which the painting itself was made, constitutes confirmation of the artist's continued existence, implying what is made explicit in his "I am still alive" telegrams. It touches on mortality without melodrama or sentimentality, conflates what is at once frankly quite funny, gentle and deadly serious. The more days that pass mean that there are fewer remaining in the lives that are lived through them, a hard fact to grasp especially in a kindergarten, a place where life is so fresh.
As an epigraph for her essay, 'The Date Paintings of On Kawara', Ann Rorimer quotes Leo Tolstoy:

I have keenly experienced consciousness of myself today, at 81 years, exactly as I was conscious of myself at 5 or 6 years. Consciousness is motionless. And it is only because of its motionlessness that we are able to see the motion of that which we call time. If time passes, it is necessary that there should be something which remains static. And it is consciousness of self which remains static.[1]

The title "Pure Consciousness" refers to the directness with which children of kindergarten age, at five or six years, apprehend the vast range of phenomena they encounter. It accords strongly with Tolstoy's observations. The novelty of experience means that this consciousness is not skewed by memories of similar experience or habituation. The possibility of its being retrievable in later life is suggested by On Kawara not only in the uncompromising here-and-now of each painting but also in his repetitious practice. Like a mantra, it encourages concentration on a simple act towards a one-ness, a direct relation, with the world.

Tolstoy asserts the static nature of consciousness, and this is reiterated by Kawara as he utilises the same basic format for each of his date paintings. The interdependence of repetition and variation is a crucial key to an understanding of the work. The children's overwhelming response to the kindergarten installation was simple: that at first glance the paintings seemed to be the same – then it became clear that they were all slightly different.

Kawara's particular consideration of the children is suggested by his choice of seven paintings – they are learning at this age that each week has seven days. The consecutive dates correspond to exercises in counting, and to begin right at the beginning (in this case 1 January) is a characteristic impulse.

Earlier works, made prior to the *Today* series (started in 1966), by Kawara have actually depicted children or pregnant women and thus the kindergarten installation has a special place in his *oeuvre.* It acquired meaning from its location – it was about children because it was literally *about* them – the juxtapositions between it and the stuff of kindergartens. Outside the walls of galleries, museums and other such spaces dedicated for art, for a distinctly non-specialist audience, it was an extraordinarily positive artistic gesture as well as being an oblique memento mori.

Kawara's acknowledgement of context, both temporal and spatial, is made clear by much of his work. The date paintings, for example, are often accompanied by press clippings from newspapers in the places, on the days – exactly where and when – they were made. The eloquence of these works with respect to historical circumstances, or a *zeitgeist* perhaps, is suggested by the *Again and Against* project, organised by Kasper König, in which works by other artists – one per year between 1966 and 1989 – were twinned with a date painting from the same year. Robert Nickas developed this concept through his exhibition *Pictures of the Real World (In Real Time)*, 1994, combining date paintings with works by American photographers.

Pure Consciousness , by contrast, was remarkable for its non-art context, the combination of On Kawara's paintings with non-art objects. The artist's work thereby was not so much encouraging a look beyond the art world as actually being beyond the art world. It had viewers essentially without a definition of art – still largely untouched by the cramping and conventional ideas of art which feature in subsequent education – but what they had instead was a kind of consciousness to which the artist aspires.

Jonathan Watkins
Sydney, November 1998

1. Ann Rorimer, 'The Date Paintings of On Kawara', *The Art Institute of Chicago Museum studies,* Volume 17, No.2 1991. Reprinted in Xavier Douroux & Franck Gautherot (eds) *Kawara: Whole and Parts, 1964 – 1995,* Les presses du réel, Dijon, 1996.

PURE CONSCIOUSNESS, REYKJAVIK, 1999

The Art and the "I"

The protagonist in Kazuo Ishiguro's novel *Artist of the Floating World* is the painter Masuji Ono. For the greater part of his life Ono has spent painting that which exists in the realm of "the floating world", and he dreams of capturing the instant which constitutes the border between day and night, dream and consciousness, reality and that which inhabits the mind. In Ono's art-world, it is the goal of the artist to fathom the complex illusion of man's ideologies and immobilize it on canvas. It takes Ono his entire life to realize that this is an impossibility since the act constitutes a fundamental paradox; as soon as a fleeting instant is captured, its vividness vanishes.

In this way it is often difficult to express abstract ideology, subjective experience or inspiration; the undefinable is no longer undefined when it has been given a distinct form, colour or tone.

In On Kawara's works it is just the contrary. He has for many years made the more subjective aspects of time and space his study, but instead of attributing form, colour or tone to time, he chooses to categorize time in a simple and neutral way, – now and again, here and there on the planet. His date paintings are symbolic for the time passing as he works on his canvas, but subsequently they belong to the past as particular instants which have passed but continue to exist as individual entities. These moments or days of On Kawara are dispersed around the world and so expose the fact that moments do not follow in succession like pearls on a string, time does not adhere to a linear morphology but can rather be compared to a tree that branches out into an infinite number of offshoots, the further away from the stem the more branches. In such a way time is perhaps multi-dimensional, even within the spatial orientation we are familiar with. It is not limited by our personal perception, and according to our idea of time its capacity to designate events in reality are endless, not dependent on how we experience it as individuals. By painting dates ubiquitously around the world, Kawara alludes to the impossibility of defining time, but gives us a clue to time's nature which we are but scantly capable of comprehending.

Despite the fact that Kawara's art specifically revolves around an infinitely vast idea, he has chosen to make only miniscule moments of endlessness or "the great void" conspicuous. It follows that a large portion of his work is materialized in the consciousness of those who experience his art. The date paintings are comparable to the stars in the heavens, they recount only a fragment of the idea of the relative endlessness which is their theme and is found in the minds of those who observe and think.

Innovative artistic creation in each epoch is characterized first and foremost by an attempt to approach our ideologies and world view in a new way. In an article written by Italo Calvino on his friend Roland Barthes, he points out that the fundamental difference between the modes of expression of photography and language is that language "is capable of speaking about things that are not."[1] In a similar way, one could postulate that On Kawara has evolved his art in such a way that it describes "that which is not", in an objective sense. By not exploiting the vastness of the subject, i.e. time, but restricting himself to recording it as it is manifested to us in our everyday life, Kawara manages to hint at infinity to the point where nothing is excluded which the mind can fathom. For as the American poet Emily Dickinson says in a poem where she is contemplating the endless capacity of the human mind:

The Brain – is wider than the sky –
For – put them side by side –
The one the other will contain
With ease – and You – beside –[2]

But then what is this vast theme? When I first contemplated On Kawara, many thoughts entered my mind. But when it came to putting them to paper, I realized they could have been about almost any other artist; any composer, writer or painter that has made the insignificance and mortal limits of human beings vis-à-vis the universe their subject. That which I found true of On Kawara was also true of so many others. In an attempt to define his art in a way which differentiated him from others, I realized that the modes of discussion and use of terminology which are dictated by tradition are most likely contradictory to the idea that permeates the works of On Kawara themselves. By analyzing and defining his art, one is immobilizing it in a way which he has rejected in his own works. I therefore decided to set my sights on that which might be unique about his work, i.e. his approach to the individual which he places in a relative spatial and temporal orientation and his mode of approaching the observer himself.

The date paintings of On Kawara are all equally modest; on a dark background we find unassuming white letters and digits which represent the date on which they are painted, in keeping with the tradition of the country in which they are created each time. They are painted with great accuracy and craftsmanship, and through these precise working methods the self of the painter is manifested, – in that which he chooses to paint. It is quite plausible that primitive images were first conceived with the intention of creating a representation of that which was not present. Later the artist becomes conscious of his function in relation to some observer – he begins to choose his perspective with purpose and to juxtapose the observer with himself and in this way we are familiar with traditional painting through the ages. The point of view that On Kawara chooses in his date paintings is practically in direct conflict with these traditions. He chooses a perspective which is so de-personalized, so non-topographic and simultaneously so everyday and simple that it might just as well be mass produced, – if it wasn't for the fact that he invests great amounts of work on each one. Instead of striving to "personalize" his imagery and cater to the emotions and perceptiveness of the onlooker, he paints the image that is the most neutral common denominator of each passing day. The time and care which he takes for the painting is of great importance and stresses the project rather than the work itself, – a project that has become the artist's life-work, who's self lies behind the work itself. In this way the date paintings have become part of a complex process, the existence of a self and its relation to (or lack of a relation to) time and space.

As an artist Kawara identifies with the idea of time as a metamorphic force and is in this way loyal to traditional ideas where the artist "stops the flow of time" by choosing particular instants and immortalizing them in an artistic rendition. Thus his paintings are surely modelled on traditional ideas despite the modesty that guides him in his choice of perspective. In his book *Ways of Seeing* John Berger explains (using like Calvino the photograph as an example) how the "photographer's way of seeing is reflected in his choice of subject. The painter's way of seeing is reconstituted by the marks he makes on the canvas or paper. Yet, although every image embodies a way of seeing, our perception or appreciation of an image depends also upon our own way of seeing"[3]. The complex process which On Kawara unfolds with his date paintings is not solely dependent on his creative input but equally dependent on the self of those who observe (and think). Each individual painting is supplied with a box which is lined with a newspaper clipping from the day and from the place where the painting is finished. The boxes, which are kept separate from the paintings, serve the purpose of alluding to the surroundings which inspire the painting on the one hand, and also to the space in which the painting was created. Thus a link is formed with that reality which is common to us all, but which each of us experiences in our own unique way.

Interestingly, while On Kawara's date paintings reject the linear flow of time, they connect to the self of the individual on a new basis in keeping with changing ideas in modernity about time, which came about when Albert Einstein realized that temporal indications were always relative to the position of the one who observes and discovers.

If On Kawara's date paintings employ time as their subject, then the idea of space is of no less importance, for without space time is non-existent according to the laws of physics. Parallel to his paintings Kawara has been putting together "spatial works" which consist of the intricate documentation of daily trips on maps, which he then collects in a book entitled "I went". In this way he not only records the time he lives but also the area of space he moves in. The same laws apply to the way he records these travels as to the way he records time, his method is objective, non-personal, only pointing to himself as an individual in an arbitrary relation to all other individuals who have moved along these same streets or similar ones. On Kawara also records in another book entitled "I Met" the names of those he meets each and every day without elaborating on who those individuals are or why he has met them. Thus the categorisation is very accurate, but as in most of his work, doesn't include information on anything other than what the observer brews in his own mind. These books are therefore primarily the catalyst for a specific context which the observer is entrusted to discover himself.

This long, objective documentation of Kawara's own life in many forms certainly recounts the self's minuteness and limitations in relation to the cosmos, – a familiar theme, commented on by many through the ages. But what differentiates his art from others is his unusual approach to the self, both his own and that of the observer, and his ability to avoid a dogmatic attitude, as he doesn't prescribe ideological lines in a conventional manner. Rather he ignites a process where the fuse is his own self, or rather the common human core that delineates its existence in time and space, and is shared by the artist and his audience. In this way he bridges the gap between artistic creation and the experience of the spectator and moulds them into a conglomerate event; in a self that is alive. Therefore it is no coincidence that Kawara has the habit of occasionally sending telegrams to those all over the world who are in some way connected to his art with the message: "I am still alive." The truth of this fundamental fact in that particular place and that particular time when he sends that message doesn't only have to do with his own self when the message leaves, but also the self of the recipient when he receives the message, as well as of anyone reading it from then on. In his works Kawara manages to elevate himself above our conventional understanding of time and space, he manages to travel in "the floating world" without the underlying paradox of the material world, where the fleeting moment vanishes on its capture.

Pure Consciousness / Tær vitund, in Reykjavík 1999:

In 1998 On Kawara participated in the 11th biennale in Sydney, with an exhibition which he called *Pure Consciousness*. The exhibition took place in a playschool which children attend before they start proper primary school. In this playschool environment the children are learning about letters and digits, – acquiring knowledge through play and various work. Here in Iceland On Kawara has chosen to open a similar exhibit. Seven date paintings are placed in the children's environment where they are preoccupied with their usual tasks. The exhibit's title Pure *Consciousness* reflects the children and their understanding of the vast amounts of disparate phenomena which they encounter at this age. The sole function of the works is to merge with the space around and they are not to be used with any educational purpose in mind, but blend into the children's everyday existence.

Reykjavík, May 1999,
Frída Björk Ingvarsdóttir

1. Italo Calvino, "In Memory of Roland Barthes", *The Uses of Literature*, p. 305. Harcourt Brace & Company 1986.
2. Emily Dickinson, *The Norton Anthology of American Literature*, ed. Gottesman, Holland, Kalstone, Murphy, Parker og Pritchard, poem number 632, p. 2369. Norton & Company 1979.
3. John Berger, *Ways of Seeing*, p. 10. British Broadcasting Corporation and Penguin Books Ltd. 1972.

PURE CONSCIOUSNESS, ABIDJAN, 2000

AND a woman who held a babe against her bosom said, Speak to us of Children.

And he said:

Your children are not your children.

They are the sons and daughters of Life's longing for itself.

They come through you but not from you,

And though they are with you yet they belong not to you.

You may give them your love but not your thoughts,

For they have their own thoughts.

You may house their bodies but not their souls,

For their souls dwell in the house of tomorrow, which you cannot visit, not even in your dreams.

You may strive to be like them, but seek not to make them like you.

For life goes not backward nor tarries with yesterday.

You are the bows from which your chidren as living arrows are sent forth.

The archer sees the mark upon the path of the infinite, and He bends you with His might that His arrows may go swift and far.

Let your bending in the archer's hand be for gladness;

For even as He loves the arrow that flies, so He loves also the bow that is stable.

THEN said a rich man, Speak to us of Giving.

And he answered:

You give but little when you give of your possessions.

It is when you give of yourself that you truly give.

For what are your possessions but things you keep and guard for fear you may need them tomorrow?

And tomorrow, what shall tomorrow bring to the overprudent dog burying bones in the trackless sand as he follows the pilgrims to the holy city?

And what is fear of need but need itself ?

Is not dread of thirst when your well is full, the thirst that is unquenchable?

There are those who give little of the much which they have – and they give it for recognition and their hidden desire makes their gifts unwholesome.

And there are those who have little and give it all.

These are the believers in life and the bounty of life, and their coffer is never empty.

There are those who give with joy, and that joy is their reward.

And there are those who give with pain, and that pain is their baptism.

And there are those who give and know not pain in giving, nor do they seek joy, nor give with mindfulness of virtue;

They give as in yonder valley the myrtle breathes its fragrance into space.

Through the hands of such as these God speaks, and from behind their eyes He
smiles upon the earth.

It is well to give when asked, but it is better to give unasked, through understanding;

And to the open-handed the search for one who shall receive is joy greater than
giving.

And is there aught you would withhold?

All you have shall some day be given;

Therefore give now, that the season of giving may be yours and not your inheritors'.

You often say, "I would give, but only to the deserving."

The trees in your orchard say not so, nor the flocks in your pasture.

They give that they may live, for to withhold is to perish.

Surely he who is worthy to receive his days and his nights, is worthy of all else from you.

And he who has deserved to drink from the ocean of life deserves to fill his cup from your little stream.

And what desert greater shall there be, than that which lies in the courage and the confidence, nay the charity, of receiving?

And who are you that men should rend their bosom and unveil their pride, that you may see their worth naked and their pride unabashed?

See first that you yourself deserve to be a giver, and an instrument of giving.

For in truth it is life that gives unto life – while you, who deem yourself a giver, are but a witness.

And you receivers – and you are all receivers – assume no weight of gratitude, lest you lay a yoke upon yourself and upon him who gives.

Rather rise together with the giver on his gifts as on wings;

For to be overmindful of your debt, is to doubt his generosity who has the freehearted earth for mother, and God for father.

AND an astronomer said, Master, what of Time?

And he answered:

You would measure time the measureless and the immeasurable.

You would adjust your conduct and even direct the course of your spirit according to hours and seasons.

Of time you would make a stream upon whose bank you would sit and watch its flowing.

Yet the timeless in you is aware of life's timelessness,

And knows that yesterday is but today's memory and tomorrow is today's dream.

And that that which sings and contemplates in you is still dwelling within the bounds of that first moment which scattered the stars into space.

Who among you does not feel that his power to love is boundless?

And yet who does not feel that very love, though boundless, encompassed within the centre of his being, and moving not from love thought to love thought, nor from love deeds to other love deeds?

And is not time even as love is, undivided and spaceless?

But if in your thought you must measure time into seasons, let each season encircle all the other seasons,

And let today embrace the past with remembrance and the future with longing.

Kahlil Gibran, from the book *The Prophet*

PURE CONSCIOUSNESS, SHANGHAI, 2000

On Kawara's *Pure Consciousness* in Shanghai

On Kawara's project for the 2000 Shanghai Biennale is a very particular one. Entitled *Pure Consciousness*, it consists of seven "Date Paintings". The sizes of the paintings are respectively 20.32 x 25.4 cm and 25.4 x 33.02 cm. The dates, from Jan. 1 to Jan. 7, 1997, are written in white against black backgrounds. He decides to show the work in a kindergarten instead of the regular venue of the biennale in the Shanghai Art Museum in order to avoid the common audience of art and enter the innocent world of children's live. Eventually, this project has been realized in Xinlei Music Kindergarten of Jing'an District, Shanghai.

In fact, On Kawara's project started in 1998 on the occasion of Sydney Biennale. This series of "Date Paintings" has been shown in kindergartens in Sydney Australia, Reykjavik, Iceland, Europe and Abidjan, Ivory Coast, Africa. Now, it is brought to Shanghai, China, Asia, To On Kawara who was born in Japan, Asia, this displacement should be considered particularly significant.

On Kawara has produced near 2000 "Date Paintings" under the name of "Today" series since 1966. The dates have been carefully and neatly written on monochrome surfaces of the canvases. They are not only records of the dates that the artist has lived. What is more important is that they reveal the states of being of both the artist and ourselves in the most radical and purest way. Facing the dates, we are aware that we are still alive. At the same time, it's matter of fact that the change from one to another implies the elapsing of time and life. If art has anything to say about the meaning of life, then, On Kawara's extremely radical expression of time lays bare the truth of life to the public eyes. On the contrary of the common understanding of his work as conceptualist, one should perceive it as "absolute" Realistic.

On Kawara's work is rich and diverse in meaning behind the extremely pure appearance. The art form is absolutely stable. But what is embodied in it are the most unstable moments of living experiences on his continuously nomadic trips across the world. He produces art work wherever he finds himself in the world. He records the process of the passing of time and life. It is the combination of the stable and unstable, between motionlessness and movement, that makes his seemly simply work full of mysteries and powerful tension. His "Date Paintings" are often conserved in special cardboard boxes accompanied by newspapers of the same days. Also, for a long period of time, he sent postcards to friends on his trips. The contents are simply: "I got up at … today", "I walked … km. today" and "I'm still alive" …

There have been numerous remarkable scholars and artists in history who have spent their lives and talents to explore and interpret the myth of life and time. However, One Kawara's succinct and pure language reaches another realm far beyond such a kind of intellectual "troubles." It is the realm of Enlightenment.

However, On Kawara's work is by no means a self-enclosing system. On the contrary, what he has achieved through developing the most "economic" form is a space open to everyone because the content of his work reveals the foundation of the existence of human being that we are all deeply concerned. In this space, people communicate each other in the simplest way. One does not have to say much to make oneself understandable to the other. Perhaps, this is the moment that we can approach the truth of life.

We often tend to divide life into all kinds of social layers, works and hierarchies in order to maintain power and interests. Art is hence separated from normal state of being and becomes the expression of a specific social class and its way of thinking. Therefore, specific circles, discourses and education systems have been created for art. In such a process of creation and development of the art world, we have made art more and more sophisticated and "sensational". However, it may also run the risk of losting the contact with people. Facing such a contradiction. On Kawara's *Pure Consciousness* becomes particularly meaningful. By putting his "Date Paintings" in kindergartens, or the naive and innocent children's world, he intends to bring art beyond the enclosure of intellectual troubles trapped by the mundane reality. It allows the children to directly communicate with "art" without being constrained by the complicated and self-limiting system of "correct education". What should be emphasized is that here the teachers are not encouraged to explain the work to the children. Their task is merely to carry on the daily games with the children…

If contemporary can facilitate trans-national, trans-cultural, trans-racial and trans-generational exchanges in the age of globalisation, then, On Kawara's project *Pure Consciousness*, with communication at it's centre, is no doubt a highly accurate and efficient one. Starting from Australia and travelling through Europe and Africa, it arrives in Shanghai to participate in the process of the reconstruction of the reborn metropolis in Eastern Asia in the significant year of 2000. It's way of participation is so original that it can achieve the most direct contact and exchange with the local culture and reality without any obstacle. It starts from the children's world, which is a kind of "zero degree" world. The unique angle, timing and approach of the project can not only dissolve it's "abstract" and "conceptual" "globality" into the most concrete and down-to-earth "locality". Also, more meaningfully, it deconstructs the oppositional division

between the "global" and the "local" in the most discrete way. However, at the end, On Kawara has never intended to produce any theory on the issue of global and local. Instead, he only presents the real to us.

Hou Hanru
13 Nov. 2000

Pure Consciousness, Leticia, 2001

Pure Consciousness

The notion of time, perceived by each individual depending on one's own cultural context is still, however, a universal notion. Day and night, morning and afternoon, noon, are all time modes which are associated in a conventional manner with local culture, and are concepts which are shared globally. This is not so with the concept of dates, however, in particular those associated with the Gregorian calendar, one of the cultural conventions most shared throughout the whole world. As a child I remember seeing on television a celebration of the Chinese New Year which took place in a completely different month to December – in a month I did not associate it with. For a six year old it was very complex to realise that the notion of a celebration so deeply rooted within me was not at all on a fixed date, nor universal; it was solely a convention.

The work of On Kawara has always been associated with the notion of time. His 'Date Paintings' make use of this convention and, by linking it to geography, reveal its relative nature. A given date is significant to each individual in that it indicates a precise event in one's personal life, in one's close environment. Or in one's context in its wider sense, that of territory, city, country. For someone who arrives at an unknown place, the date is a contingency as is the event to which it refers.

For an artist born in Asia but who lives in New York, a symbolic enclave in western culture, the notion of displacement as a form of knowledge is vital; one that the artist has emphasized through his constant travels around the world. But the work denominated 'Pure Consciousness' is of a different nature to the "Today" series. Instead of a painting carried out on site and contextualised by news articles Kawara selects from the local newspaper, seven of his "Date Paintings" have made an improbable journey through cities and continents, from Sydney to Reykjavik, from Abidjan to Shanghai and from there to Leticia, a Colombian port in the Amazon. The next step will be a village in the heart of Siberia. In all of these places the paintings have been hung in a non-artistic context (in terms what is generally understood to be a conventional 'art space'). A local school attended by children under six years of age which, according to Kawara, is the threshold of full consciousness insofar as social implications are concerned.

Leticia, capital of the Colombian province of the Amazon, is a relatively young city, the result of various contingencies. Its population has a history to construct. For us Colombians, the inhabitants of Leticia are not clearly defined in our social imaginary (we do not even know which patronymic name they should have, Leticians, Leticieños). This is due, undoubtedly, to an excessive centralization and to our profound ignorance of the country. Leticia does not bring to mind a particular bio-type, accent or music, which we certainly do have when referring to the 'paises' (those coming from Medellin and the Cafetera Zone), the 'costeños' (the coastal population from the Caribbean provinces), or more precise social groups such as the Caleños or the Bogotanos. Leticia is a young community and, at least from the outsider's point of view, they have not yet defined any social parameters which are recognizable and shared by our national imaginary.

This is probably due to their status as a settlement of colonization in a territory completely isolated from the metropolitan centres and the rest of Colombia. One facing more towards a tri-national region (Colombia-Peru-Brazil), where a jungle-river culture predominates. Leticia is a product of various successive immigrations. Initially an indigenous settlement, this port of the Amazon River (accessible solely by the route until the appearance of air transport), received an initial flow of settlers in the twenties due to the exploitation of Quinine. In later decades successive waves of settlers arrived with the rubber bonanza, as they did later on in the eighties in search of gold. The *Colombianization of Leticia* took place in 1932 as a state directive of symbolic nature to exercise sovereignty in the region. This followed a conflict with Peru, in which this country invaded part of the territory of Colombia in the Amazon due precisely to the almost non-presence of the state in the area. As a result, Leticia is a hybrid city where identity has been forged from social groups originating from the interior of the country and from the frontier with Brazil and Peru, with an important presence of local indigenous communities. The latter have, little by little, adopted some western customs such as the Spanish language, the Catholic religion, clothes and some social conventions, amongst which is the management of time.

For the native population time approximates the logic of the myth. They are events which are linked intimately to their cosmogony, to the rhythms of nature or to collective rituals. And too, to the invariable circumstances of the individual as a social being: birth, the baptism ritual, ear-piercing, the ritual of fertility when the first menstruation occurs, harvest and death. These are invariable circumstances which determine the life of an individual in relation to its community. The concept of an anniversary becomes pure convention. However, the processes of 'civilization' have consequently brought with them a gradual loss of those forms of reference to time, and gradually western notions have been integrated: week, months, year, anniversary, birthday, date. The school in which Kawara installed his paintings is situated on the outskirts of Leticia, where there is a heterogenous population: 'mestizos', settlers and natives from seven different ethnic origins (Tikunas, Uitotos, Boras, Cocamas, Yucunas,

Yaguas) each one having their own language and different customs. Children make a daily journey of three to five kilometres between byways and roads in order to get to school. School – and language – are a meeting point; and the bilingual and intercultural aspects of their life is managed by the education system.

The photographs of the school reveal the complexity of codes in which contemporary hybrid societies operate: the codes of time in the indigenous and in the western world, and the announcement of birthdays hanging on the wall. The children are probably unaware of these codes of everyday life and of art, as they calmly attend their classes at the same time as On Kawara's paintings are being exhibited.

During a recent conversation, Kawara told me that he was interested in the experience being carried out with children between four and six years old, as their consciousness was in a 'pure state', before being deformed by the conventions inherent to their entry into 'culture'. Many of these children would probably never be conscious of the presence of his works on the wall, at least not as 'art'. But this does not worry the artist. Kawara said to me that it was sufficient for him just to think that maybe, in a few years time, these children would see one of his works in another context and that maybe, an associative bond would be established with memory.

On referring to this project the critic Hou Hanru affirmed: "If the contemporary can facilitate trans-national, trans-cultural and trans-generational exchanges in the era of globalization, then On Kawara's project of *Pure Consciousness*, with communication as its central subject, is without a doubt, a very precise and efficient project". The presence of On Kawara's works in a context not distorted by conventional concepts of what is considered 'culture' and 'art' offers the possibility of generating a more direct and immediate connection not mediated by the cultural parameters of an institutional Museum nor by conventional attitudes with respect to the work of art.

Borges used to say that chance and destiny are two names for the same thing. The day on which On Kawara's exhibition was presented in Leticia, was the city's 134th birthday. The local newspaper, Anaconda, reported the celebrations as follows: "134 years delay of the once so-called *Light City of the Jungle*. Its happy and bitter history is known by its people and by outsiders. History's clock came to a standstill in the Amazon capital; oblivion and indifference, the path of misery referred to by José Eustasio Rivera remains intact from La Chornera to Leticia or from Tarapacá to El Encanto".

Despite its austere presence the work of On Kawara has the capacity of showing us that, as witnesses to the passing of time, we are alive. But our meeting with time also shows that its passing is relative and that its perception is associated with cultural notions such as that of progress. The inclusion of western time (and art) in a rural school in the Amazon does nothing but highlight the operation which is taking place there. Children coming from diverse settlements travel great distances on a daily basis – between byways and tracks - to receive 'lessons' which will assist them in un-learning concepts and forms of life which centuries of oral tradition have constructed in close relationship with the environment. Evidently from another point of view it could be argued that it is more like an intercultural process. The children travel two hours so as to arrive at school 'on time'. Consequently, the globality of On Kawara's touring project only makes sense in its most radical locations and, on doing so, reveals the tears which question the logic of the modern project.

José Roca

PURE CONSCIOUSNESS, ISTANBUL, 2001

The Chaotic point where East meets West

On Kawara's *Pure Consciousness* project has already traveled through 5 countries. The project first began in Sydney in 1998, then traveled to the Ivory Coast in Africa, Reykjavik in Iceland, Shanghai in China, Colombia in South America and is now in Istanbul, on the boundary of Asia and Europe. Seven "Date Paintings" inscribed with the dates January 1 to January 7 1997 hang on the classroom walls of Atlikarinca, Istanbul's oldest kindergarten. The children are not given any explanation about these works. They simply share their space with the paintings for 2 months. Visitors are only permitted on weekends when the children don't attend the kindergarten.

Kawara painted his first Date Paintings in 1966, and has now produced more than 2000. Using the current dates for the location he is in, Kawara paints a series of paintings one per day. The detailed typographical design remains consistent although the size of the canvas and the color of the background in each painting is different. The expansive linear flow of time has been fixed by stamping the date onto the canvas, and seven paintings from this flow of time are now traveling through gentle and innocent consciousness of children living in different continents. The seven dates from January 1 to January 7, 1997 are inscribed in white against a background of dark gray on a series of canvases in two different sizes, 8 x 10 inches and 10 x 13 inches, hung high up on the wall out of the children's reach. Their concise and static form brings a new sense of order into the chaotic classroom and at the same time, creates a strange sense of affinity.

The photographs in the catalog depict the children together with the paintings. However, the close-ups of the children often reveal their disinterest in the paintings. The children are initially all interested when the paintings first appear in the classroom. Later on, however, each child would no doubt receive the paintings in different ways. Some children, rather than remembering the numbers on the canvas, will probably remember the different sizes of the paintings and their rhythmical positioning as part of the wall as a whole. Others will probably grasp the numbers 1 to 7 as being part of the rhythm of the week.[1]

Children aged 4 to 6 do not think of shifts in terms of movement of objects. The paintings appear, but the moment they are removed from the wall, they no longer exist. The sudden appearance of the seven dark paintings in the children's world, only to disappear again, is very much a representation of coexistence as something existential.

Kawara's "Date Paintings". Very few works have managed to express the issue of time and space in such a concise manner and as such a dynamic epistemological and ontological process and event. Those who confront Kawara's "Date Paintings" experience a sense of their own past and a realization that they are still alive today. The immutable linear positioning of time acts as an agent to join, at once, the space we find ourselves in at present and the space that lay in the fixed point of the past. As reflected by the expression "realm of enlightenment", used by a critic in the past, Kawara's work opens up a clear magnetic field of consciousness. As Jonathan Watkins, the curator of the Sydney exhibition, commented, Kawara's "Date Paintings" are many, and they have also been exhibited in relation to his other works. This is because Kawara's "Date Paintings" involve the function of establishing an axis and position for time and space and creating a magnetic field of consciousness.

It is interesting that Kawara has given the title *Pure Consciousness* to this project, which involves children aged 4 to 6. When one takes into consideration the age group of the children, the meaning of "consciousness" within this context is obviously different from that used in psychology, the principle of which is the introspective analysis of self-consciousness. If anything, the former is probably closer to the concept of consciousness as theorized in neurology. In neurology, consciousness is explained in terms of the structure and the working principle. The structure consists primarily of neurons, while words such as "oscillation", "coherence" and "resonance" (resulting from external stimuli) are used to explain the working principle. For example, if water were the material, then the form of flowing water would be a river. Similarly, if neurons were the material, then consciousness would be its form. Although the word "form" in this context cannot be used to replace the "form" of a work of visual art as such, because of the oscillation that takes place between the consciousness (form) of the artist and the visitor, it could be described as an event involving the appreciation and acceptance of the work.

The neurologist Yoshiya Shinagawa[2] describes consciousness as follows:

'Information is the element of cousciousness. Consciousness itself is part of the information structure of the universe, and that information structure recognizes the universe. One extreme is that consciousness is specific to humans, while the other extreme is that consciousness is present in all matter. From the point of view of information, consciousness and matter are continuous. Just like the paradox of continuity that is represented by the following allegory.'

The paradox of continuity is expressed in the form of the clouds that can be seen by

passengers in a plane that has just taken off from the airport on a sunny day, where several clouds are floating in the sky. Initially light mist can be seen through the window, but this mist gradually becomes so heavy that eventually the air is pure white and nothing can be seen. In other words, clouds have no clear boundaries.

Consciousness is similar to this. However, while a cloud is a conglomerate of matter, consciousness is a conglomerate of information.

We can say that the consciousness of adults, whose egos are formed, is both a sophisticated conglomerate of information and a consolidated whole. By placing children aged 4 to 6 whose level of information is still low and whose egos are still being formed, in the context of his work, Kawara reveals the territory of continuity of consciousness and matter, like clouds, and he seems to be attempting to visualize the reaction (oscillation) between the work and consciousness that takes place in this territory, or magnetic field. This is an extremely metaphysical question that Kawara is posing, and a direct attempt by him to pose this question in a world that lies outside the context of understanding that is art, but within the context of the relationship between the individual, in the general sense, and the universe. The Zen-like speed of recognition that transcends the segmentation of language – Kawara, through the coexistence of his work and pure consciousness as a metaphor via the children, is attempting, in this new century, to transcend the framework of epistemology and art so characteristic of the 20th century. If we apply the premise that Kawara's work acts as an agent to create a magnetic field of oscillation of the consciousness, then this project could also be described as generating a magnetic field of the purest consciousness. Kawara's project travels between continents to join time and space. Istanbul, as the juncture of the theory of time and the theory of space of East and West, will be the 6th transit point and magnetic field.

Yuko Hasegawa
Istanbul, August 2001

1. The framework of recognition (how the world is grasped) is formed by around age 3. By age 5 or 6, the memory function of children is approaching that of adults, and the Date Paintings would probably remain in their memories as an event, but a strong interest or motive is needed for these paintings to remain as memories in the long term. Although more people understand why they remember something – because, for example, of a feeling of happiness or sadness at the time – than those who don't, there are some people who have no idea why something remains in their long-term memory. In many cases the motive is forgotten, and only the memory remains.
2. Yoshiya Shinagawa, *Ishiki to No* [Consciousness and the Brain], pp. 90-91. Kinokuniya Shoten 1982, Japan.

PURE CONSCIOUSNESS, LUND, 2002

Pure Consciousness

I am honoured to have been given the opportunity of working together with On Kawara on putting on *Pure Consciousness* for children and staff at the *Uroxen* (the Aurochs) kindergarten and the visiting public. To me, *Pure Consciousness* is one of the finest works of contemporary art that we can experience today. With the warmest feelings for On Kawara and his project I would like to take this opportunity to express my gratitude and joy in being able to participate in making this exhibition available in my native Sweden. *Pure Consciousness* is part of *Kulturbro 2002*, a biannual exhibition of art and culture in the Öresund region.

In 1972, the Modern Museum in Stockholm and its director Pontus Hulten launched the *Torpedo Institute*, putting the old torpedo workshops on the island of Skeppsholmen at the disposal of visiting artists. The idea was that artists from all over the world would be invited and given the opportunity to work and live under the same conditions as scientists within their respective areas. On Kawara spent the early spring of 1973 in Stockholm and was the first artist to visit the Institute. Here, he continued his work on "Date Paintings", a project he embarked on during the mid-60s. Up until today the artist has produced over 2,000 paintings under the title *Today* series.

In October 2002 we will once more be given the opportunity of seeing On Kawara's work in Sweden. The City of Lund is hosting *Pure Consciousness* and Sweden is thereby the eighth country visited by the project worldwide. At the *Elden* (fire) children's group at the *Uroxen* kindergarten in Lund, seven "Date paintings" are hanging in a row: 1 to 7 January 1997. In a room dedicated to play and assembly the 12 children and their teachers will, without any previous explanation, encounter the paintings, the artist and their own existence. On Kawara guides the observer into the present, but also into the future and the past. Great and small issues are brought to our attention in the presence of the as yet unaffected minds of these children. The impact of the paintings is long-term; the memory of them may well return to the child later in life.

My experience of the paintings and my contacts with On Kawara have been like a journey that has brought me through time, existence and my own self. Time and reality are relative concepts. The 1 to 7 January 1997 is a clearly defined period of time in space. On Kawara's visit to Sweden in 1973 coincided with Astrid Lindgren's completion of one of her most loved and debated stories, the fairy tale novel *The Lionheart Brothers*[1]. Just as On Kawara

transports the observer, Astrid Lindgren transports the reader through time and reality. Seeing, listening, we let ourselves go and discover aspects of time where reality is an individual experience.

Children between the ages one and six living in the Skania region, with the exception of the City of Malmö, are admitted to the Uroxen kindergarten. It is adapted for deaf, profoundly deaf, and hearing-impaired children. The kindergarten is divided into four groups in which the children's various needs for language training and communication skills are satisfied. The *Jorden* (earth) group is for the sisters and brothers of hearing-impaired children. They communicate with each other via speech. The *Vattnet* (water) group is for hearing-impaired children who use speech as their first language and sign language as a communication support. The *Solen* (sun) and *Elden* (fire) groups are for deaf and profoundly deaf children who primarily communicate via the use of sign language.

The staff is there to help the children from early on to acquire language skills that will enable them to communicate with other people later in life; to express opinions and feelings, and to convey thoughts and desires; all the things that may seem obvious. Visual communication via sign language takes place under radically different circumstances than communication via speech: "You hear with your eyes and speak with your hands". The eyes – sight – becomes an important means of communication. The children's and the observers' first meeting with On Kawara's paintings is purely visual.

The paintings communicate, in writing, from the left to the right, a month, a day and a year in white on a nearly black background. TIME. The paintings also express size relations, three of them measure 20.32 x 25.4 cm and the other four are slightly larger: 25.4 x 33.02 cm. We see black and white acrylic paint on cotton canvas over a wooden frame. The materials are taken from the Earth's natural resources: fossil fuel from the ground, cotton and wood from the plant kingdom. THE WORLD. Just as earth, water, sun and fire are all preconditions for human existence, these sources are fundamental to On Kawara's creative process. MANKIND. Each painting in the *Today* series is completed in one, single day. This is where the journey begins: with the aid of visual communication into the realm of time, via man into space.

By the entrance to the kindergarten there is a toy shed with a picture painted on it. It shows a girl with red pigtails, a short dress and unmatching stockings lifting a white horse with black spots above her head. To the right of the girl we see a yellow house. It is a picture of Pippi Longstocking. Astrid Lindgren is Sweden's best-known author of children's books and loved by all children. Children throughout all the continents have come into contact with her books, some 115[2] titles translated into 54 languages such as Azerbaijani, Kurdish and Swahili. All Swedish children love Mischievous Meg, Emil, Lotta, the brothers Lionheart and all the other characters. Fairy tales are stories through which all the wishes you can imagine come true. Stories and imagination have long been considered to be vital to children's development and their ability to handle everyday conflicts as well as a means to find their inner selves.

Among other things, *Pure Consciousness* makes me think of the story about the brothers Lionheart. Like On Kawara's paintings, *The Brothers Lionheart* takes the form of a journey; a journey in time, space, reality and life. The paintings 1 to 7 January 1997 and the visual communication they convey provide us with a tool for entering the time and reality of our imagination. In the story about the brothers Lionheart we follow Rusky, a nine-years-old boy who is about to die. It is a story about brotherly love and conquering the fear of death. The story unfolds in a different state of consciousness. We follow the boy's delirious ravings on the couch in the kitchen and accompany him and his brother through a dream vision where imagination takes over the story about the country beyond the stars. "We'll meet in Nangiyala," says Rusky to his brother Jonathan. In Cherry Valley Rusky is alive and well, the brothers live together with their horses and the air they breathe is clean. In this primeval dream the children are transported from a dull reality to a beautiful country in a faraway place: a universe beyond Earth, an ancient world beyond the Earthstar[3] transported to yet another dimension. Time and reality are relative concepts.

The reading styles of children and adults differ. The children's still "pure" and "unformed" minds often interpret the boys journey into Nangilima as the entering in to a happier world, while adults "realise" that what it is all about is the passing over to the land of the dead. Perhaps the silence of On Kawara's paintings conquers the spoken word of Astrid Lindgren's narrative.

Veronica Wiman
Lund, August 2002

"Jonathan walked ahead of me up the path to the farm, and I trotted after him with my fine straight legs. I just walked along staring at my legs and feeling how good it was to walk with them. But when we'd got a little way up the slope, I suddenly turned my head. And then – then I saw Cherry Valley at last! Oh, that valley was white with cherry blossoms everywhere. White and green, it was, with cherry blossoms and green, green grass. And through all that green and white, the river flowed like a silver ribbon. Why hadn't I even noticed it before? Had I seen nothing but Jonathan? But now I stood quite still on the path and saw how beautiful it was, and I said to Jonathan: "This must be the most beautiful valley on earth." "Yes, but not on earth," said Jonathan, and then I remembered that I was in Nangiyala"

From The Brothers Lionheart by Astrid Lindgren 1973.

1. 1907 – 2001
2. Ed.: Red. Mary Ørvig, Marianne Eriksson, Birgitta Sjöquist, *Duvdrottningen*, Stockholm,1997, p. 116.
3. Vivi Edström, Astrid Lindgren – *Vildtoring och lägereld*, Stockholm 1992, p. 224.

Colophon

Ikon Gallery
1 Oozells Square, Brindleyplace,
Birmingham, B1 2HS, UK
http://www.ikon-gallery.co.uk/ikon
tel: +44 (0) 121 248 0708
fax: +44 90) 121 248 0709
email: art@ikon-gallery.co.uk
Registered charity no: 528892

Ikon Staff
Karen Allen	Exhibitions Co-ordinator
Allison Beddoes	Marketing Assistant
Simon Bloor	Visitor Assistant
Philip Duckworth	Facilities Assistant
Siân Evans	Programme Assistant
Celine Haran	Deputy Director
Matthew Hogan	Facilities Technician IT
Jo Jones	Visitor Assistant
Helen Juffs	Gallery Facilities Manager
Deborah Kermode	Curator (Offsite)
Emma Killerby	Facilities Assistant
James Langdon	Marketing Assistant
Chris Maggs	Facilities Technician
Deborah Manning	Education Assistant
Nikki Matthews	Education Assistant
Natalia Morris	Visitor Assistant
Nasrin Newstead	Visitor Assistant
Gill Nicol	Curator (Education and Interpretation)
Jigisha Patel	Marketing Manager (from September 2002)
Vicky Skelding	Visitor Assistant
Lucy Stevens	Marketing Manager
Michael Stanley	Curator (Gallery)
Dianne Tanner	Finance Manager
Andrew Tims	Education Assistant
Jonathan Watkins	Director
Jane Williamson	PA/Office Co-ordinator

Ikon gratefully acknowledges financial support from Birmingham City Council, West Midlands Arts and the Arts Council of England.
The exhibition has been supported by the Japan Foundation

Le Consortium, centre d'art contemporain
37 rue de Longvic
21000 Dijon France
http://www.leconsortium.com
tel: +33 (0) 3 80 68 45 55
fax: +33 (0) 3 80 68 45 57
email: leconsortium@wanadoo.fr

Le Consortium
François Bernard	Technical Co-ordinator
Patricia Bobillier-Monnot	Webmaster
Catherine Bonnotte	Offsite Assistant
Irène Bony	Production Director
Xavier Douroux	Director
Arnaud Fourrier	Education Assistant
Franck Gautherot	Director
Francine Golmard	Visitor Assistant
Stéphanie Gressin	Performing arts Assistant
Jean-Paul Lapaîche	Visitor Assistant
Fabrice Magniez	Education Assistant
François Orivel	President
Eric Troncy	Director

Le Consortium gratefully acknowledges financial support from Ministère de la Culture –DRAC de Bourgogne ; Conseil régional de Bourgogne ; Ville de Dijon.

Lenders

Date Paintings (1966-2002)
Courtesy On and Hiroko Kawahara
Mr and Mrs Shuji Hirose, Japan

Sundays of 100 Years (1964)
Courtesy On and Hiroko Kawahara

One Million Years – Past (1970-1971)
One Million Years – Future (1980)
Courtesy On and Hiroko Kawahara

Telegrams (1970-2000)
Pétur Arason
Michel Assenmaker
Froehlich Collection, Stuttgart
Collection Paula Cooper, New York
Collection Hilda and Thomas Deecke, Berlin
Dietmar Elger, Hannover
Jennifer Bacon Fossati
Prof. Dr. Thomas Friedrich
Collection Marc and Josée Gensollen, Marseille
Verlag Gachnang and Springer AG, Bern
Collection Le Consortium, Dijon
Collection Von Graevenitz
Buchhandlung Walther König
Fischer Collection, Dusseldorf
Ernst Georg Kühle, Cologne
Clamencia and Peter Labin
Arnaud Lefebvre
The Lewitt Collection, Chester, CT, USA
Dora Maltz
Yutaka Matsuzawa
Philippe-André Rihoux, Brussels
Yusuke Minami
Hiroko Nonaka
Chisa Misaka
Jürgen Partenheiemer, private collection
Monica and Jean Pfaff, Ventalló, Spain
Collection Toshiki Sasanuma, Tokyo
Gabriele Schmidt Heins
Irm Sommer, Berlin
Björn Springfeldt, Sweden
Courtesy Galerie Micheline Szwajcer, Antwerp

Collection Lucien Terras
Toyota Municipal Museum of Art
Sato Tatsumi
Eleonora Villanti
Harald Vlugt
Henning Weidemann
Nino Weinstock, private Collection, Basel
Hinrich Weidemann

Aknowledgments

Hiroko and On Kawara
Kasper König
Peter Nagy
Kaye Winwood
Nigel Prince

Catalogue

Published at the occasion of an exhibition by On Kawara *Consciousness.Meditation.Watcher on the Hills* by Les presses du réel and Ikon Gallery.

Edition and graphic design: Franck Gautherot

Translation from the French (René Denizot, Michel Gauthier): Charles Penwarden;
from the Spanish (José Roca) : Katya García-Antón

Photos credits:
Sarah Blee, Robert Gomez-Godoy, Hou Hanru, Hiro Ihara, Einar Falur Ingólfsson, André Magnin, André Morin, Carl Schonebohm, Muammer Yanmaz

Scanning: Temps réel, Dijon
Printing: Edips, Dijon

Les presses du réel distribution:
Stéphanie Parizot, Romain Gigoux

ISBN 2-84066-078-4